The Art of War
& Other Classics of
Eastern Philosophy

The Art of War
& Other Classics of
Eastern Philosophy

Introduction by Ken Mondschein, PhD

Canterbury Classics

San Diego

Canterbury Classics
An imprint of Printers Row Publishing Group
10350 Barnes Canyon Road, Suite 100, San Diego, CA 92121
www.canterburyclassicsbooks.com

Printers Row Publishing Group is a division of Readerlink Distribution Services, LLC.
Canterbury Classics is a registered trademark of Readerlink Distribution Services, LLC.

All correspondence concerning the content of this book should be addressed to
Canterbury Classics, Editorial Department, at the above address.

Publisher: Peter Norton
Associate Publisher: Ana Parker
Publishing/Editorial Team: April Farr, Kelly Larsen, Kathryn C. Dalby
Editorial Team: JoAnn Padgett, Melinda Allman, Dan Mansfield, Traci Douglas
Production Team: Jonathan Lopes, Rusty von Dyl
Cover and endpaper design by Ray Caramanna

Library of Congress Cataloging-in-Publication Data

Title: The Art of war & other classics of Eastern philosophy.
Description: San Diego, California : Canterbury Classics, 2016.
Identifiers: LCCN 2016003017 | ISBN 9781626868021 (hardcover)
Subjects: LCSH: Philosophy, Asian.
Classification: LCC B121 .A78 2016 | DDC 181/.11--dc23
LC record available at http://lccn.loc.gov/2016003017

Printed in China
22 21 20 19 18 5 6 7 8 9

CONTENTS

THE TAO TE CHING

Part I

CONFUCIAN ANALECTS

THE GREAT LEARNING

THE DOCTRINE OF THE MEAN

THE WORKS OF MENCIUS

INTRODUCTION

The volume you hold in your hands contains some of the foundational texts of a great civilization. For centuries, the Confucian exam system was the means to upward mobility in Imperial China. Passing the test and acquiring status and salary required mastering a canon of books and being able to reiterate their ideas in such forms as the "eight-legged essay." Whether these books affected Chinese civilization, or the unique aspects of Chinese civilization were passed on through these texts, or if it was some combination of the two, is a moot question: If one wants to understand Chinese culture and thought—and thus understand a rising power in our modern world—then these texts must likewise be understood. They contain values, strategies, and ways of reasoning; they are in the DNA of a culture. To know the future, we must understand the past.

The first thing we must do is rid ourselves of Western ideas about the nature of this thought system. "Confucianism" and "Taoism" are not religions in the way they are understood in the West. Rather, they are a European appellation for a complicated thought system. It is important to understand that what we are presenting in this book are *jing*, or classics—books from the canon of authoritative texts. Though this volume principally presents *The Art of War*, the great classic on military strategy that provided guidance to China's leaders well through the Qing dynasty (1644–1911), it is impossible to understand Sun Tzŭ without understanding the culture from which he came and which canonized his work as a *jing*. Accordingly, we will first look at Confucius, the most revered sage in the Chinese system of thought, under whose name the entire system is often subsumed, and then continue with Mencius and Lao Tzŭ before turning to Sun Tzŭ and his work.

Life and Teachings of Confucius

K'ung Fu-tzu (in the Wade-Giles system of Romanization) or Kongfuzi (in the modern Pinyin system) is traditionally held to have been born in 551 BCE in the state of Lu, now in Shangdong Province. The name "Confucius" is a Latinization of his Chinese name, most probably by the sixteenth-century Jesuit missionary Matteo Ricci. At the time of his birth, China was experiencing the "Spring and Autumn" period of the great Zhou empire, a time of disorder following the collapse of central authority. Rulers fought among themselves and the common people suffered, caught between civil war, heavy taxation, and bandits. Lu was noted for preserving many of the Zhou traditions, and Confucius was no doubt steeped in this knowledge as a young man. At the time, there was no emperor; rather, the region that would become China was composed of petty states, each ruled by its own king. In some ways, it was comparable to the disorder of the European Middle Ages that followed the collapse of the Roman Empire.

From his writings—or, rather, the records of his teachings left by his students and his students' students—we get the idea of Confucius as a wandering scholar-administrator, traveling from court to court and advising rulers as to how best govern their states. He was not unique in this: The Spring and Autumn period, for all its disorder, was the time of the so-called Hundred Schools of philosophy and an era of tremendous cultural creativity. Other than that, we have little definite information on Confucius's early life. Sima Qian (c. 145–86 BCE), the great historian of the Han dynasty (206 BCE–220 CE), writes that he came from a noble family that had sunk into poverty, and was forced to take such jobs as working at a stable. His life was fraught with instability and danger. Yet, Sima Qian lived more than four centuries after Confucius, and records of earlier times were scant thanks to the suppression of the Hundred Schools by Qin Shi Huangdi, the ruler who united China from 220 to 210 BCE as the first emperor of the Qin dynasty.

Thus, this "everyman" depiction of Confucius may have been a romantic legend; certainly, other aspects are fanciful. For instance, Sima Qian also says that Confucius had 3,000 disciples. There are inconsistencies in his biography, as well. Was Confucius always the model of decorum he presents? Did a man who was famously adverse to capital punishment serve as the chief law enforcer of Lu? Did he really delight in the *I Ching* and other texts that came to be known as the "Confucian classics"?

We can perhaps gain a truer picture by looking at the gist of what Confucius says. First, he was strongly conservative in his outlook and admired the virtues of the Zhou. His governing philosophy placed great emphasis on hierarchy, morality, and proper relationships. The linchpins of these are *yi* (ethics) and *li* (religious rituals): In contrast to the disorder of his own day, Confucius believed everyone on the social ladder must behave properly and dutifully to those above them and those below them. By "rectification of names" (*zhengming*), he means that people's behavior should correspond to the social titles that they possess. Thus, a son who usurped his father's throne was not using his proper title or displaying proper filial piety. It is only natural that those under him would be corrupt, and the country poorly governed.

Confucius also knew the power of religion to unite people. Likewise, rulers and those under them should perform the proper ceremonies, such as sacrificing to the dead, with the proper religious music. The purpose of this is to bring oneself into harmony with the spiritual and natural world and cultivate virtue (*de*). Rituals are training in self-abnegation and self-discipline. By properly performing the rituals and keeping right thought and right feeling in his state, proper relations between people will be preserved and the ruler will maintain the "Mandate of Heaven"—the divine right to rule. Court rituals function to preserve harmony and keep the ruler in harmony with the universe, aligning the microcosm with the macrocosm. Divination, astrological observation, music, etc., are all intended to reinforce this relationship. (This also mirrors "animistic" tendencies in Western thought: The *Emerald Tablet* of Hermes Trimegistus, one of the foundational texts of Western mysticism, begins with the admonition "that which is above is like that which is below; that which is below is like that which is above.")

Most of all, Confucius is deeply humanistic. People are teachable and perfectible, and it falls upon all of us to improve one another. In his teachings, Confucius emphasizes the cultivated *junzi*, the "superior man" or "gentleman," who exercises humility and *ren*, or loving-kindness. Rather than inflicting corporal punishments, malefactors should be encouraged toward goodness by positive examples.

Life and Teachings of Mencius

Mencius (Mengzi) was a follower of Confucius who lived about a century after the latter's death. (Like Confucius's name, "Mencius" is a Latinization by seventeenth-century Jesuits.) The eponymous collection of his sayings and dialogues was posthumously collected by his disciples and edited into a compendium. He was far from a dogmatist, though: He believed that the received texts should be read creatively and usefully.

In Mencius, we can recognize the model of the Confucian as public servant. He served as a minister in the state of Qi, and his works are not just philosophy, but contain practical ideas for administration and on the morality of warfare. Ultimately, he was disappointed: The rulers of his time failed to live up to his ideals, and he retired, disappointed.

Still, Mencius's writings give an expansion and extension of Confucius's basic beliefs. For Mencius, there are four central virtues, which guide behavior, perception, and feeling: benevolence, righteousness, wisdom, and propriety. These virtues are to be cultivated through honest study and reflection, and include both active and passive components: One who has a true understanding of propriety will both address others respectfully and themselves disdain to be addressed disrespectfully. Similarly, a truly benevolent ruler will consider his subjects' well-being when considering any action. Most of all, people must be given the proper environment to cultivate their inherent goodness. This was quite in contrast to the Legalist school of Shi Huangdi's Qin state, which held that human beings are naturally bad, and must be kept in line with a system of rewards and punishments.

Life and Teachings of Lao Tzŭ

If Confucianism is the first intellectual pillar of Chinese culture, Taoism (Daoism) is the second. (The third, Buddhism, does not enter here.) However, the historicity of Lao Tzŭ (Laozi in the modern Pinyin system of transliteration) is open to debate—if he did exist, he would have lived in the sixth century BCE, well before accurate records were kept.

Sima Qian holds that Lao Tzŭ was born in Chu, a southern state, during the Spring and Autumn period of the Zhou dynasty, and worked as an archivist and historian. He was supposedly Confucius's elder, and the great sage supposedly consulted Lao Tzŭ on funeral rites. However, Lao Tzŭ did not seek fame or to promulgate his teachings. Later in life, he saw the virtue of the Zhou state diminish and sought to withdraw from China itself. An official at the northern border asked him to write down his philosophy, and the result was *The Tao Te Ching (Daodejing)*.

While Sima Qian's story is almost certainly a confabulation, and *The Tao Te Ching* might have been written down at a date later than the one the great historian specifies, Lao Tzŭ's historicity is irrelevant: *The Tao Te Ching*, the "Classic of the Way and Virtue," has had a profound effect on Chinese (and world) culture. There were active Taoist religious foundations by the time of the late Han dynasty, *The Tao Te Ching* was part of the civil service examinations since the eighth century CE, royal families traced their lineage back to Lao Tzŭ, and his putative birthday is still celebrated in many Asian countries.

Like the records of Confucius's thoughts, *The Tao Te Ching* deals with how people are to behave. Like Confucianism, Taoism emphasizes the essential unity and harmony of heaven and earth, the importance of rituals, and the importance of living a virtuous life. However, unlike Confucianism's emphasis on social action and clear directives, Taoism's central work is personal, even mystical; difficult to interpret; and rife with allusions. Furthermore, whereas the Confucian believes in improving human society through striving, the Taoist believes in nonaction. Through unambition, we are raised; through alienation from the body, we achieve long life.

Even language itself—the means by which education takes place—is suspect. *The Tao Te Ching* states, "The Tao [Way] that can be trodden is not the enduring and unchanging Tao." To speak of the Tao is impossible; it can only be expressed through cryptic and metaphysical ideas: being arises from nonbeing; beauty from ugliness; a pot takes its use from its emptiness. Desire is futile; one should empty oneself and live in accordance with nature. Only the endless flow of energy, one thing into another, is constant. The idea of flux may be encapsulated by the story of the Taoist master Chuang Tzu, who, when he awoke from dreaming he was a butterfly, did not know if he was Chuang Tzu dreaming he was a butterfly or a butterfly dreaming he was Chuang Tzu. As the story implies, the distinction is irrelevant.

Part of this accession to natural cycles and living in harmony with the universe is accepting death. Before we are born, we do not exist—why should we then fear the nonexistence that follows death? In its worldview, *The Tao Te Ching* may be seen to fall equally into the Western categories of religion, philosophy, and mythology.

Yet all of this—and the reams of scholarly papers debating *The Tao Te Ching*—is only an approximation. The Way is ineffable—an idea that would influence Japanese Zen traditions. Even in practice, there are contradictions: Taoists do not fear death, but there are many schools of alchemy intended to extend life or even grant immortality. Nonaction is an important principle, yet Taoism also speaks of government, but it is a government that does not "value and employ men of superior ability" who keep the people in a state of contented ignorance. The Taoist idea of vital energy (*chi/qui*) appears not only in meditative systems, but also as part of traditional systems of martial arts. (Of course, in Chinese thought, human society and the natural world are not separable.)

Sun Tzŭ and *The Art of War*

The art of war is of vital importance to the State." This seemingly obvious statement has been reiterated throughout history by authorities ranging from St. Augustine to Carl von Clausewitz. However, it was Sun Tzŭ who first made the case that war is part of political science, a discipline that may—and must—be studied and mastered. *The Art of War* is the world's oldest military treatise, yet one that remains relevant today, studied by generals, business leaders, sports coaches, and politicians as a general guide on strategy. Furthermore, it is a work of moral philosophy, dealing with the rightness or wrongess of the decision to wage war, as well as the proper and moral way to conduct war—what we would call *casus belli* and *jus in bello*.

Whether or not its putative author, Sun Tzŭ (Master Sun), actually existed is a matter of debate. Sima Qian recorded that he was born in the state of Qi and lived from 544 to 496 BCE, during the Spring and Autumn period. However, it is more likely that *The Art of War* was written during the disordered Warring States period that began in 475 BCE and which was only ended by the Qin ascendency in 221 BCE. Qin Shi Huangdi considered *The Art of War* an essential text, and so it escaped the book burning of his reign. During the Song dynasty of the eleventh century CE, it was placed at the head of the "seven military classics," thus ensuring its place in the canon on *jing*.

Sima Qian also relates a quite probably spurious anecdote that illuminates Sun Tzŭ's character: Before hiring the general, the king of Wu tested Sun Tzŭ by commanding him to train his harem of 180 concubines. Sun Tzŭ divided them into two companies and placed the emperor's two favorites as officers. Yet, when given marching commands, the concubines did nothing but dissolve into helpless giggles. Sun Tzŭ explained that if the soldiers did not understand the commands, then it was his own fault—that is, the fault of the commanding general. However, after patiently explaining again what he wanted, the concubines still would do nothing but laugh. Sun Tzŭ then explained that if the soldiers understood what was required but still did not obey, it was the officers' fault—and, over the king's protests, he had the two favorites he had appointed as officers executed, and chose new officers. Needless to say, the concubines now performed military maneuvers flawlessly.

As the various social contexts—as well as the history of commentary— are amply explained by the translator, Lionel Giles, I will restrict my brief remarks. What I wish to add to Giles's commentary is that Sun Tzŭ is a man writing for a premodern economy, when the state's capability to make war was limited. War is expensive, as he continually reminds us. Standing armies were expensive and time-consuming to recruit and maintain. Unlike the U.S. military, which is maintained in readiness and can be deployed anywhere at a moment's notice, an ancient Chinese state's capacity to make war was dependent on season. Raising an army, as can be seen in the chapter "Energy," took time. Best of all is to win without direct confrontation, or, as Sun Tzŭ says, "supreme excellence consists in breaking the enemy's resistance without fighting." Making war too expensive for the enemy is best; worst of all possibilities is siege warfare. Much the same was advised by the Roman military writer Publius Flavius Vegetius Renatus, which is why in the West we call this sort of delaying strategy "Vegetian warfare." However, it is a universal truth of warfare that if you deprive the enemy of the capacity to make war, victory will follow. Thus, the Allied strategic bombing campaign that deprived Nazi Germany of the capacity to make war falls wholly within Sun Tzŭ's canons of strategy.

Just as Sun Tzŭ's writing, with its references to chariots and signal fires, cannot be separated from its historical context, neither can it be separated from its unique East Asian social and military context. How else to explain verses such as "Which of the two sovereigns is imbued with the Moral law?" To Sun Tzŭ, rectitude and good generalship are inseparable. Moral weakness—anger, impatience, cowardice, even oversolicitousness of the welfare of one's troops—will lead to military weakness. To Sun Tzŭ, the ideal general is also the ideal *junzi:* "If you know the enemy and know yourself, you need not fear the result of a hundred battles. If you know yourself but not the enemy, for every victory gained you will also suffer a defeat. If you know neither the enemy nor yourself, you will succumb in every battle."

Furthermore, *The Art of War* can be seen as a Taoist work. All is flux; all is change. "Indirect tactics, efficiently applied, are inexhaustible as Heaven and Earth, unending as the flow of rivers and streams; like the sun and moon, they end but to begin anew; like the four seasons, they pass away to return once more." By comprehending the causes and nature of these changes, the general can successfully compete on the battlefield. The axioms of the Tao—the laws of the universe itself—are to be wielded to gain power over one's foes and to ensure the well-being of the human, political world.

In other words, we can see *The Art of War* as combining two of the three main streams of ancient Chinese philosophy. Sun Tzŭ's work cannot be understood otherwise: It is a work not only of military strategy but of supreme psychological insight. It gives not only the means by which to prevail in a conflict but also by which to live one's life.

Sun Tzŭ's work has been widely influential in the twentieth century. Mao Zedong, the Chinese Communist leader, was himself a military theorist whose book on guerrilla warfare was inspired by, and written in reaction to, *The Art of War*. Mao credited the defeat of both the Japanese invasion of China and Chiang Kai-shek's Nationalist forces to ideas and theories he had learned from Sun Tzŭ, and Henry Kissinger remarked that the Chinese leader "owed more to Sun Tzŭ than to Lenin." Võ Nguyên Giáp, a North Vietnamese general during the Vietnam War, was likewise inspired by *The Art of War*, and, indeed, the Vietnamese resistance to Japanese, French, and American occupiers can be seen as an application of Sun Tzŭ's principles. American generals such as Norman Schwarzkopf and Colin Powell have also praised the book, which is on the required reading list at the U.S. Military Academy at West Point.

We can even see China's recent foreign policy as following the principles of *The Art of War*. Modern China views Sun Tzŭ's classic work as part of its national patrimony, part of a cultural, if not military, expansion. Copies have been given as presents to President George W. Bush and Admiral Michael Mullen, the chair of the Joint Chiefs of Staff. The idea of ancient wisdom is certainly appealing for Westerners: Ever since Gordon Gekko, the antihero of the 1987 film *Wall Street*, quoted Sun Tzŭ, the market has seen an endless array of *Art of War* knockoffs aimed at consumers ranging from businesswomen to golfers. Whether on the battlefield or in the boardroom, there seems to be something in the Sun Tzŭ mystique for everyone. However, none of these are the real, true, and original work, which we present to you here with the translator's in-depth commentary and in the context of other books in the Chinese tradition. Without context and true understanding, even the best information is meaningless.

A History of Translation

The history of translation of the Chinese classics into European languages cannot be separated from missionary activities. The first travelers from the West to the East undertook their epic journeys to spread the European worldview: The Mongols' unification of the Eurasian landmass allowed men such as William of Rubrick and John of Montecorvino to travel to the court of the Yuan (Mongol) dynasty, where they unsuccessfully pleaded with the "Great Khan" to adopt Christianity. Later missionaries, such as Francis Xavier, likewise met with limited success, being crippled by both their lack of language skills and their inability—or unwillingness—to understand the culture that surrounded them.

Matteo Ricci marks a turning point in both missionary activity and sinology. Born in Italy in 1552, he became a Jesuit in 1571. Ricci's approach was far different from that of those who had preceded him: Rather than merely proselytizing, he tried to understand Chinese thought on its own terms and explain Christianity in ways that made sense to the Chinese. Ricci spoke admiringly of Chinese achievements and produced some of the first translations of Chinese classics for the Western world.

The two translators whose work appears in this volume are British: James Legge and Lionel Giles. The history of Great Britain and China in their lifetimes was fraught: The Opium Wars had forced the Chinese to grant extraterritorial concessions to European powers—ports such as Hong Kong and Macau were under European law, not Chinese. Furthermore, China was overpopulated and undergoverned. The result was decades of famine, rebellion, and, ultimately, the collapse of the Imperial government, which would lead to the Revolution of 1911 that overthrew the last Qing emperor.

Legge (1815–1897), the elder of the two translators, was a Scottish missionary and educator. Born in Aberdeenshire and educated at King's College, he went to the East as a missionary in 1839. His first post was as the head of the Anglo-Chinese college in Malacca; it is during this period that he conceived the project of translating the Chinese classics into English. Legge believed that it was not until Westerners understood the mindset, ideas, and culture of the Chinese that missionary activity could succeed. This project would become his life's work. After three years in Malacca, Legge moved to Hong Kong in 1844, where he remained until returning to the UK in 1867. In 1876 he became the first professor of Chinese at Oxford University, a post that he retained until his death. He was known for his tireless devotion to his translations and scholarly works on Chinese thought and religion, often rising in the middle of the night to make himself a cup of tea and work at his desk. Legge was also known for his opposition to the opium trade, which had been one of the principal means by which the British had forced an inequitable balance of trade upon the Chinese. (Chinese attempts to stop the opium trade had also given rise to two wars, the second of which resulted in the sacking and burning of the Imperial Summer Palaces in Beijing.)

Lionel Giles (1875–1958) was the fourth son of Herbert Giles, himself a well-known English diplomat and scholar of China who most famously completed what became known as the Wade-Giles system of transliterating Mandarin. The younger Giles was educated in Belgium, Austria, and Scotland, and graduated from Oxford in 1899, afterward becoming an assistant curator at the British Museum and Keeper (librarian) of the Department of Oriental Manuscripts and Printed Books. He published his translation of Sun Tzŭ in 1910, which quickly replaced the inferior and inaccurate works of the British military officer Everard Ferguson Calthrop. In his work, Giles used the Romanization system that his father helped invent, which has since been replaced by the Pinyin system. Readers should therefore be aware that the transliterations in this work are not those currently used by scholars and translators.

Conclusions

In our own era of globalization, China has recovered from the crises of the nineteenth and early twentieth centuries, civil war and anarchy, foreign imperialism, the Japanese occupation and atrocities during World War II, and the heavy hand of Mao's Communist government—and is now a world superpower. Understanding this great nation and its people requires understanding its classical literature. Competing successfully, whether in the economic or military realms, likewise requires an idea of the adversary's strategy and mindset.

We here present to you the works of four of the greatest minds the world has ever known. The Chinese classics are on par with the Bible and Qu'ran for the influence they have had on humanity. It behooves each of us to study them not only for our own self-improvement—and not just to gain advantage, but for their own sake. In doing so, we (much as Confucius taught) realize our own humanity and perfectibility.

Ken Mondschein, PhD
Northampton, Massachusetts
February 24, 2016

The Art of War

(WITHOUT COMMENTARY)

TRANSLATED FROM THE CHINESE
BY LIONEL GILES, M.A. (1910)

I

LAYING PLANS

1. Sun Tzŭ said: The art of war is of vital importance to the State.

2. It is a matter of life and death, a road either to safety or to ruin. Hence it is a subject of inquiry which can on no account be neglected.

3. The art of war, then, is governed by five constant factors, to be taken into account in one's deliberations, when seeking to determine the conditions obtaining in the field.

4. These are: (1) The Moral Law; (2) Heaven; (3) Earth; (4) The Commander; (5) Method and discipline.

5, 6. *The Moral Law* causes the people to be in complete accord with their ruler, so that they will follow him regardless of their lives, undismayed by any danger.

7. *Heaven* signifies night and day, cold and heat, times and seasons.

8. *Earth* comprises distances, great and small; danger and security; open ground and narrow passes; the chances of life and death.

9. *The Commander* stands for the virtues of wisdom, sincerity, benevolence, courage and strictness.

10. By *Method and discipline* are to be understood the marshaling of the army in its proper subdivisions, the graduations of rank among the officers, the maintenance of roads by which supplies may reach the army, and the control of military expenditure.

11. These five heads should be familiar to every general: he who knows them will be victorious; he who knows them not will fail.

12. Therefore, in your deliberations, when seeking to determine the military conditions, let them be made the basis of a comparison, in this wise:

13. (1) Which of the two sovereigns is imbued with the Moral law?
    (2) Which of the two generals has most ability?
    (3) With whom lie the advantages derived from Heaven and Earth?
    (4) On which side is discipline most rigorously enforced?

(5) Which army is stronger?

(6) On which side are officers and men more highly trained?

(7) In which army is there the greater constancy both in reward and punishment?

14. By means of these seven considerations I can forecast victory or defeat.

15. The general that hearkens to my counsel and acts upon it, will conquer: let such a one be retained in command! The general that hearkens not to my counsel nor acts upon it, will suffer defeat: let such a one be dismissed!

16. While heeding the profit of my counsel, avail yourself also of any helpful circumstances over and beyond the ordinary rules.

17. According as circumstances are favorable, one should modify one's plans.

18. All warfare is based on deception.

19. Hence, when able to attack, we must seem unable; when using our forces, we must seem inactive; when we are near, we must make the enemy believe we are far away; when far away, we must make him believe we are near.

20. Hold out baits to entice the enemy. Feign disorder, and crush him.

21. If he is secure at all points, be prepared for him. If he is in superior strength, evade him.

22. If your opponent is of choleric temper, seek to irritate him. Pretend to be weak, that he may grow arrogant.

23. If he is taking his ease, give him no rest. If his forces are united, separate them.

24. Attack him where he is unprepared, appear where you are not expected.

25. These military devices, leading to victory, must not be divulged beforehand.

26. Now the general who wins a battle makes many calculations in his temple ere the battle is fought. The general who loses a battle makes but few calculations beforehand. Thus do many calculations lead to victory, and few calculations to defeat: how much more no calculation at all! It is by attention to this point that I can foresee who is likely to win or lose.

II

WAGING WAR

1. Sun Tzŭ said: In the operations of war, where there are in the field a thousand swift chariots, as many heavy chariots, and a hundred thousand mail-clad soldiers, with provisions enough to carry them a thousand lî, the expenditure at home and at the front, including entertainment of guests, small items such as glue and paint, and sums spent on chariots and armor, will reach the total of a thousand ounces of silver per day. Such is the cost of raising an army of 100,000 men.

2. When you engage in actual fighting, if victory is long in coming, then men's weapons will grow dull and their ardor will be damped. If you lay siege to a town, you will exhaust your strength.

3. Again, if the campaign is protracted, the resources of the State will not be equal to the strain.

4. Now, when your weapons are dulled, your ardor damped, your strength exhausted and your treasure spent, other chieftains will spring up to take advantage of your extremity. Then no man, however wise, will be able to avert the consequences that must ensue.

5. Thus, though we have heard of stupid haste in war, cleverness has never been seen associated with long delays.

6. There is no instance of a country having benefited from prolonged warfare.

7. It is only one who is thoroughly acquainted with the evils of war that can thoroughly understand the profitable way of carrying it on.

8. The skillful soldier does not raise a second levy, neither are his supply-wagons loaded more than twice.

9. Bring war material with you from home, but forage on the enemy. Thus the army will have food enough for its needs.

10. Poverty of the State exchequer causes an army to be maintained by contributions from a distance. Contributing to maintain an army at a distance causes the people to be impoverished.

11. On the other hand, the proximity of an army causes prices to go up; and high prices cause the people's substance to be drained away.

12. When their substance is drained away, the peasantry will be afflicted by heavy exactions.

13,14. With this loss of substance and exhaustion of strength, the homes of the people will be stripped bare, and three-tenths of their income will be dissipated; while government expenses for broken chariots, worn-out horses, breast-plates and helmets, bows and arrows, spears and shields, protective mantelets, draught-oxen and heavy wagons, will amount to four-tenths of its total revenue.

15. Hence a wise general makes a point of foraging on the enemy. One cartload of the enemy's provisions is equivalent to twenty of one's own, and likewise a single *picul* of his provender is equivalent to twenty from one's own store.

16. Now in order to kill the enemy, our men must be roused to anger; that there may be advantage from defeating the enemy, they must have their rewards.

17. Therefore in chariot fighting, when ten or more chariots have been taken, those should be rewarded who took the first. Our own flags should be substituted for those of the enemy, and the chariots mingled and used in conjunction with ours. The captured soldiers should be kindly treated and kept.

18. This is called, using the conquered foe to augment one's own strength.

19. In war, then, let your great object be victory, not lengthy campaigns.

20. Thus it may be known that the leader of armies is the arbiter of the people's fate, the man on whom it depends whether the nation shall be in peace or in peril.

III

ATTACK BY STRATAGEM

1. Sun Tzŭ said: In the practical art of war, the best thing of all is to take the enemy's country whole and intact; to shatter and destroy it is not so good. So, too, it is better to recapture an army entire than to destroy it, to capture a regiment, a detachment or a company entire than to destroy them.

2. Hence to fight and conquer in all your battles is not supreme excellence; supreme excellence consists in breaking the enemy's resistance without fighting.

3. Thus the highest form of generalship is to balk the enemy's plans; the next best is to prevent the junction of the enemy's forces; the next in order is to attack the enemy's army in the field; and the worst policy of all is to besiege walled cities.

4. The rule is, not to besiege walled cities if it can possibly be avoided. The preparation of mantlets, movable shelters, and various implements of war, will take up three whole months; and the piling up of mounds over against the walls will take three months more.

5. The general, unable to control his irritation, will launch his men to the assault like swarming ants, with the result that one-third of his men are slain, while the town still remains untaken. Such are the disastrous effects of a siege.

6. Therefore the skillful leader subdues the enemy's troops without any fighting; he captures their cities without laying siege to them; he overthrows their kingdom without lengthy operations in the field.

7. With his forces intact he will dispute the mastery of the Empire, and thus, without losing a man, his triumph will be complete. This is the method of attacking by stratagem.

8. It is the rule in war, if our forces are ten to the enemy's one, to surround him; if five to one, to attack him; if twice as numerous, to divide our army into two.

9. If equally matched, we can offer battle; if slightly inferior in numbers, we can avoid the enemy; if quite unequal in every way, we can flee from him.

10. Hence, though an obstinate fight may be made by a small force, in the end it must be captured by the larger force.

11. Now the general is the bulwark of the State; if the bulwark is complete at all points, the State will be strong; if the bulwark is defective, the State will be weak.

12. There are three ways in which a ruler can bring misfortune upon his army:

13. (1) By commanding the army to advance or to retreat, being ignorant of the fact that it cannot obey. This is called hobbling the army.

14. (2) By attempting to govern an army in the same way as he administers a kingdom, being ignorant of the conditions which obtain in an army. This causes restlessness in the soldier's minds.

15. (3) By employing the officers of his army without discrimination, through ignorance of the military principle of adaptation to circumstances. This shakes the confidence of the soldiers.

16. But when the army is restless and distrustful, trouble is sure to come from the other feudal princes. This is simply bringing anarchy into the army, and flinging victory away.

17. Thus we may know that there are five essentials for victory:

    (1) He will win who knows when to fight and when not to fight.
    (2) He will win who knows how to handle both superior and inferior forces.
    (3) He will win whose army is animated by the same spirit throughout all its ranks.
    (4) He will win who, prepared himself, waits to take the enemy unprepared.
    (5) He will win who has military capacity and is not interfered with by the sovereign.

18. Hence the saying: If you know the enemy and know yourself, you need not fear the result of a hundred battles. If you know yourself but not the enemy, for every victory gained you will also suffer a defeat. If you know neither the enemy nor yourself, you will succumb in every battle.

IV

TACTICAL DISPOSITIONS

1. Sun Tzŭ said: The good fighters of old first put themselves beyond the possibility of defeat, and then waited for an opportunity of defeating the enemy.

2. To secure ourselves against defeat lies in our own hands, but the opportunity of defeating the enemy is provided by the enemy himself.

3. Thus the good fighter is able to secure himself against defeat, but cannot make certain of defeating the enemy.

4. Hence the saying: One may know how to conquer without being able to do it.

5. Security against defeat implies defensive tactics; ability to defeat the enemy means taking the offensive.

6. Standing on the defensive indicates insufficient strength; attacking, a superabundance of strength.

7. The general who is skilled in defense hides in the most secret recesses of the earth; he who is skilled in attack flashes forth from the topmost heights of heaven. Thus on the one hand we have ability to protect ourselves; on the other, a victory that is complete.

8. To see victory only when it is within the ken of the common herd is not the acme of excellence.

9. Neither is it the acme of excellence if you fight and conquer and the whole Empire says, "Well done!"

10. To lift an autumn hair is no sign of great strength; to see the sun and moon is no sign of sharp sight; to hear the noise of thunder is no sign of a quick ear.

11. What the ancients called a clever fighter is one who not only wins, but excels in winning with ease.

12. Hence his victories bring him neither reputation for wisdom nor credit for courage.

13. He wins his battles by making no mistakes. Making no mistakes is what establishes the certainty of victory, for it means conquering an enemy that is already defeated.

14. Hence the skillful fighter puts himself into a position which makes defeat impossible, and does not miss the moment for defeating the enemy.

15. Thus it is that in war the victorious strategist only seeks battle after the victory has been won, whereas he who is destined to defeat first fights and afterwards looks for victory.

16. The consummate leader cultivates the moral law, and strictly adheres to method and discipline; thus it is in his power to control success.

17. In respect of military method, we have, firstly, Measurement; secondly, Estimation of quantity; thirdly, Calculation; fourthly, Balancing of chances; fifthly, Victory.

18. Measurement owes its existence to Earth; Estimation of quantity to Measurement; Calculation to Estimation of quantity; Balancing of chances to Calculation; and Victory to Balancing of chances.

19. A victorious army opposed to a routed one, is as a pound's weight placed in the scale against a single grain.

20. The onrush of a conquering force is like the bursting of pent-up waters into a chasm a thousand fathoms deep.

V

ENERGY

1. Sun Tzŭ said: The control of a large force is the same principle as the control of a few men: it is merely a question of dividing up their numbers.

2. Fighting with a large army under your command is nowise different from fighting with a small one: it is merely a question of instituting signs and signals.

3. To ensure that your whole host may withstand the brunt of the enemy's attack and remain unshaken — this is effected by maneuvers direct and indirect.

4. That the impact of your army may be like a grindstone dashed against an egg — this is effected by the science of weak points and strong.

5. In all fighting, the direct method may be used for joining battle, but indirect methods will be needed in order to secure victory.

6. Indirect tactics, efficiently applied, are inexhaustible as Heaven and Earth, unending as the flow of rivers and streams; like the sun and moon, they end but to begin anew; like the four seasons, they pass away to return once more.

7. There are not more than five musical notes, yet the combinations of these five give rise to more melodies than can ever be heard.

8. There are not more than five primary colors (blue, yellow, red, white, and black), yet in combination they produce more hues than can ever been seen.

9. There are not more than five cardinal tastes (sour, acrid, salt, sweet, bitter), yet combinations of them yield more flavors than can ever be tasted.

10. In battle, there are not more than two methods of attack — the direct and the indirect; yet these two in combination give rise to an endless series of maneuvers.

11. The direct and the indirect lead on to each other in turn. It is like moving in a circle—you never come to an end. Who can exhaust the possibilities of their combination?

12. The onset of troops is like the rush of a torrent which will even roll stones along in its course.

13. The quality of decision is like the well-timed swoop of a falcon which enables it to strike and destroy its victim.

14. Therefore the good fighter will be terrible in his onset, and prompt in his decision.

15. Energy may be likened to the bending of a crossbow; decision, to the releasing of a trigger.

16. Amid the turmoil and tumult of battle, there may be seeming disorder and yet no real disorder at all; amid confusion and chaos, your array may be without head or tail, yet it will be proof against defeat.

17. Simulated disorder postulates perfect discipline, simulated fear postulates courage; simulated weakness postulates strength.

18. Hiding order beneath the cloak of disorder is simply a question of subdivision; concealing courage under a show of timidity presupposes a fund of latent energy; masking strength with weakness is to be effected by tactical dispositions.

19. Thus one who is skillful at keeping the enemy on the move maintains deceitful appearances, according to which the enemy will act. He sacrifices something, that the enemy may snatch at it.

20. By holding out baits, he keeps him on the march; then with a body of picked men he lies in wait for him.

21. The clever combatant looks to the effect of combined energy, and does not require too much from individuals. Hence his ability to pick out the right men and utilize combined energy.

22. When he utilizes combined energy, his fighting men become as it were like unto rolling logs or stones. For it is the nature of a log or stone to remain motionless on level ground, and to move when on a slope; if four-cornered, to come to a standstill, but if round-shaped, to go rolling down.

23. Thus the energy developed by good fighting men is as the momentum of a round stone rolled down a mountain thousands of feet in height. So much on the subject of energy.

VI

WEAK POINTS AND STRONG

1. Sun Tzŭ said: Whoever is first in the field and awaits the coming of the enemy, will be fresh for the fight; whoever is second in the field and has to hasten to battle will arrive exhausted.

2. Therefore the clever combatant imposes his will on the enemy, but does not allow the enemy's will to be imposed on him.

3. By holding out advantages to him, he can cause the enemy to approach of his own accord; or, by inflicting damage, he can make it impossible for the enemy to draw near.

4. If the enemy is taking his ease, he can harass him; if well supplied with food, he can starve him out; if quietly encamped, he can force him to move.

5. Appear at points which the enemy must hasten to defend; march swiftly to places where you are not expected.

6. An army may march great distances without distress, if it marches through country where the enemy is not.

7. You can be sure of succeeding in your attacks if you only attack places which are undefended. You can ensure the safety of your defense if you only hold positions that cannot be attacked.

8. Hence that general is skillful in attack whose opponent does not know what to defend; and he is skillful in defense whose opponent does not know what to attack.

9. O divine art of subtlety and secrecy! Through you we learn to be invisible, through you inaudible; and hence we can hold the enemy's fate in our hands.

10. You may advance and be absolutely irresistible, if you make for the enemy's weak points; you may retire and be safe from pursuit if your movements are more rapid than those of the enemy.

11. If we wish to fight, the enemy can be forced to an engagement even though he be sheltered behind a high rampart and a deep ditch. All

we need do is attack some other place that he will be obliged to relieve.

12. If we do not wish to fight, we can prevent the enemy from engaging us even though the lines of our encampment be merely traced out on the ground. All we need do is to throw something odd and unaccountable in his way.

13. By discovering the enemy's dispositions and remaining invisible ourselves, we can keep our forces concentrated, while the enemy's must be divided.

14. We can form a single united body, while the enemy must split up into fractions. Hence there will be a whole pitted against separate parts of a whole, which means that we shall be many to the enemy's few.

15. And if we are able thus to attack an inferior force with a superior one, our opponents will be in dire straits.

16. The spot where we intend to fight must not be made known; for then the enemy will have to prepare against a possible attack at several different points; and his forces being thus distributed in many directions, the numbers we shall have to face at any given point will be proportionately few.

17. For should the enemy strengthen his van, he will weaken his rear; should he strengthen his rear, he will weaken his van; should he strengthen his left, he will weaken his right; should he strengthen his right, he will weaken his left. If he sends reinforcements everywhere, he will everywhere be weak.

18. Numerical weakness comes from having to prepare against possible attacks; numerical strength, from compelling our adversary to make these preparations against us.

19. Knowing the place and the time of the coming battle, we may concentrate from the greatest distances in order to fight.

20. But if neither time nor place be known, then the left wing will be impotent to succor the right, the right equally impotent to succor the left, the van unable to relieve the rear, or the rear to support the van. How much more so if the furthest portions of the army are anything under a hundred lĭ apart, and even the nearest are separated by several lĭ!

21. Though according to my estimate the soldiers of Yüeh exceed our own in number, that shall advantage them nothing in the matter of victory. I say then that victory can be achieved.

22. Though the enemy be stronger in numbers, we may prevent him from fighting. Scheme so as to discover his plans and the likelihood of their success.

23. Rouse him, and learn the principle of his activity or inactivity. Force him to reveal himself, so as to find out his vulnerable spots.

24. Carefully compare the opposing army with your own, so that you may know where strength is superabundant and where it is deficient.

25. In making tactical dispositions, the highest pitch you can attain is to conceal them; conceal your dispositions, and you will be safe from the prying of the subtlest spies, from the machinations of the wisest brains.

26. How victory may be produced for them out of the enemy's own tactics—that is what the multitude cannot comprehend.

27. All men can see the tactics whereby I conquer, but what none can see is the strategy out of which victory is evolved.

28. Do not repeat the tactics which have gained you one victory, but let your methods be regulated by the infinite variety of circumstances.

29. Military tactics are like unto water; for water in its natural course runs away from high places and hastens downwards.

30. So in war, the way is to avoid what is strong and to strike at what is weak.

31. Water shapes its course according to the nature of the ground over which it flows; the soldier works out his victory in relation to the foe whom he is facing.

32. Therefore, just as water retains no constant shape, so in warfare there are no constant conditions.

33. He who can modify his tactics in relation to his opponent and thereby succeed in winning, may be called a heaven-born captain.

34. The five elements (water, fire, wood, metal, earth) are not always equally predominant; the four seasons make way for each other in turn. There are short days and long; the moon has its periods of waning and waxing.

VII

MANEUVERING

1. Sun Tzŭ said: In war, the general receives his commands from the sovereign.

2. Having collected an army and concentrated his forces, he must blend and harmonize the different elements thereof before pitching his camp.

3. After that, comes tactical maneuvering, than which there is nothing more difficult. The difficulty of tactical maneuvering consists in turning the devious into the direct, and misfortune into gain.

4. Thus, to take a long and circuitous route, after enticing the enemy out of the way, and though starting after him, to contrive to reach the goal before him, shows knowledge of the artifice of deviation.

5. Maneuvering with an army is advantageous; with an undisciplined multitude, most dangerous.

6. If you set a fully equipped army in march in order to snatch an advantage, the chances are that you will be too late. On the other hand, to detach a flying column for the purpose involves the sacrifice of its baggage and stores.

7. Thus, if you order your men to roll up their buff-coats, and make forced marches without halting day or night, covering double the usual distance at a stretch, doing a hundred lî in order to wrest an advantage, the leaders of all your three divisions will fall into the hands of the enemy.

8. The stronger men will be in front, the jaded ones will fall behind, and on this plan only one-tenth of your army will reach its destination.

9. If you march fifty lî in order to outmaneuver the enemy, you will lose the leader of your first division, and only half your force will reach the goal.

10. If you march thirty lî with the same object, two-thirds of your army will arrive.

11. We may take it then that an army without its baggage-train is lost; without provisions it is lost; without bases of supply it is lost.

12. We cannot enter into alliances until we are acquainted with the designs of our neighbors.

13. We are not fit to lead an army on the march unless we are familiar with the face of the country—its mountains and forests, its pitfalls and precipices, its marshes and swamps.

14. We shall be unable to turn natural advantage to account unless we make use of local guides.

15. In war, practice dissimulation, and you will succeed.

16. Whether to concentrate or to divide your troops, must be decided by circumstances.

17. Let your rapidity be that of the wind, your compactness that of the forest.

18. In raiding and plundering be like fire, in immovability like a mountain.

19. Let your plans be dark and impenetrable as night, and when you move, fall like a thunderbolt.

20. When you plunder a countryside, let the spoil be divided amongst your men; when you capture new territory, cut it up into allotments for the benefit of the soldiery.

21. Ponder and deliberate before you make a move.

22. He will conquer who has learnt the artifice of deviation. Such is the art of maneuvering.

23. The Book of Army Management says: On the field of battle, the spoken word does not carry far enough: hence the institution of gongs and drums. Nor can ordinary objects be seen clearly enough: hence the institution of banners and flags.

24. Gongs and drums, banners and flags, are means whereby the ears and eyes of the host may be focused on one particular point.

25. The host thus forming a single united body, is it impossible either for the brave to advance alone, or for the cowardly to retreat alone. This is the art of handling large masses of men.

26. In night-fighting, then, make much use of signal-fires and drums, and in fighting by day, of flags and banners, as a means of influencing the ears and eyes of your army.

27. A whole army may be robbed of its spirit; a commander-in-chief may be robbed of his presence of mind.

28. Now a soldier's spirit is keenest in the morning; by noonday it has begun to flag; and in the evening, his mind is bent only on returning to camp.

29. A clever general, therefore, avoids an army when its spirit is keen, but attacks it when it is sluggish and inclined to return. This is the art of studying moods.

30. Disciplined and calm, to await the appearance of disorder and hubbub amongst the enemy: this is the art of retaining self-possession.

31. To be near the goal while the enemy is still far from it, to wait at ease while the enemy is toiling and struggling, to be well-fed while the enemy is famished: this is the art of husbanding one's strength.

32. To refrain from intercepting an enemy whose banners are in perfect order, to refrain from attacking an army drawn up in calm and confident array: this is the art of studying circumstances.

33. It is a military axiom not to advance uphill against the enemy, nor to oppose him when he comes downhill.

34. Do not pursue an enemy who simulates flight; do not attack soldiers whose temper is keen.

35. Do not swallow bait offered by the enemy. Do not interfere with an army that is returning home.

36. When you surround an army, leave an outlet free. Do not press a desperate foe too hard.

37. Such is the art of warfare.

VIII

VARIATION OF TACTICS

1. Sun Tzŭ said: In war, the general receives his commands from the sovereign, collects his army and concentrates his forces.

2. When in difficult country, do not encamp. In country where high roads intersect, join hands with your allies. Do not linger in dangerously isolated positions. In hemmed-in situations, you must resort to stratagem. In desperate position, you must fight.

3. There are roads which must not be followed, armies which must be not attacked, towns which must not be besieged, positions which must not be contested, commands of the sovereign which must not be obeyed.

4. The general who thoroughly understands the advantages that accompany variation of tactics knows how to handle his troops.

5. The general who does not understand these, may be well acquainted with the configuration of the country, yet he will not be able to turn his knowledge to practical account.

6. So, the student of war who is unversed in the art of war of varying his plans, even though he be acquainted with the Five Advantages, will fail to make the best use of his men.

7. Hence in the wise leader's plans, considerations of advantage and of disadvantage will be blended together.

8. If our expectation of advantage be tempered in this way, we may succeed in accomplishing the essential part of our schemes.

9. If, on the other hand, in the midst of difficulties we are always ready to seize an advantage, we may extricate ourselves from misfortune.

10. Reduce the hostile chiefs by inflicting damage on them; and make trouble for them, and keep them constantly engaged; hold out specious allurements, and make them rush to any given point.

11. The art of war teaches us to rely not on the likelihood of the enemy's not coming, but on our own readiness to receive him; not on the

chance of his not attacking, but rather on the fact that we have made our position unassailable.

12. There are five dangerous faults which may affect a general:

(1) Recklessness, which leads to destruction;
(2) cowardice, which leads to capture;
(3) a hasty temper, which can be provoked by insults;
(4) a delicacy of honor which is sensitive to shame;
(5) over-solicitude for his men, which exposes him to worry and trouble.

13. These are the five besetting sins of a general, ruinous to the conduct of war.

14. When an army is overthrown and its leader slain, the cause will surely be found among these five dangerous faults. Let them be a subject of meditation.

IX

THE ARMY ON THE MARCH

1. Sun Tzŭ said: We come now to the question of encamping the army, and observing signs of the enemy. Pass quickly over mountains, and keep in the neighborhood of valleys.

2. Camp in high places, facing the sun. Do not climb heights in order to fight. So much for mountain warfare.

3. After crossing a river, you should get far away from it.

4. When an invading force crosses a river in its onward march, do not advance to meet it in mid-stream. It will be best to let half the army get across, and then deliver your attack.

5. If you are anxious to fight, you should not go to meet the invader near a river which he has to cross.

6. Moor your craft higher up than the enemy, and facing the sun. Do not move up-stream to meet the enemy. So much for river warfare.

7. In crossing salt-marshes, your sole concern should be to get over them quickly, without any delay.

8. If forced to fight in a salt-marsh, you should have water and grass near you, and get your back to a clump of trees. So much for operations in salt-marshes.

9. In dry, level country, take up an easily accessible position with rising ground to your right and on your rear, so that the danger may be in front, and safety lie behind. So much for campaigning in flat country.

10. These are the four useful branches of military knowledge which enabled the Yellow Emperor to vanquish four several sovereigns.

11. All armies prefer high ground to low and sunny places to dark.

12. If you are careful of your men, and camp on hard ground, the army will be free from disease of every kind, and this will spell victory.

13. When you come to a hill or a bank, occupy the sunny side, with the slope on your right rear. Thus you will at once act for the benefit of your soldiers and utilize the natural advantages of the ground.

14. When, in consequence of heavy rains up-country, a river which you wish to ford is swollen and flecked with foam, you must wait until it subsides.

15. Country in which there are precipitous cliffs with torrents running between, deep natural hollows, confined places, tangled thickets, quagmires and crevasses, should be left with all possible speed and not approached.

16. While we keep away from such places, we should get the enemy to approach them; while we face them, we should let the enemy have them on his rear.

17. If in the neighborhood of your camp there should be any hilly country, ponds surrounded by aquatic grass, hollow basins filled with reeds, or woods with thick undergrowth, they must be carefully routed out and searched; for these are places where men in ambush or insidious spies are likely to be lurking.

18. When the enemy is close at hand and remains quiet, he is relying on the natural strength of his position.

19. When he keeps aloof and tries to provoke a battle, he is anxious for the other side to advance.

20. If his place of encampment is easy of access, he is tendering a bait.

21. Movement amongst the trees of a forest shows that the enemy is advancing. The appearance of a number of screens in the midst of thick grass means that the enemy wants to make us suspicious.

22. The rising of birds in their flight is the sign of an ambuscade. Startled beasts indicate that a sudden attack is coming.

23. When there is dust rising in a high column, it is the sign of chariots advancing; when the dust is low, but spread over a wide area, it betokens the approach of infantry. When it branches out in different directions, it shows that parties have been sent to collect firewood. A few clouds of dust moving to and fro signify that the army is encamping.

24. Humble words and increased preparations are signs that the enemy is about to advance. Violent language and driving forward as if to the attack are signs that he will retreat.

25. When the light chariots come out first and take up a position on the wings, it is a sign that the enemy is forming for battle.

26. Peace proposals unaccompanied by a sworn covenant indicate a plot.

27. When there is much running about and the soldiers fall into rank, it means that the critical moment has come.

28. When some are seen advancing and some retreating, it is a lure.

29. When the soldiers stand leaning on their spears, they are faint from want of food.

30. If those who are sent to draw water begin by drinking themselves, the army is suffering from thirst.

31. If the enemy sees an advantage to be gained and makes no effort to secure it, the soldiers are exhausted.

32. If birds gather on any spot, it is unoccupied. Clamor by night betokens nervousness.

33. If there is disturbance in the camp, the general's authority is weak. If the banners and flags are shifted about, sedition is afoot. If the officers are angry, it means that the men are weary.

34. When an army feeds its horses with grain and kills its cattle for food, and when the men do not hang their cooking-pots over the camp-fires, showing that they will not return to their tents, you may know that they are determined to fight to the death.

35. The sight of men whispering together in small knots or speaking in subdued tones points to disaffection amongst the rank and file.

36. Too frequent rewards signify that the enemy is at the end of his resources; too many punishments betray a condition of dire distress.

37. To begin by bluster, but afterwards to take fright at the enemy's numbers, shows a supreme lack of intelligence.

38. When envoys are sent with compliments in their mouths, it is a sign that the enemy wishes for a truce.

39. If the enemy's troops march up angrily and remain facing ours for a long time without either joining battle or taking themselves off again, the situation is one that demands great vigilance and circumspection.

40. If our troops are no more in number than the enemy, that is amply sufficient; it only means that no direct attack can be made. What we can do is simply to concentrate all our available strength, keep a close watch on the enemy, and obtain reinforcements.

41. He who exercises no forethought but makes light of his opponents is sure to be captured by them.

42. If soldiers are punished before they have grown attached to you, they will not prove submissive; and, unless submissive, then will be practically useless. If, when the soldiers have become attached to you, punishments are not enforced, they will still be useless.

43. Therefore soldiers must be treated in the first instance with humanity, but kept under control by means of iron discipline. This is a certain road to victory.

44. If in training soldiers commands are habitually enforced, the army will be well-disciplined; if not, its discipline will be bad.

45. If a general shows confidence in his men but always insists on his orders being obeyed, the gain will be mutual.

X

TERRAIN

1. Sun Tzŭ said: We may distinguish six kinds of terrain, to wit:

   (1) Accessible ground;
   (2) entangling ground;
   (3) temporizing ground;
   (4) narrow passes;
   (5) precipitous heights;
   (6) positions at a great distance from the enemy.

2. Ground which can be freely traversed by both sides is called accessible.

3. With regard to ground of this nature, be before the enemy in occupying the raised and sunny spots, and carefully guard your line of supplies. Then you will be able to fight with advantage.

4. Ground which can be abandoned but is hard to re-occupy is called entangling.

5. From a position of this sort, if the enemy is unprepared, you may sally forth and defeat him. But if the enemy is prepared for your coming, and you fail to defeat him, then, return being impossible, disaster will ensue.

6. When the position is such that neither side will gain by making the first move, it is called temporizing ground.

7. In a position of this sort, even though the enemy should offer us an attractive bait, it will be advisable not to stir forth, but rather to retreat, thus enticing the enemy in his turn; then, when part of his army has come out, we may deliver our attack with advantage.

8. With regard to narrow passes, if you can occupy them first, let them be strongly garrisoned and await the advent of the enemy.

9. Should the army forestall you in occupying a pass, do not go after him if the pass is fully garrisoned, but only if it is weakly garrisoned.

10. With regard to precipitous heights, if you are beforehand with your adversary, you should occupy the raised and sunny spots, and there wait for him to come up.

11. If the enemy has occupied them before you, do not follow him, but retreat and try to entice him away.

12. If you are situated at a great distance from the enemy, and the strength of the two armies is equal, it is not easy to provoke a battle, and fighting will be to your disadvantage.

13. These six are the principles connected with Earth. The general who has attained a responsible post must be careful to study them.

14. Now an army is exposed to six several calamities, not arising from natural causes, but from faults for which the general is responsible. These are: (1) flight; (2) insubordination; (3) collapse; (4) ruin; (5) disorganization; (6) rout.

15. Other conditions being equal, if one force is hurled against another ten times its size, the result will be the flight of the former.

16. When the common soldiers are too strong and their officers too weak, the result is insubordination. When the officers are too strong and the common soldiers too weak, the result is collapse.

17. When the higher officers are angry and insubordinate, and on meeting the enemy give battle on their own account from a feeling of resentment, before the commander-in-chief can tell whether or not he is in a position to fight, the result is ruin.

18. When the general is weak and without authority; when his orders are not clear and distinct; when there are no fixed duties assigned to officers and men, and the ranks are formed in a slovenly haphazard manner, the result is utter disorganization.

19. When a general, unable to estimate the enemy's strength, allows an inferior force to engage a larger one, or hurls a weak detachment against a powerful one, and neglects to place picked soldiers in the front rank, the result must be rout.

20. These are six ways of courting defeat, which must be carefully noted by the general who has attained a responsible post.

21. The natural formation of the country is the soldier's best ally; but a power of estimating the adversary, of controlling the forces

of victory, and of shrewdly calculating difficulties, dangers and distances, constitutes the test of a great general.

22. He who knows these things, and in fighting puts his knowledge into practice, will win his battles. He who knows them not, nor practices them, will surely be defeated.

23. If fighting is sure to result in victory, then you must fight, even though the ruler forbid it; if fighting will not result in victory, then you must not fight even at the ruler's bidding.

24. The general who advances without coveting fame and retreats without fearing disgrace, whose only thought is to protect his country and do good service for his sovereign, is the jewel of the kingdom.

25. Regard your soldiers as your children, and they will follow you into the deepest valleys; look upon them as your own beloved sons, and they will stand by you even unto death.

26. If, however, you are indulgent, but unable to make your authority felt; kind-hearted, but unable to enforce your commands; and incapable, moreover, of quelling disorder: then your soldiers must be likened to spoilt children; they are useless for any practical purpose.

27. If we know that our own men are in a condition to attack, but are unaware that the enemy is not open to attack, we have gone only halfway towards victory.

28. If we know that the enemy is open to attack, but are unaware that our own men are not in a condition to attack, we have gone only halfway towards victory.

29. If we know that the enemy is open to attack, and also know that our men are in a condition to attack, but are unaware that the nature of the ground makes fighting impracticable, we have still gone only halfway towards victory.

30. Hence the experienced soldier, once in motion, is never bewildered; once he has broken camp, he is never at a loss.

31. Hence the saying: If you know the enemy and know yourself, your victory will not stand in doubt; if you know Heaven and know Earth, you may make your victory complete.

XI

THE NINE SITUATIONS

1. Sun Tzŭ said: The art of war recognizes nine varieties of ground:

    (1) dispersive ground;
    (2) facile ground;
    (3) contentious ground;
    (4) open ground;
    (5) ground of intersecting highways;
    (6) serious ground;
    (7) difficult ground;
    (8) hemmed-in ground;
    (9) desperate ground.

2. When a chieftain is fighting in his own territory, it is dispersive ground.

3. When he has penetrated into hostile territory, but to no great distance, it is facile ground.

4. Ground the possession of which imports great advantage to either side, is contentious ground.

5. Ground on which each side has liberty of movement is open ground.

6. Ground which forms the key to three contiguous states, so that he who occupies it first has most of the Empire at his command, is a ground of intersecting highways.

7. When an army has penetrated into the heart of a hostile country, leaving a number of fortified cities in its rear, it is serious ground.

8. Mountain forests, rugged steeps, marshes and fens—all country that is hard to traverse: this is difficult ground.

9. Ground which is reached through narrow gorges, and from which we can only retire by tortuous paths, so that a small number of the enemy would suffice to crush a large body of our men: this is hemmed-in ground.

10. Ground on which we can only be saved from destruction by fighting without delay, is desperate ground.

11. On dispersive ground, therefore, fight not. On facile ground, halt not. On contentious ground, attack not.

12. On open ground, do not try to block the enemy's way. On the ground of intersecting highways, join hands with your allies.

13. On serious ground, gather in plunder. In difficult ground, keep steadily on the march.

14. On hemmed-in ground, resort to stratagem. On desperate ground, fight.

15. Those who were called skillful leaders of old knew how to drive a wedge between the enemy's front and rear; to prevent co-operation between his large and small divisions; to hinder the good troops from rescuing the bad, the officers from rallying their men.

16. When the enemy's men were united, they managed to keep them in disorder.

17. When it was to their advantage, they made a forward move; when otherwise, they stopped still.

18. If asked how to cope with a great host of the enemy in orderly array and on the point of marching to the attack, I should say: "Begin by seizing something which your opponent holds dear; then he will be amenable to your will."

19. Rapidity is the essence of war: take advantage of the enemy's unreadiness, make your way by unexpected routes, and attack unguarded spots.

20. The following are the principles to be observed by an invading force: The further you penetrate into a country, the greater will be the solidarity of your troops, and thus the defenders will not prevail against you.

21. Make forays in fertile country in order to supply your army with food.

22. Carefully study the well-being of your men, and do not overtax them. Concentrate your energy and hoard your strength. Keep your army continually on the move, and devise unfathomable plans.

23. Throw your soldiers into positions whence there is no escape, and they will prefer death to flight. If they will face death, there is nothing they may not achieve. Officers and men alike will put forth their uttermost strength.

24. Soldiers when in desperate straits lose the sense of fear. If there is no place of refuge, they will stand firm. If they are in hostile country, they will show a stubborn front. If there is no help for it, they will fight hard.

25. Thus, without waiting to be marshaled, the soldiers will be constantly on the *qui vive*; without waiting to be asked, they will do your will; without restrictions, they will be faithful; without giving orders, they can be trusted.

26. Prohibit the taking of omens, and do away with superstitious doubts. Then, until death itself comes, no calamity need be feared.

27. If our soldiers are not overburdened with money, it is not because they have a distaste for riches; if their lives are not unduly long, it is not because they are disinclined to longevity.

28. On the day they are ordered out to battle, your soldiers may weep, those sitting up bedewing their garments, and those lying down letting the tears run down their cheeks. But let them once be brought to bay, and they will display the courage of a Chu or a Kuei.

29. The skillful tactician may be likened to the *shuai-jan*. Now the *shuai-jan* is a snake that is found in the Ch'ang mountains. Strike at its head, and you will be attacked by its tail; strike at its tail, and you will be attacked by its head; strike at its middle, and you will be attacked by head and tail both.

30. Asked if an army can be made to imitate the *shuai-jan*, I should answer, Yes. For the men of Wu and the men of Yüeh are enemies; yet if they are crossing a river in the same boat and are caught by a storm, they will come to each other's assistance just as the left hand helps the right.

31. Hence it is not enough to put one's trust in the tethering of horses, and the burying of chariot wheels in the ground.

32. The principle on which to manage an army is to set up one standard of courage which all must reach.

33. How to make the best of both strong and weak—that is a question involving the proper use of ground.

34. Thus the skillful general conducts his army just as though he were leading a single man, willy-nilly, by the hand.

35. It is the business of a general to be quiet and thus ensure secrecy; upright and just, and thus maintain order.

36. He must be able to mystify his officers and men by false reports and appearances, and thus keep them in total ignorance.

37. By altering his arrangements and changing his plans, he keeps the enemy without definite knowledge. By shifting his camp and taking circuitous routes, he prevents the enemy from anticipating his purpose.

38. At the critical moment, the leader of an army acts like one who has climbed up a height and then kicks away the ladder behind him. He carries his men deep into hostile territory before he shows his hand.

39. He burns his boats and breaks his cooking-pots; like a shepherd driving a flock of sheep, he drives his men this way and that, and none knows whither he is going.

40. To muster his host and bring it into danger: this may be termed the business of the general.

41. The different measures suited to the nine varieties of ground; the expediency of aggressive or defensive tactics; and the fundamental laws of human nature: these are things that must most certainly be studied.

42. When invading hostile territory, the general principle is, that penetrating deeply brings cohesion; penetrating but a short way means dispersion.

43. When you leave your own country behind, and take your army across neighborhood territory, you find yourself on critical ground. When there are means of communication on all four sides, the ground is one of intersecting highways.

44. When you penetrate deeply into a country, it is serious ground. When you penetrate but a little way, it is facile ground.

45. When you have the enemy's strongholds on your rear, and narrow passes in front, it is hemmed-in ground. When there is no place of refuge at all, it is desperate ground.

46. Therefore, on dispersive ground, I would inspire my men with unity of purpose. On facile ground, I would see that there is close connection between all parts of my army.

47. On contentious ground, I would hurry up my rear.

48. On open ground, I would keep a vigilant eye on my defenses. On ground of intersecting highways, I would consolidate my alliances.

49. On serious ground, I would try to ensure a continuous stream of supplies. On difficult ground, I would keep pushing on along the road.

50. On hemmed-in ground, I would block any way of retreat. On desperate ground, I would proclaim to my soldiers the hopelessness of saving their lives.

51. For it is the soldier's disposition to offer an obstinate resistance when surrounded, to fight hard when he cannot help himself, and to obey promptly when he has fallen into danger.

52. We cannot enter into alliance with neighboring princes until we are acquainted with their designs. We are not fit to lead an army on the march unless we are familiar with the face of the country—its mountains and forests, its pitfalls and precipices, its marshes and swamps. We shall be unable to turn natural advantages to account unless we make use of local guides.

53. To be ignored of any one of the following four or five principles does not befit a warlike prince.

54. When a warlike prince attacks a powerful state, his generalship shows itself in preventing the concentration of the enemy's forces. He overawes his opponents, and their allies are prevented from joining against him.

55. Hence he does not strive to ally himself with all and sundry, nor does he foster the power of other states. He carries out his own secret designs, keeping his antagonists in awe. Thus he is able to capture their cities and overthrow their kingdoms.

56. Bestow rewards without regard to rule, issue orders without regard to previous arrangements; and you will be able to handle a whole army as though you had to do with but a single man.

57. Confront your soldiers with the deed itself; never let them know your design. When the outlook is bright, bring it before their eyes; but tell them nothing when the situation is gloomy.

58. Place your army in deadly peril, and it will survive; plunge it into desperate straits, and it will come off in safety.

59. For it is precisely when a force has fallen into harm's way that is capable of striking a blow for victory.

60. Success in warfare is gained by carefully accommodating ourselves to the enemy's purpose.

61. By persistently hanging on the enemy's flank, we shall succeed in the long run in killing the commander-in-chief.

62. This is called ability to accomplish a thing by sheer cunning.

63. On the day that you take up your command, block the frontier passes, destroy the official tallies, and stop the passage of all emissaries.

64. Be stern in the council-chamber, so that you may control the situation.

65. If the enemy leaves a door open, you must rush in.

66. Forestall your opponent by seizing what he holds dear, and subtly contrive to time his arrival on the ground.

67. Walk in the path defined by rule, and accommodate yourself to the enemy until you can fight a decisive battle.

68. At first, then, exhibit the coyness of a maiden, until the enemy gives you an opening; afterwards emulate the rapidity of a running hare, and it will be too late for the enemy to oppose you.

XII

THE ATTACK BY FIRE

1. Sun Tzŭ said: There are five ways of attacking with fire. The first is to burn soldiers in their camp; the second is to burn stores; the third is to burn baggage trains; the fourth is to burn arsenals and magazines; the fifth is to hurl dropping fire amongst the enemy.

2. In order to carry out an attack, we must have means available. The material for raising fire should always be kept in readiness.

3. There is a proper season for making attacks with fire, and special days for starting a conflagration.

4. The proper season is when the weather is very dry; the special days are those when the moon is in the constellations of the Sieve, the Wall, the Wing or the Cross-bar; for these four are all days of rising wind.

5. In attacking with fire, one should be prepared to meet five possible developments:

6. (1) When fire breaks out inside to enemy's camp, respond at once with an attack from without.

7. (2) If there is an outbreak of fire, but the enemy's soldiers remain quiet, bide your time and do not attack.

8. (3) When the force of the flames has reached its height, follow it up with an attack, if that is practicable; if not, stay where you are.

9. (4) If it is possible to make an assault with fire from without, do not wait for it to break out within, but deliver your attack at a favorable moment.

10. (5) When you start a fire, be to windward of it. Do not attack from the leeward.

11. A wind that rises in the daytime lasts long, but a night breeze soon falls.

12. In every army, the five developments connected with fire must be known, the movements of the stars calculated, and a watch kept for the proper days.

13. Hence those who use fire as an aid to the attack show intelligence; those who use water as an aid to the attack gain an accession of strength.

14. By means of water, an enemy may be intercepted, but not robbed of all his belongings.

15. Unhappy is the fate of one who tries to win his battles and succeed in his attacks without cultivating the spirit of enterprise; for the result is waste of time and general stagnation.

16. Hence the saying: The enlightened ruler lays his plans well ahead; the good general cultivates his resources.

17. Move not unless you see an advantage; use not your troops unless there is something to be gained; fight not unless the position is critical.

18. No ruler should put troops into the field merely to gratify his own spleen; no general should fight a battle simply out of pique.

19. If it is to your advantage, make a forward move; if not, stay where you are.

20. Anger may in time change to gladness; vexation may be succeeded by content.

21. But a kingdom that has once been destroyed can never come again into being; nor can the dead ever be brought back to life.

22. Hence the enlightened ruler is heedful, and the good general full of caution. This is the way to keep a country at peace and an army intact.

XIII

THE USE OF SPIES

1. Sun Tzŭ said: Raising a host of a hundred thousand men and marching them great distances entails heavy loss on the people and a drain on the resources of the State. The daily expenditure will amount to a thousand ounces of silver. There will be commotion at home and abroad, and men will drop down exhausted on the highways. As many as seven hundred thousand families will be impeded in their labor.

2. Hostile armies may face each other for years, striving for the victory which is decided in a single day. This being so, to remain in ignorance of the enemy's condition simply because one grudges the outlay of a hundred ounces of silver in honors and emoluments, is the height of inhumanity.

3. One who acts thus is no leader of men, no present help to his sovereign, no master of victory.

4. Thus, what enables the wise sovereign and the good general to strike and conquer, and achieve things beyond the reach of ordinary men, is foreknowledge.

5. Now this foreknowledge cannot be elicited from spirits; it cannot be obtained inductively from experience, nor by any deductive calculation.

6. Knowledge of the enemy's dispositions can only be obtained from other men.

7. Hence the use of spies, of whom there are five classes: (1) Local spies; (2) inward spies; (3) converted spies; (4) doomed spies; (5) surviving spies.

8. When these five kinds of spy are all at work, none can discover the secret system. This is called "divine manipulation of the threads." It is the sovereign's most precious faculty.

9. Having local spies means employing the services of the inhabitants of a district.

10. Having inward spies, making use of officials of the enemy.

11. Having converted spies, getting hold of the enemy's spies and using them for our own purposes.

12. Having doomed spies, doing certain things openly for purposes of deception, and allowing our spies to know of them and report them to the enemy.

13. Surviving spies, finally, are those who bring back news from the enemy's camp.

14. Hence it is that which none in the whole army are more intimate relations to be maintained than with spies. None should be more liberally rewarded. In no other business should greater secrecy be preserved.

15. Spies cannot be usefully employed without a certain intuitive sagacity.

16. They cannot be properly managed without benevolence and straightforwardness.

17. Without subtle ingenuity of mind, one cannot make certain of the truth of their reports.

18. Be subtle! be subtle! and use your spies for every kind of business.

19. If a secret piece of news is divulged by a spy before the time is ripe, he must be put to death together with the man to whom the secret was told.

20. Whether the object be to crush an army, to storm a city, or to assassinate an individual, it is always necessary to begin by finding out the names of the attendants, the aides-de-camp, and door-keepers and sentries of the general in command. Our spies must be commissioned to ascertain these.

21. The enemy's spies who have come to spy on us must be sought out, tempted with bribes, led away and comfortably housed. Thus they will become converted spies and available for our service.

22. It is through the information brought by the converted spy that we are able to acquire and employ local and inward spies.

23. It is owing to his information, again, that we can cause the doomed spy to carry false tidings to the enemy.

24. Lastly, it is by his information that the surviving spy can be used on appointed occasions.

25. The end and aim of spying in all its five varieties is knowledge of the enemy; and this knowledge can only be derived, in the first instance, from the converted spy. Hence it is essential that the converted spy be treated with the utmost liberality.

26. Of old, the rise of the Yin dynasty was due to I Chih who had served under the Hsia. Likewise, the rise of the Chou dynasty was due to Lu Ya who had served under the Yin.

27. Hence it is only the enlightened ruler and the wise general who will use the highest intelligence of the army for purposes of spying and thereby they achieve great results. Spies are a most important element in water, because on them depends an army's ability to move.

The Art of War

(WITH COMMENTARY)

INTRODUCTION

SUN TZŬ AND HIS BOOK

Ssŭ-ma Ch'ien gives the following biography of Sun Tzŭ:

Sun Tzŭ Wu was a native of the Ch'i State. His *Art of War* brought him to the notice of Ho Lü, King of Wu. Ho Lü said to him: "I have carefully perused your thirteen chapters. May I submit your theory of managing soldiers to a slight test?"

Sun Tzŭ replied: "You may."

Ho Lü asked: "May the test be applied to women?"

The answer was again in the affirmative, so arrangements were made to bring 180 ladies out of the Palace. Sun Tzŭ divided them into two companies, and placed one of the King's favorite concubines at the head of each. He then bade them all take spears in their hands, and addressed them thus: "I presume you know the difference between front and back, right hand and left hand?"

The girls replied: Yes.

Sun Tzŭ went on: "When I say 'Eyes front,' you must look straight ahead. When I say 'Left turn,' you must face towards your left hand. When I say 'Right turn,' you must face towards your right hand. When I say 'About turn,' you must face right round towards your back."

Again the girls assented. The words of command having been thus explained, he set up the halberds and battle-axes in order to begin the drill. Then, to the sound of drums, he gave the order "Right turn." But the girls only burst out laughing. Sun Tzŭ said: "If words of command are not clear and distinct, if orders are not thoroughly understood, then the general is to blame."

So he started drilling them again, and this time gave the order "Left turn," whereupon the girls once more burst into fits of laughter. Sun Tzŭ: "If words of command are not clear and distinct, if orders are not thoroughly understood, the general is to blame. But if his orders are clear, and the soldiers nevertheless disobey, then it is the fault of their officers."

So saying, he ordered the leaders of the two companies to be beheaded. Now the king of Wu was watching the scene from the top of a raised pavilion; and when he saw that his favorite concubines were about to be executed, he was greatly alarmed and hurriedly sent down the following message: "We are now quite satisfied as to our general's ability to handle troops. If we are bereft of these two concubines, our meat and drink will lose their savor. It is our wish that they shall not be beheaded."

Sun Tzŭ replied: "Having once received His Majesty's commission to be the general of his forces, there are certain commands of His Majesty which, acting in that capacity, I am unable to accept."

Accordingly, he had the two leaders beheaded, and straightway installed the pair next in order as leaders in their place. When this had been done, the drum was sounded for the drill once more; and the girls went through all the evolutions, turning to the right or to the left, marching ahead or wheeling back, kneeling or standing, with perfect accuracy and precision, not venturing to utter a sound. Then Sun Tzŭ sent a messenger to the King saying: "Your soldiers, Sire, are now properly drilled and disciplined, and ready for your majesty's inspection. They can be put to any use that their sovereign may desire; bid them go through fire and water, and they will not disobey."

But the King replied: "Let our general cease drilling and return to camp. As for us, We have no wish to come down and inspect the troops."

Thereupon Sun Tzŭ said: "The King is only fond of words, and cannot translate them into deeds."

After that, Ho Lü saw that Sun Tzŭ was one who knew how to handle an army, and finally appointed him general. In the west, he defeated the Ch'u State and forced his way into Ying, the capital; to the north he put fear into the States of Ch'i and Chin, and spread his fame abroad amongst the feudal princes. And Sun Tzŭ shared in the might of the King.

About Sun Tzŭ himself this is all that Ssŭ-ma Ch'ien has to tell us in this chapter. But he proceeds to give a biography of his descendant, Sun Pin, born about a hundred years after his famous ancestor's death, and also the outstanding military genius of his time. The historian speaks of him too as Sun Tzŭ, and in his preface we read: "Sun Tzŭ had his feet cut off and yet continued to discuss the art of war." It seems likely, then, that "Pin" was a nickname bestowed on him after his mutilation, unless the story was invented in order to account for the name. (The crowning incident of his career, the crushing defeat of his treacherous rival P'ang Chüan, will be found briefly related in Ch. Five, paragraph 19, of *The Art of War*.) To return to the elder Sun Tzŭ, he is mentioned in two other passages of the *Shih Chi*:

> In the third year of his reign [512 BC] Ho Lü, king of Wu, took the field with Tzŭ-hsu [i.e., Wu Yuan] and Po P'ei, and attacked Ch'u. He captured the town of Shu and slew the two prince's sons who had formerly been generals of Wu. He was then meditating a descent on Ying [the capital]; but the general Sun Wu [another name for Sun Tzŭ] said: "The army is exhausted. It is not yet possible. We must wait . . ." [After further successful fighting,] "in the ninth year [506 BC], King Ho Lü addressed Wu Tzŭ-hsu and Sun Wu, saying: "Formerly, you declared that it was not yet possible for us to enter Ying. Is the time ripe now?" The two men replied: "Ch'u's general Tzŭ-ch'ang, is grasping and covetous, and the princes of T'ang and Ts'ai both have a grudge against him. If Your Majesty has resolved to make a grand attack, you must win over T'ang and Ts'ai, and then you may succeed." Ho Lü followed this advice [and beat Ch'u in five pitched battles and marched into Ying].

This is the latest date at which anything is recorded of Sun Wu. He does not appear to have survived his patron, who died from the effects of a wound in 496. In another chapter there occurs this passage:

> From this time onward, a number of famous soldiers arose, one after the other: Kao-fan, who was employed by the Chin State; Wang-Tzŭ, in the service of Ch'i; and Sun Wu, in the service of Wu. These men developed and threw light upon the principles of war.

It is obvious enough that Ssŭ-ma Ch'ien at least had no doubt about the reality of Sun Wu as an historical personage; and with one exception, to be noticed presently, he is by far the most important authority on the period in question. It will not be necessary, therefore, to say much of such a work as the *Wu Yüeh Ch'un Ch'iu*, which is supposed to have been written by Chao Yeh of the 1st century AD. The attribution is somewhat doubtful; but even if it were otherwise, his account would be of little value, based as it is on the *Shih Chi* and expanded with romantic details. The story of Sun Tzŭ will be found, for what it is worth, in ch. 2. The only new points in it worth noting are: (1) Sun Tzŭ was first recommended to Ho Lü by Wu Tzŭ-hsü. (2) He is called a native of Wu. (3) He had previously lived a retired life, and his contemporaries were unaware of his ability.

The following passage occurs in the Huai-nan Tzŭ: "When sovereign and ministers show perversity of mind, it is impossible even for a Sun Tzŭ to encounter the foe." Assuming that this work is genuine (and hitherto no doubt has been cast upon it), we have here the earliest direct reference for Sun Tzŭ, for Huai-nan Tzŭ died in 122 BC, many years before the *Shih Chi* was given to the world.

Liu Hsiang (80–9 BC) says: "The reason why Sun Tzŭ at the head of 30,000 men beat Ch'u with 200,000 is that the latter were undisciplined."

Teng Ming-shih informs us that the surname "Sun" was bestowed on Sun Wu's grandfather by Duke Ching of Ch'i [547–490 BC]. Sun Wu's father Sun P'ing, rose to be a Minister of State in Ch'i, and Sun Wu himself, whose style was Ch'ang-ch'ing, fled to Wu on account of the rebellion which was being fomented by the kindred of T'ien Pao. He had three sons, of whom the second, named Ming, was the father of Sun Pin. According to this account then, Pin was the grandson of Wu, which, considering that Sun Pin's victory over Wei was gained in 341 BC, may be dismissed as chronological impossible. Whence these data were obtained by Teng Ming-shih I do not know, but of course no reliance whatever can be placed in them.

An interesting document which has survived from the close of the Han period is the short preface written by the Great Ts'ao Ts'ao, or Wei Wu Ti, for his edition of Sun Tzŭ. I shall give it in full:

> I have heard that the ancients used bows and arrows to their advantage. The Shu Chu mentions "the army" among the "eight objects of government." The *I Ching* says: "'army' indicates firmness and justice; the experienced leader will have good fortune." The Shih Ching says: "The King rose majestic in his wrath, and he marshaled his troops." The Yellow Emperor, T'ang the Completer and Wu Wang all used spears and battle-axes in order to succor their generation. The Ssŭ-Ma Fa says: "If one man slay another of set purpose, he himself may

rightfully be slain." He who relies solely on warlike measures shall be exterminated; he who relies solely on peaceful measures shall perish. Instances of this are Fu Ch'ai on the one hand and Yen Wang on the other. In military matters, the Sage's rule is normally to keep the peace, and to move his forces only when occasion requires. He will not use armed force unless driven to it by necessity.

Many books have I read on the subject of war and fighting; but the work composed by Sun Wu is the profoundest of them all. [Sun Tzŭ was a native of the Ch'i state, his personal name was Wu. He wrote *The Art of War* in thirteen chapters for Ho Lü, King of Wu. Its principles were tested on women, and he was subsequently made a general. He led an army westwards, crushed the Ch'u state and entered Ying the capital. In the north, he kept Ch'i and Chin in awe. A hundred years and more after his time, Sun Pin lived. He was a descendant of Wu.] In his treatment of deliberation and planning, the importance of rapidity in taking the field, clearness of conception, and depth of design, Sun Tzŭ stands beyond the reach of carping criticism. My contemporaries, however, have failed to grasp the full meaning of his instructions, and while putting into practice the smaller details in which his work abounds, they have overlooked its essential purport. That is the motive which has led me to outline a rough explanation of the whole.

One thing to be noticed in the above is the explicit statement that the thirteen chapters were specially composed for King Ho Lü. This is supported by the internal evidence of Ch. One, paragraph 15, in which it seems clear that some ruler is addressed.

In the bibliographic section of the *Han Shu*, there is an entry which has given rise to much discussion: "The works of Sun Tzŭ of Wu in 82 *p'ien* (or chapters), with diagrams in 9 *chüan*." It is evident that this cannot be merely the thirteen chapters known to Ssŭ-ma Ch'ien, or those we possess today. Chang Shou-chieh refers to an edition of Sun Tzŭ's *Art of War* of which the "thirteen chapters" formed the first chüan, adding that there were two other *chüan* besides. This has brought forth a theory, that the bulk of these eighty-two chapters consisted of other writings of Sun Tzŭ — we should call them apocryphal — similar to the *Wen Ta*, of which a specimen dealing with the Nine Situations is preserved in the *T'ung Tien*, and another in Ho Shin's commentary. It is suggested that before his interview with Ho Lü, Sun Tzŭ had only written the thirteen chapters, but afterwards composed a sort of exegesis in the form of question and answer between himself and the King. Pi I-hsün, the author of the *Sun Tzŭ Hsu Lü*, backs this up with a quotation from the *Wu Yüeh Ch'un Ch'iu*: "The King of Wu summoned Sun Tzŭ, and asked him questions about the art of war. Each time he set forth a chapter of his work, the King could not find words enough to praise him." As he points out, if the whole work was expounded on the same scale as in the above-mentioned fragments, the total number of chapters could not fail to be considerable. Then the numerous other treatises attributed to Sun Tzŭ might be included. The fact that the *Han Chih* mentions no work of Sun Tzŭ except the 82 *p'ien*, whereas the Sui and T'ang bibliographies give the titles of others in addition to the "thirteen chapters," is good proof, Pi I-hsun thinks, that all of these were contained in the 82 *p'ien*. Without pinning our faith to the accuracy of details supplied by the *Wu Yüeh Ch'un Ch'iu*, or admitting the genuineness of any of the treatises cited by Pi I-hsün, we may see in this theory a probable solution of the mystery. Between Ssŭ-ma Ch'ien and Pan Ku there was plenty of time for a luxuriant crop of forgeries to have grown up under the magic name of Sun Tzŭ, and the 82 *p'ien* may very well represent a collected edition of these lumped together with the original work. It is also possible, though less likely, that some of them existed in the time of the earlier historian and were purposely ignored by him.

Tu Mu, after Tsao Kung the most important commentator on Sun Tzŭ, composed the preface to his edition about the middle of the ninth century. After a somewhat lengthy defense of the military art, he comes at last to Sun Tzŭ himself, and makes two startling asssertions: "The writings of Sun Wu," he said, "originally comprise several hundred thousand words, but Ts'ao Ts'ao, the Emperor Wu Wei, pruned away all redundancies and wrote out the essence of the whole, so as to form a single book in thirteen chapters." He goes on to remark that Ts'ao Ts'ao's commentary on Sun Wu leaves a certain proportion of difficulties unexplained. This, in Tu Mu's opinion, does not necessarily imply that he was unable to furnish a complete commentary. According to the *Wei Chih*, Ts'ao himself wrote a book on war in something over one hundred thousand words, known as the *Hsin Shu*. It appears to have been of such exceptional merit that he suspects Ts'ao to have used for it the surplus mateiral he found in Sun Tzŭ. He concludes, however, by saying "the *Hsin Shu* is now lost, so that the truth cannot be known for certain."

Tu Mu's conjecture seems to be based on a passage which states: "Wei Wu Ti strung together Sun Wu's *Art of War*," which in turn may have resulted from a misunderstanding of the final words of Ts'ao King's preface. This, as Sun Hsing-yen points out, is only a modest way of saying that he made an explanatory paraphrase, or in other words, wrote a commentary on it. On the whole, this theory has met with very little acceptance. Thus, the *Ssu K'u Ch'uan Shu* says: "The mention of the thirteen chapters in the *Shih Chi* shows that they were in existence before the *Han Chih*, and that latter accretions are not to be considered part of the original work. Tu Mu's assertion can certainly not be taken as proof."

There is every reason to suppose, then, that the thirteen chapters existed in the time of Ssŭ-ma Ch'ien practically as we have them now. That the work was then well known he tells us in so many words. Sun Tzŭ's thirteen Chapters and Wu Ch'i's *Art of War* are the two books that people commonly refer to on the subject of military matters. Both of them are widely distributed, so I will not discuss them here." But as we go further back, serious difficulties begin to arise. The salient fact which has to be faced is that the *Tso Chuan*, the greatest contemporary record, makes no mention whatsoever of Sun Wu, either as a general or as a writer. It is natural, in view of this awkward circumstance, that many scholars should not only cast doubt on the story of Sun Wu as given in the *Shih Chi*, but even show themselves frankly skeptical as to the existence of the man at all. The most powerful presentment of this side of the case is to be found in the following disposition by Yeh Shui-hsin [1151–1223]:

> It is stated in Ssŭ-ma Ch'ien's history that Sun Wu was a native of the Ch'i State, and employed by Wu; and that in the reign of Ho Lü he crushed Ch'u, entered Ying, and was a great general. But in Tso's Commentary no Sun Wu appears at all. It is true that Tso's Commentary need not contain absolutely everything that other histories contain. But Tso has not omitted to mention vulgar plebeians and hireling ruffians such as Ying K'ao-shu, Ts'ao Kuei, Chu Chih-wu and Chüan She-chu. In the case of Sun Wu, whose fame and achievements were so brilliant, the omission is much more glaring. Again, details are given, in their due order, about his contemporaries Wu Yuan and the Minister P'ei. Is it credible that Sun Wu alone should have been passed over?

In point of literary style, Sun Tzŭ's work belongs to the same school as *Kuan Tzŭ, Liu T'ao*, and the *Yüeh Yü* and may have been the production of some private scholar living towards the end of the "Spring and Autumn" or the beginning of the "Warring States" period. The story that his precepts were actually applied by the Wu State, is merely the outcome of big talk on the part of his followers.

From the flourishing period of the Chou dynasty down to the time of the "Spring and Autumn," all military commanders were statesmen as well, and the class of professional generals, for conducting external campaigns, did not then exist. It was not until the period of the "Six States" that this custom changed. Now although Wu was an uncivilized State, it is conceivable that Tso should have left unrecorded the fact that Sun Wu was a great general and yet held no civil office? What we are told, therefore, about Jang-chu and Sun Wu, is not authentic matter, but the reckless fabrication of theorizing pundits. The story of Ho Lü's experiment on the women, in particular, is utterly preposterous and incredible.

Yeh Shui-hsin represents Ssŭ-ma Ch'ien as having said that Sun Wu crushed Ch'u and entered Ying. This is not quite correct. No doubt the impression left on the reader's mind is that he at least shared in these exploits. The fact may or may not be significant; but it is nowhere explicitly stated in the *Shih Chi* either that Sun Tzŭ was general on the occasion of the taking of Ying, or that he even went there at all. Moreover, as we know that Wu Yuan and Po P'ei both took part in the expedition, and also that its success was largely due to the dash and enterprise of Fu Kai, Ho Lü's younger brother, it is not easy to see how yet another general could have played a very prominent part in the same campaign.

Ch'ên Chên-sun of the Sung dynasty has the note:

Military writers look upon Sun Wu as the father of their art. But the fact that he does not appear in the *Tso Chuan*, although he is said to have served under Ho Lü King of Wu, makes it uncertain what period he really belonged to.

He also says:

The works of Sun Wu and Wu Ch'i may be of genuine antiquity.

It is noticeable that both Yeh Shui-hsin and Ch'en Chen-sun, while rejecting the personality of Sun Wu as he figures in Ssŭ-ma Ch'ien's history, are inclined to accept the date traditionally assigned to the work which passes under his name. The author of the *Hsu Lü* fails to appreciate this distinction, and consequently his bitter attack on Ch'en Chen-sun really misses its mark. He makes one of two points, however, which certainly tell in favor of the high antiquity of our "thirteen chapters." "Sun Tzŭ," he says, "must have lived in the age of Ching Wang [519–476], because he is frequently plagiarized in subsequent works of the Chou, Ch'in and Han dynasties." The two most shameless offenders in this respect are Wu Ch'i and Huai-nan Tzŭ, both of them important historical personages in their day. The former lived only a century after the alleged date of Sun Tzŭ, and his death is known to have taken place in 381 BC. It was to him, according to Liu Hsiang, that Tseng Shen delivered the *Tso Chuan*, which had been entrusted to him by its author. Now the fact that quotations from *The Art of War*, acknowledged or otherwise, are to be found in so many authors of different epochs, establishes a very strong anterior to them all — in other words, that Sun Tzŭ's treatise was already in existence towards the end of the 5th century BC. Further proof of Sun Tzŭ's antiquity is furnished by the archaic or wholly obsolete meanings attaching to a number of the words he uses. A list of these, which might perhaps be extended, is given in the *Hsü Lu*; and though some of the interpretations are doubtful, the main argument is hardly affected thereby. Again, it must not be forgotten that Yeh Shui-hsin, a scholar and critic of the first rank, deliberately pronounces the style of the thirteen chapters to belong to the early part of the fifth century. Seeing that he is actually engaged in an attempt to disprove the existence of Sun Wu himself, we may be sure that he would not have hesitated to assign the work to a later date had he not honestly believed the contrary. And it is precisely on such a point that the judgment of an educated Chinaman will carry most weight. Other internal evidence is not far to seek. Thus in Ch. 13, paragraph 1, there is an unmistakable allusion to the ancient system of land-tenure which had already passed away by the time of Mencius, who was anxious to see it revived in a modified form. The only warfare Sun Tzŭ knows is that carried on between the various feudal princes, in which armored chariots play a large part. Their use seems to have entirely died out before the end of the Chou dynasty. He speaks as a man of Wu, a state which ceased to exist as early as 473 BC. On this I shall touch presently.

But once refer the work to the 5th century or earlier, and the chances of its being other than a *bona fide* production are sensibly diminished. The great age of forgeries did not come until long after. That it should have been forged in the period immediately following 473 is particularly unlikely, for no one, as a rule, hastens to identify himself with a lost cause. As for Yeh Shui-hsin's theory, that the author was a literary recluse, that seems to me quite untenable. If one thing is more apparent than another after reading the maxims of Sun Tzŭ, it is that their essence has been distilled from a large store of personal observation and experience. They reflect the mind not only of a born strategist, gifted with a rare faculty of generalization, but also of a practical soldier closely acquainted with the military conditions of his time. To say nothing of the fact that these sayings have been accepted and endorsed by all the greatest captains of Chinese history, they offer a combination of freshness and sincerity, acuteness and common sense, which quite excludes the idea that they were artificially concocted in the study. If we admit, then, that the thirteen chapters were the genuine production of a military man living towards the end of the "Ch'un Ch'iu" period, are we not bound, in spite of the silence of the *Tso Chuan*, to accept Ssŭ-ma Ch'ien's account in its entirety? In view of his high repute as a sober historian, must we not hesitate to assume that the records he drew upon for Sun Wu's biography were false and untrustworthy? The answer, I fear, must be in the negative. There is still one grave, if not fatal, objection to the chronology involved in the story as told in the *Shih Chi*, which, so far as I am aware, nobody has yet pointed out. There are two passages in Sun Tzŭ in which he alludes to contemporary affairs. The first in in Ch. Six, paragraph 21:

> Though according to my estimate the soldiers of Yüeh exceed our own in number, that shall advantage them nothing in the matter of victory. I say then that victory can be achieved.

The other is in Ch. Eleven, paragraph 30:

> Asked if an army can be made to imitate the *shuai-jan*, I should answer, Yes. For the men of Wu and the men of Yüeh are enemies; yet if they are crossing a river in the same boat and are

caught by a storm, they will come to each other's assistance just as the left hand helps the right.

These two paragraphs are extremely valuable as evidence of the date of composition. They assign the work to the period of the struggle between Wu and Yüeh. So much has been observed by Pi I-hsün. But what has hitherto escaped notice is that they also seriously impair the credibility of Ssŭ-ma Ch'ien's narrative. As we have seen above, the first positive date given in connection with Sun Wu is 512 BC. He is then spoken of as a general, acting as confidential adviser to Ho Lü, so that his alleged introduction to that monarch had already taken place, and of course the thirteen chapters must have been written earlier still. But at that time, and for several years after, down to the capture of Ying in 506, Ch'u and not Yüeh, was the great hereditary enemy of Wu. The two states, Ch'u and Wu, had been constantly at war for over half a century, whereas the first war between Wu and Yüeh was waged only in 510, and even then was no more than a short interlude sandwiched in the midst of the fierce struggle with Ch'u. Now Ch'u is not mentioned in the thirteen chapters at all. The natural inference is that they were written at a time when Yüeh had become the prime antagonist of Wu, that is, after Ch'u had suffered the great humiliation of 506. At this point, a table of dates may be found useful.

BC

514   Accession of Ho Lü.

512   Ho Lü attacks Ch'u, but is dissuaded from entering Ying, the capital. Shih Chi mentions Sun Wu as general.

511   Another attack on Ch'u.

510   Wu makes a successful attack on Yüeh. This is the first war between the two states.

509 or 508 Ch'u invades Wu, but is signally defeated at Yu-chang.

506   Ho Lü attacks Ch'u with the aid of T'ang and Ts'ai. Decisive battle of Po-chu, and capture of Ying. Last mention of Sun Wu in Shih Chi.

505   Yüeh makes a raid on Wu in the absence of its army. Wu is beaten by Ch'in and evacuates Ying.

504   Ho Lü sends Fu Ch'ai to attack Ch'u.

497   Kou Chien becomes King of Yüeh.

496   Wu attacks Yüeh, but is defeated by Kou Chien at Tsui-li. Ho Lü is killed.

494   Fu Ch'ai defeats Kou Chien in the great battle of Fu-chaio, and
       enters the capital of Yüeh.
485 or 484 Kou Chien renders homage to Wu. Death of Wu Tzŭ-hsü.
482   Kou Chien invades Wu in the absence of Fu Ch'ai.
478 to 476 Further attacks by Yüeh on Wu.
475   Kou Chien lays siege to the capital of Wu.
473   Final defeat and extinction of Wu.

The sentence quoted above from ch. 6, paragraph 21 hardly strikes
me as one that could have been written in the full flush of victory. It
seems rather to imply that, for the moment at least, the tide had turned
against Wu, and that she was getting the worst of the struggle. Hence
we may conclude that our treatise was not in existence in 505, before
which date Yüeh does not appear to have scored any notable success
against Wu. Ho Lü died in 496, so that if the book was written for him,
it must have been during the period 505–496, when there was a lull in
the hostilities, Wu having presumably exhausted by its supreme effort
against Ch'u. On the other hand, if we choose to disregard the tradition
connecting Sun Wu's name with Ho Lü, it might equally well have
seen the light between 496 and 494, or possibly in the period 482–473,
when Yüeh was once again becoming a very serious menace. We may
feel fairly certain that the author, whoever he may have been, was not
a man of any great eminence in his own day. On this point the negative
testimony of the *Chuan: Tso Chuan* far outweighs any shred of authority
still attaching to the *Shih Chi*, if once its other facts are discredited. Sun
Hsing-yen, however, makes a feeble attempt to explain the omission of
his name from the great commentary. It was Wu Tzŭ-hsü, he says, who
got all the credit of Sun Wu's exploits, because the latter (being an alien)
was not rewarded with an office in the State.

How then did the Sun Tzŭ legend originate? It may be that the
growing celebrity of the book imparted by degrees a kind of factitious
renown to its author. It was felt to be only right and proper that one so
well versed in the science of war should have solid achievements to his
credit as well. Now the capture of Ying was undoubtedly the greatest
feat of arms in Ho Lü's reign; it made a deep and lasting impression
on all the surrounding states, and raised Wu to the short-lived zenith
of her power. Hence, what more natural, as time went on, than that
the acknowledged master of strategy, Sun Wu, should be popularly
identified with that campaign, at first perhaps only in the sense that his

brain conceived and planned it; afterwards, that it was actually carried out by him in conjunction with Wu Yuan, Po P'ei and Fu Kai?

It is obvious that any attempt to reconstruct even the outline of Sun Tzŭ's life must be based almost wholly on conjecture. With this necessary proviso, I should say that he probably entered the service of Wu about the time of Ho Lü's accession, and gathered experience, though only in the capacity of a subordinate officer, during the intense military activity which marked the first half of the prince's reign. If he rose to be a general at all, he certainly was never on an equal footing with the three above mentioned. He was doubtless present at the investment and occupation of Ying, and witnessed Wu's sudden collapse in the following year. Yüeh's attack at this critical juncture, when her rival was embarrassed on every side, seems to have convinced him that this upstart kingdom was the great enemy against whom every effort would henceforth have to be directed. Sun Wu was thus a well-seasoned warrior when he sat down to write his famous book, which according to my reckoning must have appeared towards the end, rather than the beginning of Ho Lü's reign. The story of the women may possibly have grown out of some real incident occurring about the same time. As we hear no more of Sun Wu after this from any source, he is hardly likely to have survived his patron or to have taken part in the death-struggle with Yüeh, which began with the disaster at Tsui-li.

If these inferences are approximately correct, there is a certain irony in the fate which decreed that China's most illustrious man of peace should be contemporary with her greatest writer on war.

THE TEXT OF SUN TZŬ

I have found it difficult to glean much about the history of Sun Tzŭ's text. The quotations that occur in early authors go to show that the "thirteen chapters" of which Ssŭ-ma Ch'ien speaks were essentially the same as those now extant. We have his word for it that they were widely circulated in his day, and can only regret that he refrained from discussing them on that account. Sun Hsing-yen says in his preface:

> During the Ch'in and Han dynasties Sun Tzŭ's *Art of War* was in general use amongst military commanders, but they seem to have treated it as a work of mysterious import, and were unwilling to expound it for the benefit of posterity. Thus it came about that Wei Wu was the first to write a commentary on it.

As we have already seen, there is no reasonable ground to suppose that Ts'ao Kung tampered with the text. But the text itself is often so obscure, and the number of editions which appeared from that time onward so great, especially during the T'ang and Sung dynasties, that it would be surprising if numerous corruptions had not managed to creep in. Towards the middle of the Sung period, by which time all the chief commentaries on Sun Tzŭ were in existence, a certain Chi T'ien-pao published a work in 15 *chüan* entitled "Sun Tzŭ with the collected commentaries of ten writers." There was another text, with variant readings put forward by Chu Fu of Ta-hsing, which also had supporters among the scholars of that period; but in the Ming editions, Sun Hsing-yen tells us, these readings were for some reason or other no longer put into circulation. Thus, until the end of the 18th century, the text in sole possession of the field was one derived from Chi T'ien-pao's edition, although no actual copy of that important work was known to have survived. That, therefore, is the text of Sun Tzŭ which appears in the War section of the great Imperial encyclopedia printed in 1726, the *Ku Chin T'u Shu Chich'êng*. Another copy at my disposal of what is practically the same text, with slight variations, is that contained in the "Eleven philosophers of the Chou and Ch'in dynasties" [1758]. And the Chinese printed in Capt. Calthrop's first edition is evidently a similar version which has filtered through Japanese channels.

So things remained until Sun Hsing-yen [1752–1818], a distinguished antiquarian and classical scholar, who claimed to be an actual descendant of Sun Wu, accidentally discovered a copy of Chi T'ien-pao's long-lost work, when on a visit to the library of the Hua-yin temple. Appended to it was the *I Shuo* of Cheng Yu-Hsien, mentioned in the *T'ung Chih*, and also believed to have perished. This is what Sun Hsing-yen designates as the "original edition (or text)"—a rather misleading name, for it cannot by any means claim to set before us the text of Sun Tzŭ in its pristine purity. Chi T'ien-pao was a careless compiler, and appears to have been content to reproduce the somewhat debased version current in his day, without troubling to collate it with the earliest editions then available. Fortunately, two versions of Sun Tzŭ, even older than the newly discovered work, were still extant, one buried in the *T'ung Tien*, Tu Yu's great treatise on the Constitution, the other similarly enshrined in the *T'ai P'ing Yü Lan* encyclopedia. In both the complete text is to be found, though split up into fragments, intermixed with other matter, and scattered piecemeal over a number of different sections. Considering that the *Yü Lan* takes us back to the year 983, and the *T'ung Tien* about 200 years further still, to the middle of the T'ang dynasty, the value of these early transcripts of Sun Tzŭ can hardly be overestimated. Yet the idea of utilizing them does not seem to have occurred to anyone until Sun Hsing-yen, acting under Government instructions, undertook a thorough recension of the text. This is his own account:

> Because of the numerous mistakes in the text of Sun Tzŭ which his editors had handed down, the Government ordered that the ancient edition [of Chi T'ien-pao] should be used, and that the text should be revised and corrected throughout. It happened that Wu Nien-hu, the Governor Pi Kua, and Hsi, a graduate of the second degree, had all devoted themselves to this study, probably surpassing me therein. Accordingly, I have had the whole work cut on blocks as a textbook for military men.

The three individuals here referred to had evidently been occupied on the text of Sun Tzŭ prior to Sun Hsing-yen's commission, but we are left in doubt as to the work they really accomplished. At any rate, the new edition, when ultimately produced, appeared in the names of Sun Hsing-yen and only one co-editor Wu Jên-shi. They took the "original edition" as their basis, and by careful comparison with older versions, as well as the extant commentaries and other sources of information such as the *I Shuo*, succeeded in restoring a very large number of doubtful passages, and turned out, on the whole, what must be accepted as the closest approximation we are ever likely to get to Sun Tzŭ's original work. This is what will hereafter be denominated the "standard text."

The copy which I have used belongs to a reissue dated 1877. It is in 6 *pên*, forming part of a well-printed set of 23 early philosophical works in 83 *pên*. It opens with a preface by Sun Hsing-yen (largely quoted in this introduction), vindicating the traditional view of Sun Tzŭ's life and performances, and summing up in remarkably concise fashion the evidence in its favor. This is followed by Ts'ao Kung's preface to his edition, and the biography of Sun Tzŭ from the *Shih Chi*, both translated above. Then come, firstly, Cheng Yu-hsien's *I Shuo*, with author's preface, and next, a short miscellany of historical and bibliographical information entitled *Sun Tzŭ Hsü Lu*, compiled by Pi I-hsun. As regards the body of the work, each separate sentence is followed by a note on the text, if required, and then by the various commentaries appertaining to it, arranged in chronological order. These we shall now proceed to discuss briefly, one by one.

THE COMMENTATORS

Sun Tzŭ can boast an exceptionally long distinguished roll of commentators, which would do honor to any classic. Ou-yang Hsiu remarks on this fact, though he wrote before the tale was complete, and rather ingeniously explains it by saying that the artifices of war, being inexhaustible, must therefore be susceptible of treatment in a great variety of ways.

1. *Ts'ao Ts'ao* or Ts'ao Kung, afterwards known as Wei Wu Ti (AD 155–220). There is hardly any room for doubt that the earliest commentary on Sun Tzŭ actually came from the pen of this extraordinary man, whose biography in the *San Kuo Chih* reads like a romance. One of the greatest military geniuses that the world has seen, and Napoleonic in the scale of his operations, he was especially famed for the marvelous rapidity of his marches, which has found expression in the line "Talk of Ts'ao Ts'ao, and Ts'ao Ts'ao will appear." Ou-yang Hsiu says of him that he was a great captain who "measured his strength against Tung Cho, Lu Pu and the two Yuan, father and son, and vanquished them all; whereupon he divided the Empire of Han with Wu and Shu, and made himself king. It is recorded that whenever a council of war was held by Wei on the eve of a far-reaching campaign, he had all his calculations ready; those generals who made use of them did not lose one battle in ten; those who ran counter to them in any particular saw their armies incontinently beaten and put to flight." Ts'ao Kung's notes on Sun Tzŭ, models of austere brevity, are so thoroughly characteristic of the stern commander known to history, that it is hard indeed to conceive of them as the work of a mere *litterateur*. Sometimes, indeed, owing to extreme compression, they are scarcely intelligible and stand no less in need of a commentary than the text itself.

2. *Meng Shih.* The commentary which has come down to us under this name is comparatively meager, and nothing about the author is known. Even his personal name has not been recorded. Chi T'ien-pao's edition places him after Chia Lin, and Ch'ao Kung-wu also assigns him to the T'ang dynasty, but this is a mistake. In Sun Hsing-yen's preface, he appears as Meng Shih of the Liang

dynasty [502–557]. Others would identify him with Meng K'ang of the 3rd century. He is named in one work as the last of the "Five Commentators," the others being Wei Wu Ti, Tu Mu, Ch'ên Hao and Chia Lin.

3. *Li Ch'uan* of the 8th century was a well-known writer on military tactics. One of his works has been in constant use down to the present day. The *T'ung Chih* mentions "Lives of famous generals from the Chou to the T'ang dynasty" as written by him. According to Ch'ao Kung-wu and the *Tien-i-ko* catalogue, he followed a variant of the text of Sun Tzŭ which differs considerably from those now extant. His notes are mostly short and to the point, and he frequently illustrates his remarks by anecdotes from Chinese history.

4. *Tu Yu* (died 812) did not publish a separate commentary on Sun Tzŭ, his notes being taken from the *T'ung Tien*, the encyclopedic treatise on the Constitution which was his life-work. They are largely repetitions of Ts'ao Kung and Meng Shih, besides which it is believed that he drew on the ancient commentaries of Wang Ling and others. Owing to the peculiar arrangement of *T'ung Tien*, he has to explain each passage on its merits, apart from the context, and sometimes his own explanation does not agree with that of Ts'ao Kung, whom he always quotes first. Though not strictly to be reckoned as one of the "Ten Commentators," he was added to their number by Chi T'ien-pao, being wrongly placed after his grandson Tu Mu.

5. *Tu Mu* (803–852) is perhaps the best known as a poet—a bright star even in the glorious galaxy of the T'ang period. We learn from Ch'ao Kung-wu that although he had no practical experience of war, he was extremely fond of discussing the subject, and was moreover well read in the military history of the *Ch'un Ch'iu* and *Chan Kuo* eras. His notes, therefore, are well worth attention. They are very copious, and replete with historical parallels. The gist of Sun Tzŭ's work is thus summarized by him: "Practice benevolence and justice, but on the other hand make full use of artifice and measures of expediency." He further declared that all the military triumphs and disasters of the thousand years which had elapsed since Sun Tzŭ's death would, upon examination, be found to uphold and corroborate, in every particular, the maxims contained in his book. Tu Mu's somewhat spiteful charge against Ts'ao Kung has already been considered elsewhere.

6. *Ch'ên Hao* appears to have been a contemporary of Tu Mu. Ch'ao Kung-wu says that he was impelled to write a new commentary on Sun Tzŭ because Ts'ao Kung's on the one hand was too obscure and subtle, and that of Tu Mu on the other too long-winded and diffuse. Ou-yang Hsiu, writing in the middle of the 11th century, calls Ts'ao Kung, Tu Mu and Ch'ên Hao the three chief commentators on Sun Tzŭ, and observes that Ch'ên Hao is continually attacking Tu Mu's shortcomings. His commentary, though not lacking in merit, must rank below those of his predecessors.

7. *Chia Lin* is known to have lived under the T'ang dynasty, for his commentary on Sun Tzŭ is mentioned in the *T'ang Shu* and was afterwards republished by Chi Hsieh of the same dynasty together with those of Meng Shih and Tu Yu. It is of somewhat scanty texture, and in point of quality, too, perhaps the least valuable of the eleven.

8. *Mei Yao-Ch'ên* (1002–1060), commonly known by his "style" as Mei Sheng-yu, was, like Tu Mu, a poet of distinction. His commentary was published with a laudatory preface by the great Ou-yang Hsiu, from which we may cull the following:

Later scholars have misread Sun Tzŭ, distorting his words and trying to make them square with their own one-sided views. Thus, though commentators have not been lacking, only a few have proved equal to the task. My friend Sheng-yu has not fallen into this mistake. In attempting to provide a critical commentary for Sun Tzŭ's work, he does not lose sight of the fact that these sayings were intended for states engaged in internecine warfare; that the author is not concerned with the military conditions prevailing under the sovereigns of the three ancient dynasties, nor with the nine punitive measures prescribed to the Minister of War. Again, Sun Wu loved brevity of diction, but his meaning is always deep. Whether the subject be marching an army, or handling soldiers, or estimating the enemy, or controlling the forces of victory, it is always systematically treated; the sayings are bound together in strict logical sequence, though this has been obscured by commentators who have probably failed to grasp their meaning. In his own commentary, Mei Sheng-yu has brushed aside all the obstinate prejudices of these critics, and has tried to bring out the true meaning of Sun Tzŭ himself. In this way, the clouds of confusion have been dispersed and the sayings made clear. I am convinced that the present work deserves to be handed down side by side with the three great commentaries; and for a great deal that they find in the sayings, coming generations will have constant reason to thank my friend Sheng-yu.

Making some allowance for the exuberance of friendship, I am inclined to endorse this favorable judgment, and would certainly place him above Ch'ên Hao in order of merit.

9.   *Wang Hsi*, also of the Sung dynasty, is decidedly original in some of his interpretations, but much less judicious than Mei Yao-ch'ên, and on the whole not a very trustworthy guide. He is fond of comparing his own commentary with that of Ts'ao Kung, but the comparison is not often flattering to him. We learn from Ch'ao Kung-wu that Wang Hsi revised the ancient text of Sun Tzŭ, filling up lacunae and correcting mistakes.

10. *Ho Yen-Hsi* of the Sung dynasty. The personal name of this commentator is given as above by Cheng Ch'iao in the *Tung Chih*, written about the middle of the twelfth century, but he appears simply as Ho Shih in the *Yu Hai*, and Ma Tuan-lin quotes Ch'ao Kung-wu as saying that his personal name is unknown. There seems to be no reason to doubt Cheng Ch'iao's statement, otherwise I should have been inclined to hazard a guess and identify him with one Ho Ch'u-fei, the author of a short treatise on war, who lived in the latter part of the 11th century. Ho Shih's commentary, in the words of the *T'ien-i-ko* catalogue, "contains helpful additions" here and there, but is chiefly remarkable for the copious extracts taken, in adapted form, from the dynastic histories and other sources.

11. *Chang Yu*. The list closes with a commentator of no great originality perhaps, but gifted with admirable powers of lucid exposition. His commentator is based on that of Ts'ao Kung, whose terse sentences he contrives to expand and develop in masterly fashion. Without Chang Yu, it is safe to say that much of Ts'ao Kung's commentary would have remained cloaked in its pristine obscurity and therefore valueless. His work is not mentioned in the Sung history, the *T'ung K'ao*, or the *Yü Hai*, but it finds a niche in the *T'ung Chih*, which also names him as the author of the "Lives of Famous Generals." It is rather remarkable that the last-named four should all have flourished within so short a space of time. Ch'ao Kung-wu accounts

for it by saying: "During the early years of the Sung dynasty the Empire enjoyed a long spell of peace, and men ceased to practice the art of war. But when (Chao) Yuan-hao's rebellion came [1038–42] and the frontier generals were defeated time after time, the Court made strenuous inquiry for men skilled in war, and military topics became the vogue amongst all the high officials. Hence it is that the commentators of Sun Tzŭ in our dynasty belong mainly to that period.

Besides these eleven commentators, there are several others whose work has not come down to us. The *Sui Shu* mentions four, namely Wang Ling (often quoted by Tu Yu as Wang Tzŭ); Chang Tzŭ-shang; Chia Hsü of Wei; [48] and Shen Yü of Wu. The *T'ang Shu* adds Sun Hao, and the *T'ung Chih* Hsiao Chi, while the *T'u Shu* mentions a Ming commentator, Huang Jun-yu. It is possible that some of these may have been merely collectors and editors of other commentaries, like Chi T'ien-pao and Chi Hsieh, mentioned above.

APPRECIATIONS OF SUN TZŬ

智

Sun Tzŭ has exercised a potent fascination over the minds of some of China's greatest men. Among the famous generals who are known to have studied his pages with enthusiasm may be mentioned Han Hsin (∂. 196 BC), Feng I (∂. AD 34), Lü Meng (∂. 219), and Yo Fei (1103–1141). The opinion of Ts'ao Kung, who disputes with Han Hsin the highest place in Chinese military annals, has already been recorded. Still more remarkable, in one way, is the testimony of purely literary men, such as Su Hsun (the father of Su Tung-p'o), who wrote several essays on military topics, all of which owe their chief inspiration to Sun Tzŭ. The following short passage by him is preserved in the *Yu Hai*:

> Sun Wu's saying, that in war one cannot make certain of conquering, is very different indeed from what other books tell us. Wu Ch'i was a man of the same stamp as Sun Wu: they both wrote books on war, and they are linked together in popular speech as "Sun and Wu." But Wu Ch'i's remarks on war are less weighty, his rules are rougher and more crudely stated, and there is not the same unity of plan as in Sun Tzŭ's work, where the style is terse, but the meaning fully brought out.

The following is an extract from the "Impartial Judgments in the Garden of Literature" by Cheng Hou:

> Sun Tzŭ's thirteen chapters are not only the staple and base of all military men's training, but also compel the most careful attention of scholars and men of letters. His sayings are terse yet elegant, simple yet profound, perspicuous and eminently practical. Such works as the *Lun Yu*, the *I Ching* and the great Commentary, as well as the writings of Mencius, Hsün K'uang and Yang Chu, all fall below the level of Sun Tzŭ.

Chu Hsi, commenting on this, fully admits the first part of the criticism, although he dislikes the audacious comparison with the venerated classical works. Language of this sort, he says, "encourages a ruler's bent towards unrelenting warfare and reckless militarism."

APOLOGIES FOR WAR

Accustomed as we are to think of China as the greatest peace-loving nation on earth, we are in some danger of forgetting that her experience of war in all its phases has also been such as no modern State can parallel. Her long military annals stretch back to a point at which they are lost in the mists of time. She had built the Great Wall and was maintaining a huge standing army along her frontier centuries before the first Roman legionary was seen on the Danube. What with the perpetual collisions of the ancient feudal States, the grim conflicts with Huns, Turks and other invaders after the centralization of government, the terrific upheavals which accompanied the overthrow of so many dynasties, besides the countless rebellions and minor disturbances that have flamed up and flickered out again one by one, it is hardly too much to say that the clash of arms has never ceased to resound in one portion or another of the Empire.

No less remarkable is the succession of illustrious captains to whom China can point with pride. As in all countries, the greatest are fond of emerging at the most fateful crises of her history. Thus, Po Ch'i stands out conspicuous in the period when Ch'in was entering upon her final struggle with the remaining independent states. The stormy years which followed the break-up of the Ch'in dynasty are illuminated by the transcendent genius of Han Hsin. When the House of Han in turn is tottering to its fall, the great and baleful figure of Ts'ao Ts'ao dominates the scene. And in the establishment of the T'ang dynasty, one of the mightiest tasks achieved by man, the superhuman energy of Li Shih-min (afterwards the Emperor T'ai Tsung) was seconded by the brilliant strategy of Li Ching. None of these generals need fear comparison with the greatest names in the military history of Europe.

In spite of all this, the great body of Chinese sentiment, from Lao Tzŭ downwards, and especially as reflected in the standard literature of Confucianism, has been consistently pacific and intensely opposed to militarism in any form. It is such an uncommon thing to find any of the literati defending warfare on principle, that I have thought it worth while to collect and translate a few passages in which the unorthodox view is upheld. The following, by Ssŭ-ma Ch'ien, shows that for all his ardent admiration of Confucius, he was yet no advocate of peace at any price:

Military weapons are the means used by the Sage to punish violence and cruelty, to give peace to troublous times, to remove difficulties and dangers, and to succor those who are in peril. Every animal with blood in its veins and horns on its head will fight when it is attacked. How much more so will man, who carries in his breast the faculties of love and hatred, joy and anger! When he is pleased, a feeling of affection springs up within him; when angry, his poisoned sting is brought into play. That is the natural law which governs his being.... What then shall be said of those scholars of our time, blind to all great issues, and without any appreciation of relative values, who can only bark out their stale formulas about "virtue" and "civilization," condemning the use of military weapons? They will surely bring our country to impotence and dishonor and the loss of her rightful heritage; or, at the very least, they will bring about invasion and rebellion, sacrifice of territory and general enfeeblement. Yet they obstinately refuse to modify the position they have taken up. The truth is that, just as in the family the teacher must not spare the rod, and punishments cannot be dispensed with in the State, so military chastisement can never be allowed to fall into abeyance in the Empire. All one can say is that this power will be exercised wisely by some, foolishly by others, and that among those who bear arms some will be loyal and others rebellious.

The next piece is taken from Tu Mu's preface to his commentary on Sun Tzŭ:

War may be defined as punishment, which is one of the functions of government. It was the profession of Chung Yu and Jan Ch'iu, both disciples of Confucius. Nowadays, the holding of trials and hearing of litigation, the imprisonment of offenders and their execution by flogging in the market-place, are all done by officials. But the wielding of huge armies, the throwing down of fortified cities, the hauling of women and children into captivity, and the beheading of traitors—this is also work which is done by officials. The objects of the rack and of military weapons are essentially the same. There is no intrinsic difference between the punishment of flogging and cutting off heads in war. For the lesser infractions of law, which are easily dealt with, only a small amount of force need be employed: hence the use of military weapons and wholesale decapitation. In both cases, however, the end in view is to get rid of wicked people, and to give comfort and relief to the good . . .

Chi-sun asked Jan Yu, saying: "Have you, Sir, acquired your military aptitude by study, or is it innate?" Jan Yu replied: "It has been acquired by study." "How can that be so," said Chi-sun, "seeing that you are a disciple of Confucius?" "It is a fact," replied Jan Yu; "I was taught by Confucius. It is fitting that the great Sage should exercise both civil and military functions, though to be sure my instruction in the art of fighting has not yet gone very far."

Now, who the author was of this rigid distinction between the "civil" and the "military," and the limitation of each to a separate sphere of action, or in what year of which dynasty it was first introduced, is more than I can say. But, at any rate, it has come about that the members of the governing class are quite afraid of enlarging on military topics, or do so only in a shamefaced manner. If any are bold enough to discuss the subject, they are at once set down as eccentric individuals of coarse and brutal propensities. This is an extraordinary instance in which, through sheer lack of reasoning, men unhappily lose sight of fundamental principles.

When the Duke of Chou was minister under Ch'eng Wang, he regulated ceremonies and made music, and venerated the arts of scholarship and learning; yet when the barbarians of the River Huai revolted, he sallied forth and chastised them. When Confucius held office under the Duke of Lu, and a meeting was convened at Chia-ku, he said: "If pacific negotiations are in progress, warlike preparations should have been made beforehand." He rebuked and shamed the Marquis of Ch'i, who cowered under him and dared not proceed to violence. How can it be said that these two great Sages had no knowledge of military matters?

We have seen that the great Chu Hsi held Sun Tzŭ in high esteem. He also appeals to the authority of the Classics:

Our Master Confucius, answering Duke Ling of Wei, said: "I have never studied matters connected with armies and battalions."

Replying to K'ung Wen-Tzŭ, he said: I have not been instructed about buff-coats and weapons." But if we turn to the meeting at Chia-ku, we find that he used armed force against the men of Lai, so that the marquis of Ch'i was overawed. Again, when the inhabitants of Pi revolted; he ordered his officers to attack them, whereupon they were defeated and fled in confusion. He once uttered the words: "If I fight, I conquer." And Jan Yu also said: "The Sage exercises both civil and military functions." Can it be a fact that Confucius never studied or received instruction in the art of war? We can only say that he did not specially choose matters connected with armies and fighting to be the subject of his teaching.

Sun Hsing-yen, the editor of Sun Tzŭ, writes in similar strain:

Confucius said: "I am unversed in military matters." He also said: "If I fight, I conquer." Confucius ordered ceremonies and regulated music. Now war constitutes one of the five classes of State ceremonial, and must not be treated as an independent branch of study. Hence, the words "I am unversed in" must be taken to mean that there are things which even an inspired Teacher does not know. Those who have to lead an army and devise stratagems, must learn the art of war. But if one can command the services of a good general like Sun Tzŭ, who was employed by Wu Tzŭ-hsü, there is no need to learn it oneself. Hence the remark added by Confucius: "If I fight, I conquer."

The men of the present day, however, willfully interpret these words of Confucius in their narrowest sense, as though he meant that books on the art of war were not worth reading. With blind persistency, they adduce the example of Chao Kua, who pored over his father's books to no purpose, as a proof that all military theory is useless. Again, seeing that books on war have to do with such things as opportunism in designing plans, and the conversion of spies, they hold that the art is immoral and unworthy of a sage. These people ignore the fact that the studies of our scholars and the civil administration of our officials also require steady application and practice before efficiency is reached. The ancients were particularly chary of allowing mere novices to botch their work. Weapons are baneful and fighting perilous; and useless unless a general is in constant practice, he ought not to hazard other men's lives in battle. Hence it is essential that Sun Tzǔ's thirteen chapters should be studied. Hsiang Liang used to instruct his nephew Chi in the art of war. Chi got a rough idea of the art in its general bearings, but would not pursue his studies to their proper outcome, the consequence being that he was finally defeated and overthrown. He did not realize that the tricks and artifices of war are beyond verbal computation. Duke Hsiang of Sung and King Yen of Hsü were brought to destruction by their misplaced humanity. The treacherous and underhand nature of war necessitates the use of guile and stratagem suited to the occasion. There is a case on record of Confucius himself having violated an extorted oath, and also of his having left the Sung State in disguise. Can we then recklessly arraign Sun Tzǔ for disregarding truth and honesty?

BIBLIOGRAPHY

The following are the oldest Chinese treatises on war, after Sun Tzŭ. The notes on each have been drawn principally from the *Sŭu K'u Ch'üan Shu Chien Ming Mu Lu*.

Wu Tzŭ, in 1 *chüan* or 6 chapters. By Wu Ch'i (∂. 381 BC). A genuine work. See *Shih Chi*.

Sŭ-Ma Fa, in 1 *chüan* or 5 chapters. Wrongly attributed to Ssŭ-ma Jang-chu of the 6th century BC. Its date, however, must be early, as the customs of the three ancient dynasties are constantly to be met within its pages. See *Shih Chi*, Ch. 64. The *Sŭ K'u Ch'üan Shu* remarks that the oldest three treatises on war, *Sun Tzŭ*, *Wu Tzŭ* and *Sŭ-Ma Fa*, are, generally speaking, only concerned with things strictly military—the art of producing, collecting, training and drilling troops, and the correct theory with regard to measures of expediency, laying plans, transport of goods and the handling of soldiers—in strong contrast to later works, in which the science of war is usually blended with metaphysics, divination and magical arts in general.

Liu T'ao, in 6 *chüan* or 60 chapters. Attributed to Lu Wang (or Lu Shang, also known as T'ai Kung) of the 12th century BC. But its style does not belong to the era of the Three Dynasties. Lu Te-ming (AD 550–625) mentions the work, and enumerates the headings of the six sections so that the forgery cannot have been later than Sui dynasty.

Wei Liao Tzŭ, in 5 *chüan*. Attributed to Wei Liao (4th cent. BC), who studied under the famous Kuei-ku Tzŭ. The work appears to have been originally in 31 chapters, whereas the text we possess contains only 24. Its matter is sound enough in the main, though the strategical devices differ considerably from those of the Warring States period. It is been furnished with a commentary by the well-known Sung philosopher Chang Tsai.

San Lüeh, in 3 *chüan*. Attributed to Huang-shih Kung, a legendary personage who is said to have bestowed it on Chang Liang (∂. 187 BC) in an interview on a bridge. But here again, the style is not that of works dating from the Ch'in or Han period. The Han Emperor Kuang Wu [AD 25–57] apparently quotes from it in one of his proclamations; but the passage in question may have been inserted later on, in order to prove the genuineness of the work. We shall not be far out if we refer it to the Northern Sung period [AD 420–478], or somewhat earlier.

Li Wei Kung Wen Tui, in 3 sections. Written in the form of a dialogue between T'ai Tsung and his great general Li Ching, it is usually ascribed to the latter. Competent authorities consider it a forgery, though the author was evidently well versed in the art of war.

Li Ching Ping Fa (not to be confounded with the foregoing) is a short treatise in 8 chapters, preserved in the *T'ung Tien*, but not published separately. This fact explains its omission from the *Ssŭ K'u Ch'üan Shu*.

Wu Ch'i Ching, in 1 *chüan*. Attributed to the legendary minister Feng Hou, with exegetical notes by Kung-sun Hung of the Han dynasty (∂. 121 BC), and said to have been eulogized by the celebrated general Ma Lüng (∂. AD 300). Yet the earliest mention of it is in the *Sung Chih*. Although a forgery, the work is well put together.

Considering the high popular estimation in which Chu-ko Liang has always been held, it is not surprising to find more than one work on war ascribed to his pen. Such are (1) the *Shih Liu Ts'ê* (1 *chüan*), preserved in the *Yung Lo Ta Tien*; (2) *Chiang Yüan* (1 *chüan*); and (3) *Hsin Shu* (1 *chüan*), which steals wholesale from Sun Tzŭ. None of these has the slightest claim to be considered genuine. Most of the large Chinese encyclopedias contain extensive sections devoted to the literature of war. The following references may be found useful:

T'ung Tien (circa 800 AD), ch. 148–162.
T'ai P'ing Yü Lan (983), ch. 270–359.
Wen Hsien Tung K'ao (13th cent.), ch. 221.
Yu Hai (13th cent.), ch. 140, 141.
San Ts'ai T'u Hui (16th cent.).
Kuang Po Wu Chih (1607), ch. 31, 32.
Ch'ien Ch'io Lei Shu (1632), ch. 75.
Yuan Chien Lei Han (1710), ch. 206–229.
Ku Chin T'u Shu Chi Ch'êng (1726), section XXX, esp. ch. 81–90.
Hsü Wen Hsien T'ung K'ao (1784), ch. 121–134.
Huang Ch'ao Ching Shih Wên Pien (1826), ch. 76, 77.

The bibliographical sections of certain historical works also deserve mention:

Ch'ien Han Shu, ch. 30.
Sui Shu, ch. 32–35.

Chiu T'ang Shu, ch. 46, 47.
Hsin T'ang Shu, ch. 57, 60.
Sung Shih, ch. 202–209.
T'ung Chih (circa 1150), ch. 68.

To these of course must be added the great Catalogue of the Imperial Library:

Ssu K'u Ch'üan Shu Tsung Mu T'i Yao (1790), ch. 99, 100.

The Art of War
(The Oldest Military Treatise in the World)

TRANSLATED FROM THE CHINESE WITH
INTRODUCTION AND CRITICAL NOTES
BY LIONEL GILES, M.A.

ASSISTANT IN THE DEPARTMENT OF
ORIENTAL PRINTED BOOKS AND MSS.
IN THE BRITISH MUSEUM
FIRST PUBLISHED IN 1910

I

LAYING PLANS

[Ts'ao Kung, in defining the meaning of the Chinese for the title of this chapter, says it refers to the deliberations in the temple selected by the general for his temporary use, or as we should say, in his tent. See paragraph 26.]

1. Sun Tzŭ said: The art of war is of vital importance to the State.

2. It is a matter of life and death, a road either to safety or to ruin. Hence it is a subject of inquiry which can on no account be neglected.

3. The art of war, then, is governed by five constant factors, to be taken into account in one's deliberations, when seeking to determine the conditions obtaining in the field.

4. These are: (1) The Moral Law; (2) Heaven; (3) Earth; (4) The Commander; (5) Method and discipline.

   [It appears from what follows that Sun Tzŭ means by "Moral Law" a principle of harmony, not unlike the Tao of Lao Tzŭ in its moral aspect. One might be tempted to render it by "morale," were it not considered as an attribute of the ruler in paragraph 13.]

5, 6. *The Moral Law* causes the people to be in complete accord with their ruler, so that they will follow him regardless of their lives, undismayed by any danger.

   [Tu Yu quotes Wang Tzŭ as saying: "Without constant practice, the officers will be nervous and undecided when mustering for battle; without constant practice, the general will be wavering and irresolute when the crisis is at hand."]

7. Heaven signifies night and day, cold and heat, times and seasons.

   [The commentators, I think, make an unnecessary mystery of two words here. Meng Shih refers to "the hard and the soft, waxing and waning" of Heaven. Wang Hsi, however, may be right in saying that what is meant is "the general economy of Heaven," including the five elements, the four seasons, wind and clouds, and other phenomena.]

8. Earth comprises distances, great and small; danger and security; open ground and narrow passes; the chances of life and death.

9. The Commander stands for the virtues of wisdom, sincerity, benevolence, courage and strictness.

    [The five cardinal virtues of the Chinese are (1) humanity or benevolence; (2) uprightness of mind; (3) self-respect, self-control, or "proper feeling"; (4) wisdom; (5) sincerity or good faith. Here "wisdom" and "sincerity" are put before "humanity or benevolence," and the two military virtues of "courage" and "strictness" substituted for "uprightness of mind" and "self-respect, self-control, or 'proper feeling.' "]

10. By Method and Discipline are to be understood the marshaling of the army in its proper subdivisions, the graduations of rank among the officers, the maintenance of roads by which supplies may reach the army, and the control of military expenditure.

11. These five heads should be familiar to every general: he who knows them will be victorious; he who knows them not will fail.

12. Therefore, in your deliberations, when seeking to determine the military conditions, let them be made the basis of a comparison, in this wise:

13. (1) Which of the two sovereigns is imbued with the Moral law?

    [I.e., "is in harmony with his subjects." See paragraph 5.]

        (2) Which of the two generals has most ability?
        (3) With whom lie the advantages derived from Heaven and Earth?

    [See paragraphs 7, 8]

        (4) On which side is discipline most rigorously enforced?

[Tu Mu alludes to the remarkable story of Ts'ao Ts'ao (AD 155–220), who was such a strict disciplinarian that once, in accordance with his own severe regulations against injury to standing crops, he condemned himself to death for having allowed his horse to shy into a field of corn! However, in lieu of losing his head, he was persuaded to satisfy his sense of justice by cutting off his hair. Ts'ao Ts'ao's own comment on the present passage is characteristically curt: "when you lay down a law, see that it is not disobeyed; if it is disobeyed the offender must be put to death."]

(5) Which army is stronger?

[Morally as well as physically. As Mei Yao-ch'ên puts it, freely rendered, "esprit de corps and 'big battalions.' "]

(6) On which side are officers and men more highly trained?

[Tu Yu quotes Wang Tzŭ as saying: "Without constant practice, the officers will be nervous and undecided when mustering for battle; without constant practice, the general will be wavering and irresolute when the crisis is at hand."]

(7) In which army is there the greater constancy both in reward and punishment?

[On which side is there the most absolute certainty that merit will be properly rewarded and misdeeds summarily punished?]

14. By means of these seven considerations I can forecast victory or defeat.

15. The general that hearkens to my counsel and acts upon it, will conquer: let such a one be retained in command! The general that hearkens not to my counsel nor acts upon it, will suffer defeat: let such a one be dismissed!

[The form of this paragraph reminds us that Sun Tzŭ's treatise was composed expressly for the benefit of his patron Ho Lu, king of the Wu State.]

16. While heeding the profit of my counsel, avail yourself also of any helpful circumstances over and beyond the ordinary rules.

17. According as circumstances are favorable, one should modify one's plans.

[Sun Tzŭ, as a practical soldier, will have none of the "bookish theoric." He cautions us here not to pin our faith to abstract principles; "for," as Chang Yü puts it, "while the main laws of strategy can be stated clearly enough for the benefit of all and sundry, you must be guided by the actions of the enemy in attempting to secure a favorable position in actual warfare." On the eve of the battle of Waterloo, Lord Uxbridge, commanding the cavalry, went to the Duke of Wellington in order to learn what his plans and calculations were for the morrow, because, as he explained, he might suddenly find himself Commander-in-chief and would be unable to frame new plans in a critical moment. The Duke listened quietly and then said: "Who will attack the first tomorrow—I or Bonaparte?" "Bonaparte," replied Lord Uxbridge. "Well," continued the Duke, "Bonaparte has not given me any idea of his projects; and as my plans will depend upon his, how can you expect me to tell you what mine are?" (*Words on Wellington*, by Sir. W. Fraser.)]

18. All warfare is based on deception.

[The truth of this pithy and profound saying will be admitted by every soldier. Col. Henderson tells us that Wellington, great in so many military qualities, was especially distinguished by "the extraordinary skill with which he concealed his movements and deceived both friend and foe."]

19. Hence, when able to attack, we must seem unable; when using our forces, we must seem inactive; when we are near, we must make the enemy believe we are far away; when far away, we must make him believe we are near.

20. Hold out baits to entice the enemy. Feign disorder, and crush him.

[All commentators, except Chang Yü, say, "When he is in disorder, crush him." It is more natural to suppose that Sun Tzŭ is still illustrating the uses of deception in war.]

21. If he is secure at all points, be prepared for him. If he is in superior strength, evade him.

22. If your opponent is of choleric temper, seek to irritate him. Pretend to be weak, that he may grow arrogant.

[Wang Tzŭ, quoted by Tu Yu, says that the good tactician plays with his adversary as a cat plays with a mouse, first feigning weakness and immobility, and then suddenly pouncing upon him.]

23. If he is taking his ease, give him no rest.

[This is probably the meaning, though Mei Yao-ch'ên has the note: "while we are taking our ease, wait for the enemy to tire himself out." The *Yu Lan* has "lure him on and tire him out."]

If his forces are united, separate them.

[Less plausible is the interpretation favored by most of the commentators: "If sovereign and subject are in accord, put division between them."]

24. Attack him where he is unprepared, appear where you are not expected.

25. These military devices, leading to victory, must not be divulged beforehand.

26. Now the general who wins a battle makes many calculations in his temple ere the battle is fought.

[Chang Yü tells us that in ancient times it was customary for a temple to be set apart for the use of a general who was about to take the field, in order that he might there elaborate his plan of campaign.]

The general who loses a battle makes but few calculations beforehand. Thus do many calculations lead to victory, and few calculations to defeat: how much more no calculation at all! It is by attention to this point that I can foresee who is likely to win or lose.

II

WAGING WAR

[Ts'ao Kung has the note: "He who wishes to fight must first count the cost," which prepares us for the discovery that the subject of the chapter is not what we might expect from the title, but is primarily a consideration of ways and means.]

1. Sun Tzŭ said: In the operations of war, where there are in the field a thousand swift chariots, as many heavy chariots, and a hundred thousand mail-clad soldiers,

[The "swift chariots" were lightly built and, according to Chang Yü, used for the attack; the "heavy chariots" were heavier, and designed for purposes of defense. Li Ch'üan, it is true, says that the latter were light, but this seems hardly probable. It is interesting to note the analogies between early Chinese warfare and that of the Homeric Greeks. In each case, the war-chariot was the important factor, forming as it did the nucleus round which was grouped a certain number of foot-soldiers. With regard to the numbers given here, we are informed that each swift chariot was accompanied by seventy-five footmen, and each heavy chariot by twenty-five footmen, so that the whole army would be divided up into a thousand battalions, each consisting of two chariots and a hundred men.]

with provisions enough to carry them a thousand lî,

[2.78 modern lî go to a mile. The length may have varied slightly since Sun Tzŭ's time.]

the expenditure at home and at the front, including entertainment of guests, small items such as glue and paint, and sums spent on chariots and armor, will reach the total of a thousand ounces of silver per day. Such is the cost of raising an army of 100,000 men.

2. When you engage in actual fighting, if victory is long in coming, then men's weapons will grow dull and their ardor will be damped. If you lay siege to a town, you will exhaust your strength.

3. Again, if the campaign is protracted, the resources of the State will not be equal to the strain.

4. Now, when your weapons are dulled, your ardor damped, your strength exhausted and your treasure spent, other chieftains will spring up to take advantage of your extremity. Then no man, however wise, will be able to avert the consequences that must ensue.

5. Thus, though we have heard of stupid haste in war, cleverness has never been seen associated with long delays.

[This concise and difficult sentence is not well explained by any of the commentators. Ts'ao Kung, Li Ch'üan, Mêng Shih, Tu Yu, Tu Mu and Mei Yao-ch'ên have notes to the effect that a general, though naturally stupid, may nevertheless conquer through sheer force of rapidity. Ho Shih says: "Haste may be stupid, but at any rate it saves expenditure of energy and treasure; protracted operations may be very clever, but they bring calamity in their train." Wang Hsi evades the difficulty by remarking: "Lengthy operations mean an army growing old, wealth being expended, an empty exchequer and distress among the people; true cleverness insures against the occurrence of such calamities." Chang Yü says: "So long as victory can be attained, stupid haste is preferable to clever dilatoriness." Now Sun Tzŭ says nothing whatever, except possibly by implication, about ill-considered haste being better than ingenious but lengthy operations. What he does say is something much more guarded, namely that, while speed may sometimes be injudicious, tardiness can never be anything but foolish—if only because it means impoverishment to the nation. In considering the point raised here by Sun Tzŭ, the classic example of Fabius Cunctator will inevitably occur to the mind. That general deliberately measured the endurance of Rome against that of Hannibal's isolated army, because it seemed to him that the latter was more likely to suffer from a long campaign in a strange country. But it is quite a moot question whether his tactics would have proved successful in the long run. Their reversal it is true, led to Cannae; but this only establishes a negative presumption in their favor.]

6. There is no instance of a country having benefited from prolonged warfare.

7. It is only one who is thoroughly acquainted with the evils of war that can thoroughly understand the profitable way of carrying it on.

   [That is, with rapidity. Only one who knows the disastrous effects of a long war can realize the supreme importance of rapidity in bringing it to a close. Only two commentators seem to favor this interpretation, but it fits well into the logic of the context, whereas the rendering, "He who does not know the evils of war cannot appreciate its benefits," is distinctly pointless.]

8. The skillful soldier does not raise a second levy, neither are his supply-wagons loaded more than twice.

   [Once war is declared, he will not waste precious time in waiting for reinforcements, nor will he return his army back for fresh supplies, but crosses the enemy's frontier without delay. This may seem an audacious policy to recommend, but with all great strategists, from Julius Caesar to Napoleon Bonaparte, the value of time—that is, being a little ahead of your opponent—has counted for more than either numerical superiority or the nicest calculations with regard to commissariat.]

9. Bring war material with you from home, but forage on the enemy. Thus the army will have food enough for its needs.

   [The Chinese word translated here as "war material" literally means "things to be used," and is meant in the widest sense. It includes all the impedimenta of an army, apart from provisions.]

10. Poverty of the State exchequer causes an army to be maintained by contributions from a distance. Contributing to maintain an army at a distance causes the people to be impoverished.

    [The beginning of this sentence does not balance properly with the next, though obviously intended to do so. The arrangement, moreover, is so awkward that I cannot help suspecting some corruption in the text. It never seems to occur to Chinese commentators that an emendation may be necessary for the sense, and we get no help from them there. The Chinese words Sun Tzŭ used to indicate the cause of the people's impoverishment clearly have reference to some system by which the husbandmen sent their contributions of corn to the army direct. But why should it fall on them to maintain an army in this way, except because the State or Government is too poor to do so?]

11. On the other hand, the proximity of an army causes prices to go up; and high prices cause the people's substance to be drained away.

[Wang Hsi says high prices occur before the army has left its own territory. Ts'ao Kung understands it of an army that has already crossed the frontier.]

12. When their substance is drained away, the peasantry will be afflicted by heavy exactions.

13, 14. With this loss of substance and exhaustion of strength, the homes of the people will be stripped bare, and three-tenths of their income will be dissipated;

[Tu Mu and Wang Hsi agree that the people are not mulcted not of three-tenths, but of seven-tenths, of their income. But this is hardly to be extracted from our text. Ho Shih has a characteristic tag: "The people being regarded as the essential part of the State, and food as the people's heaven, is it not right that those in authority should value and be careful of both?"]

while government expenses for broken chariots, worn-out horses, breast-plates and helmets, bows and arrows, spears and shields, protective mantelets, draught-oxen and heavy wagons, will amount to four-tenths of its total revenue.

15. Hence a wise general makes a point of foraging on the enemy. One cartload of the enemy's provisions is equivalent to twenty of one's own, and likewise a single *picul* of his provender is equivalent to twenty from one's own store.

[Because twenty cartloads will be consumed in the process of transporting one cartload to the front. A picul is a unit of measure equal to 133.3 pounds (65.5 kilograms).]

16. Now in order to kill the enemy, our men must be roused to anger; that there may be advantage from defeating the enemy, they must have their rewards.

[Tu Mu says: "Rewards are necessary in order to make the soldiers see the advantage of beating the enemy; thus, when you capture spoils from the enemy, they must be used as rewards, so that all your men may have a keen desire to fight, each on his own account."]

17. Therefore in chariot fighting, when ten or more chariots have been taken, those should be rewarded who took the first. Our own flags should be substituted for those of the enemy, and the chariots mingled and used in conjunction with ours. The captured soldiers should be kindly treated and kept.

18. This is called, using the conquered foe to augment one's own strength.

19. In war, then, let your great object be victory, not lengthy campaigns.

[As Ho Shih remarks: "War is not a thing to be trifled with." Sun Tzŭ here reiterates the main lesson which this chapter is intended to enforce.]

20. Thus it may be known that the leader of armies is the arbiter of the people's fate, the man on whom it depends whether the nation shall be in peace or in peril.

III

ATTACK BY STRATAGEM

1. Sun Tzŭ said: In the practical art of war, the best thing of all is to take the enemy's country whole and intact; to shatter and destroy it is not so good. So, too, it is better to recapture an army entire than to destroy it, to capture a regiment, a detachment or a company entire than to destroy them.

    [The equivalent to an army corps, according to Ssŭ-a Fa, consisted nominally of 12,500 men; according to Ts'ao Kung, the equivalent of a regiment contained 500 men, the equivalent to a detachment consists from any number between 100 and 500, and the equivalent of a company contains from 5 to 100 men. For the last two, however, Chang Yü gives the exact figures of 100 and 5 respectively.]

2. Hence to fight and conquer in all your battles is not supreme excellence; supreme excellence consists in breaking the enemy's resistance without fighting.

    [Here again, no modern strategist but will approve the words of the old Chinese general. Moltke's greatest triumph, the capitulation of the huge French army at Sedan, was won practically without bloodshed.]

3. Thus the highest form of generalship is to balk the enemy's plans;

    [Perhaps the word "balk" falls short of expressing the full force of the Chinese word, which implies not an attitude of defense, whereby one might be content to foil the enemy's stratagems one after another, but an active policy of counter-attack. Ho Shih puts this very clearly in his note: "When the enemy has made a plan of attack against us, we must anticipate him by delivering our own attack first."]

the next best is to prevent the junction of the enemy's forces;

[Isolating him from his allies. We must not forget that Sun Tzŭ, in speaking of hostilities, always has in mind the numerous states or principalities into which the China of his day was split up.]

the next in order is to attack the enemy's army in the field;

[When he is already at full strength.]

and the worst policy of all is to besiege walled cities.

4. The rule is, not to besiege walled cities if it can possibly be avoided.

[Another sound piece of military theory. Had the Boers acted upon it in 1899, and refrained from dissipating their strength before Kimberley, Mafeking, or even Ladysmith, it is more than probable that they would have been masters of the situation before the British were ready seriously to oppose them.]

The preparation of mantlets, movable shelters, and various implements of war, will take up three whole months;

[It is not quite clear what the Chinese word, here translated as "mantlets," described. Ts'ao Kung simply defines them as "large shields," but we get a better idea of them from Li Ch'üan, who says they were to protect the heads of those who were assaulting the city walls at close quarters. This seems to suggest a sort of Roman *testudo*, ready made. Tu Mu says they were wheeled vehicles used in repelling attacks, but this is denied by Ch'ên Hao. See *supra* 2, 14. The name is also applied to turrets on city walls. Of the "movable shelters" we get a fairly clear description from several commentators. They were wooden missile-proof structures on four wheels, propelled from within, covered over with raw hides, and used in sieges to convey parties of men to and from the walls, for the purpose of filling up the encircling moat with earth. Tu Mu adds that they are now called "wooden donkeys."]

and the piling up of mounds over against the walls will take three months more.

[These were great mounds or ramparts of earth heaped up to the level of the enemy's walls in order to discover the weak points in the defense, and also to destroy the fortified turrets mentioned in the preceding note.]

5. The general, unable to control his irritation, will launch his men to the assault like swarming ants,

    [This vivid simile of Ts'ao Kung is taken from the spectacle of an army of ants climbing a wall. The meaning is that the general, losing patience at the long delay, may make a premature attempt to storm the place before his engines of war are ready.]

    with the result that one-third of his men are slain, while the town still remains untaken. Such are the disastrous effects of a siege.

    [We are reminded of the terrible losses of the Japanese before Port Arthur, in the most recent siege which history has to record.]

6. Therefore the skillful leader subdues the enemy's troops without any fighting; he captures their cities without laying siege to them; he overthrows their kingdom without lengthy operations in the field.

    [Chia Lin notes that he only overthrows the Government, but does no harm to individuals. The classical instance is Wu Wang, who after having put an end to the Yin dynasty was acclaimed "Father and mother of the people."]

7. With his forces intact he will dispute the mastery of the Empire, and thus, without losing a man, his triumph will be complete.

    [Owing to the double meanings in the Chinese text, the latter part of the sentence is susceptible of quite a different meaning: "And thus, the weapon not being blunted by use, its keenness remains perfect."]

    This is the method of attacking by stratagem.

8. It is the rule in war, if our forces are ten to the enemy's one, to surround him; if five to one, to attack him;

[Straightway, without waiting for any further advantage.]

if twice as numerous, to divide our army into two.

[Tu Mu takes exception to the saying; and at first sight, indeed, it appears to violate a fundamental principle of war. Ts'ao Kung, however, gives a clue to Sun Tzŭ's meaning: "Being two to the enemy's one, we may use one part of our army in the regular way, and the other for some special diversion." Chang Yü thus further elucidates the point: "If our force is twice as numerous as that of the enemy, it should be split up into two divisions, one to meet the enemy in front, and one to fall upon his rear; if he replies to the frontal attack, he may be crushed from behind; if to the rearward attack, he may be crushed in front." This is what is meant by saying that "one part may be used in the regular way, and the other for some special diversion." Tu Mu does not understand that dividing one's army is simply an irregular, just as concentrating it is the regular, strategical method, and he is too hasty in calling this a mistake.]

9. If equally matched, we can offer battle;

[Li Ch'üan, followed by Ho Shih, gives the following paraphrase: "If attackers and attacked are equally matched in strength, only the able general will fight."]

if slightly inferior in numbers, we can avoid the enemy;

[The meaning, "we can watch the enemy," is certainly a great improvement on the above; but unfortunately there appears to be no very good authority for the variant. Chang Yü reminds us that the saying only applies if the other factors are equal; a small difference in numbers is often more than counterbalanced by superior energy and discipline.]

if quite unequal in every way, we can flee from him.

10. Hence, though an obstinate fight may be made by a small force, in the end it must be captured by the larger force.

11. Now the general is the bulwark of the State; if the bulwark is complete at all points; the State will be strong; if the bulwark is defective, the State will be weak.

[As Li Ch'üan tersely puts it: "Gap indicates deficiency; if the general's ability is not perfect (i.e. if he is not thoroughly versed in his profession), his army will lack strength."]

12. There are three ways in which a ruler can bring misfortune upon his army:

13. (1) By commanding the army to advance or to retreat, being ignorant of the fact that it cannot obey. This is called hobbling the army.

[Li Ch'üan adds the comment: "It is like tying together the legs of a thoroughbred, so that it is unable to gallop." One would naturally think of "the ruler" in this passage as being at home, and trying to direct the movements of his army from a distance. But the commentators understand just the reverse, and quote the saying of T'ai Kung: "A kingdom should not be governed from without, and army should not be directed from within." Of course it is true that, during an engagement, or when in close touch with the enemy, the general should not be in the thick of his own troops, but a little distance apart. Otherwise, he will be liable to misjudge the position as a whole, and give wrong orders.]

14. (2) By attempting to govern an army in the same way as he administers a kingdom, being ignorant of the conditions which obtain in an army. This causes restlessness in the soldier's minds.

[Ts'ao Kung's note is, freely translated: "The military sphere and the civil sphere are wholly distinct; you can't handle an army in kid gloves." And Chang Yü says: "Humanity and justice are the principles on which to govern a state, but not an army; opportunism and flexibility, on the other hand, are military rather than civil virtues to assimilate the governing of an army"—to that of a State, understood.]

15. (3) By employing the officers of his army without discrimination,

[That is, he is not careful to use the right man in the right place.]

through ignorance of the military principle of adaptation to circumstances. This shakes the confidence of the soldiers.

[I follow Mei Yao-ch'ên here. The other commentators refer not to the ruler, as in paragraph 13, 14, but to the officers he employs. Thus Tu Yu says: "If a general is ignorant of the principle of adaptability, he must not be entrusted with a position of authority." Tu Mu quotes: "The skillful employer of men will employ the wise man, the brave man, the covetous man, and the stupid man. For the wise man delights in establishing his merit, the brave man likes to show his courage in action, the covetous man is quick at seizing advantages, and the stupid man has no fear of death."]

16. But when the army is restless and distrustful, trouble is sure to come from the other feudal princes. This is simply bringing anarchy into the army, and flinging victory away.

17. Thus we may know that there are five essentials for victory:

(1) He will win who knows when to fight and when not to fight.

[Chang Yü says: If he can fight, he advances and takes the offensive; if he cannot fight, he retreats and remains on the defensive. He will invariably conquer who knows whether it is right to take the offensive or the defensive.]

(2) He will win who knows how to handle both superior and inferior forces.

[This is not merely the general's ability to estimate numbers correctly, as Li Ch'üan and others make out. Chang Yü expounds the saying more satisfactorily: "By applying the art of war, it is possible with a lesser force to defeat a greater, and vice versa. The secret lies in an eye for locality, and in not letting the right moment slip. Thus Wu Tzŭ says: 'With a superior force, make for easy ground; with an inferior one, make for difficult ground.' "]

(3) He will win whose army is animated by the same spirit throughout all its ranks.

(4) He will win who, prepared himself, waits to take the enemy unprepared.

(5) He will win who has military capacity and is not interfered with by the sovereign.

[Tu Yu quotes Wang Tzŭ as saying: "It is the sovereign's function to give broad instructions, but to decide on battle it is the function of the general." It is needless to dilate on the military disasters which have been caused by undue interference with operations in the field on the part of the home government. Napoleon undoubtedly owed much of his extraordinary success to the fact that he was not hampered by central authority.]

18. Hence the saying: If you know the enemy and know yourself, you need not fear the result of a hundred battles. If you know yourself but not the enemy, for every victory gained you will also suffer a defeat.

[Li Ch'üan cites the case of Fu Chien, prince of Ch'in, who in AD 383 marched with a vast army against the Chin Emperor. When warned not to despise an enemy who could command the services of such men as Hsieh An and Huan Ch'ung, he boastfully replied: "I have the population of eight provinces at my back, infantry and horsemen to the number of one million; why, they could dam up the Yangtsze River itself by merely throwing their whips into the stream. What danger have I to fear?" Nevertheless, his forces were soon after disastrously routed at the Fei River, and he was obliged to beat a hasty retreat.]

If you know neither the enemy nor yourself, you will succumb in every battle.

[Chang Yü said: "Knowing the enemy enables you to take the offensive, knowing yourself enables you to stand on the defensive." He adds: "Attack is the secret of defense; defense is the planning of an attack." It would be hard to find a better epitome of the root-principle of war.]

IV

TACTICAL DISPOSITIONS

[Ts'ao Kung explains the Chinese meaning of the words for the title of this chapter: "marching and countermarching on the part of the two armies with a view to discovering each other's condition." Tu Mu says: "It is through the dispositions of an army that its condition may be discovered. Conceal your dispositions, and your condition will remain secret, which leads to victory; show your dispositions, and your condition will become patent, which leads to defeat." Wang Hsi remarks that the good general can "secure success by modifying his tactics to meet those of the enemy."]

1. Sun Tzŭ said: The good fighters of old first put themselves beyond the possibility of defeat, and then waited for an opportunity of defeating the enemy.

2. To secure ourselves against defeat lies in our own hands, but the opportunity of defeating the enemy is provided by the enemy himself.

    [That is, of course, by a mistake on the enemy's part.]

3. Thus the good fighter is able to secure himself against defeat,

    [Chang Yü says this is done, "By concealing the disposition of his troops, covering up his tracks, and taking unremitting precautions."]

    but cannot make certain of defeating the enemy.

4. Hence the saying: One may know how to conquer without being able to do it.

5. Security against defeat implies defensive tactics; ability to defeat the enemy means taking the offensive.

[I retain the sense found in a similar passage in paragraph 1–3, in spite of the fact that the commentators are all against me. The meaning they give, "He who cannot conquer takes the defensive," is plausible enough.]

6. Standing on the defensive indicates insufficient strength; attacking, a superabundance of strength.

7. The general who is skilled in defense hides in the most secret recesses of the earth;

    [Literally, "hides under the ninth earth," which is a metaphor indicating the utmost secrecy and concealment, so that the enemy may not know his whereabouts.]

    he who is skilled in attack flashes forth from the topmost heights of heaven.

    [Another metaphor, implying that he falls on his adversary like a thunderbolt, against which there is no time to prepare. This is the opinion of most of the commentators.]

    Thus on the one hand we have ability to protect ourselves; on the other, a victory that is complete.

8. To see victory only when it is within the ken of the common herd is not the acme of excellence.

    [As Ts'ao Kung remarks, "the thing is to see the plant before it has germinated," to foresee the event before the action has begun. Li Ch'üan alludes to the story of Han Hsin who, when about to attack the vastly superior army of Chao, which was strongly entrenched in the city of Ch'êng-an, said to his officers: "Gentlemen, we are going to annihilate the enemy, and shall meet again at dinner." The officers hardly took his words seriously, and gave a very dubious assent. But Han Hsin had already worked out in his mind the details of a clever stratagem, whereby, as he foresaw, he was able to capture the city and inflict a crushing defeat on his adversary.]

9. Neither is it the acme of excellence if you fight and conquer and the whole Empire says, "Well done!"

[True excellence being, as Tu Mu says: "To plan secretly, to move surreptitiously, to foil the enemy's intentions and balk his schemes, so that at last the day may be won without shedding a drop of blood." Sun Tzǔ reserves his approbation for things that "the world's coarse thumb/And finger fail to plumb."]

10. To lift an autumn hair is no sign of great strength;

["Autumn hair" is explained as the fur of a hare, which is finest in autumn, when it begins to grow afresh. The phrase is a very common one in Chinese writers.]

to see the sun and moon is no sign of sharp sight; to hear the noise of thunder is no sign of a quick ear.

[Ho Shih gives as real instances of strength, sharp sight and quick hearing: Wu Huo, who could lift a tripod weighing 250 stone; Li Chu, who at a distance of a hundred paces could see objects no bigger than a mustard seed; and Shih K'uang, a blind musician who could hear the footsteps of a mosquito.]

11. What the ancients called a clever fighter is one who not only wins, but excels in winning with ease.

[The last half is literally "one who, conquering, excels in easy conquering." Mei Yao-ch'ên says: "He who only sees the obvious, wins his battles with difficulty; he who looks below the surface of things, wins with ease."]

12. Hence his victories bring him neither reputation for wisdom nor credit for courage.

[Tu Mu explains this very well: "Inasmuch as his victories are gained over circumstances that have not come to light, the world at large knows nothing of them, and he wins no reputation for wisdom; inasmuch as the hostile state submits before there has been any bloodshed, he receives no credit for courage."]

13. He wins his battles by making no mistakes.

[Ch'ên Hao says: "He plans no superfluous marches, he devises no futile attacks." The connection of ideas is thus explained by Chang Yü: "One who seeks to conquer by sheer strength, clever though he may be at winning pitched battles, is also liable on occasion to be vanquished; whereas he who can look into the future and discern conditions that are not yet manifest, will never make a blunder and therefore invariably win."]

Making no mistakes is what establishes the certainty of victory, for it means conquering an enemy that is already defeated.

14. Hence the skillful fighter puts himself into a position which makes defeat impossible, and does not miss the moment for defeating the enemy.

[A "counsel of perfection" as Tu Mu truly observes. "Position" need not be confined to the actual ground occupied by the troops. It includes all the arrangements and preparations which a wise general will make to increase the safety of his army.]

15. Thus it is that in war the victorious strategist only seeks battle after the victory has been won, whereas he who is destined to defeat first fights and afterwards looks for victory.

[Ho Shih thus expounds the paradox: "In warfare, first lay plans which will ensure victory, and then lead your army to battle; if you will not begin with stratagem but rely on brute strength alone, victory will no longer be assured."]

16. The consummate leader cultivates the moral law, and strictly adheres to method and discipline; thus it is in his power to control success.

17. In respect of military method, we have, firstly, Measurement; secondly, Estimation of quantity; thirdly, Calculation; fourthly, Balancing of chances; fifthly, Victory.

18. Measurement owes its existence to Earth; Estimation of quantity to Measurement; Calculation to Estimation of quantity; Balancing of chances to Calculation; and Victory to Balancing of chances.

[It is not easy to distinguish the four terms very clearly in the Chinese. The first seems to be surveying and measurement of the ground, which enable us to form an estimate of the enemy's strength, and to make calculations based on the data thus obtained; we are thus led to a general weighing-up, or comparison of the enemy's chances with our own; if the latter turn the scale, then victory ensues. The chief difficulty lies in third term, which in the Chinese some commentators take as a calculation of numbers, thereby making it nearly synonymous with the second term. Perhaps the second term should be thought of as a consideration of the enemy's general position or condition, while the third term is the estimate of his numerical strength. On the other hand, Tu Mu says: "The question of relative strength having been settled, we can bring the varied resources of cunning into play." Ho Shih seconds this interpretation, but weakens it. However, it points to the third term as being a calculation of numbers.]

19. A victorious army opposed to a routed one, is as a pound's weight placed in the scale against a single grain.

[Literally, "a victorious army is like an *i* (20 oz.) weighed against a *ʃhu* (¹⁄₂₄oz.); a routed army is a *ʃhu* weighed against an *i*." The point is simply the enormous advantage which a disciplined force, flushed with victory, has over one demoralized by defeat." Legge, in his note on Mencius, I. 2. ix. 2, makes the *i* to be 24 Chinese ounces, and corrects Chu Hsi's statement that it equaled 20 oz. only. But Li Ch'üan of the T'ang dynasty here gives the same figure as Chu Hsi.]

20. The onrush of a conquering force is like the bursting of pent-up waters into a chasm a thousand fathoms deep.

V

ENERGY

1. Sun Tzŭ said: The control of a large force is the same principle as the control of a few men: it is merely a question of dividing up their numbers.

   [That is, cutting up the army into regiments, companies, etc., with subordinate officers in command of each. Tu Mu reminds us of Han Hsin's famous reply to the first Han Emperor, who once said to him: "How large an army do you think I could lead?" "Not more than 100,000 men, your Majesty." "And you?" asked the Emperor. "Oh!" he answered, "the more the better."]

2. Fighting with a large army under your command is nowise different from fighting with a small one: it is merely a question of instituting signs and signals.

3. To ensure that your whole host may withstand the brunt of the enemy's attack and remain unshaken — this is effected by maneuvers direct and indirect.

   [We now come to one of the most interesting parts of Sun Tzŭ's treatise, the discussion of the *chêng* and the *ch'i*." As it is by no means easy to grasp the full significance of these two terms, or to render them consistently by good English equivalents; it may be as well to tabulate some of the commentators' remarks on the subject before proceeding further. Li Ch'üan: "Facing the enemy is *chêng*, making lateral diversion is *ch'i*. Chia Lin: "In presence of the enemy, your troops should be arrayed in normal fashion, but in order to secure victory abnormal maneuvers must be employed." Mei Yao-ch'en: "*ch'i* is active, *chêng* is passive; passivity means waiting for an opportunity, activity beings the victory itself." Ho Shih: "We must cause the enemy to regard our straightforward attack as one that is secretly designed, and vice versa; thus *chêng* may also be *ch'i*, and *ch'i* may also be *chêng*." He instances the famous exploit of Han Hsin, who when marching ostensibly against Lin-chin (now Chao-i in Shensi), suddenly threw a large force across the Yellow River in wooden tubs, utterly disconcerting his opponent. (Ch'ien Han Shu) Here, we are told, the march on Lin-chin was *chêng*, and the surprise maneuver was *ch'i*." Chang Yü gives the following summary of opinions on the words: "Military writers do not agree with regard to the meaning of *ch'i* and *chêng*. Wei Liao Tzŭ (4th cent. BC) says: 'Direct warfare favors frontal attacks, indirect warfare attacks from the rear.' Ts'ao Kung says: 'Going straight out to join battle is a direct operation; appearing on the enemy's rear is an indirect maneuver.' Li Wei-kung (6th and 7th cent. AD) says: 'In war, to march straight ahead is *chêng*; turning movements, on the other hand, are *ch'i*.' These writers simply regard *chêng* as *chêng*, and *ch'i* as *ch'i*; they do not note that the two are mutually interchangeable and run into each other like the two sides of a circle (see *infra*, paragraph 11). A comment on the T'ang Emperor T'ai Tsung goes to the root of the matter: 'A *ch'i* maneuver may be *chêng*, if we make the enemy look upon it as *chêng*; then our real attack will be *ch'i*, and vice versa. The whole secret lies in confusing the enemy, so that he cannot fathom our real intent.' " To put it perhaps a little more clearly: any attack or other operation is *chêng*, on which the enemy has had his attention fixed; whereas that is *ch'i*, which takes him by surprise or comes from an unexpected quarter. If the enemy perceives a movement which is meant to be *ch'i*, it immediately becomes *chêng*.]

4. That the impact of your army may be like a grindstone dashed against an egg—this is effected by the science of weak points and strong.

5. In all fighting, the direct method may be used for joining battle, but indirect methods will be needed in order to secure victory.

[Chang Yü says: "Steadily develop indirect tactics, either by pounding the enemy's flanks or falling on his rear." A brilliant example of "indirect tactics" which decided the fortunes of a campaign was Lord Roberts' night march round the Peiwar Kotal in the second Afghan war, as recounted in *Forty-One Years in India*.]

6. Indirect tactics, efficiently applied, are inexhausible as Heaven and Earth, unending as the flow of rivers and streams; like the sun and moon, they end but to begin anew; like the four seasons, they pass away to return once more.

   [Tu Yu and Chang Yü understand this of the permutations of *ch'i* and *chêng*. But at present Sun Tzŭ is not speaking of *chêng* at all, unless, indeed, we suppose with Chêng Yu-hsien that a clause relating to it has fallen out of the text. Of course, as has already been pointed out, the two are so inextricably interwoven in all military operations, that they cannot really be considered apart. Here we simply have an expression, in figurative language, of the almost infinite resource of a great leader.]

7. There are not more than five musical notes, yet the combinations of these five give rise to more melodies than can ever be heard.

8. There are not more than five primary colors (blue, yellow, red, white, and black), yet in combination they produce more hues than can ever been seen.

9 There are not more than five cardinal tastes (sour, acrid, salt, sweet, bitter), yet combinations of them yield more flavors than can ever be tasted.

10. In battle, there are not more than two methods of attack — the direct and the indirect; yet these two in combination give rise to an endless series of maneuvers.

11. The direct and the indirect lead on to each other in turn. It is like moving in a circle — you never come to an end. Who can exhaust the possibilities of their combination?

12. The onset of troops is like the rush of a torrent which will even roll stones along in its course.

13. The quality of decision is like the well-timed swoop of a falcon which enables it to strike and destroy its victim.

   [The Chinese here is tricky and a certain key word in the context it is used defies the best efforts of the translator. Tu Mu defines this word as "the measurement or estimation of distance." But this meaning does not quite fit the illustrative simile in paragraph 15. Applying this definition to the falcon, it seems to me to denote that instinct of self-restraint which keeps the bird from swooping on its quarry until the right moment, together with the power of judging when the right moment has arrived. The analogous quality in soldiers is the highly important one of being able to reserve their fire until the very instant at which it will be most effective. When the "Victory" went into action at Trafalgar at hardly more than drifting pace, she was for several minutes exposed to a storm of shot and shell before replying with a single gun. Nelson coolly waited until he was within close range, when the broadside he brought to bear worked fearful havoc on the enemy's nearest ships.]

14. Therefore the good fighter will be terrible in his onset, and prompt in his decision.

[The word "decision" would have reference to the measurement of distance mentioned above, letting the enemy get near before striking. But I cannot help thinking that Sun Tzŭ meant to use the word in a figurative sense comparable to our own idiom "short and sharp." Cf. Wang Hsi's note, which after describing the falcon's mode of attack, proceeds: "This is just how the 'psychological moment' should be seized in war."]

15. Energy may be likened to the bending of a crossbow; decision, to the releasing of a trigger.

[None of the commentators seem to grasp the real point of the simile of energy and the force stored up in the bent crossbow until released by the finger on the trigger.]

16. Amid the turmoil and tumult of battle, there may be seeming disorder and yet no real disorder at all; amid confusion and chaos, your array may be without head or tail, yet it will be proof against defeat.

[Mei Yao-ch'ên says: "The subdivisions of the army having been previously fixed, and the various signals agreed upon, the separating and joining, the dispersing and collecting which will take place in the course of a battle, may give the appearance of disorder when no real disorder is possible. Your formation may be without head or tail, your dispositions all topsy-turvy, and yet a rout of your forces quite out of the question."]

17. Simulated disorder postulates perfect discipline, simulated fear postulates courage; simulated weakness postulates strength.

[In order to make the translation intelligible, it is necessary to tone down the sharply paradoxical form of the original. Ts'ao Kung throws out a hint of the meaning in his brief note: "These things all serve to destroy formation and conceal one's condition." But Tu Mu is the first to put it quite plainly: "If you wish to feign confusion in order to lure the enemy on, you must first have perfect discipline; if you wish to display timidity in order to entrap the enemy, you must have extreme courage; if you wish to parade your weakness in order to make the enemy over-confident, you must have exceeding strength."]

18. Hiding order beneath the cloak of disorder is simply a question of subdivision;

[See *supra*, paragraph 1.]

concealing courage under a show of timidity presupposes a fund of latent energy;

[The commentators strongly understand a certain Chinese word here differently than anywhere else in this chapter. Thus Tu Mu says: "seeing that we are favorably circumstanced and yet make no move, the enemy will believe that we are really afraid."]

masking strength with weakness is to be effected by tactical dispositions.

[Chang Yü relates the following anecdote of Kao Tsu, the first Han Emperor: "Wishing to crush the Hsiung-nu, he sent out spies to report on their condition. But the Hsiung-nu, forewarned, carefully concealed all their able-bodied men and well-fed horses, and only allowed infirm soldiers and emaciated cattle to be seen. The result was that spies one and all recommended the Emperor to deliver his attack. Lou Ching alone opposed them, saying:

"When two countries go to war, they are naturally inclined to make an ostentatious display of their strength. Yet our spies have seen nothing but old age and infirmity. This is surely some ruse on the part of the enemy, and it would be unwise for us to attack." The Emperor, however, disregarding this advice, fell into the trap and found himself surrounded at Po-têng.]

19. Thus one who is skillful at keeping the enemy on the move maintains deceitful appearances, according to which the enemy will act.

[Ts'ao Kung's note is "Make a display of weakness and want." Tu Mu says: "If our force happens to be superior to the enemy's, weakness may be simulated in order to lure him on; but if inferior, he must be led to believe that we are strong, in order that he may keep off. In fact, all the enemy's movements should be determined by the signs that we choose to give him." Note the following anecdote of Sun Pin, a descendent of Sun Wu: In 341 BC, the Ch'i State being at war with Wei, sent T'ien Chi and Sun Pin against the general P'ang Chüan, who happened to be a deadly personal enemy of the latter. Sun Pin said: "The Ch'i State has a reputation for cowardice, and therefore our adversary despises us. Let us turn this circumstance to account." Accordingly, when the army had crossed the border into Wei territory, he gave orders to show 100,000 fires on the first night, 50,000 on the next, and the night after only 20,000. P'ang Chüan pursued them hotly, saying to himself: "I knew these men of Ch'i were cowards: their numbers have already fallen away by more than half." In his retreat, Sun Pin came to a narrow defile, which he calculated that his pursuers would reach after dark. Here he had a tree stripped of its bark, and inscribed upon it the words: "Under this tree shall P'ang Chüan die." Then, as night began to fall, he placed a strong body of archers in ambush nearby, with orders to shoot directly if they saw a light. Later on, P'ang Chüan arrived at the spot, and noticing the tree, struck a light in order to read what was written on it. His body was immediately riddled by a volley of arrows, and his whole army thrown into confusion. (The above is Tu Mu's version of the story; the *Shih Chi*, less dramatically but probably with more historical truth, makes P'ang Chüan cut his own throat with an exclamation of despair, after the rout of his army.)]

He sacrifices something, that the enemy may snatch at it.

20. By holding out baits, he keeps him on the march; then with a body of picked men he lies in wait for him.

   [With an emendation suggested by Li Ching, this then reads, "He lies in wait with the main body of his troops."]

21. The clever combatant looks to the effect of combined energy, and does not require too much from individuals.

   [Tu Mu says: "He first of all considers the power of his army in the bulk; afterwards he takes individual talent into account, and uses each man according to his capabilities. He does not demand perfection from the untalented."]

   Hence his ability to pick out the right men and utilize combined energy.

22. When he utilizes combined energy, his fighting men become as it were like unto rolling logs or stones. For it is the nature of a log or stone to remain motionless on level ground, and to move when on a slope; if four-cornered, to come to a standstill, but if round-shaped, to go rolling down.

   [Ts'au Kung calls this "the use of natural or inherent power."]

23. Thus the energy developed by good fighting men is as the momentum of a round stone rolled down a mountain thousands of feet in height. So much on the subject of energy.

   [The chief lesson of this chapter, in Tu Mu's opinion, is the paramount importance in war of rapid evolutions and sudden rushes. "Great results," he adds, "can thus be achieved with small forces."]

VI

WEAK POINTS AND STRONG

[Chang Yü attempts to explain the sequence of chapters as follows: "Ch. Four, on Tactical Dispositions, treated of the offensive and the defensive; Ch. Five, on Energy, dealt with direct and indirect methods. The good general acquaints himself first with the theory of attack and defense, and then turns his attention to direct and indirect methods. He studies the art of varying and combining these two methods before proceeding to the subject of weak and strong points. For the use of direct or indirect methods arises out of attack and defense, and the perception of weak and strong points depends again on the above methods. Hence the present chapter comes immediately after the chapter on Energy."]

1. Sun Tzŭ said: Whoever is first in the field and awaits the coming of the enemy, will be fresh for the fight; whoever is second in the field and has to hasten to battle will arrive exhausted.

2. Therefore the clever combatant imposes his will on the enemy, but does not allow the enemy's will to be imposed on him.

    [One mark of a great soldier is that he fights on his own terms or fights not at all.]

3. By holding out advantages to him, he can cause the enemy to approach of his own accord; or, by inflicting damage, he can make it impossible for the enemy to draw near.

    [In the first case, he will entice him with a bait; in the second, he will strike at some important point which the enemy will have to defend.]

4. If the enemy is taking his ease, he can harass him;

[This passage may be cited as evidence against Mei Yao-ch'ên's interpretation of Ch. One, paragraph 23.]

if well supplied with food, he can starve him out; if quietly encamped, he can force him to move.

5. Appear at points which the enemy must hasten to defend; march swiftly to places where you are not expected.

6. An army may march great distances without distress, if it marches through country where the enemy is not.

[Ts'ao Kung sums up very well: "Emerge from the void [q.d., like 'a bolt from the blue'], strike at vulnerable points, shun places that are defended, attack in unexpected quarters."]

7. You can be sure of succeeding in your attacks if you only attack places which are undefended.

[Wang Hsi explains "undefended places" as "weak points; that is to say, where the general is lacking in capacity, or the soldiers in spirit; where the walls are not strong enough, or the precautions not strict enough; where relief comes too late, or provisions are too scanty, or the defenders are variance amongst themselves."]

You can ensure the safety of your defense if you only hold positions that cannot be attacked.

[i.e., Where there are none of the weak points mentioned above. There is rather a nice point involved in the interpretation of this later clause. Tu Mu, Ch'ên Hao, and Mei Yao-ch'ên assume the meaning to be: "In order to make your defense quite safe, you must defend even those places that are not likely to be attacked"; and Tu Mu adds: "How much more, then, those that will be attacked." Taken thus, however, the clause balances less well with the preceding—always a consideration in the highly antithetical style which is natural to the Chinese. Chang Yü, therefore, seems to come nearer the mark in saying: "He who is skilled in attack flashes forth from the topmost heights of heaven, making it impossible for the enemy to guard against him. This being so, the places that I shall attack are precisely those that the enemy cannot defend.... He who is skilled in defense hides in the most secret recesses of the earth, making it impossible for the enemy to estimate his whereabouts. This being so, the places that I shall hold are precisely those that the enemy cannot attack."]

8. Hence that general is skillful in attack whose opponent does not know what to defend; and he is skillful in defense whose opponent does not know what to attack.

   [An aphorism which puts the whole art of war in a nutshell.]

9. O divine art of subtlety and secrecy! Through you we learn to be invisible, through you inaudible;

   [Literally, "without form or sound," but it is said of course with reference to the enemy.]

   and hence we can hold the enemy's fate in our hands.

10. You may advance and be absolutely irresistible, if you make for the enemy's weak points; you may retire and be safe from pursuit if your movements are more rapid than those of the enemy.

11. If we wish to fight, the enemy can be forced to an engagement even though he be sheltered behind a high rampart and a deep ditch. All we need do is attack some other place that he will be obliged to relieve.

    [Tu Mu says: "If the enemy is the invading party, we can cut his line of communications and occupy the roads by which he will have to return; if we are the invaders, we may direct our attack against the sovereign himself." It is clear that Sun Tzŭ, unlike certain generals in the late Boer war, was no believer in frontal attacks.]

12. If we do not wish to fight, we can prevent the enemy from engaging us even though the lines of our encampment be merely traced out on the ground. All we need do is to throw something odd and unaccountable in his way.

    [This extremely concise expression is intelligibly paraphrased by Chia Lin: "even though we have constructed neither wall nor ditch." Li Ch'üan says: "we puzzle him by strange and unusual dispositions"; and Tu Mu finally clinches the meaning by three illustrative anecdotes—one of Chu-ko Liang, who when occupying Yang-p'ing and about to be attacked by Ssŭ-ma I, suddenly struck his colors, stopped the beating of the drums, and flung open the city gates, showing only a few men engaged in sweeping and sprinkling the ground. This unexpected proceeding had the intended effect; for Ssŭ-ma I, suspecting an ambush, actually drew off his army and retreated. What Sun Tzŭ is advocating here, therefore, is nothing more nor less than the timely use of "bluff."]

13. By discovering the enemy's dispositions and remaining invisible ourselves, we can keep our forces concentrated, while the enemy's must be divided.

[The conclusion is perhaps not very obvious, but Chang Yü (after Mei Yao-ch'ên) rightly explains it thus: "If the enemy's dispositions are visible, we can make for him in one body; whereas, our own dispositions being kept secret, the enemy will be obliged to divide his forces in order to guard against attack from every quarter."]

14. We can form a single united body, while the enemy must split up into fractions. Hence there will be a whole pitted against separate parts of a whole, which means that we shall be many to the enemy's few.

15. And if we are able thus to attack an inferior force with a superior one, our opponents will be in dire straits.

16. The spot where we intend to fight must not be made known; for then the enemy will have to prepare against a possible attack at several different points;

[Sheridan once explained the reason of General Grant's victories by saying that "while his opponents were kept fully employed wondering what he was going to do, he was thinking most of what he was going to do himself."]

and his forces being thus distributed in many directions, the numbers we shall have to face at any given point will be proportionately few.

17. For should the enemy strengthen his van, he will weaken his rear; should he strengthen his rear, he will weaken his van; should he strengthen his left, he will weaken his right; should he strengthen his right, he will weaken his left. If he sends reinforcements everywhere, he will everywhere be weak.

[In Frederick the Great's *Instructions to His Generals* we read: "A defensive war is apt to betray us into too frequent detachment. Those generals who have had but little experience attempt to protect every point, while those who are better acquainted with their profession, having only the capital object in view, guard against a decisive blow, and acquiesce in small misfortunes to avoid greater."]

18. Numerical weakness comes from having to prepare against possible attacks; numerical strength, from compelling our adversary to make these preparations against us.

[The highest generalship, in Col. Henderson's words, is "to compel the enemy to disperse his army, and then to concentrate superior force against each fraction in turn."]

19. Knowing the place and the time of the coming battle, we may concentrate from the greatest distances in order to fight.

[What Sun Tzŭ evidently has in mind is that nice calculation of distances and that masterly employment of strategy which enable a general to divide his army for the purpose of a long and rapid march, and afterwards to effect a junction at precisely the right spot and the right hour in order to confront the enemy in overwhelming strength. Among many such successful junctions which military history records, one of the most dramatic and decisive was the appearance of Blücher just at the critical moment on the field of Waterloo.]

20. But if neither time nor place be known, then the left wing will be impotent to succor the right, the right equally impotent to succor the left, the van unable to relieve the rear, or the rear to support the van. How much more so if the furthest portions of the army are anything

under a hundred lǐ apart, and even the nearest are separated by several lǐ!

[The Chinese of this last sentence is a little lacking in precision, but the mental picture we are required to draw is probably that of an army advancing towards a given rendezvous in separate columns, each of which has orders to be there on a fixed date. If the general allows the various detachments to proceed at haphazard, without precise instructions as to the time and place of meeting, the enemy will be able to annihilate the army in detail. Chang Yü's note may be worth quoting here: "If we do not know the place where our opponents mean to concentrate or the day on which they will join battle, our unity will be forfeited through our preparations for defense, and the positions we hold will be insecure. Suddenly happening upon a powerful foe, we shall be brought to battle in a flurried condition, and no mutual support will be possible between wings, vanguard or rear, especially if there is any great distance between the foremost and hindmost divisions of the army."]

21. Though according to my estimate the soldiers of Yüeh exceed our own in number, that shall advantage them nothing in the matter of victory. I say then that victory can be achieved.

[Alas for these brave words! The long feud between the two states ended in 473 BC with the total defeat of Wu by Kou Chien and its incorporation in Yüeh. This was doubtless long after Sun Tzŭ's death. With his present assertion compare Ch. Four, paragraph 4. Chang Yü is the only one to point out the seeming discrepancy, which he thus goes on to explain: "In the chapter on Tactical Dispositions it is said, 'One may know how to conquer without being able to do it,' whereas here we have the statement that 'victory can be achieved.'" The explanation is, that in the former chapter, where the offensive and defensive are under discussion, it is said that if the enemy is fully prepared, one cannot make certain of beating him. But the present passage refers particularly to the soldiers of Yüeh who, according to Sun Tzŭ's calculations, will be kept in ignorance of the time and place of the impending struggle. That is why he says here that victory can be achieved.]

22. Though the enemy be stronger in numbers, we may prevent him from fighting. Scheme so as to discover his plans and the likelihood of their success.

[An alternative reading offered by Chia Lin is: "Know beforehand all plans conducive to our success and to the enemy's failure."]

23. Rouse him, and learn the principle of his activity or inactivity.

[Chang Yü tells us that by noting the joy or anger shown by the enemy on being thus disturbed, we shall be able to conclude whether his policy is to lie low or the reverse. He instances the action of Cho-ku Liang, who sent the scornful present of a woman's head-dress to Ssŭ-ma I, in order to goad him out of his Fabian tactics.]

Force him to reveal himself, so as to find out his vulnerable spots.

24. Carefully compare the opposing army with your own, so that you may know where strength is superabundant and where it is deficient.

[See Ch. 4, paragraph 6.]

25. In making tactical dispositions, the highest pitch you can attain is to conceal them;

[The piquancy of the paradox evaporates in translation. Concealment is perhaps not so much actual invisibility (see *supra* paragraph 9) as "showing no sign" of what you mean to do, of the plans that are formed in your brain.]

conceal your dispositions, and you will be safe from the prying of the subtlest spies, from the machinations of the wisest brains.

[Tu Mu explains: "Though the enemy may have clever and capable officers, they will not be able to lay any plans against us."]

26. How victory may be produced for them out of the enemy's own tactics—that is what the multitude cannot comprehend.

27. All men can see the tactics whereby I conquer, but what none can see is the strategy out of which victory is evolved.

[i.e., everybody can see superficially how a battle is won; what they cannot see is the long series of plans and combinations which has preceded the battle.]

28. Do not repeat the tactics which have gained you one victory, but let your methods be regulated by the infinite variety of circumstances.

[As Wang Hsi sagely remarks: "There is but one root-principle underlying victory, but the tactics which lead up to it are infinite in number." With this compare Col. Henderson: "The rules of strategy are few and simple. They may be learned in a week. They may be taught by familiar illustrations or a dozen diagrams. But such knowledge will no more teach a man to lead an army like Napoleon than a knowledge of grammar will teach him to write like Gibbon."]

29. Military tactics are like unto water; for water in its natural course runs away from high places and hastens downwards.

30. So in war, the way is to avoid what is strong and to strike at what is weak.

[Like water, taking the line of least resistance.]

31. Water shapes its course according to the nature of the ground over which it flows; the soldier works out his victory in relation to the foe whom he is facing.

32. Therefore, just as water retains no constant shape, so in warfare there are no constant conditions.

33. He who can modify his tactics in relation to his opponent and thereby succeed in winning, may be called a heaven-born captain.

34. The five elements (water, fire, wood, metal, earth) are not always equally predominant;

[That is, as Wang Hsi says: "they predominate alternately."]

the four seasons make way for each other in turn.

[Literally, "have no invariable seat."]

There are short days and long; the moon has its periods of waning and waxing.

[See Ch. Five, paragraph 6. The purport of the passage is simply to illustrate the want of fixity in war by the changes constantly taking place in Nature. The comparison is not very happy, however, because the regularity of the phenomena which Sun Tzŭ mentions is by no means paralleled in war.]

VII

MANEUVERING

1. Sun Tzŭ said: In war, the general receives his commands from the sovereign.

2. Having collected an army and concentrated his forces, he must blend and harmonize the different elements thereof before pitching his camp.

   ["Chang Yü says: "the establishment of harmony and confidence between the higher and lower ranks before venturing into the field"; and he quotes a saying of Wu Tzŭ (ch. 1, ad initium.): "Without harmony in the State, no military expedition can be undertaken; without harmony in the army, no battle array can be formed." In an historical romance Sun Tzŭ is represented as saying to Wu Yuan: "As a general rule, those who are waging war should get rid of all the domestic troubles before proceeding to attack the external foe."]

3. After that, comes tactical maneuvering, than which there is nothing more difficult.

   [I have departed slightly from the traditional interpretation of Ts'ao Kung, who says: "From the time of receiving the sovereign's instructions until our encampment over against the enemy, the tactics to be pursued are most difficult." It seems to me that the tactics or maneuvers can hardly be said to begin until the army has sallied forth and encamped, and Ch'iên Hao's note gives color to this view: "For levying, concentrating, harmonizing and entrenching an army, there are plenty of old rules which will serve. The real difficulty comes when we engage in tactical operations." Tu Yu also observes that "the great difficulty is to be beforehand with the enemy in seizing favorable position."]

   The difficulty of tactical maneuvering consists in turning the devious into the direct, and misfortune into gain.

[This sentence contains one of those highly condensed and somewhat enigmatical expressions of which Sun Tzŭ is so fond. This is how it is explained by Ts'ao Kung: "Make it appear that you are a long way off, then cover the distance rapidly and arrive on the scene before your opponent." Tu Mu says: "Hoodwink the enemy, so that he may be remiss and leisurely while you are dashing along with utmost speed." Ho Shih gives a slightly different turn: "Although you may have difficult ground to traverse and natural obstacles to encounter this is a drawback which can be turned into actual advantage by celerity of movement." Signal examples of this saying are afforded by the two famous passages across the Alps — that of Hannibal, which laid Italy at his mercy, and that of Napoleon two thousand years later, which resulted in the great victory of Marengo.]

4. Thus, to take a long and circuitous route, after enticing the enemy out of the way, and though starting after him, to contrive to reach the goal before him, shows knowledge of the artifice of deviation.

[Tu Mu cites the famous march of Chao Shê in 270 BC to relieve the town of O-yü, which was closely invested by a Ch'in army. The King of Chao first consulted Lien P'o on the advisability of attempting a relief, but the latter thought the distance too great, and the intervening country too rugged and difficult. His Majesty then turned to Chao Shê, who fully admitted the hazardous nature of the march, but finally said: "We shall be like two rats fighting in a hole — and the pluckier one will win!" So he left the capital with his army, but had only gone a distance of 30 lî when he stopped and began throwing up entrenchments. For 28 days he continued strengthening his fortifications, and took care that spies should carry the intelligence to the enemy. The Ch'in general was overjoyed, and attributed his adversary's tardiness to the fact that the beleaguered city was in the Han State, and thus not actually part of Chao territory. But the spies had no sooner departed than Chao Shê began a forced march lasting for two days and one night, and arrive on the scene of action with such astonishing rapidity that he was able to occupy a commanding position on the "North hill" before the enemy had got wind of his movements. A crushing defeat followed for the Ch'in forces, who were obliged to raise the siege of O-yü in all haste and retreat across the border.]

5. Maneuvering with an army is advantageous; with an undisciplined multitude, most dangerous.

[I adopt the reading of the *T'ung Tien*, Chêng Yu-hsien and the *T'u Shu*, since they appear to apply the exact nuance required in order to make sense. The commentators using the standard text take this line to mean that maneuvers may be profitable, or they may be dangerous: it all depends on the ability of the general.]

6. If you set a fully equipped army in march in order to snatch an advantage, the chances are that you will be too late. On the other hand, to detach a flying column for the purpose involves the sacrifice of its baggage and stores.

[Some of the Chinese text is unintelligible to the Chinese commentators, who paraphrase the sentence. I submit my own rendering without much enthusiasm, being convinced that there is some deep-seated corruption in the text. On the whole, it is clear that Sun Tzŭ does not approve of a lengthy march being undertaken without supplies. *Cf. infra*, paragraph 11.]

7. Thus, if you order your men to roll up their buff-coats, and make forced marches without halting day or night, covering double the usual distance at a stretch,

[The ordinary day's march, according to Tu Mu, was 30 lî; but on one occasion, when pursuing Liu Pei, Ts'ao Ts'ao is said to have covered the incredible distance of 300 lî within twenty-four hours.]

doing a hundred lî in order to wrest an advantage, the leaders of all your three divisions will fall into the hands of the enemy.

8. The stronger men will be in front, the jaded ones will fall behind, and on this plan only one-tenth of your army will reach its destination.

[The moral is, as Ts'ao Kung and others point out: Don't march a hundred lî to gain a tactical advantage, either with or without impedimenta. Maneuvers of this description should be confined to short distances. Stonewall Jackson said: "The hardships of forced marches are often more painful than the dangers of battle." He did not often call upon his troops for extraordinary exertions. It was only when he intended a surprise, or when a rapid retreat was imperative, that he sacrificed everything for speed.]

9. If you march fifty lî in order to outmaneuver the enemy, you will lose the leader of your first division, and only half your force will reach the goal.

   [Literally, "the leader of the first division will be torn away."]

10. If you march thirty lî with the same object, two-thirds of your army will arrive.

    [In the *T'ung Tien* is added: "From this we may know the difficulty of maneuvering."]

11. We may take it then that an army without its baggage-train is lost; without provisions it is lost; without bases of supply it is lost.

    [I think Sun Tzŭ meant "stores accumulated in depots." But Tu Yu says "fodder and the like," Chang Yü says "Goods in general," and Wang Hsi says "fuel, salt, foodstuffs, etc."]

12. We cannot enter into alliances until we are acquainted with the designs of our neighbors.

13. We are not fit to lead an army on the march unless we are familiar with the face of the country—its mountains and forests, its pitfalls and precipices, its marshes and swamps.

14. We shall be unable to turn natural advantage to account unless we make use of local guides.

    [paragraphs 12–14 are repeated in Ch. Eleven, paragraph 52.]

15. In war, practice dissimulation, and you will succeed.

[In the tactics of Turenne, deception of the enemy, especially as to the numerical strength of his troops, took a very prominent position.]

16. Whether to concentrate or to divide your troops, must be decided by circumstances.

17. Let your rapidity be that of the wind,

[The simile is doubly appropriate, because the wind is not only swift but, as Mei Yao-ch'ên points out, "invisible and leaves no tracks."]

your compactness that of the forest.

[Mêng Shih comes nearer to the mark in his note: "When slowly marching, order and ranks must be preserved"—so as to guard against surprise attacks. But natural forest do not grow in rows, whereas they do generally possess the quality of density or compactness.]

18. In raiding and plundering be like fire,

[See *Shih Ching* IV. 3. iv. 6: "Fierce as a blazing fire which no man can check."]

in immovability like a mountain.

[That is, when holding a position from which the enemy is trying to dislodge you, or perhaps, as Tu Yu says, when he is trying to entice you into a trap.]

19. Let your plans be dark and impenetrable as night, and when you move, fall like a thunderbolt.

[Tu Yu quotes a saying of T'ai Kung which has passed into a proverb: "You cannot shut your ears to the thunder or your eyes to the lighting—so rapid are they." Likewise, an attack should be made so quickly that it cannot be parried.]

20. When you plunder a countryside, let the spoil be divided amongst your men;

[Sun Tzŭ wishes to lessen the abuses of indiscriminate plundering by insisting that all booty shall be thrown into a common stock, which may afterwards be fairly divided amongst all.]

when you capture new territory, cut it up into allotments for the benefit of the soldiery.

[Ch'ên Hao says "quarter your soldiers on the land, and let them sow and plant it." It is by acting on this principle, and harvesting the lands they invaded, that the Chinese have succeeded in carrying out some of their most memorable and triumphant expeditions, such as that of Pan Ch'ao who penetrated to the Caspian, and in more recent years, those of Fu-k'ang-an and Tso Tsung-t'ang.]

21. Ponder and deliberate before you make a move.

[Chang Yü quotes Wei Liao Tzŭ as saying that we must not break camp until we have gained the resisting power of the enemy and the cleverness of the opposing general. Cf. the "seven comparisons" in Ch. One, paragraph 13.]

22. He will conquer who has learnt the artifice of deviation.

[See *supra*, paragraph 3, 4.]

Such is the art of maneuvering.

[With these words, the chapter would naturally come to an end. But there now follows a long appendix in the shape of an extract from an earlier book on War, now lost, but apparently extant at the time when Sun Tzŭ wrote. The style of this fragment is not noticeably different from that of Sun Tzŭ himself, but no commentator raises a doubt as to its genuineness.]

23. The Book of Army Management says:

[It is perhaps significant that none of the earlier commentators give us any information about this work. Mei Yao-ch'ên calls it "an ancient military classic," and Wang Hsi, "an old book on war." Considering the enormous amount of fighting that had gone on for centuries before Sun Tzŭ's time between the various kingdoms and principalities of China, it is not in itself improbable that a collection of military maxims should have been made and written down at some earlier period.]

On the field of battle,

[Implied, though not actually in the Chinese.]

the spoken word does not carry far enough: hence the institution of gongs and drums. Nor can ordinary objects be seen clearly enough: hence the institution of banners and flags.

24. Gongs and drums, banners and flags, are means whereby the ears and eyes of the host may be focused on one particular point.

[Chang Yü says: "If sight and hearing converge simultaneously on the same object, the evolutions of as many as a million soldiers will be like those of a single man!"]

25. The host thus forming a single united body, is it impossible either for the brave to advance alone, or for the cowardly to retreat alone.

[Chuang Yu quotes a saying: "Equally guilty are those who advance against orders and those who retreat against orders." Tu Mu tells a story in this connection of Wu Ch'i, when he was fighting against the Ch'in State. Before the battle had begun, one of his soldiers, a man of matchless daring, sallied forth by himself, captured two heads from the enemy, and returned to camp. Wu Ch'i had the man instantly executed, whereupon an officer ventured to remonstrate, saying: "This man was a good soldier, and ought not to have been beheaded." Wu Ch'i replied: "I fully believe he was a good soldier, but I had him beheaded because he acted without orders."]

This is the art of handling large masses of men.

26. In night-fighting, then, make much use of signal-fires and drums, and in fighting by day, of flags and banners, as a means of influencing the ears and eyes of your army.

[Ch'ên Hao alludes to Li Kuang-pi's night ride to Ho-yang at the head of 500 mounted men; they made such an imposing display with torches, that though the rebel leader Shih Ssŭ-ming had a large army, he did not dare to dispute their passage.]

27. A whole army may be robbed of its spirit;

["In war," says Chang Yü, "if a spirit of anger can be made to pervade all ranks of an army at one and the same time, its onset will be irresistible. Now the spirit of the enemy's soldiers will be keenest when they have newly arrived on the scene, and it is therefore our cue not to fight at once, but to wait until their ardor and enthusiasm have worn off, and then strike. It is in this way that they may be robbed of their keen spirit." Li Ch'üan and others tell an anecdote (to be found in the *Tso Chuan*, year 10, paragraph 1) of Ts'ao Kuei, a protégé of Duke Chuang of Lü. The latter State was attacked by Ch'i, and the duke was about to join battle at Ch'ang-cho, after the first roll of the enemy's drums, when Ts'ao said: "Not just yet." Only after their drums had beaten for the third time, did he give the word for attack. Then they fought, and the men of Ch'i were utterly defeated. Questioned afterwards by the Duke as to the meaning of his delay, Ts'ao Kuei replied: "In battle, a courageous spirit is everything. Now the first roll of the drum tends to create this spirit, but with the second it is already on the wane, and after the third it is gone altogether. I attacked when their spirit was gone and ours was at its height. Hence our victory." Wu Tzŭ (Ch. 4) puts "spirit" first among the "four important influences" in war, and continues: "The value of a whole army—a mighty host of a million men—is dependent on one man alone: such is the influence of spirit!"]

a commander-in-chief may be robbed of his presence of mind.

[Chang Yü says: "Presence of mind is the general's most important asset. It is the quality which enables him to discipline disorder and to inspire courage into the panic-stricken." The great general Li Ching (AD 571–649) has a saying: "Attacking does not merely consist in assaulting walled cities or striking at an army in battle array; it must include the art of assailing the enemy's mental equilibrium."]

28. Now a soldier's spirit is keenest in the morning;

[Always provided, I suppose, that he has had breakfast. At the battle of the Trebia, the Romans were foolishly allowed to fight fasting, whereas Hannibal's men had breakfasted at their leisure. See Livy, XXI, *liv.* 8, *lv.* 1 and 8.]

by noonday it has begun to flag; and in the evening, his mind is bent only on returning to camp.

29. A clever general, therefore, avoids an army when its spirit is keen, but attacks it when it is sluggish and inclined to return. This is the art of studying moods.

30. Disciplined and calm, to await the appearance of disorder and hubbub amongst the enemy: this is the art of retaining self-possession.

31. To be near the goal while the enemy is still far from it, to wait at ease while the enemy is toiling and struggling, to be well-fed while the enemy is famished: this is the art of husbanding one's strength.

32. To refrain from intercepting an enemy whose banners are in perfect order, to refrain from attacking an army drawn up in calm and confident array: this is the art of studying circumstances.

33. It is a military axiom not to advance uphill against the enemy, nor to oppose him when he comes downhill.

34. Do not pursue an enemy who simulates flight; do not attack soldiers whose temper is keen.

35. Do not swallow bait offered by the enemy.

[Li Ch'üan and Tu Mu, with extraordinary inability to see a metaphor, take these words quite literally of food and drink that have been poisoned by the enemy. Ch'ên Hao and Chang Yü carefully point out that the saying has a wider application.]

Do not interfere with an army that is returning home.

[The commentators explain this rather singular piece of advice by saying that a man whose heart is set on returning home will fight to the death against any attempt to bar his way, and is therefore too dangerous an opponent to be tackled. Chang Yü quotes the words of Han Hsin: "Invincible is the soldier who hath his desire and returneth homewards." A marvelous tale is told of Ts'ao Ts'ao's courage and resource in the *San Kuo Chi*: In AD 198, he was besieging Chang Hsiu in Jang, when Liu Piao sent reinforcements with a view to cutting off Ts'ao's retreat. The latter was obliged to draw off his troops, only to find himself hemmed in between two enemies, who were guarding each outlet of a narrow pass in which he had engaged himself. In this desperate plight Ts'ao waited until nightfall, when he bored a tunnel into the mountain side and laid an ambush in it. As soon as the whole army had passed by, the hidden troops fell on his rear, while Ts'ao himself turned and met his pursuers in front, so that they were thrown into confusion and annihilated. Ts'ao Ts'ao said afterwards: "The brigands tried to check my army in its retreat and brought me to battle in a desperate position: hence I knew how to overcome them."]

36. When you surround an army, leave an outlet free.

[This does not mean that the enemy is to be allowed to escape. The object, as Tu Mu puts it, is "to make him believe that there is a road to safety, and thus prevent his fighting with the courage of despair." Tu Mu adds pleasantly: "After that, you may crush him."]

Do not press a desperate foe too hard.

[Ch'ên Hao quotes the saying: "Birds and beasts when brought to bay will use their claws and teeth." Chang Yü says: "If your adversary has burned his boats and destroyed his cooking-pots, and is ready to stake all on the issue of a battle, he must not be pushed to extremities." Ho Shih illustrates the meaning by a story taken from the life of Yen-ch'ing. That general, together with his colleague Tu Chung-wei was surrounded by a vastly superior army of Khitans in the year AD 945. The country was bare and desert-like, and the little Chinese force was soon in dire straits for want of water. The wells they bored ran dry, and the men were reduced to squeezing lumps of mud and sucking out the moisture. Their ranks thinned rapidly, until at last Fu Yen-ch'ing exclaimed: "We are desperate men. Far better to die for our country than to go with fettered hands into captivity!" A strong gale happened to be blowing from the northeast and darkening the air with dense clouds of sandy dust. Tu Chung-wei was for waiting until this had abated before deciding on a final attack; but luckily another officer, Li Shou-chêng by name, was quicker to see an opportunity, and said: "They are many and we are few, but in the midst of this sandstorm our numbers will not be discernible; victory will go to the strenuous fighter, and the wind will be our best ally." Accordingly, Fu Yen-ch'ing made a sudden and wholly unexpected onslaught with his cavalry, routed the barbarians and succeeded in breaking through to safety.]

37. Such is the art of warfare.

VIII

VARIATION OF TACTICS

[The heading means literally "The Nine Variations," but as Sun Tzŭ does not appear to enumerate these, and as, indeed, he has already told us (Ch. Five, paragraphs 6–11) that such deflections from the ordinary course are practically innumerable, we have little option but to follow Wang Hsi, who says that "Nine" stands for an indefinitely large number. "All it means is that in warfare we ought to vary our tactics to the utmost degree . . . I do not know what Ts'ao Kung makes these Nine Variations out to be, but it has been suggested that they are connected with the Nine Situations." This is the view adopted by Chang Yü. The only other alternative is to suppose that something has been lost—a supposition to which the unusual shortness of the chapter lends some weight.]

1. Sun Tzŭ said: In war, the general receives his commands from the sovereign, collects his army and concentrates his forces.

   [Repeated from Ch. Seven, paragraph 1, where it is certainly more in place. It may have been interpolated here merely in order to supply a beginning to the chapter.]

2. When in difficult country, do not encamp. In country where high roads intersect, join hands with your allies. Do not linger in dangerously isolated positions.

   [The last situation is not one of the Nine Situations as given in the beginning of Ch. Eleven, but occurs later on (*ibid*. paragraph 43. *q.v.*). Chang Yü defines this situation as being situated across the frontier, in hostile territory. Li Ch'üan says it is "country in which there are no springs or wells, flocks or herds, vegetables or firewood"; Chia Lin, "one of gorges, chasms and precipices, without a road by which to advance."]

In hemmed-in situations, you must resort to stratagem. In desperate position, you must fight.

3. There are roads which must not be followed,

["Especially those leading through narrow defiles," says Li Ch'üan, "where an ambush is to be feared."]

armies which must be not attacked,

[More correctly, perhaps, "there are times when an army must not be attacked." Ch'ên Hao says: "When you see your way to obtain a rival advantage, but are powerless to inflict a real defeat, refrain from attacking, for fear of overtaxing your men's strength."]

towns which must not be besieged,

[*Cf.* Ch. Three, paragraph 4: Ts'ao Kung gives an interesting illustration from his own experience. When invading the territory of Hsu-chou, he ignored the city of Hua-pi, which lay directly in his path, and pressed on into the heart of the country. This excellent strategy was rewarded by the subsequent capture of no fewer than fourteen important district cities. Chang Yü says: "No town should be attacked which, if taken, cannot be held, or if left alone, will not cause any trouble." Hsun Ying, when urged to attack Pi-yang, replied: "The city is small and well-fortified; even if I succeed in taking it, it will be no great feat of arms; whereas if I fail, I shall make myself a laughing-stock." In the seventeenth century, sieges still formed a large proportion of war. It was Turenne who directed attention to the importance of marches, countermarches and maneuvers. He said: "It is a great mistake to waste men in taking a town when the same expenditure of soldiers will gain a province."]

positions which must not be contested, commands of the sovereign which must not be obeyed.

[This is a hard saying for the Chinese, with their reverence for authority, and Wei Liao Tzŭ (quoted by Tu Mu) is moved to exclaim: "Weapons are baleful instruments, strife is antagonistic to virtue, a military commander is the negation of civil order!" The unpalatable fact remains, however, that even Imperial wishes must be subordinated to military necessity.]

4. The general who thoroughly understands the advantages that accompany variation of tactics knows how to handle his troops.

5. The general who does not understand these, may be well acquainted with the configuration of the country, yet he will not be able to turn his knowledge to practical account.

   [Literally, "get the advantage of the ground," which means not only securing good positions, but availing oneself of natural advantages in every possible way. Chang Yü says: "Every kind of ground is characterized by certain natural features, and also gives scope for a certain variability of plan. How it is possible to turn these natural features to account unless topographical knowledge is supplemented by versatility of mind?"]

6. So, the student of war who is unversed in the art of war of varying his plans, even though he be acquainted with the Five Advantages, will fail to make the best use of his men.

   [Chia Lin tells us that these imply five obvious and generally advantageous lines of action, namely: "if a certain road is short, it must be followed; if an army is isolated, it must be attacked; if a town is in a parlous condition, it must be besieged; if a position can be stormed, it must be attempted; and if consistent with military operations, the ruler's commands must be obeyed." But there are circumstances which sometimes forbid a general to use these advantages. For instance, "a certain road may be the shortest way for him, but if he knows that it abounds in natural obstacles, or that the enemy has laid an ambush on it, he will not follow that road. A hostile force may be open to attack, but if he knows that it is hard-pressed and likely to fight with desperation, he will refrain from striking," and so on.]

7. Hence in the wise leader's plans, considerations of advantage and of disadvantage will be blended together.

["Whether in an advantageous position or a disadvantageous one," says Ts'ao Kung, "the opposite state should be always present to your mind."]

8. If our expectation of advantage be tempered in this way, we may succeed in accomplishing the essential part of our schemes.

[Tu Mu says: "If we wish to wrest an advantage from the enemy, we must not fix our minds on that alone, but allow for the possibility of the enemy also doing some harm to us, and let this enter as a factor into our calculations."]

9. If, on the other hand, in the midst of difficulties we are always ready to seize an advantage, we may extricate ourselves from misfortune.

[Tu Mu says: "If I wish to extricate myself from a dangerous position, I must consider not only the enemy's ability to injure me, but also my own ability to gain an advantage over the enemy. If in my counsels these two considerations are properly blended, I shall succeed in liberating myself. . . . For instance; if I am surrounded by the enemy and only think of effecting an escape, the nervelessness of my policy will incite my adversary to pursue and crush me; it would be far better to encourage my men to deliver a bold counter-attack, and use the advantage thus gained to free myself from the enemy's toils." See the story of Ts'ao Ts'ao, Ch. Seven, paragraph 35.]

10. Reduce the hostile chiefs by inflicting damage on them;

[Chia Lin enumerates several ways of inflicting this injury, some of which would only occur to the Oriental mind: "Entice away the enemy's best and wisest men, so that he may be left without counselors. Introduce traitors into his country, that the government policy may be rendered futile. Foment intrigue and deceit, and thus sow dissension between the ruler and his ministers. By means of every artful contrivance, cause deterioration amongst his men and waste of his treasure. Corrupt his morals by insidious gifts leading him into excess. Disturb and unsettle his mind by presenting him with lovely women." Chang Yü (after Wang Hsi) makes a different interpretation of

Sun Tzŭ here: "Get the enemy into a position where he must suffer injury, and he will submit of his own accord."]

and make trouble for them,

[Tu Mu, in this phrase, in his interpretation indicates that trouble should be made for the enemy affecting their "possessions," or, as we might say, "assets," which he considers to be "a large army, a rich exchequer, harmony amongst the soldiers, punctual fulfillment of commands." These give us a whip-hand over the enemy.]

and keep them constantly engaged;

[Literally, "make servants of them." Tu Yu says "prevent them from having any rest."]

hold out specious allurements, and make them rush to any given point.

11. The art of war teaches us to rely not on the likelihood of the enemy's not coming, but on our own readiness to receive him; not on the chance of his not attacking, but rather on the fact that we have made our position unassailable.

12. There are five dangerous faults which may affect a general:

(1) Recklessness, which leads to destruction;

["Bravery without forethought," as Ts'ao Kung analyzes it, which causes a man to fight blindly and desperately like a mad bull. Such an opponent, says Chang Yü, "must not be encountered with brute force, but may be lured into an ambush and slain." *Cf.* Wu Tzŭ, Ch. Four, *ad initium*: "In estimating the character of a general, men are wont to pay exclusive attention to his courage, forgetting that courage is only one out of many qualities which a general should possess. The merely brave man is prone to fight recklessly; and he who fights recklessly, without any perception of what is expedient, must be condemned." The *Sŭ-Ma Fa*, too, make the incisive remark: "Simply going to one's death does not bring about victory."]

(2) cowardice, which leads to capture;

[Ts'ao Kung defines the Chinese word translated here as "cowardice" as being of the man "whom timidity prevents from advancing to seize an advantage," and Wang Hsi adds "who is quick to flee at the sight of danger." Mêng Shih gives the closer paraphrase "he who is bent on returning alive," this is, the man who will never take a risk. But, as Sun Tzŭ knew, nothing is to be achieved in war unless you are willing to take risks. T'ai Kung said: "He who lets an advantage slip will subsequently bring upon himself real disaster." In AD 404, Liu Yu pursued the rebel Huan Hsuan up the Yangtsze and fought a naval battle with him at the island of Ch'êng-hung. The loyal troops numbered only a few thousands, while their opponents were in great force. But Huan Hsuan, fearing the fate which was in store for him should be overcome, had a light boat made fast to the side of his war-junk, so that he might escape, if necessary, at a moment's notice. The natural result was that the fighting spirit of his soldiers was utterly quenched, and when the loyalists made an attack from windward with fireships, all striving with the utmost ardor to be first in the fray, Huan Hsuan's forces were routed, had to burn all their baggage and fled for two days and nights without stopping. Chang Yü tells a somewhat similar story of Chao Ying-ch'i, a general of the Chin State who during a battle with the army of Ch'u in 597 BC had a boat kept in readiness for him on the river, wishing in case of defeat to be the first to get across.]

(3) a hasty temper, which can be provoked by insults;

[Tu Mu tells us that Yao Hsing, when opposed in AD 357 by Huang Mei, Teng Ch'iang and others shut himself up behind his walls and refused to fight. Teng Ch'iang said: "Our adversary is of a choleric temper and easily provoked; let us make constant sallies and break down his walls, then he will grow angry and come out. Once we can bring his force to battle, it is doomed to be our prey." This plan was acted upon, Yao Hsiang came out to fight, was lured as far as San-yuan by the enemy's pretended flight, and finally attacked and slain.]

(4) a delicacy of honor which is sensitive to shame;

[This need not be taken to mean that a sense of honor is really a defect in a general. What Sun Tzŭ condemns is rather an exaggerated sensitiveness to slanderous reports, the thin-skinned man who is stung by opprobrium, however undeserved. Mei Yao-ch'ên truly observes, though somewhat paradoxically: "The seeker after glory should be careless of public opinion."]

(5) over-solicitude for his men, which exposes him to worry and
   trouble.

[Here again, Sun Tzŭ does not mean that the general is to be careless of the welfare of his troops. All he wishes to emphasize is the danger of sacrificing any important military advantage to the immediate comfort of his men. This is a shortsighted policy, because in the long run the troops will suffer more from the defeat, or, at best, the prolongation of the war, which will be the consequence. A mistaken feeling of pity will often induce a general to relieve a beleaguered city, or to reinforce a hard-pressed detachment, contrary to his military instincts. It is now generally admitted that our repeated efforts to relieve Ladysmith in the South African War were so many strategical blunders which defeated their own purpose. And in the end, relief came through the very man who started out with the distinct resolve no longer to subordinate the interests of the whole to sentiment in favor of a part. An old soldier of one of our generals who failed most conspicuously in this war, tried once, I remember, to defend him to me on the ground that he was always "so good to his men." By this plea, had he but known it, he was only condemning him out of Sun Tzŭ's mouth.]

13. These are the five besetting sins of a general, ruinous to the conduct
   of war.

14. When an army is overthrown and its leader slain, the cause will
   surely be found among these five dangerous faults. Let them be a
   subject of meditation.

IX

THE ARMY ON THE MARCH

1. Sun Tzŭ said: We come now to the question of encamping the army, and observing signs of the enemy. Pass quickly over mountains, and keep in the neighborhood of valleys.

   [The idea is, not to linger among barren uplands, but to keep close to supplies of water and grass. *Cf.* Wu Tzŭ: "Abide not in natural ovens," i.e. "the openings of valleys." Chang Yü tells the following anecdote: Wu-tu Ch'iang was a robber captain in the time of the Later Han, and Ma Yuan was sent to exterminate his gang. Ch'iang having found a refuge in the hills, Ma Yuan made no attempt to force a battle, but seized all the favorable positions commanding supplies of water and forage. Ch'iang was soon in such a desperate plight for want of provisions that he was forced to make a total surrender. He did not know the advantage of keeping in the neighborhood of valleys."]

2. Camp in high places,

   [Not on high hills, but on knolls or hillocks elevated above the surrounding country.]

   facing the sun.

   [Tu Mu takes this to mean "facing south," and Ch'ên Hao "facing east." *Cf. infra*, paragraph 11, 13. Do not climb heights in order to fight. So much for mountain warfare.]

3. After crossing a river, you should get far away from it.

   ["In order to tempt the enemy to cross after you," according to Ts'ao Kung, and also, says Chang Yü, "in order not to be impeded in your evolutions." The *T'ung Tien* reads, "If the enemy crosses a river," etc. But in view of the next sentence, this is almost certainly an interpolation.]

4.   When an invading force crosses a river in its onward march, do not advance to meet it in mid-stream. It will be best to let half the army get across, and then deliver your attack.

[Li Ch'üan alludes to the great victory won by Han Hsin over Lung Chu at the Wei River. In the *Ch'ien Han Shu*, we find the battle described as follows: "The two armies were drawn up on opposite sides of the river. In the night, Han Hsin ordered his men to take some ten thousand sacks filled with sand and construct a dam higher up. Then, leading half his army across, he attacked Lung Chu; but after a time, pretending to have failed in his attempt, he hastily withdrew to the other bank. Lung Chu was much elated by this unlooked-for success, and exclaiming: "I felt sure that Han Hsin was really a coward!" he pursued him and began crossing the river in his turn. Han Hsin now sent a party to cut open the sandbags, thus releasing a great volume of water, which swept down and prevented the greater portion of Lung Chu's army from getting across. He then turned upon the force which had been cut off, and annihilated it, Lung Chu himself being amongst the slain. The rest of the army, on the further bank, also scattered and fled in all directions.]

5.   If you are anxious to fight, you should not go to meet the invader near a river which he has to cross.

[For fear of preventing his crossing.]

6.   Moor your craft higher up than the enemy, and facing the sun.

[See *supra*, paragraph 2. The repetition of these words in connection with water is very awkward. Chang Yü has the note: "Said either of troops marshaled on the river-bank, or of boats anchored in the stream itself; in either case it is essential to be higher than the enemy and facing the sun." The other commentators are not at all explicit.]

Do not move up-stream to meet the enemy.

[Tu Mu says: "As water flows downwards, we must not pitch our camp on the lower reaches of a river, for fear the enemy should open the sluices and sweep us away in a flood. Chu-ko Wu-hou has remarked that 'in river warfare we must not advance against the stream,' which is as much as to say that our fleet must not be anchored below that of the enemy, for then they would be able to take advantage of the current and make short work of us." There is also the danger, noted by other commentators, that the enemy may throw poison on the water to be carried down to us.]

So much for river warfare.

7. In crossing salt-marshes, your sole concern should be to get over them quickly, without any delay.

    [Because of the lack of fresh water, the poor quality of the herbage, and last but not least, because they are low, flat, and exposed to attack.]

8. If forced to fight in a salt-marsh, you should have water and grass near you, and get your back to a clump of trees.

    [Li Ch'üan remarks that the ground is less likely to be treacherous where there are trees, while Tu Mu says that they will serve to protect the rear.]

    So much for operations in salt-marshes.

9. In dry, level country, take up an easily accessible position with rising ground to your right and on your rear,

    [Tu Mu quotes T'ai Kung as saying: "An army should have a stream or a marsh on its left, and a hill or tumulus on its right."]

    so that the danger may be in front, and safety lie behind. So much for campaigning in flat country.

10. These are the four useful branches of military knowledge

    [Those, namely, concerned with (1) mountains, (2) rivers, (3) marshes, and (4) plains. Compare Napoleon's *Military Maxims*, no. 1.]

which enabled the Yellow Emperor to vanquish four several sovereigns.

[Regarding the "Yellow Emperor": Mei Yao-ch'ên asks, with some plausibility, whether there is an error in the text as nothing is known of Huang Ti having conquered four other Emperors. The *Shih Chi* (Ch. 1, *ad initium*) speaks only of his victories over Yen Ti and Ch'ih Yu. In the *Liu T'ao* it is mentioned that he "fought seventy battles and pacified the Empire." Ts'ao Kung's explanation is, that the Yellow Emperor was the first to institute the feudal system of vassals princes, each of whom (to the number of four) originally bore the title of Emperor. Li Ch'üan tells us that the art of war originated under Huang Ti, who received it from his Minister Feng Hou.]

11. All armies prefer high ground to low.

["High Ground," says Mei Yao-ch'ên, "is not only more agreeable and salubrious, but more convenient from a military point of view; low ground is not only damp and unhealthy, but also disadvantageous for fighting."]

and sunny places to dark.

12. If you are careful of your men,

[Ts'ao Kung says: "Make for fresh water and pasture, where you can turn out your animals to graze."]

and camp on hard ground, the army will be free from disease of every kind,

[Chang Yü says: "The dryness of the climate will prevent the outbreak of illness."]

and this will spell victory.

13. When you come to a hill or a bank, occupy the sunny side, with the slope on your right rear. Thus you will at once act for the benefit of your soldiers and utilize the natural advantages of the ground.

14. When, in consequence of heavy rains up-country, a river which you wish to ford is swollen and flecked with foam, you must wait until it subsides.

15. Country in which there are precipitous cliffs with torrents running between, deep natural hollows,

[The latter defined as "places enclosed on every side by steep banks, with pools of water at the bottom."]

confined places,

[Defined as "natural pens or prisons" or "places surrounded by precipices on three sides—easy to get into, but hard to get out of."]

tangled thickets,

[Defined as "places covered with such dense undergrowth that spears cannot be used."]

quagmires

[Defined as "low-lying places, so heavy with mud as to be impassable for chariots and horsemen."]

and crevasses,

[Defined by Mei Yao-ch'ên as "a narrow difficult way between beetling cliffs." Tu Mu's note is "ground covered with trees and rocks, and intersected by numerous ravines and pitfalls." This is very vague, but Chia Lin explains it clearly enough as a defile or narrow pass, and Chang Yü takes much the same view. On the whole, the weight of the commentators certainly inclines to the rendering "defile." But the ordinary meaning of the Chinese in one place is "a crack or fissure" and the fact that the meaning of the Chinese elsewhere in the sentence indicates something in the nature of a defile, make me think that Sun Tzŭ is here speaking of crevasses.]

should be left with all possible speed and not approached.

16. While we keep away from such places, we should get the enemy to approach them; while we face them, we should let the enemy have them on his rear.

17. If in the neighborhood of your camp there should be any hilly country, ponds surrounded by aquatic grass, hollow basins filled with reeds, or woods with thick undergrowth, they must be carefully routed out and searched; for these are places where men in ambush or insidious spies are likely to be lurking.

[Chang Yü has the note: "We must also be on our guard against traitors who may lie in close covert, secretly spying out our weaknesses and overhearing our instructions."]

18. When the enemy is close at hand and remains quiet, he is relying on the natural strength of his position.

[Here begin Sun Tzǔ's remarks on the reading of signs, much of which is so good that it could almost be included in a modern manual like Gen. Baden-Powell's *Aids to Scouting*.]

19. When he keeps aloof and tries to provoke a battle, he is anxious for the other side to advance.

[Probably because we are in a strong position from which he wishes to dislodge us. "If he came close up to us," says Tu Mu, "and tried to force a battle, he would seem to despise us, and there would be less probability of our responding to the challenge."]

20. If his place of encampment is easy of access, he is tendering a bait.

21. Movement amongst the trees of a forest shows that the enemy is advancing.

[Ts'ao Kung explains this as "felling trees to clear a passage," and Chang Yü says: "Every man sends out scouts to climb high places and observe the enemy. If a scout sees that the trees of a forest are moving and shaking, he may know that they are being cut down to clear a passage for the enemy's march."]

The appearance of a number of screens in the midst of thick grass means that the enemy wants to make us suspicious.

[Tu Yu's explanation, borrowed from Ts'ao Kung's, is as follows: "The presence of a number of screens or sheds in the midst of thick vegetation is a sure sign that the enemy has fled and, fearing pursuit, has constructed these hiding-places in order to make us suspect an ambush." It appears that these "screens" were hastily knotted together out of any long grass which the retreating enemy happened to come across.]

22. The rising of birds in their flight is the sign of an ambuscade.

[Chang Yü's explanation is doubtless right: "When birds that are flying along in a straight line suddenly shoot upwards, it means that soldiers are in ambush at the spot beneath."]

Startled beasts indicate that a sudden attack is coming.

23. When there is dust rising in a high column, it is the sign of chariots advancing; when the dust is low, but spread over a wide area, it betokens the approach of infantry.

["High and sharp," or rising to a peak, is of course somewhat exaggerated as applied to dust. The commentators explain the phenomenon by saying that horses and chariots, being heavier than men, raise more dust, and also follow one another in the same wheel-track, whereas foot-soldiers would be marching in ranks, many abreast. According to Chang Yü, "every army on the march must have scouts some way in advance, who on sighting dust raised by the enemy, will gallop back and report it to the commander-in-chief." *Cf.* Gen. Baden-Powell, *Aids to Scouting*: "As you move along, say, in a hostile country, your eyes should be looking afar for the enemy or any signs of him: figures, dust rising, birds getting up, glitter of arms, etc."]

When it branches out in different directions, it shows that parties have been sent to collect firewood. A few clouds of dust moving to and fro signify that the army is encamping.

[Chang Yü says: "In apportioning the defenses for a cantonment, light horse will be sent out to survey the position and ascertain the weak and strong points all along its circumference. Hence the small quantity of dust and its motion."]

24. Humble words and increased preparations are signs that the enemy is about to advance.

["As though they stood in great fear of us," says Tu Mu. "Their object is to make us contemptuous and careless, after which they will attack us." Chang Yü alludes to the story of T'ien Tan of the Ch'i-mo against the Yen forces, led by Ch'i Chieh. In Ch. 82 of the *Shih Chi* we read: "T'ien Tan openly said: 'My only fear is that the Yen army may cut off the noses of their Ch'i prisoners and place them in the front rank to fight against us; that would be the undoing of our city.' The other side being informed of this speech, at once acted on the suggestion; but those within the city were enraged at seeing their fellow-countrymen thus mutilated, and fearing only lest they should fall into the enemy's hands, were nerved to defend themselves more obstinately than ever. Once again T'ien Tan sent back converted spies who reported these words to the enemy: 'What I dread most is that the men of Yen may dig up the ancestral tombs outside the town, and by inflicting this indignity on our forefathers cause us to become faint-hearted.' Forthwith the besiegers dug up all the graves and burned the corpses lying in them. And the inhabitants of Chi-mo, witnessing the outrage from the city-walls, wept passionately and were all impatient to go out and fight, their fury being increased tenfold. T'ien Tan knew then that his soldiers were ready for any enterprise. But instead of a sword, he himself took a mattock in his hands, and ordered others to be distributed amongst his best warriors, while the ranks were filled up with their wives and concubines. He then served out all the remaining rations and bade his men eat their fill. The regular soldiers were told to keep out of sight, and the walls were manned with the old and weaker men and with women. This done, envoys were dispatched to the enemy's camp to arrange terms of surrender, whereupon the Yen army began shouting for joy. T'ien Tan also collected 20,000 ounces of silver from the people, and got the wealthy citizens of Chi-mo to send it to the Yen general with the prayer that, when the town capitulated, he would allow their homes to be plundered or their women to be maltreated. Ch'i Chieh, in high good humor, granted their prayer; but his army now became increasingly slack and careless. Meanwhile, T'ien Tan got together a thousand oxen, decked them with pieces of red silk, painted their bodies, dragon-like, with colored stripes, and fastened sharp blades on their horns and well-greased rushes on their tails. When night came on, he lighted the ends of the rushes, and drove the oxen through a number of holes which he had pierced in the walls, backing them up with a force of 5,000 picked warriors. The animals, maddened with pain, dashed furiously into the enemy's camp where they caused the utmost confusion and dismay; for their tails acted as torches, showing up the hideous pattern on their bodies, and the weapons on their horns killed or wounded any with whom they came into contact. In the meantime, the band of 5,000 had crept up with gags in their mouths, and now threw themselves on the enemy. At the same moment a frightful din arose in the city itself, all those that remained behind making as much noise as possible by banging drums and hammering on bronze vessels, until heaven and earth were convulsed by the uproar. Terror-stricken, the Yen army fled in disorder, hotly pursued by the men of Ch'i, who succeeded in slaying their general Ch'i Chien . . . The result of the battle was the ultimate recovery of some seventy cities which had belonged to the Ch'i State."]

Violent language and driving forward as if to the attack are signs that he will retreat.

25. When the light chariots come out first and take up a position on the wings, it is a sign that the enemy is forming for battle.

26. Peace proposals unaccompanied by a sworn covenant indicate a plot.

[The reading here is uncertain. Li Ch'uan indicates "a treaty confirmed by oaths and hostages." Wang Hsi and Chang Yü, on the other hand, simply say "without reason," "on a frivolous pretext."]

27. When there is much running about

[Every man hastening to his proper place under his own regimental banner.]

and the soldiers fall into rank, it means that the critical moment has come.

28. When some are seen advancing and some retreating, it is a lure.

29. When the soldiers stand leaning on their spears, they are faint from want of food.

30. If those who are sent to draw water begin by drinking themselves, the army is suffering from thirst.

[As Tu Mu remarks: "One may know the condition of a whole army from the behavior of a single man."]

31. If the enemy sees an advantage to be gained and makes no effort to secure it, the soldiers are exhausted.

32. If birds gather on any spot, it is unoccupied.

[A useful fact to bear in mind when, for instance, as Ch'ên Hao says, the enemy has secretly abandoned his camp.]

Clamor by night betokens nervousness.

33. If there is disturbance in the camp, the general's authority is weak. If the banners and flags are shifted about, sedition is afoot. If the officers are angry, it means that the men are weary.

[Tu Mu understands the sentence differently: "If all the officers of an army are angry with their general, it means that they are broken with fatigue" owing to the exertions which he has demanded from them.]

34. When an army feeds its horses with grain and kills its cattle for food,

[In the ordinary course of things, the men would be fed on grain and the horses chiefly on grass.]

and when the men do not hang their cooking-pots over the camp-fires, showing that they will not return to their tents, you may know that they are determined to fight to the death.

[I may quote here the illustrative passage from the *Hou Han Shu*, Ch. 71, given in abbreviated form by the *P'ei Wen Yun Fu*: "The rebel Wang Kuo of Liang was besieging the town of Ch'ên-ts'ang, and Huang-fu Sung, who was in supreme command,

and Tung Cho were sent out against him. The latter pressed for hasty measures, but Sung turned a deaf ear to his counsel. At last the rebels were utterly worn out, and began to throw down their weapons of their own accord. Sung was not advancing to the attack, but Cho said: 'It is a principle of war not to pursue desperate men and not to press a retreating host.' Sung answered: 'That does not apply here. What I am about to attack is a jaded army, not a retreating host; with disciplined troops I am falling on a disorganized multitude, not a band of desperate men.' Thereupon he advances to the attack unsupported by his colleague, and routed the enemy, Wang Kuo being slain."]

35. The sight of men whispering together in small knots or speaking in subdued tones points to disaffection amongst the rank and file.

36. Too frequent rewards signify that the enemy is at the end of his resources;

[Because, when an army is hard pressed, as Tu Mu says, there is always a fear of mutiny, and lavish rewards are given to keep the men in good temper.]

too many punishments betray a condition of dire distress.

[Because in such case discipline becomes relaxed, and unwonted severity is necessary to keep the men to their duty.]

37. To begin by bluster, but afterwards to take fright at the enemy's numbers, shows a supreme lack of intelligence.

[I follow the interpretation of Ts'ao Kung, also adopted by Li Ch'üan, Tu Mu, and Chang Yü. Another possible meaning set forth by Tu Yu, Chia Lin, Mei Tao-ch'ên and Wang Hsi, is: "The general who is first tyrannical towards his men, and then in terror lest they should mutiny, etc." This would connect the sentence with what went before about rewards and punishments.]

38. When envoys are sent with compliments in their mouths, it is a sign that the enemy wishes for a truce.

[Tu Mu says: "If the enemy open friendly relations by sending hostages, it is a sign that they are anxious for an armistice, either because their strength is exhausted or for some other reason." But it hardly needs a Sun Tzŭ to draw such an obvious inference.]

39. If the enemy's troops march up angrily and remain facing ours for a long time without either joining battle or taking themselves off again, the situation is one that demands great vigilance and circumspection.

[Ts'ao Kung says a maneuver of this sort may be only a ruse to gain time for an unexpected flank attack or the laying of an ambush.]

40. If our troops are no more in number than the enemy, that is amply sufficient; it only means that no direct attack can be made.

[Literally, "no martial advance." That is to say, *chêng* tactics and frontal attacks must be eschewed, and stratagem resorted to instead.]

What we can do is simply to concentrate all our available strength, keep a close watch on the enemy, and obtain reinforcements.

[This is an obscure sentence, and none of the commentators succeed in squeezing very good sense out of it. I follow Li Ch'üan, who appears to offer the simplest explanation: "Only the side that gets more men will win." Fortunately we have Chang Yü to expound its meaning to us in language which is lucidity itself: "When the numbers are even, and no favorable opening presents itself, although we may not be strong enough to deliver a sustained attack, we can find additional recruits amongst our sutlers and camp-followers, and then, concentrating our forces and keeping a close watch on the enemy, contrive to snatch the victory. But we must avoid borrowing foreign soldiers to help us." He then quotes from Wei Liao Tzŭ, Ch. 3: "The nominal strength of mercenary troops may be 100,000, but their real value will be not more than half that figure."]

41. He who exercises no forethought but makes light of his opponents is sure to be captured by them.

[Ch'ên Hao, quoting from the *Tso Chuan*, says: "If bees and scorpions carry poison, how much more will a hostile state! Even a puny opponent, then, should not be treated with contempt."]

42. If soldiers are punished before they have grown attached to you, they will not prove submissive; and, unless submissive, then will be practically useless. If, when the soldiers have become attached to you, punishments are not enforced, they will still be useless.

43. Therefore soldiers must be treated in the first instance with humanity, but kept under control by means of iron discipline.

[Yen Tzǔ (493 BC) said of Ssǔ-ma Jang-chu: "His civil virtues endeared him to the people; his martial prowess kept his enemies in awe." *Cf.* Wu Tzǔ: "The ideal commander unites culture with a warlike temper; the profession of arms requires a combination of hardness and tenderness."]

This is a certain road to victory.

44. If in training soldiers commands are habitually enforced, the army will be well-disciplined; if not, its discipline will be bad.

45. If a general shows confidence in his men but always insists on his orders being obeyed,

[Tu Mu says: "A general ought in time of peace to show kindly confidence in his men and also make his authority respected, so that when they come to face the enemy, orders may be executed and discipline maintained, because they all trust and look up to him." What Sun Tzǔ has said in paragraph 44, however, would lead one rather to expect something like this: "If a general is always confident that his orders will be carried out," etc.]

the gain will be mutual.

[Chang Yü says: "The general has confidence in the men under his command, and the men are docile, having confidence in him. Thus the gain is mutual." He quotes a pregnant sentence from Wei Liao Tzŭ: "The art of giving orders is not to try to rectify minor blunders and not to be swayed by petty doubts." Vacillation and fussiness are the surest means of sapping the confidence of an army.]

X

TERRAIN

[Only about a third of the chapter, comprising paragraphs 1–13, deals with "terrain," the subject being more fully treated in Ch. Eleven. The "six calamities" are discussed in paragraphs 14–20, and the rest of the chapter is again a mere string of desultory remarks, though not less interesting, perhaps, on that account.]

1. Sun Tzŭ said: We may distinguish six kinds of terrain, to wit:

   (1) Accessible ground;

   [Mei Yao-ch'ên says: "plentifully provided with roads and means of communications."]

   (2) entangling ground;

   [The same commentator says: "Net-like country, venturing into which you become entangled."]

   (3) temporizing ground;

   [Ground which allows you to "stave off" or "delay."]

   (4) narrow passes;
   (5) precipitous heights;
   (6) positions at a great distance from the enemy.

   [It is hardly necessary to point out the faultiness of this classification. A strange lack of logical perception is shown in the Chinaman's unquestioning acceptance of glaring cross-divisions such as the above.]

2. Ground which can be freely traversed by both sides is called accessible.

3. With regard to ground of this nature, be before the enemy in occupying the raised and sunny spots, and carefully guard your line of supplies.

[The general meaning of the last phrase is doubtlessly, as Tu Yu says, "not to allow the enemy to cut your communications." In view of Napoleon's dictum, "the secret of war lies in the communications"(*Pensées de Napoléon1er*, no. 47), we could wish that Sun Tzŭ had done more than skirt the edge of this important subject here and in Ch. One, paragraph 10 and Ch. Seven, paragraph 11. Col. Henderson says (in Ch. 2 of *The Science of War*): "The line of supply may be said to be as vital to the existence of an army as the heart to the life of a human being. Just as the duelist who finds his adversary's point menacing him with certain death, and his own guard astray, is compelled to conform to his adversary's movements, and to content himself with warding off his thrusts, so the commander whose communications are suddenly threatened finds himself in a false position, and he will be fortunate if he has not to change all his plans, to split up his force into more or less isolated detachments, and to fight with inferior numbers on ground which he has not had time to prepare, and where defeat will not be an ordinary failure, but will entail the ruin or surrender of his whole army."]

Then you will be able to fight with advantage.

4. Ground which can be abandoned but is hard to re-occupy is called entangling.

5. From a position of this sort, if the enemy is unprepared, you may sally forth and defeat him. But if the enemy is prepared for your coming, and you fail to defeat him, then, return being impossible, disaster will ensue.

6. When the position is such that neither side will gain by making the first move, it is called temporizing ground.

[Tu Mu says: "Each side finds it inconvenient to move, and the situation remains at a deadlock."]

7. In a position of this sort, even though the enemy should offer us an attractive bait,

[Tu Yu says, "turning their backs on us and pretending to flee." But this is only one of the lures which might induce us to quit our position.]

it will be advisable not to stir forth, but rather to retreat, thus enticing the enemy in his turn; then, when part of his army has come out, we may deliver our attack with advantage.

8. With regard to narrow passes, if you can occupy them first, let them be strongly garrisoned and await the advent of the enemy.

[Because then, as Tu Yu observes, "the initiative will lie with us, and by making sudden and unexpected attacks we shall have the enemy at our mercy."]

9. Should the army forestall you in occupying a pass, do not go after him if the pass is fully garrisoned, but only if it is weakly garrisoned.

10. With regard to precipitous heights, if you are beforehand with your adversary, you should occupy the raised and sunny spots, and there wait for him to come up.

[Ts'ao Kung says: "The particular advantage of securing heights and defiles is that your actions cannot then be dictated by the enemy." (For the enunciation of the grand principle alluded to, see Ch. Six, paragraph 2). Chang Yü tells the following anecdote of P'ei Hsing-chien (AD 619–682), who was sent on a punitive expedition against the Turkic tribes. "At night he pitched his camp as usual, and it had already been completely fortified by wall and ditch, when suddenly he gave orders that the army should shift its quarters to a hill near by. This was highly displeasing to his officers, who protested loudly against the extra fatigue which it would entail on the men. P'ei Hsing-chien, however, paid no heed to their remonstrances and had the camp moved as quickly as possible. The same night, a terrific storm came on, which flooded their former place of encampment to the depth of over twelve feet. The recalcitrant officers were amazed at the sight, and owned that they had been in the wrong. 'How did you know what was going to happen?' they asked. P'ei Hsing-chien replied: 'From this time forward be content to obey orders without asking unnecessary questions.' From this it may be seen," Chang Yü continues, "that high and sunny places are advantageous not only for fighting, but also because they are immune from disastrous floods."]

11. If the enemy has occupied them before you, do not follow him, but retreat and try to entice him away.

[The turning point of Li Shih-min's campaign in AD 621 against the two rebels, Tou Chien-tê, King of Hsia, and Wang Shih-ch'ung, Prince of Chêng, was his seizure of the heights of Wu-lao, in spite of which Tou Chien-tê persisted in his attempt to relieve his ally in Lo-yang, was defeated and taken prisoner. See *Chiu T'ang*.]

12. If you are situated at a great distance from the enemy, and the strength of the two armies is equal, it is not easy to provoke a battle,

[The point is that we must not think of undertaking a long and wearisome march, at the end of which, as Tu Yu says, "we should be exhausted and our adversary fresh and keen."]

and fighting will be to your disadvantage.

13. These six are the principles connected with Earth.

[Or perhaps, "the principles relating to ground." See, however, Ch. One, paragraph 8.]

The general who has attained a responsible post must be careful to study them.

14. Now an army is exposed to six several calamities, not arising from natural causes, but from faults for which the general is responsible. These are: (1) Flight; (2) insubordination; (3) collapse; (4) ruin; (5) disorganization; (6) rout.

15. Other conditions being equal, if one force is hurled against another ten times its size, the result will be the *flight* of the former.

16. When the common soldiers are too strong and their officers too weak, the result is *insubordination*.

[Tu Mu cites the unhappy case of T'ien Pu (Hsin T'ang Shu), who was sent to Wei in AD 821 with orders to lead an army against Wang T'ing-ts'ou. But the whole time he was in command, his soldiers treated him with the utmost contempt, and openly flouted his authority by riding about the camp on donkeys, several thousands at a time. T'ien Pu was powerless to put a stop to this conduct, and when, after some months had passed, he made an attempt to engage the enemy, his troops turned tail and dispersed in every direction. After that, the unfortunate man committed suicide by cutting his throat.]

When the officers are too strong and the common soldiers too weak, the result is *collapse*.

[Ts'ao Kung says: "The officers are energetic and want to press on, the common soldiers are feeble and suddenly collapse."]

17. When the higher officers are angry and insubordinate, and on meeting the enemy give battle on their own account from a feeling of resentment, before the commander-in-chief can tell whether or no he is in a position to fight, the result is *ruin*.

[Wang Hsi's note is: "This means, the general is angry without cause, and at the same time does not appreciate the ability of his subordinate officers; thus he arouses fierce resentment and brings an avalanche of ruin upon his head."]

18. When the general is weak and without authority; when his orders are not clear and distinct;

[Wei Liao Tzŭ (Ch. 4) says: "If the commander gives his orders with decision, the soldiers will not wait to hear them twice; if his moves are made without vacillation, the soldiers will not be in two minds about doing their duty." General Baden-Powell says (in *Aids to Scouting*, p. xii), italicizing the words: "The secret of getting successful work out of your trained men lies in one nutshell—in the clearness of the instructions they receive." *Cf.* also Wu Tzŭ: "the most fatal defect in a military leader is difference; the worst calamities that befall an army arise from hesitation."]

when there are no fixed duties assigned to officers and men,

[Tu Mu says: "Neither officers nor men have any regular routine."]

and the ranks are formed in a slovenly haphazard manner, the result is utter *disorganization*.

19. When a general, unable to estimate the enemy's strength, allows an inferior force to engage a larger one, or hurls a weak detachment against a powerful one, and neglects to place picked soldiers in the front rank, the result must be *rout*.

[Chang Yü paraphrases the latter part of the sentence and continues: "Whenever there is fighting to be done, the keenest spirits should be appointed to serve in the front ranks, both in order to strengthen the resolution of our own men and to demoralize the enemy." *Cf.* the *primi ordines* of Caesar (*De Bello Gallico*).]

20. These are six ways of courting defeat, which must be carefully noted by the general who has attained a responsible post.

[See *supra*, paragraph 13.]

21. The natural formation of the country is the soldier's best ally;

[Ch'ên Hao says: "The advantages of weather and season are not equal to those connected with ground."]

but a power of estimating the adversary, of controlling the forces of victory, and of shrewdly calculating difficulties, dangers and distances, constitutes the test of a great general.

22. He who knows these things, and in fighting puts his knowledge into practice, will win his battles. He who knows them not, nor practices them, will surely be defeated.

23. If fighting is sure to result in victory, then you must fight, even though the ruler forbid it; if fighting will not result in victory, then you must not fight even at the ruler's bidding.

[*Cf*. Ch. Eight, paragraph 3 *fin*. Huang-Shih Kung of the Ch'in dynasty, who is said to have been the patron of Chang Liang and to have written the *San Lueh*, has these words attributed to him: "The responsibility of setting an army in motion must devolve on the general alone; if advance and retreat are controlled from the Palace, brilliant results will hardly be achieved. Hence the god-like ruler and the enlightened monarch are content to play a humble part in furthering their country's cause (literally, kneel down to push the chariot wheel)." This means that "in matters lying outside the *zenana*, the decision of the military commander must be absolute." Chang Yü also quote the saying: "Decrees from the Son of Heaven do not penetrate the walls of a camp."]

24. The general who advances without coveting fame and retreats without fearing disgrace,

[It was Wellington, I think, who said that the hardest thing of all for a soldier is to retreat.]

whose only thought is to protect his country and do good service for his sovereign, is the jewel of the kingdom.

[A noble presentiment, in few words, of the Chinese "happy warrior." Such a man, says Ho Shih, "even if he had to suffer punishment, would not regret his conduct."]

25. Regard your soldiers as your children, and they will follow you into the deepest valleys; look upon them as your own beloved sons, and they will stand by you even unto death.

[*Cf*. Ch. One, paragraph 6. In this connection, Tu Mu draws for us an engaging picture of the famous general Wu Ch'i, from whose treatise on war I have frequently had occasion to quote: "He wore the same clothes and ate the same food as the meanest of his soldiers, refused to have either a horse to ride or a mat to sleep on, carried his own surplus rations wrapped in a parcel, and shared every hardship with his men. One of his soldiers was suffering from an abscess, and Wu Ch'i himself sucked out the virus. The soldier's mother, hearing this, began wailing and lamenting. Somebody asked her, saying: 'Why do you cry? Your son is only a common soldier, and yet the commander-in-chief himself has sucked the poison from his sore.' The woman replied, 'Many years ago, Lord Wu performed a similar service for my husband, who never left him afterwards, and finally met his death at the hands of the enemy. And now that he has done the same for my son, he too will fall fighting I know not where.'" Li Ch'üan mentions the Viscount of Ch'u, who invaded the small state of Hsiao during the winter. The Duke of Shen said to him: "Many of the soldiers are suffering severely from the cold." So he made a round of the whole army, comforting and encouraging the men; and straightway they felt as if they were clothed in garments lined with floss silk.]

26. If, however, you are indulgent, but unable to make your authority felt; kind-hearted, but unable to enforce your commands; and incapable, moreover, of quelling disorder: then your soldiers must be likened to spoilt children; they are useless for any practical purpose.

[Li Ching once said that if you could make your soldiers afraid of you, they would not be afraid of the enemy. Tu Mu recalls an instance of stern military discipline which occurred in AD 219, when Lu Mêng was occupying the town of Chiang-ling. He had given stringent orders to his army not to molest the inhabitants nor take anything from them by force. Nevertheless, a certain officer serving under his banner, who happened to be a fellow-townsman, ventured to appropriate a bamboo hat belonging to one of the people, in order to wear it over his regulation helmet as a protection against the rain. Lu Mêng considered that the fact of his being also a native of Ju-nan should not be allowed to palliate a clear breach of discipline, and accordingly he ordered his summary execution, the tears rolling down his face, however, as he did so. This act of severity filled the army with wholesome awe, and from that time forth even articles dropped in the highway were not picked up.]

27. If we know that our own men are in a condition to attack, but are unaware that the enemy is not open to attack, we have gone only halfway towards victory.

[That is, Ts'ao Kung says, "the issue in this case is uncertain."]

28. If we know that the enemy is open to attack, but are unaware that our own men are not in a condition to attack, we have gone only halfway towards victory.

[*Cf.* Ch. Three, paragraph 13 (1).]

29. If we know that the enemy is open to attack, and also know that our men are in a condition to attack, but are unaware that the nature of the ground makes fighting impracticable, we have still gone only halfway towards victory.

30. Hence the experienced soldier, once in motion, is never bewildered; once he has broken camp, he is never at a loss.

[The reason being, according to Tu Mu, that he has taken his measures so thoroughly as to ensure victory beforehand. "He does not move recklessly," says Chang Yü, "so that when he does move, he makes no mistakes."]

31. Hence the saying: If you know the enemy and know yourself, your victory will not stand in doubt; if you know Heaven and know Earth, you may make your victory complete.

[Li Ch'üan sums up as follows: "Given a knowledge of three things—the affairs of men, the seasons of heaven and the natural advantages of earth—victory will invariably crown your battles."]

XI

THE NINE SITUATIONS

1. Sun Tzŭ said: The art of war recognizes nine varieties of ground:

    (1) Dispersive ground;
    (2) facile ground;
    (3) contentious ground;
    (4) open ground;
    (5) ground of intersecting highways;
    (6) serious ground;
    (7) difficult ground;
    (8) hemmed-in ground;
    (9) desperate ground.

2. When a chieftain is fighting in his own territory, it is dispersive ground.

    [So called because the soldiers, being near to their homes and anxious to see their wives and children, are likely to seize the opportunity afforded by a battle and scatter in every direction. "In their advance," observes Tu Mu, "they will lack the valor of desperation, and when they retreat, they will find harbors of refuge."]

3. When he has penetrated into hostile territory, but to no great distance, it is facile ground.

    [Li Ch'üan and Ho Shih say "because of the facility for retreating," and the other commentators give similar explanations. Tu Mu remarks: "When your army has crossed the border, you should burn your boats and bridges, in order to make it clear to everybody that you have no hankering after home."]

4. Ground the possession of which imports great advantage to either side, is contentious ground.

[Tu Mu defines the ground as ground "to be contended for." Ts'ao Kung says: "ground on which the few and the weak can defeat the many and the strong," such as "the neck of a pass," instanced by Li Ch'üan. Thus, Thermopylae was of this classification because the possession of it, even for a few days only, meant holding the entire invading army in check and thus gaining invaluable time. Wu Tzŭ writes: "For those who have to fight in the ratio of one to ten, there is nothing better than a narrow pass." When Lu Kuang was returning from his triumphant expedition to Turkestan in AD 385, and had got as far as I-ho, laden with spoils, Liang Hsi, administrator of Liang-chou, taking advantage of the death of Fu Chien, King of Ch'in, plotted against him and was for barring his way into the province. Yang Han, governor of Kao-ch'ang, counseled him, saying: "Lu Kuang is fresh from his victories in the west, and his soldiers are vigorous and mettlesome. If we oppose him in the shifting sands of the desert, we shall be no match for him, and we must therefore try a different plan. Let us hasten to occupy the defile at the mouth of the Kao-wu pass, thus cutting him off from supplies of water, and when his troops are prostrated with thirst, we can dictate our own terms without moving. Or if you think that the pass I mention is too far off, we could make a stand against him at the I-wu pass, which is nearer. The cunning and resource of Tzŭ-fang himself would be expended in vain against the enormous strength of these two positions." Liang Hsi, refusing to act on this advice, was overwhelmed and swept away by the invader.]

5.   Ground on which each side has liberty of movement is open ground.

[There are various interpretations of the Chinese adjective for this type of ground. Ts'ao Kung says it means "ground covered with a network of roads," like a chessboard. Ho Shih suggested: "ground on which intercommunication is easy."]

6.   Ground which forms the key to three contiguous states,

[Ts'au Kung defines this as: "Our country adjoining the enemy's and a third country conterminous with both." Mêng Shih instances the small principality of Cheng, which was bounded on the north-east by Ch'i, on the west by Chin, and on the south by Ch'u.]

so that he who occupies it first has most of the Empire at his command,

[The belligerent who holds this dominating position can constrain most of them to become his allies.]

is a ground of intersecting highways.

7. When an army has penetrated into the heart of a hostile country, leaving a number of fortified cities in its rear, it is serious ground.

[Wang Hsi explains the name by saying that "when an army has reached such a point, its situation is serious."]

8. Mountain forests,

[Or simply "forests."]

rugged steeps, marshes and fens — all country that is hard to traverse: this is difficult ground.

9. Ground which is reached through narrow gorges, and from which we can only retire by tortuous paths, so that a small number of the enemy would suffice to crush a large body of our men: this is hemmed-in ground.

10. Ground on which we can only be saved from destruction by fighting without delay, is desperate ground.

[The situation, as pictured by Ts'ao Kung, is very similar to the "hemmed-in ground" except that here escape is no longer possible: "A lofty mountain in front, a large river behind, advance impossible, retreat blocked." Ch'ên Hao says: "to be on 'desperate ground' is like sitting in a leaking boat or crouching in a burning house." Tu Mu quotes from Li Ching a vivid description of the plight of an army thus entrapped: "Suppose an army invading hostile territory without the aid of local guides: it falls into a fatal snare and is at the enemy's mercy. A ravine on the left, a mountain on the right, a pathway so perilous that the horses have to be roped together and the chariots carried in slings, no passage open in front, retreat cut off behind, no choice but to proceed in single file. Then, before there is time to range our soldiers in order of battle, the enemy in overwhelming strength suddenly appears on the scene. Advancing, we can nowhere take a breathing-space; retreating, we have no haven of refuge. We seek a pitched battle, but in vain; yet standing on the defensive, none of us has a moment's respite. If we simply maintain our ground, whole days and months will crawl by; the moment we make a move, we have to sustain the enemy's attacks on front and rear. The country is wild, destitute of water and plants; the army is lacking in the necessaries of life, the horses are jaded and the men worn-out, all the resources of strength and skill unavailing, the pass so narrow that a single man defending it can check the onset of ten thousand; all means of offense in the hands of the enemy, all points of vantage already forfeited by ourselves: in this terrible plight, even though we had the most valiant soldiers and the keenest of weapons, how could they be employed with the slightest effect?" Students of Greek history may be reminded of the awful close to the Sicilian expedition, and the agony of the Athenians under Nicias and Demonsthenes.]

11. On dispersive ground, therefore, fight not. On facile ground, halt not. On contentious ground, attack not.

[But rather let all your energies be bent on occupying the advantageous position first. So Ts'ao Kung. Li Ch'üan and others, however, suppose the meaning to be that the enemy has already forestalled us, so that it would be sheer madness to attack. In the *Sun Tzŭ Hsu Liu*, when the King of Wu inquires what should be done in this case, Sun Tzŭ replies: "The rule with regard to contentious ground is that those in possession have the advantage over the other side. If a position of this kind is secured first by the enemy, beware of attacking him. Lure him away by pretending to flee—show your banners and sound your drums—make a dash for other places that he cannot afford to lose—trail brushwood and raise a dust—confound his ears and eyes—detach a body of your best troops, and place it secretly in ambuscade. Then your opponent will sally forth to the rescue."]

12. On open ground, do not try to block the enemy's way.

[Because the attempt would be futile, and would expose the blocking force itself to serious risks. There are two interpretations available here. I follow that of Chang Yü. The other is indicated in Ts'ao Kung's brief note: "Draw closer together"—i.e., see that a portion of your own army is not cut off.]

On the ground of intersecting highways, join hands with your allies.

[Or perhaps, "form alliances with neighboring states."]

13. On serious ground, gather in plunder.

[On this, Li Ch'üan has the following delicious note: "When an army penetrates far into the enemy's country, care must be taken not to alienate the people by unjust treatment. Follow the example of the Han Emperor Kao Tsu, whose march into Ch'in territory was marked by no violation of women or looting of valuables. (*Nota bene*: this was in 207 BC, and may well cause us to blush for the Christian armies that entered Peking in AD 1900.) Thus he won the hearts of all. In the present passage, then, I think that the true reading must be, not 'plunder,' but 'do not plunder.'" Alas, I fear that in this instance the worthy commentator's feelings outran his judgment. Tu Mu, at least, has no such illusions. He says: "When encamped on 'serious ground,' there being no inducement as yet to advance further, and no possibility of retreat, one ought to take measures for a protracted resistance by bringing in provisions from all sides, and keep a close watch on the enemy."]

In difficult ground, keep steadily on the march.

[Or, in the words of Ch. Eight, paragraph 2, "do not encamp."]

14. On hemmed-in ground, resort to stratagem.

[Ts'au Kung says: "Try the effect of some unusual artifice"; and Tu Yu amplifies this by saying: "In such a position, some scheme must be devised which will suit the circumstances, and if we

can succeed in deluding the enemy, the peril may be escaped."
This is exactly what happened on the famous occasion when
Hannibal was hemmed in among the mountains on the road
to Casilinum, and to all appearances entrapped by the dictator
Fabius. The stratagem which Hannibal devised to baffle his foes
was remarkably like that which T'ien Tan had also employed
with success exactly 62 years before. (See Ch. Nine, paragraph
24, note.) When night came on, bundles of twigs were fastened to
the horns of some 2,000 oxen and set on fire, the terrified animals
being then quickly driven along the mountain side towards the
passes which were beset by the enemy. The strange spectacle
of these rapidly moving lights so alarmed and discomfited the
Romans that they withdrew from their position, and Hannibal's
army passed safely through the defile.]

On desperate ground, fight.

[For, as Chia Lin remarks: "if you fight with all your might,
there is a chance of life; whereas death is certain if you cling to
your corner."]

15. Those who were called skillful leaders of old knew how to drive a
wedge between the enemy's front and rear;

[More literally, "cause the front and rear to lose touch with each
other."]

to prevent cooperation between his large and small divisions; to
hinder the good troops from rescuing the bad, the officers from
rallying their men.

16. When the enemy's men were united, they managed to keep them in
disorder.

17. When it was to their advantage, they made a forward move; when
otherwise, they stopped still.

[Mei Yao-ch'ên connects this with the foregoing: "Having
succeeded in thus dislocating the enemy, they would push
forward in order to secure any advantage to be gained; if there
was no advantage to be gained, they would remain where they
were."]

18. If asked how to cope with a great host of the enemy in orderly array and on the point of marching to the attack, I should say: "Begin by seizing something which your opponent holds dear; then he will be amenable to your will."

[Opinions differ as to what Sun Tzŭ had in mind. Ts'ao Kung thinks it is "some strategical advantage on which the enemy is depending." Tu Mu says: "The three things which an enemy is anxious to do, and on the accomplishment of which his success depends, are: (1) to capture our favorable positions; (2) to ravage our cultivated land; (3) to guard his own communications." Our object then must be to thwart his plans in these three directions and thus render him helpless. (*Cf.* Ch. Three, paragraph 3.) By boldly seizing the initiative in this way, you at once throw the other side on the defensive.]

19. Rapidity is the essence of war:

[According to Tu Mu, "this is a summary of leading principles in warfare," and he adds: "These are the profoundest truths of military science, and the chief business of the general." The following anecdotes, told by Ho Shih, shows the importance attached to speed by two of China's greatest generals. In AD 227, Mêng Ta, governor of Hsin-ch'êng under the Wei Emperor Wên Ti, was meditating defection to the House of Shu, and had entered into correspondence with Chu-ko Liang, Prime Minister of that State. The Wei general Ssŭ-ma I was then military governor of Wan, and getting wind of Mêng Ta's treachery, he at once set off with an army to anticipate his revolt, having previously cajoled him by a specious message of friendly import. Ssŭ-ma's officers came to him and said: "If Mêng Ta has leagued himself with Wu and Shu, the matter should be thoroughly investigated before we make a move." Ssŭ-ma I replied: "Mêng Ta is an unprincipled man, and we ought to go and punish him at once, while he is still wavering and before he has thrown off the mask." Then, by a series of forced marches, be brought his army under the walls of Hsin-ch'êng within a space of eight days. Now Mêng Ta had previously said in a letter to Chu-ko Liang: "Wan is 1200 lî from here. When the news of my revolt reaches Ssŭ-ma I, he will at once inform his imperial master, but it will be a whole month before any steps can be taken, and by that time my city will be well fortified. Besides, Ssŭ-ma I is sure not to come himself, and the generals that will be sent against us are not worth troubling about." The next letter, however, was filled with consternation: "Though only eight days have passed since I threw off my allegiance, an army is already at the city-gates. What miraculous rapidity is this!" A fortnight later, Hsin-ch'êng had fallen and Mêng Ta had lost his head. In AD 621, Li Ching was sent from K'uei-chou in Ssŭ-ch'üan to reduce the successful rebel Hsiao Hsien, who had set up as Emperor at the modern Ching-chou Fu in Hupeh. It was autumn, and the Yangtsze being then in flood, Hsiao Hsien never dreamt that his adversary would venture to come down through the gorges, and consequently made no preparations. But Li Ching embarked his army without loss of time, and was just about to start when the other generals implored him to postpone his departure until the river was in a less dangerous state for navigation. Li Ching replied: "To the soldier, overwhelming speed is of paramount importance, and he must never miss opportunities. Now is the time to strike, before Hsiao Hsien even knows that we have got an army together. If we seize the present moment when the river is in flood, we shall appear before his capital with startling suddenness, like the thunder which is heard before you have time to stop your ears against it. (See Ch. Seven, paragraph 19, note.) This is the great principle in war. Even if he gets to know of our approach, he will have to levy his soldiers in such a hurry that they will not be fit to oppose us. Thus the full fruits of victory will be ours." All came about as he predicted, and Hsiao Hsien was obliged to surrender, nobly stipulating that his people should be spared and he alone suffer the penalty of death.]

take advantage of the enemy's unreadiness, make your way by unexpected routes, and attack unguarded spots.

20. The following are the principles to be observed by an invading force: The further you penetrate into a country, the greater will be the solidarity of your troops, and thus the defenders will not prevail against you.

21. Make forays in fertile country in order to supply your army with food.

[*Cf. supra*, paragraph 13. Li Ch'üan does not venture on a note here.]

22. Carefully study the well-being of your men,

[For "well-being," Wang Hsi means, "Pet them, humor them, give them plenty of food and drink, and look after them generally."]

and do not overtax them. Concentrate your energy and hoard your strength.

[Ch'ên Hao recalls the line of action adopted in 224 BC by the famous general Wang Chien, whose military genius largely contributed to the success of the First Emperor. He had invaded the Ch'u State, where a universal levy was made to oppose him. But, being doubtful of the temper of his troops, he declined all invitations to fight and remained strictly on the defensive. In vain did the Ch'u general try to force a battle: day after day Wang Chien kept inside his walls and would not come out, but devoted his whole time and energy to winning the affection and confidence of his men. He took care that they should be well fed, sharing his own meals with them, provided facilities for bathing, and employed every method of judicious indulgence to weld them into a loyal and homogenous body. After some time had elapsed, he told off certain persons to find out how the men were amusing themselves. The answer was, that they were contending with one another in putting the weight and long-jumping. When Wang Chien heard that they were engaged in these athletic pursuits, he knew that their spirits had been strung up to the required pitch and that they were now ready for fighting. By this time the Ch'u army, after repeating their challenge again and again, had marched away eastwards in disgust. The Ch'in general immediately broke up his camp and followed them, and in the battle that ensued they were routed with great slaughter. Shortly afterwards, the whole of Ch'u was conquered by Ch'in, and the king Fu-ch'u led into captivity.]

Keep your army continually on the move,

[In order that the enemy may never know exactly where you are. It has struck me, however, that the true reading might be "link your army together."]

and devise unfathomable plans.

23. Throw your soldiers into positions whence there is no escape, and they will prefer death to flight. If they will face death, there is nothing they may not achieve.

[Chang Yü quotes his favorite Wei Liao Tzŭ: "If one man were to run amok with a sword in the market-place, and everybody else tried to get out of his way, I should not allow that this man alone had courage and that all the rest were contemptible cowards. The truth is, that a desperado and a man who sets some value on his life do not meet on even terms."]

Officers and men alike will put forth their uttermost strength.

[Chang Yü says: "If they are in an awkward place together, they will surely exert their united strength to get out of it."]

24. Soldiers when in desperate straits lose the sense of fear. If there is no place of refuge, they will stand firm. If they are in hostile country, they will show a stubborn front. If there is no help for it, they will fight hard.

25. Thus, without waiting to be marshaled, the soldiers will be constantly on the *qui vive*; without waiting to be asked, they will do your will;

[Literally, "without asking, you will get."]

without restrictions, they will be faithful; without giving orders, they can be trusted.

26. Prohibit the taking of omens, and do away with superstitious doubts. Then, until death itself comes, no calamity need be feared.

[The superstitious, "bound in to saucy doubts and fears," degenerate into cowards and "die many times before their deaths." Tu Mu quotes Huang Shih-kung: "'Spells and incantations should be strictly forbidden, and no officer allowed to inquire by divination into the fortunes of an army, for fear the soldiers' minds should be seriously perturbed.' The meaning is," he continues, "that if all doubts and scruples are discarded, your men will never falter in their resolution until they die."]

27. If our soldiers are not overburdened with money, it is not because they have a distaste for riches; if their lives are not unduly long, it is not because they are disinclined to longevity.

[Chang Yü has the best note on this passage: "Wealth and long life are things for which all men have a natural inclination. Hence, if they burn or fling away valuables, and sacrifice their own lives, it is not that they dislike them, but simply that they have no choice." Sun Tzŭ is slyly insinuating that, as soldiers are but human, it is for the general to see that temptations to shirk fighting and grow rich are not thrown in their way.]

28. On the day they are ordered out to battle, your soldiers may weep,

[The word in the Chinese is "snivel." This is taken to indicate more genuine grief than tears alone.]

those sitting up bedewing their garments, and those lying down letting the tears run down their cheeks.

[Not because they are afraid, but because, as Ts'ao Kung says, "all have embraced the firm resolution to do or die." We may remember that the heroes of the *Iliad* were equally childlike in showing their emotion. Chang Yü alludes to the mournful parting at the I River between Ching K'o and his friends, when the former was sent to attempt the life of the King of Ch'in (afterwards First Emperor) in 227 BC. The tears of all flowed down like rain as he bade them farewell and uttered the following lines: "The shrill blast is blowing, Chilly the burn; Your champion is going—Not to return."]

But let them once be brought to bay, and they will display the courage of a Chu or a Kuei.

[Chu was the personal name of Chuan Chu, a native of the Wu State and contemporary with Sun Tzŭ himself, who was employed by Kung-Tzŭ Kuang, better known as Ho Lü Wang, to assassinate his sovereign Wang Liao with a dagger which he secreted in the belly of a fish served up at a banquet. He succeeded in his attempt, but was immediately hacked to pieces by the king's bodyguard. This was in 515 BC. The other hero referred to, Ts'ao Kuei (or Ts'ao Mo), performed the exploit which has made his name famous 166 years earlier, in 681 BC Lu had been thrice defeated by Ch'i, and was just about to conclude a treaty surrendering a large slice of territory, when Ts'ao Kuei suddenly seized Huan Kung, the Duke of Ch'i, as he stood on the altar steps and held a dagger against his chest. None of the duke's retainers dared to move a muscle, and Ts'ao Kuei proceeded to demand full restitution, declaring the Lu was being unjustly treated because she was a smaller and a weaker state. Huan Kung, in peril of his life, was obliged to consent, whereupon Ts'ao Kuei flung away his dagger and quietly resumed his place amid the terrified assemblage without having so much as changed color. As was to be expected, the Duke wanted afterwards to repudiate the bargain, but his wise old counselor Kuan Chung pointed out to him the impolicy of breaking his word, and the upshot was that this bold stroke regained for Lu the whole of what she had lost in three pitched battles.]

29. The skillful tactician may be likened to the *shuai-jan*. Now the *shuai-jan* is a snake that is found in the Ch'ang mountains.

["Shuai-jan" means "suddenly" or "rapidly," and the snake in question was doubtless so called owing to the rapidity of its movements. Through this passage, the term in the Chinese has now come to be used in the sense of "military maneuvers."]

Strike at its head, and you will be attacked by its tail; strike at its tail, and you will be attacked by its head; strike at its middle, and you will be attacked by head and tail both.

30. Asked if an army can be made to imitate the *shuai-jan*,

[That is, as Mei Yao-ch'en says, "Is it possible to make the front and rear of an army each swiftly responsive to attack on the other, just as though they were part of a single living body?"]

I should answer, Yes. For the men of Wu and the men of Yüeh are enemies;

[Cf. Ch. Six, paragraph 21.]

yet if they are crossing a river in the same boat and are caught by a storm, they will come to each other's assistance just as the left hand helps the right.

[The meaning is: If two enemies will help each other in a time of common peril, how much more should two parts of the same army, bound together as they are by every tie of interest and fellow-feeling. Yet it is notorious that many a campaign has been ruined through lack of cooperation, especially in the case of allied armies.]

31. Hence it is not enough to put one's trust in the tethering of horses, and the burying of chariot wheels in the ground.

[These quaint devices to prevent one's army from running away recall the Athenian hero Sophanes, who carried the anchor with him at the battle of Plataea, by means of which he fastened himself firmly to one spot. It is not enough, says Sun Tzŭ, to render flight impossible by such mechanical means. You will not succeed unless your men have tenacity and unity of purpose, and, above all, a spirit of sympathetic cooperation. This is the lesson which can be learned from the *shuai-jan.*]

32. The principle on which to manage an army is to set up one standard of courage which all must reach.

[Literally, "level the courage (of all) as though (it were that of) one." If the ideal army is to form a single organic whole, then it follows that the resolution and spirit of its component parts must be of the same quality, or at any rate must not fall below a certain standard. Wellington's seemingly ungrateful description of his army at Waterloo as "the worst he had ever commanded" meant no more than that it was deficient in this important particular—unity of spirit and courage. Had he not foreseen the Belgian defections and carefully kept those troops in the background, he would almost certainly have lost the day.]

33. How to make the best of both strong and weak—that is a question involving the proper use of ground.

[Mei Yao-ch'ên's paraphrase is: "The way to eliminate the differences of strong and weak and to make both serviceable is to utilize accidental features of the ground." Less reliable troops, if posted in strong positions, will hold out as long as better troops on more exposed terrain. The advantage of position neutralizes the inferiority in stamina and courage. Col. Henderson, in *The Science of War*, says: "With all respect to the text books, and to the ordinary tactical teaching, I am inclined to think that the study of ground is often overlooked, and that by no means sufficient importance is attached to the selection of positions . . . and to the immense advantages that are to be derived, whether you are defending or attacking, from the proper utilization of natural features."]

34. Thus the skillful general conducts his army just as though he were leading a single man, willy-nilly, by the hand.

[Tu Mu says: "The simile has reference to the ease with which he does it."]

35. It is the business of a general to be quiet and thus ensure secrecy; upright and just, and thus maintain order.

36. He must be able to mystify his officers and men by false reports and appearances,

[Literally, "to deceive their eyes and ears."]

and thus keep them in total ignorance.

[Ts'ao Kung gives us one of his excellent apophthegms: "The troops must not be allowed to share your schemes in the beginning; they may only rejoice with you over their happy outcome." "To mystify, mislead, and surprise the enemy," is one of the first principles in war, as had been frequently pointed out. But how about the other process—the mystification of one's own men? Those who may think that Sun Tzŭ is over-emphatic on this point would do well to read Col. Henderson's remarks on Stonewall Jackson's Valley campaign: "The infinite pains," he says, "with which Jackson sought to conceal, even from his most trusted staff officers, his movements, his intentions, and his thoughts, a commander less thorough would have pronounced useless"—etc. etc. In the year AD 88, as we read in Ch. 47 of the *Hou Han Shu*, "Pan Ch'ao took the field with 25,000 men from Khotan and other Central Asian states with the object of crushing Yarkand. The King of Kutcha replied by dispatching his chief commander to succor the place with an army drawn from the kingdoms of Wen-su, Ku-mo, and Wei-t'ou, totaling 50,000 men. Pan Ch'ao summoned his officers and also the King of Khotan to a council of war, and said: 'Our forces are now outnumbered and unable to make head against the enemy. The best plan, then, is for us to separate and disperse, each in a different direction. The King of Khotan will march away by the easterly route, and I will then return myself towards the west. Let us wait until the evening drum has sounded and then start.' Pan Ch'ao now secretly released the prisoners whom he had taken alive, and the King of Kutcha was thus informed of his plans. Much elated by the news, the latter set off at once at the head of 10,000 horsemen to bar Pan Ch'ao's retreat in the west, while the King of Wen-su rode eastward with 8,000 horse in order to intercept the King of Khotan. As soon as Pan Ch'ao knew that the two chieftains had gone, he called his divisions together, got them well in hand, and at cock-crow hurled them against the army of Yarkand, as it lay encamped. The barbarians, panic-stricken, fled in confusion, and were closely pursued by Pan Ch'ao. Over 5000 heads were brought back as trophies, besides immense spoils in the shape of horses and cattle and valuables of every description. Yarkand then capitulating, Kutcha and the other kingdoms drew off their respective forces. From that time forward, Pan Ch'ao's prestige completely overawed the countries of the west." In this case, we see that the Chinese general not only kept his own officers in ignorance of his real plans, but actually took the bold step of dividing his army in order to deceive the enemy.]

37. By altering his arrangements and changing his plans,

[Wang Hsi thinks that this means not using the same stratagem twice.]

he keeps the enemy without definite knowledge.

[Chang Yü, in a quotation from another work, says: "The axiom, that war is based on deception, does not apply only to deception of the enemy. You must deceive even your own soldiers. Make them follow you, but without letting them know why."]

By shifting his camp and taking circuitous routes, he prevents the enemy from anticipating his purpose.

38. At the critical moment, the leader of an army acts like one who has climbed up a height and then kicks away the ladder behind him. He carries his men deep into hostile territory before he shows his hand.

[Literally, "releases the spring" (see Ch. Five, paragraph 15), that is, takes some decisive step which makes it impossible for the army to return — like Hsiang Yu, who sunk his ships after crossing a river. Ch'ên Hao , followed by Chia Lin, understands the words less well as "puts forth every artifice at his command."]

39. He burns his boats and breaks his cooking-pots; like a shepherd driving a flock of sheep, he drives his men this way and that, and nothing knows whither he is going.

[Tu Mu says: "The army is only cognizant of orders to advance or retreat; it is ignorant of the ulterior ends of attacking and conquering."]

40. To muster his host and bring it into danger: — this may be termed the business of the general.

[Sun Tzŭ means that after mobilization there should be no delay in aiming a blow at the enemy's heart. Note how he returns again and again to this point. Among the warring states of ancient China, desertion was no doubt a much more present fear and serious evil than it is in the armies of today.]

41. The different measures suited to the nine varieties of ground;

[Chang Yü says: "One must not be hide-bound in interpreting the rules for the nine varieties of ground.]

the expediency of aggressive or defensive tactics; and the fundamental laws of human nature: these are things that must most certainly be studied.

42. When invading hostile territory, the general principle is, that penetrating deeply brings cohesion; penetrating but a short way means dispersion.

[*Cf. supra*, paragraph 20.]

43. When you leave your own country behind, and take your army across neighborhood territory, you find yourself on critical ground.

[This "ground" is curiously mentioned in Ch. Eight, paragraph 2, but it does not figure among the Nine Situations or the Six Calamities in Ch. Ten. One's first impulse would be to translate it "distant ground," but this, if we can trust the commentators, is precisely what is not meant here. Mei Yao-ch'ên says it is "a position not far enough advanced to be called 'facile,' and not near enough to home to be 'dispersive,' but something between the two." Wang Hsi says: "It is ground separated from home by an interjacent state, whose territory we have had to cross in order to reach it. Hence, it is incumbent on us to settle our business there quickly." He adds that this position is of rare occurrence, which is the reason why it is not included among the Nine Situations.]

When there are means of communication on all four sides, the ground is one of intersecting highways.

44. When you penetrate deeply into a country, it is serious ground. When you penetrate but a little way, it is facile ground.

45. When you have the enemy's strongholds on your rear, and narrow passes in front, it is hemmed-in ground. When there is no place of refuge at all, it is desperate ground.

46. Therefore, on dispersive ground, I would inspire my men with unity of purpose.

[This end, according to Tu Mu, is best attained by remaining on the defensive, and avoiding battle. *Cf. supra*, paragraph 11.]

On facile ground, I would see that there is close connection between all parts of my army.

[As Tu Mu says, the object is to guard against two possible contingencies: "(1) the desertion of our own troops; (2) a sudden attack on the part of the enemy." *Cf.* Ch. Seven, paragraph 17. Mei Yao-ch'ên says: "On the march, the regiments should be in close touch; in an encampment, there should be continuity between the fortifications."]

47. On contentious ground, I would hurry up my rear.

[This is Ts'ao Kung's interpretation. Chang Yü adopts it, saying: "We must quickly bring up our rear, so that head and tail may both reach the goal." That is, they must not be allowed to straggle up a long way apart. Mei Yao-ch'ên offers another equally plausible explanation: "Supposing the enemy has not yet reached the coveted position, and we are behind him, we should advance with all speed in order to dispute its possession." Ch'ên Hao, on the other hand, assuming that the enemy has had time to select his own ground, quotes Ch. Six, paragraph 1, where Sun Tzŭ warns us against coming exhausted to the attack. His own idea of the situation is rather vaguely expressed: "If there is a favorable position lying in front of you, detach a picked body of troops to occupy it, then if the enemy, relying on their numbers, come up to make a fight for it, you may fall quickly on their rear with your main body, and victory will be assured." It was thus, he adds, that Chao Shê beat the army of Ch'in.]

48. On open ground, I would keep a vigilant eye on my defenses. On ground of intersecting highways, I would consolidate my alliances.

49. On serious ground, I would try to ensure a continuous stream of supplies.

[The commentators take this as referring to forage and plunder, not, as one might expect, to an unbroken communication with a home base.]

On difficult ground, I would keep pushing on along the road.

50. On hemmed-in ground, I would block any way of retreat.

[Mêng Shih says: "To make it seem that I meant to defend the position, whereas my real intention is to burst suddenly through the enemy's lines." Mei Yao-ch'ên says: "in order to make my soldiers fight with desperation." Wang Hsi says, "fearing lest my men be tempted to run away." Tu Mu points out that this is the converse of Ch. Seven, paragraph 36, where it is the enemy who is surrounded. In AD 532, Kao Huan, afterwards Emperor and canonized as Shen-wu, was surrounded by a great army under Erh-chu Chao and others. His own force was comparatively small, consisting only of 2,000 horse and something under 30,000 foot. The lines of investment had not been drawn very closely together, gaps being left at certain points. But Kao Huan, instead of trying to escape, actually made a shift to block all the remaining outlets himself by driving into them a number of oxen and donkeys roped together. As soon as his officers and men saw that there was nothing for it but to conquer or die, their spirits rose to an extraordinary pitch of exaltation, and they charged with such desperate ferocity that the opposing ranks broke and crumbled under their onslaught.]

On desperate ground, I would proclaim to my soldiers the hopelessness of saving their lives.

[Tu Yu says: "Burn your baggage and impedimenta, throw away your stores and provisions, choke up the wells, destroy your cooking-stoves, and make it plain to your men that they cannot survive, but must fight to the death." Mei Yao-ch'ên says: "The only chance of life lies in giving up all hope of it." This concludes what Sun Tzŭ has to say about "grounds" and the "variations" corresponding to them. Reviewing the passages which bear on this important subject, we cannot fail to be struck by the desultory and unmethodical fashion in which it is treated. Sun Tzŭ begins abruptly in Ch. Eight, paragraph 2 to enumerate "variations" before touching on "grounds" at all, but only mentions five, namely nos. 7, 5, 8 and 9 of the subsequent list, and one that is not included in it. A few varieties of ground are dealt with in the earlier portion of Ch. Nine, and then Ch. Ten sets forth six new grounds, with six variations of plan to match. None of these is mentioned again, though the first is hardly to be distinguished from ground no. 4 in the next chapter. At last, in Ch. Eleven, we come to the Nine Grounds par excellence, immediately followed by the variations. This takes us down to paragraph 14. In paragraphs 43–45, fresh definitions are provided for nos. 5, 6, 2, 8 and 9 (in the order given), as well as for the tenth ground noticed in Ch. Eight; and finally, the nine variations are enumerated once more from beginning to end, all, with the exception of 5, 6 and 7, being different from those previously given. Though it is impossible to account for the present state of Sun Tzŭ's text, a few suggestive facts may be brought into prominence: (1) Ch. Eight, according to the title, should deal with nine variations, whereas only five appear. (2) It is an abnormally short chapter. (3) Ch. Eleven is entitled The Nine Grounds. Several of these are defined twice over, besides which there are two distinct lists of the corresponding variations. (4) The length of the chapter is disproportionate, being double that of any other except Nine. I do not propose to draw any inferences from these facts, beyond the general conclusion that Sun Tzŭ's work cannot have come down to us in the shape in which it left his hands: Ch. Eight is obviously defective and probably out of place, while Eleven seems to contain matter that has either been added by a later hand or ought to appear elsewhere.]

51. For it is the soldier's disposition to offer an obstinate resistance when surrounded, to fight hard when he cannot help himself, and to obey promptly when he has fallen into danger.

[Chang Yü alludes to the conduct of Pan Ch'ao's devoted followers in AD 73. The story runs thus in the *Hou Han Shu*, ch. 47: "When Pan Ch'ao arrived at Shan-shan, Kuang, the King of the country, received him at first with great politeness and respect; but shortly afterwards his behavior underwent a sudden change, and he became remiss and negligent. Pan Ch'ao spoke about this to the officers of his suite: 'Have you noticed,' he said, 'that Kuang's polite intentions are on the wane? This must signify that envoys have come from the Northern barbarians, and that consequently he is in a state of indecision, not knowing with which side to throw in his lot. That surely is the reason. The truly wise man, we are told, can perceive things before they have come to pass; how much more, then, those that are already manifest!' Thereupon he called one of the natives who had been assigned to his service, and set a trap for him, saying: 'Where are those envoys from the Hsiung-nu who arrived some day ago?' The man was so taken aback that between surprise and fear he presently blurted out the whole truth. Pan Ch'ao, keeping his informant carefully under lock and key, then summoned a general gathering of his officers, thirty-six in all, and began drinking with them. When the wine had mounted into their heads a little, he tried to rouse their spirit still further by addressing them thus: 'Gentlemen, here we are in the heart of an isolated region, anxious to achieve riches and honor by some great exploit. Now it happens that an ambassador from the Hsiung-nu arrived in this kingdom only a few days ago, and the result is that the respectful courtesy extended towards us by our royal host has disappeared. Should this envoy prevail upon him to seize our party and hand us over to the Hsiung-nu, our bones will become food for the wolves of the desert. What are we to do?' With one accord, the officers replied: 'Standing as we do in peril of our lives, we will follow our commander through life and death.'" For the sequel of this adventure, see Ch. Twelve, paragraph 1, note.]

52. We cannot enter into alliance with neighboring princes until we are acquainted with their designs. We are not fit to lead an army on the march unless we are familiar with the face of the country—its mountains and forests, its pitfalls and precipices, its marshes and swamps. We shall be unable to turn natural advantages to account unless we make use of local guides.

[These three sentences are repeated from Ch. Seven, paragraphs 12–14 — in order to emphasize their importance, the commentators seem to think. I prefer to regard them as interpolated here in order to form an antecedent to the following words. With regard to local guides, Sun Tzŭ might have added that there is always the risk of going wrong, either through their treachery or some misunderstanding such as Livy records: Hannibal, we are told, ordered a guide to lead him into the neighborhood of Casinum, where there was an important pass to be occupied; but his Carthaginian accent, unsuited to the pronunciation of Latin names, caused the guide to understand Casilinum instead of Casinum, and turning from his proper route, he took the army in that direction, the mistake not being discovered until they had almost arrived.]

53. To be ignored of any one of the following four or five principles does not befit a warlike prince.

54. When a warlike prince attacks a powerful state, his generalship shows itself in preventing the concentration of the enemy's forces. He overawes his opponents, and their allies are prevented from joining against him.

[Mei Tao-ch'ên constructs one of the chains of reasoning that are so much affected by the Chinese: "In attacking a powerful state, if you can divide her forces, you will have a superiority in strength; if you have a superiority in strength, you will overawe the enemy; if you overawe the enemy, the neighboring states will be frightened; and if the neighboring states are frightened, the enemy's allies will be prevented from joining her." The following gives a stronger meaning: "If the great state has once been defeated (before she has had time to summon her allies), then the lesser states will hold aloof and refrain from massing their forces." Ch'ên Hao and Chang Yü take the sentence in quite another way. The former says: "Powerful though a prince may be, if he attacks a large state, he will be unable to raise enough troops, and must rely to some extent on external aid; if he dispenses with this, and with overweening confidence in his own strength, simply tries to intimidate the enemy, he will surely be defeated." Chang Yü puts his view thus: "If we recklessly attack a large state, our own people will be discontented and hang back. But if (as will then be the case) our display of military force is inferior by half to that of the enemy, the other chieftains will take fright and refuse to join us."]

55. Hence he does not strive to ally himself with all and sundry, nor does he foster the power of other states. He carries out his own secret designs, keeping his antagonists in awe.

[The train of thought, as said by Li Ch'üan, appears to be this: Secure against a combination of his enemies, "he can afford to reject entangling alliances and simply pursue his own secret designs, his prestige enable him to dispense with external friendships."]

Thus he is able to capture their cities and overthrow their kingdoms.

[This paragraph, though written many years before the Ch'in State became a serious menace, is not a bad summary of the policy by which the famous Six Chancellors gradually paved the way for her final triumph under Shih Huang Ti. Chang Yü, following up his previous note, thinks that Sun Tzŭ is condemning this attitude of cold-blooded selfishness and haughty isolation.]

56. Bestow rewards without regard to rule,

[Wu Tzŭ (Ch. 3) less wisely says: "Let advance be richly rewarded and retreat be heavily punished."]

issue orders

[Literally, "hang" or "post up."]

without regard to previous arrangements;

["In order to prevent treachery," says Wang Hsi. The general meaning is made clear by Ts'ao Kung's quotation from the *Sŭ-Ma Fa*: "Give instructions only on sighting the enemy; give rewards when you see deserving deeds." Ts'ao Kung's paraphrase: "The final instructions you give to your army should not correspond with those that have been previously posted up."

Chang Yü simplifies this into "your arrangements should not be divulged beforehand." And Chia Lin says: "there should be no fixity in your rules and arrangements." Not only is there danger in letting your plans be known, but war often necessitates the entire reversal of them at the last moment.]

and you will be able to handle a whole army as though you had to do with but a single man.

[*Cf. supra*, paragraph 34.]

57. Confront your soldiers with the deed itself; never let them know your design.

[Literally, "do not tell them words"; i.e. do not give your reasons for any order. Lord Mansfield once told a junior colleague to "give no reasons" for his decisions, and the maxim is even more applicable to a general than to a judge.]

When the outlook is bright, bring it before their eyes; but tell them nothing when the situation is gloomy.

58. Place your army in deadly peril, and it will survive; plunge it into desperate straits, and it will come off in safety.

[These words of Sun Tzŭ were once quoted by Han Hsin in explanation of the tactics he employed in one of his most brilliant battles, already alluded to in Ch. Four, paragraph 8 note. In 204 BC, he was sent against the army of Chao, and halted ten miles from the mouth of the Ching-hsing pass, where the enemy had mustered in full force. Here, at midnight, he detached a body of 2,000 light cavalry, every man of which was furnished with a red flag. Their instructions were to make their way through narrow defiles and keep a secret watch on the enemy. "When the men of Chao see me in full flight," Han Hsin said, "they will abandon their fortifications and give chase. This must be the sign for you to rush in, pluck down the Chao standards and set up the red banners of Han in their stead." Turning then to his other officers, he remarked: "Our adversary holds a strong position, and is not likely to come out and attack us until he sees the standard and drums of the commander-in-chief, for fear I should turn back and escape through the mountains." So saying, he first of all sent out a division consisting of 10,000 men, and ordered them to form in line of battle with their backs to the River Ti. Seeing this maneuver, the whole army of Chao broke into loud laughter. By this time it was broad daylight, and Han Hsin, displaying the generalissimo's flag, marched out of the pass with drums beating, and was immediately engaged by the enemy. A great battle followed, lasting for some time; until at length Han Hsin and his colleague Chang Ni, leaving drums and banner on the field, fled to the division on the river bank, where another fierce battle was raging. The enemy rushed out to pursue them and to secure the trophies, thus denuding their ramparts of men; but the two generals succeeded in joining the other army, which was fighting with the utmost desperation. The time had now come for the 2,000 horsemen to play their part. As soon as they saw the men of Chao following up their advantage, they galloped behind the deserted walls, tore up the enemy's flags and replaced them by those of Han. When the Chao army looked back from the pursuit, the sight of these red flags struck them with terror. Convinced that the Hans had got in and overpowered their king, they broke up in wild disorder, every effort of their leader to stay the panic being in vain. Then the Han army fell on them from both sides and completed the rout, killing a number and capturing the rest, amongst whom was King Ya himself . . . After the battle, some of Han Hsin's officers came to him and said: "In *The Art of War* we are told to have a hill or tumulus on the right rear, and a river or marsh on the left front. (This appears to be a blend of Sun Tzŭ and T'ai Kung. See Ch. Nine, paragraph 9, and note.) You, on the contrary, ordered us to draw up our troops with the river at our back. Under these conditions, how did you manage to gain the victory?" The general replied: "I fear you gentlemen have not studied *The Art of War* with sufficient care. Is it not written there: 'Plunge your army into desperate straits and it will come off in safety; place it in deadly peril and it will survive'? Had I taken the usual course, I should never have been able to bring my colleague round. What says the Military Classic — 'Swoop down on the market-place and drive the men off to fight.' (This passage does not occur in the present text of Sun Tzŭ.) If I had not placed my troops in a position where they were obliged to fight for their lives, but had allowed each man to follow his own discretion, there would have been a general *débandade*, and it would have been impossible to do anything with them." The officers admitted the force of his argument, and said: "These are higher tactics than we should have been capable of."]

59. For it is precisely when a force has fallen into harm's way that is capable of striking a blow for victory.

[Danger has a bracing effect.]

60. Success in warfare is gained by carefully accommodating ourselves to the enemy's purpose.

[Ts'ao Kung says: "Feign stupidity"—by an appearance of yielding and falling in with the enemy's wishes. Chang Yü's note makes the meaning clear: "If the enemy shows an inclination to advance, lure him on to do so; if he is anxious to retreat, delay on purpose that he may carry out his intention." The object is to make him remiss and contemptuous before we deliver our attack.]

61. By persistently hanging on the enemy's flank,

[I understand the first four words to mean "accompanying the enemy in one direction." Ts'ao Kung says: "unite the soldiers and make for the enemy." But such a violent displacement of characters is quite indefensible.]

we shall succeed in the long run

[Literally, "after a thousand lî."]

in killing the commander-in-chief.

[Always a great point with the Chinese.]

62. This is called ability to accomplish a thing by sheer cunning.

63. On the day that you take up your command, block the frontier passes, destroy the official tallies,

[These were tablets of bamboo or wood, one half of which was issued as a permit or passport by the official in charge of a gate. *Cf.* the "border-warden" of *Lun Yu* III. 24, who may have had similar duties. When this half was returned to him, within a fixed period, he was authorized to open the gate and let the traveler through.]

and stop the passage of all emissaries.

[Either to or from the enemy's country.]

64. Be stern in the council-chamber,

[Show no weakness, and insist on your plans being ratified by the sovereign.]

so that you may control the situation.

[Mei Yao-ch'ên understands the whole sentence to mean: Take the strictest precautions to ensure secrecy in your deliberations.]

65. If the enemy leaves a door open, you must rush in.

66. Forestall your opponent by seizing what he holds dear,

[*Cf. supra*, paragraph 18.]

and subtly contrive to time his arrival on the ground.

[Ch'ên Hao's explanation: "If I manage to seize a favorable position, but the enemy does not appear on the scene, the advantage thus obtained cannot be turned to any practical account. He who intends therefore, to occupy a position of importance to the enemy, must begin by making an artful appointment, so to speak, with his antagonist, and cajole him into going there as well." Mei Yao-ch'ên explains that this "artful appointment" is to be made through the medium of the enemy's own spies, who will carry back just the amount of information that we choose to give them. Then, having cunningly disclosed our intentions, "we must manage, though starting after the enemy, to arrive before him (Ch. Seven, paragraph 4). We must start after him in order to ensure his marching thither; we must arrive before him in order to capture the place without trouble. Taken thus, the present passage lends some support to Mei Yao-ch'ên's interpretation of paragraph 47.]

67. Walk in the path defined by rule,

[Chia Lin says: "Victory is the only thing that matters, and this cannot be achieved by adhering to conventional canons." It is unfortunate that this variant rests on very slight authority, for the sense yielded is certainly much more satisfactory. Napoleon, as we know, according to the veterans of the old school whom he defeated, won his battles by violating every accepted canon of warfare.]

and accommodate yourself to the enemy until you can fight a decisive battle.

[Tu Mu says: "Conform to the enemy's tactics until a favorable opportunity offers; then come forth and engage in a battle that shall prove decisive."]

68. At first, then, exhibit the coyness of a maiden, until the enemy gives you an opening; afterwards emulate the rapidity of a running hare, and it will be too late for the enemy to oppose you.

[As the hare is noted for its extreme timidity, the comparison hardly appears felicitous. But of course Sun Tzŭ was thinking only of its speed. The words have been taken to mean: You must flee from the enemy as quickly as an escaping hare; but this is rightly rejected by Tu Mu.]

XII

THE ATTACK BY FIRE

[Rather more than half the chapter (paragraphs 1–13) is devoted to the subject of fire, after which the author branches off into other topics.]

1. Sun Tzŭ said: There are five ways of attacking with fire. The first is to burn soldiers in their camp;

[So Tu Mu. Li Ch'üan says: "Set fire to the camp, and kill the soldiers" (when they try to escape from the flames). Pan Ch'ao, sent on a diplomatic mission to the King of Shan-shan (see Ch. Eleven, paragraph 51, note), found himself placed in extreme peril by the unexpected arrival of an envoy from the Hsiung-nu (the mortal enemies of the Chinese). In consultation with his officers, he exclaimed: "'Never venture, never win! The only course open to us now is to make an assault by fire on the barbarians under cover of night, when they will not be able to discern our numbers. Profiting by their panic, we shall exterminate them completely; this will cool the King's courage and cover us with glory, besides ensuring the success of our mission.' The officers all replied that it would be necessary to discuss the matter first with the Intendant. Pan Ch'ao then fell into a passion: 'It is today,' he cried, 'that our fortunes must be decided! The Intendant is only a humdrum civilian, who on hearing of our project will certainly be afraid, and everything will be brought to light. An inglorious death is no worthy fate for valiant warriors.' All then agreed to do as he wished. Accordingly, as soon as night came on, he and his little band quickly made their way to the barbarian camp. A strong gale was blowing at the time. Pan Ch'ao ordered ten of the party to take drums and hide behind the enemy's barracks, it being arranged that when they saw flames shoot up, they should begin drumming and yelling with all their might. The rest of his men, armed with bows and crossbows, he posted in ambuscade at the gate of the camp. He then set fire to the place from the windward side, whereupon a deafening noise of drums and shouting arose on the front and rear of the Hsiung-nu, who rushed out pell-mell in frantic disorder. Pan Ch'ao slew three of them with his own hand, while his companions cut off the heads of the envoy and thirty of his suite. The remainder, more than a hundred in all, perished in the flames. On the following day, Pan Ch'ao, divining his thoughts, said with uplifted hand: 'Although you did not go with us last night, I should not think, Sir, of taking sole credit for our exploit.' This satisfied Kuo Hsun, and Pan Ch'ao, having sent for Kuang, King of Shan-shan, showed him the head of the barbarian envoy. The whole kingdom was seized with fear and trembling, which Pan Ch'ao took steps to allay by issuing a public proclamation. Then, taking the king's sons as hostage, he returned to make his report to Tou Ku." *Hou Han Shu*, Ch. 47, ff. 1, 2.]

the second is to burn stores;

[Tu Mu says: "Provisions, fuel and fodder." In order to subdue the rebellious population of Kiangnan, Kao Keng recommended Wen Ti of the Sui dynasty to make periodical raids and burn their stores of grain, a policy which in the long run proved entirely successful.]

the third is to burn baggage trains;

[An example given is the destruction of Yuan Shao's wagons and impedimenta by Ts'ao Ts'ao in AD 200.]

the fourth is to burn arsenals and magazines;

[Tu Mu says that the things contained in "arsenals" and "magazines" are the same. He specifies weapons and other implements, bullion and clothing. *Cf.* Ch. Seven, paragraph 11.]

the fifth is to hurl dropping fire amongst the enemy.

[Tu Yu says in the *T'ung Tien*: "To drop fire into the enemy's camp. The method by which this may be done is to set the tips of arrows alight by dipping them into a brazier, and then shoot them from powerful crossbows into the enemy's lines."]

2. In order to carry out an attack, we must have means available.

    [T'sao Kung thinks that "traitors in the enemy's camp" are referred to. But Ch'ên Hao is more likely to be right in saying: "We must have favorable circumstances in general, not merely traitors to help us." Chia Lin says: "We must avail ourselves of wind and dry weather."]

    the material for raising fire should always be kept in readiness.

    [Tu Mu suggests as material for making fire: "dry vegetable matter, reeds, brushwood, straw, grease, oil, etc." Here we have the material cause. Chang Yü says: "vessels for hoarding fire, stuff for lighting fires."]

3. There is a proper season for making attacks with fire, and special days for starting a conflagration.

4. The proper season is when the weather is very dry; the special days are those when the moon is in the constellations of the Sieve, the Wall, the Wing or the Cross-bar;

    [These are, respectively, the 7th, 14th, 27th, and 28th of the Twenty-eight Stellar Mansions, corresponding roughly to Sagittarius, Pegasus, Crater and Corvus.]

    for these four are all days of rising wind.

5. In attacking with fire, one should be prepared to meet five possible developments:

6. (1) When fire breaks out inside to enemy's camp, respond at once with an attack from without.

7. (2) If there is an outbreak of fire, but the enemy's soldiers remain quiet, bide your time and do not attack.

    [The prime object of attacking with fire is to throw the enemy into confusion. If this effect is not produced, it means that the enemy is ready to receive us. Hence the necessity for caution.]

8. (3) When the force of the flames has reached its height, follow it up with an attack, if that is practicable; if not, stay where you are.

[Ts'ao Kung says: "If you see a possible way, advance; but if you find the difficulties too great, retire."]

9. (4) If it is possible to make an assault with fire from without, do not wait for it to break out within, but deliver your attack at a favorable moment.

[Tu Mu says that the previous paragraphs had reference to the fire breaking out (either accidentally, we may suppose, or by the agency of incendiaries) inside the enemy's camp. "But," he continues, "if the enemy is settled in a waste place littered with quantities of grass, or if he has pitched his camp in a position which can be burnt out, we must carry our fire against him at any seasonable opportunity, and not await on in hopes of an outbreak occurring within, for fear our opponents should themselves burn up the surrounding vegetation, and thus render our own attempts fruitless." The famous Li Ling once baffled the leader of the Hsiung-nu in this way. The latter, taking advantage of a favorable wind, tried to set fire to the Chinese general's camp, but found that every scrap of combustible vegetation in the neighborhood had already been burnt down. On the other hand, Po-ts'ai, a general of the Yellow Turban rebels, was badly defeated in AD 184 through his neglect of this simple precaution. "At the head of a large army he was besieging Ch'ang-she, which was held by Huang-fu Sung. The garrison was very small, and a general feeling of nervousness pervaded the ranks; so Huang-fu Sung called his officers together and said: 'In war, there are various indirect methods of attack, and numbers do not count for everything. (The commentator here quotes Sun Tzŭ, Ch. Five, paragraphs 5, 6 and 10.) Now the rebels have pitched their camp in the midst of thick grass which will easily burn when the wind blows. If we set fire to it at night, they will be thrown into a panic, and we can make a sortie and attack them on all sides at once, thus emulating the achievement of T'ien Tan.' That same evening, a strong breeze sprang up; so Huang-fu Sung instructed his soldiers to bind reeds together into torches and mount guard on the city walls, after which he sent out a band of daring men, who stealthily made their way through the lines and started the fire with loud shouts and yells. Simultaneously, a glare of light shot up from the city walls, and Huang-fu Sung, sounding his drums, led a rapid charge, which threw the rebels into confusion and put them to headlong flight." (*Hou Han Shu*, Ch. 71.)]

10. (5) When you start a fire, be to windward of it. Do not attack from the leeward.

[Chang Yü, following Tu Yu, says: "When you make a fire, the enemy will retreat away from it; if you oppose his retreat and attack him then, he will fight desperately, which will not conduce to your success." A rather more obvious explanation is given by Tu Mu: "If the wind is in the east, begin burning to the east of the enemy, and follow up the attack yourself from that side. If you start the fire on the east side, and then attack from the west, you will suffer in the same way as your enemy."]

11. A wind that rises in the daytime lasts long, but a night breeze soon falls.

[*Cf.* Lao Tzǔ's saying: "A violent wind does not last the space of a morning." (*Tao Te Ching*, Ch. 23.) Mei Yao-ch'ên and Wang Hsi say: "A day breeze dies down at nightfall, and a night breeze at daybreak. This is what happens as a general rule." The phenomenon observed may be correct enough, but how this sense is to be obtained is not apparent.]

12. In every army, the five developments connected with fire must be known, the movements of the stars calculated, and a watch kept for the proper days.

[Tu Mu says: "We must make calculations as to the paths of the stars, and watch for the days on which wind will rise, before making our attack with fire." Chang Yü seems to interpret the text differently: "We must not only know how to assail our opponents with fire, but also be on our guard against similar attacks from them."]

13. Hence those who use fire as an aid to the attack show intelligence; those who use water as an aid to the attack gain an accession of strength.

14. By means of water, an enemy may be intercepted, but not robbed of all his belongings.

[Ts'ao Kung's note is: "We can merely obstruct the enemy's road or divide his army, but not sweep away all his accumulated stores." Water can do useful service, but it lacks the terrible destructive power of fire. This is the reason, Chang Yü concludes, why the former is dismissed in a couple of sentences, whereas the attack by fire is discussed in detail. Wu Tzŭ speaks thus of the two elements: "If an army is encamped on low-lying marshy ground, from which the water cannot run off, and where the rainfall is heavy, it may be submerged by a flood. If an army is encamped in wild marsh lands thickly overgrown with weeds and brambles, and visited by frequent gales, it may be exterminated by fire."]

15. Unhappy is the fate of one who tries to win his battles and succeed in his attacks without cultivating the spirit of enterprise; for the result is waste of time and general stagnation.

[This is one of the most perplexing passages in Sun Tzŭ. Ts'ao Kung says: "Rewards for good service should not be deferred a single day." And Tu Mu: "If you do not take opportunity to advance and reward the deserving, your subordinates will not carry out your commands, and disaster will ensue." For several reasons, however, and in spite of the formidable array of scholars on the other side, I prefer the interpretation suggested by Mei Yao-ch'ên alone, whose words I will quote: "Those who want to make sure of succeeding in their battles and assaults must seize the favorable moments when they come and not shrink on occasion from heroic measures: that is to say, they must resort to such means of attack of fire, water and the like. What they must not do, and what will prove fatal, is to sit still and simply hold to the advantages they have got."]

16. Hence the saying: The enlightened ruler lays his plans well ahead; the good general cultivates his resources.

[Tu Mu quotes the following from the *San Lueh*, Ch. 2: "The warlike prince controls his soldiers by his authority, kits them together by good faith, and by rewards makes them serviceable. If faith decays, there will be disruption; if rewards are deficient, commands will not be respected."]

17. Move not unless you see an advantage; use not your troops unless there is something to be gained; fight not unless the position is critical.

[Sun Tzŭ may at times appear to be over-cautious, but he never goes so far in that direction as the remarkable passage in the *Tao Te Ching*, Ch. 69. "I dare not take the initiative, but prefer to act on the defensive; I dare not advance an inch, but prefer to retreat a foot."]

18. No ruler should put troops into the field merely to gratify his own spleen; no general should fight a battle simply out of pique.

19. If it is to your advantage, make a forward move; if not, stay where you are.

[This is repeated from Ch. Eleven, paragraph 17. Here I feel convinced that it is an interpolation, for it is evident that paragraph 20 ought to follow immediately on paragraph 18.]

20. Anger may in time change to gladness; vexation may be succeeded by content.

21. But a kingdom that has once been destroyed can never come again into being;

[The Wu State was destined to be a melancholy example of this saying.]

nor can the dead ever be brought back to life.

22. Hence the enlightened ruler is heedful, and the good general full of caution. This is the way to keep a country at peace and an army intact.

XIII

THE USE OF SPIES

1. Sun Tzŭ said: Raising a host of a hundred thousand men and marching them great distances entails heavy loss on the people and a drain on the resources of the State. The daily expenditure will amount to a thousand ounces of silver.

[*Cf.* Chapter Two, paragraph 1, 13, 14.]

There will be commotion at home and abroad, and men will drop down exhausted on the highways.

[*Cf. Tao Te Ching*, Ch. 30: "Where troops have been quartered, brambles and thorns spring up." Chang Yü has the note: "We may be reminded of the saying: 'On serious ground, gather in plunder.' Why then should carriage and transportation cause exhaustion on the highways? The answer is, that not victuals alone, but all sorts of munitions of war have to be conveyed to the army. Besides, the injunction to 'forage on the enemy' only means that when an army is deeply engaged in hostile territory, scarcity of food must be provided against. Hence, without being solely dependent on the enemy for corn, we must forage in order that there may be an uninterrupted flow of supplies. Then, again, there are places like salt deserts where provisions being unobtainable, supplies from home cannot be dispensed with."]

As many as seven hundred thousand families will be impeded in their labor.

[Mei Yao-ch'ên says: "Men will be lacking at the plough-tail." The allusion is to the system of dividing land into nine parts, each consisting of about 15 acres, the plot in the center being cultivated on behalf of the State by the tenants of the other eight. It was here also, so Tu Mu tells us, that their cottages were built and a well sunk, to be used by all in common. (See Ch. Two, paragraph 12, note.) In time of war, one of the families had to serve in the army, while the other seven contributed to its support. Thus, by a levy of 100,000 men (reckoning one able-bodied soldier to each family) the husbandry of 700,000 families would be affected.]

2. Hostile armies may face each other for years, striving for the victory which is decided in a single day. This being so, to remain in ignorance of the enemy's condition simply because one grudges the outlay of a hundred ounces of silver in honors and emoluments,

["For spies" is of course the meaning, though it would spoil the effect of this curiously elaborate exordium if spies were actually mentioned at this point.]

is the height of inhumanity.

[Sun Tzŭ's agreement is certainly ingenious. He begins by adverting to the frightful misery and vast expenditure of blood and treasure which war always brings in its train. Now, unless you are kept informed of the enemy's condition, and are ready to strike at the right moment, a war may drag on for years. The only way to get this information is to employ spies, and it is impossible to obtain trustworthy spies unless they are properly paid for their services. But it is surely false economy to grudge a comparatively trifling amount for this purpose, when every day that the war lasts eats up an incalculably greater sum. This grievous burden falls on the shoulders of the poor, and hence Sun Tzŭ concludes that to neglect the use of spies is nothing less than a crime against humanity.]

3. One who acts thus is no leader of men, no present help to his sovereign, no master of victory.

[This idea, that the true object of war is peace, has its root in the national temperament of the Chinese. Even so far back as 597 BC, these memorable words were uttered by Prince Chuang of the Ch'u State: "The (Chinese) character for 'prowess' is made up of (the characters for) 'to stay' and 'a spear' (cessation of hostilities). Military prowess is seen in the repression of cruelty, the calling in of weapons, the preservation of the appointment of Heaven, the firm establishment of merit, the bestowal of happiness on the people, putting harmony between the princes, the diffusion of wealth."]

4. Thus, what enables the wise sovereign and the good general to strike and conquer, and achieve things beyond the reach of ordinary men, is *foreknowledge*.

[That is, knowledge of the enemy's dispositions, and what he means to do.]

5. Now this foreknowledge cannot be elicited from spirits; it cannot be obtained inductively from experience,

[Tu Mu's note is: "(knowledge of the enemy) cannot be gained by reasoning from other analogous cases."]

nor by any deductive calculation.

[Li Ch'üan says: "Quantities like length, breadth, distance and magnitude, are susceptible of exact mathematical determination; human actions cannot be so calculated."]

6. Knowledge of the enemy's dispositions can only be obtained from other men.

[Mei Yao-ch'ên has rather an interesting note: "Knowledge of the spirit-world is to be obtained by divination; information in natural science may be sought by inductive reasoning; the laws of the universe can be verified by mathematical calculation: but the dispositions of an enemy are ascertainable through spies and spies alone."]

7. Hence the use of spies, of whom there are five classes: (1) Local spies; (2) inward spies; (3) converted spies; (4) doomed spies; (5) surviving spies.

8. When these five kinds of spy are all at work, none can discover the secret system. This is called "divine manipulation of the threads." It is the sovereign's most precious faculty.

[According to Baden-Powell, in *Aids to Scouting*, "Cromwell, one of the greatest and most practical of all cavalry leaders, had officers styled 'scout masters,' whose business it was to collect all possible information regarding the enemy, through scouts and spies, etc., and much of his success in war was traceable to the previous knowledge of the enemy's moves thus gained."]

9. Having local spies means employing the services of the inhabitants of a district.

[Tu Mu says: "In the enemy's country, win people over by kind treatment, and use them as spies."]

10. Having *inward spies*, making use of officials of the enemy.

[Tu Mu enumerates the following classes as likely to do good service in this respect: "Worthy men who have been degraded from office, criminals who have undergone punishment; also, favorite concubines who are greedy for gold, men who are aggrieved at being in subordinate positions, or who have been passed over in the distribution of posts, others who are anxious that their side should be defeated in order that they may have a chance of displaying their ability and talents, fickle turncoats who always want to have a foot in each boat. Officials of these several kinds," he continues, "should be secretly approached and bound to one's interests by means of rich presents. In this way you will be able to find out the state of affairs in the enemy's country, ascertain the plans that are being formed against you, and moreover disturb the harmony and create a breach between the sovereign and his ministers." The necessity for extreme caution, however, in dealing with "inward spies," appears from an historical incident related by Ho Shih: "Lo Shang, Governor of I-Chou, sent his general Wei Po to attack the rebel Li Hsiung of Shu in his stronghold at P'i. After each side had experienced a number of victories and defeats, Li Hsiung had recourse to the services of a certain P'o-t'ai, a native of Wu-tu. He began to have him whipped until the blood came, and then sent him off to Lo Shang, whom he was to delude by offering to cooperate with him from inside the city, and to give a fire signal at the right moment for making a general assault. Lo Shang, confiding in these promises, march out all his best troops, and placed Wei Po and others at their head with orders to attack at P'o-t'ai's bidding. Meanwhile, Li Hsiung's general, Li Hsiang, had prepared an ambuscade on their line of march; and P'o-t'ai, having reared long scaling-ladders against the city walls, now lighted the beacon-fire. Wei Po's men raced up on seeing the signal and began climbing the ladders as fast as they could, while others were drawn up by ropes lowered from above. More than a hundred of Lo Shang's soldiers entered the city in this way, every one of whom was forthwith beheaded. Li Hsiung then charged with all his forces, both inside and outside the city, and routed the enemy completely." [This happened in AD 303. I do not know where Ho Shih got the story from. It is not given in the biography of Li Hsiung or that of his father Li T'e, *Chin Shu*, Ch. 120, 121.]

11. Having *converted spies*, getting hold of the enemy's spies and using them for our own purposes.

[By means of heavy bribes and liberal promises detaching them from the enemy's service, and inducing them to carry back false information as well as to spy in turn on their own countrymen. On the other hand, Hsiao Shih-hsien says that we pretend not to have detected him, but contrive to let him carry away a false impression of what is going on. Several of the commentators accept this as an alternative definition; but that it is not what Sun Tzŭ meant is conclusively proved by his subsequent remarks about treating the converted spy generously (paragraph 21 *sqq*.). Ho Shih notes three occasions on which converted spies were used with conspicuous success: (1) by T'ien Tan in his defense of Chi-mo; (2) by Chao Shê on his march to O-yü (see p. 57); and by the wily Fan Chu in 260 BC, when Lien P'o was conducting a defensive campaign against Ch'in. The King of Chao strongly disapproved of Lien P'o's cautious and dilatory methods, which had been unable to avert a series of minor disasters, and therefore lent a ready ear to the reports of his spies, who had secretly gone over to the enemy and were already in Fan Chu's pay. They said: "The only thing which causes Ch'in anxiety is lest Chao Kua should be made general. Lien P'o they consider an easy opponent, who is sure to be vanquished in the long run." Now this Chao Kua was a son of the famous Chao Shê. From his boyhood, he had been wholly engrossed in the study of war and military matters, until at last he came to believe that there was no commander in the whole Empire who could stand against him. His father was much disquieted by this overweening conceit, and the flippancy with which he spoke of such a serious thing as war, and solemnly declared that if ever Kua was appointed general, he would bring ruin on the armies of Chao. This was the man who, in spite of earnest protests from his own mother and the veteran statesman Lin Hsiang-ju, was now sent to succeed Lien P'o. Needless to say, he proved no match for the redoubtable Po Ch'i and the great military power of Ch'in. He fell into a trap by which his army was divided into two and his communications cut; and after a desperate resistance lasting 46 days, during which the famished soldiers devoured one another, he was himself killed by an arrow, and his whole force, amounting, it is said, to 400,000 men, ruthlessly put to the sword.]

12. Having *doomed spies*, doing certain things openly for purposes of deception, and allowing our spies to know of them and report them to the enemy.

[Tu Yu gives the best exposition of the meaning: "We ostentatiously do things calculated to deceive our own spies, who must be led to believe that they have been unwittingly disclosed. Then, when these spies are captured in the enemy's lines, they will make an entirely false report, and the enemy will take measures accordingly, only to find that we do something quite different. The spies will thereupon be put to death." As an example of doomed spies, Ho Shih mentions the prisoners released by Pan Ch'ao in his campaign against Yarkand. He also refers to T'ang Chien, who in AD 630 was sent by T'ai Tsung to lull the Turkish Kahn Chieh-li into fancied security, until Li Ching was able to deliver a crushing blow against him. Chang Yü says that the Turks revenged themselves by killing

T'ang Chien, but this is a mistake, for we read in both the old and the New T'ang History (Ch. 58, fol. 2 and Ch. 89, fol. 8 respectively) that he escaped and lived on until 656. Li I-chi played a somewhat similar part in 203 BC, when sent by the King of Han to open peaceful negotiations with Ch'i. He has certainly more claim to be described a "doomed spy," for the king of Ch'i, being subsequently attacked without warning by Han Hsin, and infuriated by what he considered the treachery of Li I-chi, ordered the unfortunate envoy to be boiled alive.]

13. *Surviving spies*, finally, are those who bring back news from the enemy's camp.

[This is the ordinary class of spies, properly so called, forming a regular part of the army. Tu Mu says: "Your surviving spy must be a man of keen intellect, though in outward appearance a fool; of shabby exterior, but with a will of iron. He must be active, robust, endowed with physical strength and courage; thoroughly accustomed to all sorts of dirty work, able to endure hunger and cold, and to put up with shame and ignominy." Ho Shih tells the following story of Ta-hsi Wu of the Sui dynasty: "When he was governor of Eastern Ch'in, Shen-wu of Ch'i made a hostile movement upon Sha-yuan. The Emperor T'ai Tsu sent Ta-hsi Wu to spy upon the enemy. He was accompanied by two other men. All three were on horseback and wore the enemy's uniform. When it was dark, they dismounted a few hundred feet away from the enemy's camp and stealthily crept up to listen, until they succeeded in catching the passwords used in the army. Then they got on their horses again and boldly passed through the camp under the guise of night-watchmen; and more than once, happening to come across a soldier who was committing some breach of discipline, they actually stopped to give the culprit a sound cudgeling! Thus they managed to return with the fullest possible information about the enemy's dispositions, and received warm commendation from the Emperor, who in consequence of their report was able to inflict a severe defeat on his adversary."]

14. Hence it is that which none in the whole army are more intimate relations to be maintained than with spies.

[Tu Mu and Mei Yao-ch'en point out that the spy is privileged to enter even the general's private sleeping-tent.]

None should be more liberally rewarded. In no other business should greater secrecy be preserved.

[Tu Mu gives a graphic touch: all communication with spies should be carried "mouth-to-ear." The following remarks on spies may be quoted from Turenne, who made perhaps larger use of them than any previous commander: "Spies are attached to those who give them most, he who pays them ill is never served. They should never be known to anybody; nor should they know one another. When they propose anything very material, secure their persons, or have in your possession their wives and children as hostages for their fidelity. Never communicate anything to them but what is absolutely necessary that they should know.]

15. Spies cannot be usefully employed without a certain intuitive sagacity.

[Mei Yao-ch'ên says: "In order to use them, one must know fact from falsehood, and be able to discriminate between honesty and double-dealing." Wang Hsi in a different interpretation thinks more along the lines of "intuitive perception" and "practical intelligence." Tu Mu strangely refers these attributes to the spies themselves: "Before using spies we must assure ourselves as to their integrity of character and the extent of their experience and skill." But he continues: "A brazen face and a crafty disposition are more dangerous than mountains or rivers; it takes a man of genius to penetrate such." So that we are left in some doubt as to his real opinion on the passage.]

16. They cannot be properly managed without benevolence and straightforwardness.

[Chang Yü says: "When you have attracted them by substantial offers, you must treat them with absolute sincerity; then they will work for you with all their might."]

17. Without subtle ingenuity of mind, one cannot make certain of the truth of their reports.

[Mei Yao-ch'ên says: "Be on your guard against the possibility of spies going over to the service of the enemy."]

18. Be subtle! be subtle! and use your spies for every kind of business.

[*Cf.* Ch. Six, paragraph 9.]

19. If a secret piece of news is divulged by a spy before the time is ripe, he must be put to death together with the man to whom the secret was told.

[Word for word, the translation here is: "If spy matters are heard before (our plans) are carried out," etc. Sun Tzǔ's main point in this passage is: Whereas you kill the spy himself "as a punishment for letting out the secret," the object of killing the other man is only, as Ch'ên Hao puts it, "to stop his mouth" and prevent news leaking any further. If it had already been repeated to others, this object would not be gained. Either way, Sun Tzǔ lays himself open to the charge of inhumanity, though Tu Mu tries to defend him by saying that the man deserves to be put to death, for the spy would certainly not have told the secret unless the other had been at pains to worm it out of him.]

20. Whether the object be to crush an army, to storm a city, or to assassinate an individual, it is always necessary to begin by finding out the names of the attendants, the aides-de-camp,

[Literally "visitors," is equivalent, as Tu Yu says, to "those whose duty it is to keep the general supplied with information," which naturally necessitates frequent interviews with him.]

and door-keepers and sentries of the general in command. Our spies must be commissioned to ascertain these.

[As the first step, no doubt towards finding out if any of these important functionaries can be won over by bribery.]

21. The enemy's spies who have come to spy on us must be sought out, tempted with bribes, led away and comfortably housed. Thus they will become converted spies and available for our service.

22. It is through the information brought by the converted spy that we are able to acquire and employ local and inward spies.

[Tu Yu says: "through conversion of the enemy's spies we learn the enemy's condition." And Chang Yü says: "We must tempt the converted spy into our service, because it is he that knows which of the local inhabitants are greedy of gain, and which of the officials are open to corruption."]

23. It is owing to his information, again, that we can cause the doomed spy to carry false tidings to the enemy.

[Chang Yü says, "because the converted spy knows how the enemy can best be deceived."]

24. Lastly, it is by his information that the surviving spy can be used on appointed occasions.

25. The end and aim of spying in all its five varieties is knowledge of the enemy; and this knowledge can only be derived, in the first instance, from the converted spy.

[As explained in paragraphs 22–24. He not only brings information himself, but makes it possible to use the other kinds of spy to advantage.]

Hence it is essential that the converted spy be treated with the utmost liberality.

26. Of old, the rise of the Yin dynasty

[Sun Tzŭ means the Shang dynasty, founded in 1766 BC. Its name was changed to Yin by P'an Keng in 1401.

was due to I Chih

[Better known as I Yin, the famous general and statesman who took part in Ch'eng T'ang's campaign against Chieh Kuei.]

who had served under the Hsia. Likewise, the rise of the Chou dynasty was due to Lü Ya

[Lu Shang rose to high office under the tyrant Chou Hsin, whom he afterwards helped to overthrow. Popularly known as T'ai Kung, a title bestowed on him by Wen Wang, he is said to have composed a treatise on war, erroneously identified with the *Liu T'ao*.]

who had served under the Yin.

[There is less precision in the Chinese than I have thought it well to introduce into my translation, and the commentaries on the passage are by no means explicit. But, having regard to the context, we can hardly doubt that Sun Tzŭ is holding up I Chih and Lü Ya as illustrious examples of the converted spy, or something closely analogous. His suggestion is, that the Hsia and Yin dynasties were upset owing to the intimate knowledge of their weaknesses and shortcoming which these former ministers were able to impart to the other side. Mei Yao-ch'ên appears to resent any such aspersion on these historic names: "I Yin and Lü Ya," he says, "were not rebels against the Government. Hsia could not employ the former, hence Yin employed him. Yin could not employ the latter, hence Hou employed him. Their great achievements were all for the good of the people." Ho Shih is also indignant: "How should two divinely inspired men such as I and Lü have acted as common spies? Sun Tzŭ's mention of them simply means that the proper use of the five classes of spies is a matter which requires men of the highest mental caliber like I and Lü, whose wisdom and capacity qualified them for the task. The above words only emphasize this point." Ho Shih believes then that the two heroes are mentioned on account of their supposed skill in the use of spies. But this is very weak.]

27. Hence it is only the enlightened ruler and the wise general who will use the highest intelligence of the army for purposes of spying and thereby they achieve great results.

[Tu Mu closes with a note of warning: "Just as water, which carries a boat from bank to bank, may also be the means of sinking it, so reliance on spies, while production of great results, is oft-times the cause of utter destruction."]

Spies are a most important element in war, because on them depends an army's ability to move.

[Chia Lin says that an army without spies is like a man without ears or eyes.]

The Tao
Te Ching

BY LAO-TZŬ

TRANSLATED BY JAMES LEGGE

PART I

I
EMBODYING THE TAO

1. The Tao that can be trodden is not the enduring and unchanging Tao. The name that can be named is not the enduring and unchanging name.

2. (Conceived of as) having no name, it is the Originator of Heaven and Earth; (conceived of as) having a name, it is the Mother of all things.

3. Always without desire we must be found,
   If its deep mystery we would sound;
   But if desire always within us be,
   Its outer fringe is all that we shall see.

4. Under these two aspects, it is really the same; but as development takes place, it receives the different names. Together we call them the Mystery. Where the Mystery is the deepest is the gate of all that is subtle and wonderful.

II
THE NOURISHMENT OF THE PERSON

1. All in the world know the beauty of the beautiful, and in doing this they have (the idea of) what ugliness is; they all know the skill of the skillful, and in doing this they have (the idea of) what the want of skill is.

2. So it is that existence and non-existence give birth the one to (the idea of) the other; that difficulty and ease produce the one (the idea of) the other; that length and shortness fashion out the one the figure of the other; that (the ideas of) height and lowness arise from the contrast of the one with the other; that the musical notes and tones become harmonious through the relation of one with another; and that being before and behind give the idea of one following another.

3. Therefore the sage manages affairs without doing anything, and conveys his instructions without the use of speech.

4. All things spring up, and there is not one which declines to show itself; they grow, and there is no claim made for their ownership; they go through their processes, and there is no expectation (of a reward for the results). The work is accomplished, and there is no resting in it (as an achievement).

> The work is done, but how no one can see;
> 'Tis this that makes the power not cease to be.

III
KEEPING THE PEOPLE AT REST

1. Not to value and employ men of superior ability is the way to keep the people from rivalry among themselves; not to prize articles which are difficult to procure is the way to keep them from becoming thieves; not to show them what is likely to excite their desires is the way to keep their minds from disorder.

2. Therefore the sage, in the exercise of his government, empties their minds, fills their bellies, weakens their wills, and strengthens their bones.

3. He constantly (tries to) keep them without knowledge and without desire, and where there are those who have knowledge, to keep them from presuming to act (on it). When there is this abstinence from action, good order is universal.

IV
THE FOUNTAINLESS

1. The Tao is (like) the emptiness of a vessel; and in our employment of it we must be on our guard against all fullness. How deep and unfathomable it is, as if it were the Honored Ancestor of all things!

2. We should blunt our sharp points, and unravel the complications of things; we should attemper our brightness, and bring ourselves into agreement with the obscurity of others. How pure and still the Tao is, as if it would ever so continue!

3. I do not know whose son it is. It might appear to have been before God.

V
THE USE OF EMPTINESS

1. Heaven and Earth do not act from (the impulse of) any wish to be benevolent; they deal with all things as the dogs of grass are dealt with. The sages do not act from (any wish to be) benevolent; they deal with the people as the dogs of grass are dealt with.

2. May not the space between Heaven and Earth be compared to a bellows?

> 'Tis emptied, yet it loses not its power;
> 'Tis moved again, and sends forth air the more.
> Much speech to swift exhaustion lead we see;
> Your inner being guard, and keep it free.

VI
THE COMPLETION OF MATERIAL FORMS

> The valley spirit dies not, aye the same;
> The female mystery thus do we name.
> Its gate, from which at first they issued forth,
> Is called the root from which grew Heaven and Earth.
> Long and unbroken does its power remain,
> Used gently, and without the touch of pain.

VII
SHEATHING THE LIGHT

1. Heaven is long-enduring and Earth continues long. The reason why Heaven and Earth are able to endure and continue thus long is because they do not live of, or for, themselves. This is how they are able to continue and endure.

2. Therefore the sage puts his own person last, and yet it is found in the foremost place; he treats his person as if it were foreign to him, and yet that person is preserved. Is it not because he has no personal and private ends, that therefore such ends are realized?

VIII
THE PLACID AND CONTENTED NATURE

1. The highest excellence is like (that of) water. The excellence of water appears in its benefiting all things, and in its occupying, without

striving (to the contrary), the low place which all men dislike. Hence (its way) is near to (that of) the Tao.

2. The excellence of a residence is in (the suitability of) the place; that of the mind is in abysmal stillness; that of associations is in their being with the virtuous; that of government is in its securing good order; that of (the conduct of) affairs is in its ability; and that of (the initiation of) any movement is in its timeliness.

3. And when (one with the highest excellence) does not wrangle (about his low position), no one finds fault with him.

IX
FULLNESS AND COMPLACENCY IN SUCCESS CONTRARY TO THE TAO

1. It is better to leave a vessel unfilled, than to attempt to carry it when it is full. If you keep feeling a point that has been sharpened, the point cannot long preserve its sharpness.

2. When gold and jade fill the hall, their possessor cannot keep them safe. When wealth and honors lead to arrogancy, this brings its evil on itself. When the work is done, and one's name is becoming distinguished, to withdraw into obscurity is the way of Heaven.

X
POSSIBILITIES

1. When the intelligent and animal souls are held together in one embrace, they can be kept from separating. When one gives undivided attention to the (vital) breath, and brings it to the utmost degree of pliancy, he can become as a (tender) babe. When he has cleansed away the most mysterious sights (of his imagination), he can become without a flaw.

2. In loving the people and ruling the state, cannot he proceed without any (purpose of) action? In the opening and shutting of his gates of Heaven, cannot he do so as a female bird? While his intelligence reaches in every direction, cannot he (appear to) be without knowledge?

3. (The Tao) produces (all things) and nourishes them; it produces them and does not claim them as its own; it does all, and yet does not boast of it; it presides over all, and yet does not control them. This is what is called "The mysterious Quality" (of the Tao).

XI
THE USE OF WHAT HAS NO SUBSTANTIVE EXISTENCE

The thirty spokes unite in the one nave; but it is on the empty space (for the axle), that the use of the wheel depends. Clay is fashioned into vessels; but it is on their empty hollowness, that their use depends. The door and windows are cut out (from the walls) to form an apartment; but it is on the empty space (within), that its use depends. Therefore, what has a (positive) existence serves for profitable adaptation, and what has not that for (actual) usefulness.

XII
THE REPRESSION OF THE DESIRES

1. Color's five hues from th' eyes their sight will take;
   Music's five notes the ears as deaf can make;
   The flavors five deprive the mouth of taste;
   The chariot course, and the wild hunting waste
   Make mad the mind; and objects rare and strange,
   Sought for, men's conduct will to evil change.

2. Therefore the sage seeks to satisfy (the craving of) the belly, and not the (insatiable longing of the) eyes. He puts from him the latter, and prefers to seek the former.

XIII
LOATHING SHAME

1. Favor and disgrace would seem equally to be feared; honor and great calamity, to be regarded as personal conditions (of the same kind).

2. What is meant by speaking thus of favor and disgrace? Disgrace is being in a low position (after the enjoyment of favor). The getting of (favor) leads to the apprehension (of losing it), and the losing of it leads to the fear of (still greater calamity): this is what is meant by saying that favor and disgrace would seem equally to be feared.

   And what is meant by saying that honor and great calamity are to be (similarly) regarded as personal conditions? What makes me liable to great calamity is my having the body (which I call myself); if I had not the body, what great calamity could come to me?

3. Therefore he who would administer the kingdom, honoring it as he honors his own person, may be employed to govern it, and he who

would administer it with the love which he bears to his own person may be entrusted with it.

XIV
THE MANIFESTATION OF MYSTERY

1. We look at it, and we do not see it, and we name it "the Equable." We listen to it, and we do not hear it, and we name it "the Inaudible." We try to grasp it, and do not get hold of it, and we name it "the Subtle." With these three qualities, it cannot be made the subject of description; and hence we blend them together and obtain The One.

2. Its upper part is not bright, and its lower part is not obscure. Ceaseless in its action, it yet cannot be named, and then it again returns and becomes nothing. This is called the Form of the Formless, and the Semblance of the Invisible; this is called the Fleeting and Indeterminable.

3. We meet it and do not see its Front; we follow it, and do not see its Back. When we can lay hold of the Tao of old to direct the things of the present day, and are able to know it as it was of old in the beginning, this is called (unwinding) the clue of Tao.

XV
THE EXHIBITION OF THE QUALITY

1. The skillful masters (of the Tao) in old times, with a subtle and exquisite penetration, comprehended its mysteries, and were deep (also) so as to elude men's knowledge. As they were thus beyond men's knowledge, I will make an effort to describe of what sort they appeared to be.

2. Shrinking looked they like those who wade through a stream in winter; irresolute like those who are afraid of all around them; grave like a guest (in awe of his host); evanescent like ice that is melting away; unpretentious like wood that has not been fashioned into anything; vacant like a valley, and dull like muddy water.

3. Who can (make) the muddy water (clear)? Let it be still, and it will gradually become clear. Who can secure the condition of rest? Let movement go on, and the condition of rest will gradually arise.

4. They who preserve this method of the Tao do not wish to be full (of themselves). It is through their not being full of themselves that they can afford to seem worn and not appear new and complete.

XVI
RETURNING TO THE ROOT

1. The (state of) vacancy should be brought to the utmost degree, and that of stillness guarded with unwearying vigor. All things alike go through their processes of activity, and (then) we see them return (to their original state). When things (in the vegetable world) have displayed their luxuriant growth, we see each of them return to its root. This returning to their root is what we call the state of stillness; and that stillness may be called a reporting that they have fulfilled their appointed end.

2. The report of that fulfillment is the regular, unchanging rule. To know that unchanging rule is to be intelligent; not to know it leads to wild movements and evil issues. The knowledge of that unchanging rule produces a (grand) capacity and forbearance, and that capacity and forbearance lead to a community (of feeling with all things). From this community of feeling comes a kingliness of character; and he who is king-like goes on to be Heaven-like. In that likeness to Heaven he possesses the Tao. Possessed of the Tao, he endures long; and to the end of his bodily life, is exempt from all danger of decay.

XVII
THE UNADULTERATED INFLUENCE

1. In the highest antiquity, (the people) did not know that there were (their rulers). In the next age they loved them and praised them. In the next they feared them; in the next they despised them. Thus it was that when faith (in the Tao) was deficient (in the rulers) a want of faith in them ensued (in the people).

2. How irresolute did those (earliest rulers) appear, showing (by their reticence) the importance which they set upon their words! Their work was done and their undertakings were successful, while the people all said, 'We are as we are, of ourselves!'

XVIII
THE DECAY OF MANNERS

1. When the Great Tao (Way or Method) ceased to be observed, benevolence and righteousness came into vogue. (Then) appeared wisdom and shrewdness, and there ensued great hypocrisy.

2. When harmony no longer prevailed throughout the six kinships, filial sons found their manifestation; when the states and clans fell into disorder, loyal ministers appeared.

XIX
RETURNING TO THE UNADULTERATED INFLUENCE

1. If we could renounce our sageness and discard our wisdom, it would be better for the people a hundredfold. If we could renounce our benevolence and discard our righteousness, the people would again become filial and kindly. If we could renounce our artful contrivances and discard our (scheming for) gain, there would be no thieves nor robbers.

2. Those three methods (of government)
   Thought olden ways in elegance did fail
   And made these names their want of worth to veil;
   But simple views, and courses plain and true
   Would selfish ends and many lusts eschew.

XX
BEING DIFFERENT FROM ORDINARY MEN

1. When we renounce learning we have no troubles.

   The (ready) "yes," and (flattering) "yea";
   Small is the difference they display.
   But mark their issues, good and ill;
   What space the gulf between shall fill?

   What all men fear is indeed to be feared; but how wide and without end is the range of questions (asking to be discussed)!

2. The multitude of men look satisfied and pleased; as if enjoying a full banquet, as if mounted on a tower in spring. I alone seem listless and still, my desires having as yet given no indication of their presence. I am like an infant which has not yet smiled. I look dejected and forlorn, as if I had no home to go to. The multitude of men all have enough and to spare. I alone seem to have lost everything. My mind is that of a stupid man; I am in a state of chaos.

   Ordinary men look bright and intelligent, while I alone seem to be benighted. They look full of discrimination, while I alone am dull and confused. I seem to be carried about as on the sea, drifting as if I had nowhere to rest. All men have their spheres of action, while I alone seem dull and incapable, like a rude borderer. (Thus) I alone am different from other men, but I value the nursing-mother (the Tao).

XXI
THE EMPTY HEART

The grandest forms of active force
From Tao come, their only source.
Who can of Tao the nature tell?
Our sight it flies, our touch as well.
Eluding sight, eluding touch,
The forms of things all in it crouch;
Eluding touch, eluding sight,
There are their semblances, all right.
Profound it is, dark and obscure;
Things' essences all there endure.
Those essences the truth enfold
Of what, when seen, shall then be told.
Now it is so; 'twas so of old.
Its name—what passes not away;
So, in their beautiful array,
Things form and never know decay.

How know I that it is so with all the beauties of existing things? By this (nature of the Tao).

XXII
THE INCREASE GRANTED TO HUMILITY

1. The partial becomes complete; the crooked, straight; the empty, full; the worn out, new. He whose (desires) are few gets them; he whose (desires) are many goes astray.

2. Therefore the sage holds in his embrace the one thing (of humility), and manifests it to all the world. He is free from self-display, and therefore he shines; from self-assertion, and therefore he is distinguished; from self-boasting, and therefore his merit is acknowledged; from self-complacency, and therefore he acquires superiority. It is because he is thus free from striving that therefore no one in the world is able to strive with him.

3. That saying of the ancients that "the partial becomes complete" was not vainly spoken: all real completion is comprehended under it.

XXIII
ABSOLUTE VACANCY

1. Abstaining from speech marks him who is obeying the spontaneity of his nature. A violent wind does not last for a whole morning; a sudden rain does not last for the whole day. To whom is it that these (two) things are owing? To Heaven and Earth. If Heaven and Earth cannot make such (spasmodic) actings last long, how much less can man!

2. Therefore when one is making the Tao his business, those who are also pursuing it, agree with him in it, and those who are making the manifestation of its course their object agree with him in that; while even those who are failing in both these things agree with him where they fail.

3. Hence, those with whom he agrees as to the Tao have the happiness of attaining to it; those with whom he agrees as to its manifestation have the happiness of attaining to it; and those with whom he agrees in their failure have also the happiness of attaining (to the Tao). (But) when there is not faith sufficient (on his part), a want of faith (in him) ensues (on the part of the others).

XXIV
PAINFUL GRACIOUSNESS

He who stands on his tiptoes does not stand firm; he who stretches his legs does not walk (easily). (So), he who displays himself does not shine; he who asserts his own views is not distinguished; he who vaunts himself does not find his merit acknowledged; he who is self-conceited has no superiority allowed to him. Such conditions, viewed from the standpoint of the Tao, are like remnants of food, or a tumor on the body, which all dislike. Hence those who pursue (the course) of the Tao do not adopt and allow them.

XXV
REPRESENTATIONS OF THE MYSTERY

1. There was something undefined and complete, coming into existence before Heaven and Earth. How still it was and formless, standing alone, and undergoing no change, reaching everywhere and in no danger (of being exhausted)! It may be regarded as the Mother of all things.

2. I do not know its name, and I give it the designation of the Tao (the Way or Course). Making an effort (further) to give it a name I call it The Great.

3. Great, it passes on (in constant flow). Passing on, it becomes remote. Having become remote, it returns. Therefore the Tao is great; Heaven is great; Earth is great; and the (sage) king is also great. In the universe there are four that are great, and the (sage) king is one of them.

4. Man takes his law from the Earth; the Earth takes its law from Heaven; Heaven takes its law from the Tao. The law of the Tao is its being what it is.

XXVI
THE QUALITY OF GRAVITY

1. Gravity is the root of lightness; stillness, the ruler of movement.

2. Therefore a wise prince, marching the whole day, does not go far from his baggage wagons. Although he may have brilliant prospects to look at, he quietly remains (in his proper place), indifferent to them. How should the lord of a myriad chariots carry himself lightly before the kingdom? If he do act lightly, he has lost his root (of gravity); if he proceed to active movement, he will lose his throne.

XXVII
DEXTERITY IN USING THE TAO

1. The skillful traveler leaves no traces of his wheels or footsteps; the skillful speaker says nothing that can be found fault with or blamed; the skillful reckoner uses no tallies; the skillful closer needs no bolts or bars, while to open what he has shut will be impossible; the skillful binder uses no strings or knots, while to unloose what he has bound will be impossible. In the same way the sage is always skillful at saving men, and so he does not cast away any man; he is always skillful at saving things, and so he does not cast away anything. This is called "Hiding the light of his procedure."

2. Therefore the man of skill is a master (to be looked up to) by him who has not the skill; and he who has not the skill is the helper of (the reputation of) him who has the skill. If the one did not honor his master, and the other did not rejoice in his helper, an (observer), though intelligent, might greatly err about them. This is called "The utmost degree of mystery."

XXVIII
RETURNING TO SIMPLICITY

1. Who knows his manhood's strength,
   Yet still his female feebleness maintains;
   As to one channel flow the many drains,
   All come to him, yea, all beneath the sky.
   Thus he the constant excellence retains;
   The simple child again, free from all stains.

   Who knows how white attracts,
   Yet always keeps himself within black's shade,
   The pattern of humility displayed,
   Displayed in view of all beneath the sky;
   He in the unchanging excellence arrayed,
   Endless return to man's first state has made.

   Who knows how glory shines,
   Yet loves disgrace, nor e'er for it is pale;
   Behold his presence in a spacious vale,
   To which men come from all beneath the sky.
   The unchanging excellence completes its tale;
   The simple infant man in him we hail.

2. The unwrought material, when divided and distributed, forms vessels. The sage, when employed, becomes the Head of all the Officers (of government); and in his greatest regulations he employs no violent measures.

XXIX
TAKING NO ACTION

1. If any one should wish to get the kingdom for himself, and to effect this by what he does, I see that he will not succeed. The kingdom is a spirit-like thing, and cannot be got by active doing. He who would so win it destroys it; he who would hold it in his grasp loses it.

2. The course and nature of things is such that
   What was in front is now behind;
   What warmed anon we freezing find.
   Strength is of weakness oft the spoil;
   The store in ruins mocks our toil.

Hence the sage puts away excessive effort, extravagance, and easy indulgence.

XXX
A CAVEAT AGAINST WAR

1. He who would assist a lord of men in harmony with the Tao will not assert his mastery in the kingdom by force of arms. Such a course is sure to meet with its proper return.

2. Wherever a host is stationed, briars and thorns spring up. In the sequence of great armies there are sure to be bad years.

3. A skillful (commander) strikes a decisive blow, and stops. He does not dare (by continuing his operations) to assert and complete his mastery. He will strike the blow, but will be on his guard against being vain or boastful or arrogant in consequence of it. He strikes it as a matter of necessity; he strikes it, but not from a wish for mastery.

4. When things have attained their strong maturity they become old. This may be said to be not in accordance with the Tao: and what is not in accordance with it soon comes to an end.

XXXI
STILLING WAR

1. Now arms, however beautiful, are instruments of evil omen, hateful, it may be said, to all creatures. Therefore they who have the Tao do not like to employ them.

2. The superior man ordinarily considers the left hand the most honorable place, but in time of war the right hand. Those sharp weapons are instruments of evil omen, and not the instruments of the superior man; he uses them only on the compulsion of necessity. Calm and repose are what he prizes; victory (by force of arms) is to him undesirable. To consider this desirable would be to delight in the slaughter of men; and he who delights in the slaughter of men cannot get his will in the kingdom.

3. On occasions of festivity to be on the left hand is the prized position; on occasions of mourning, the right hand. The second in command of the army has his place on the left; the general commanding in chief has his on the right; his place, that is, is assigned to him as in the rites of mourning. He who has killed multitudes of men should weep for them with the bitterest grief; and the victor in battle has his place (rightly) according to those rites.

XXXII
THE TAO WITH NO NAME

1. The Tao, considered as unchanging, has no name.

2. Though in its primordial simplicity it may be small, the whole world dares not deal with (one embodying) it as a minister. If a feudal prince or the king could guard and hold it, all would spontaneously submit themselves to him.

3. Heaven and Earth (under its guidance) unite together and send down the sweet dew, which, without the directions of men, reaches equally everywhere as of its own accord.

4. As soon as it proceeds to action, it has a name. When it once has that name, (men) can know to rest in it. When they know to rest in it, they can be free from all risk of failure and error.

5. The relation of the Tao to all the world is like that of the great rivers and seas to the streams from the valleys.

XXXIII
DISCRIMINATING BETWEEN (DIFFERENT) ATTRIBUTES

1. He who knows other men is discerning; he who knows himself is intelligent. He who overcomes others is strong; he who overcomes himself is mighty. He who is satisfied with his lot is rich; he who goes on acting with energy has a (firm) will.

2. He who does not fail in the requirements of his position, continues long; he who dies and yet does not perish, has longevity.

XXXIV
THE TASK OF ACHIEVEMENT

1. All-pervading is the Great Tao! It may be found on the left hand and on the right.

2. All things depend on it for their production, which it gives to them, not one refusing obedience to it. When its work is accomplished, it does not claim the name of having done it. It clothes all things as with a garment, and makes no assumption of being their lord; it may be named in the smallest things. All things return (to their root and disappear), and do not know that it is it which presides over their doing so; it may be named in the greatest things.

3. Hence the sage is able (in the same way) to accomplish his great achievements. It is through his not making himself great that he can accomplish them.

XXXV
THE ATTRIBUTE OF BENEVOLENCE

1. To him who holds in his hands the Great Image (of the invisible Tao), the whole world repairs. Men resort to him, and receive no hurt, but (find) rest, peace, and the feeling of ease.

2. Music and dainties will make the passing guest stop (for a time). But though the Tao as it comes from the mouth, seems insipid and has no flavor, though it seems not worth being looked at or listened to, the use of it is inexhaustible.

XXXVI
MINIMIZING THE LIGHT

1. When one is about to take an inspiration, he is sure to make a (previous) expiration; when he is going to weaken another, he will first strengthen him; when he is going to overthrow another, he will first have raised him up; when he is going to despoil another, he will first have made gifts to him: this is called "Hiding the light (of his procedure)."

2. The soft overcomes the hard; and the weak the strong.

3. Fishes should not be taken from the deep; instruments for the profit of a state should not be shown to the people.

XXXVII
THE EXERCISE OF GOVERNMENT

1. The Tao in its regular course does nothing (for the sake of doing it), and so there is nothing which it does not do.

2. If princes and kings were able to maintain it, all things would of themselves be transformed by them.

3. If this transformation became to me an object of desire, I would express the desire by the nameless simplicity.

> Simplicity without a name
> Is free from all external aim.
> With no desire, at rest and still,
> All things go right as of their will.

PART II

XXXVIII
ABOUT THE ATTRIBUTES OF THE TAO

1. (Those who) possessed in highest degree the attributes (of the Tao) did not (seek) to show them, and therefore they possessed them (in fullest measure). (Those who) possessed in a lower degree those attributes (sought how) not to lose them, and therefore they did not possess them (in fullest measure).

2. (Those who) possessed in the highest degree those attributes did nothing (with a purpose), and had no need to do anything. (Those who) possessed them in a lower degree were (always) doing, and had need to be so doing.

3. (Those who) possessed the highest benevolence were (always seeking) to carry it out, and had no need to be doing so. (Those who) possessed the highest righteousness were (always seeking) to carry it out, and had need to be so doing.

4. (Those who) possessed the highest (sense of) propriety were (always seeking) to show it, and when men did not respond to it, they bared the arm and marched up to them.

5. Thus it was that when the Tao was lost, its attributes appeared; when its attributes were lost, benevolence appeared; when benevolence was lost, righteousness appeared; and when righteousness was lost, the proprieties appeared.

6. Now propriety is the attenuated form of leal-heartedness and good faith, and is also the commencement of disorder; swift apprehension is (only) a flower of the Tao, and is the beginning of stupidity.

7. Thus it is that the Great man abides by what is solid, and eschews what is flimsy; dwells with the fruit and not with the flower. It is thus that he puts away the one and makes choice of the other.

XXXIX
THE ORIGIN OF THE LAW

1. The things which from of old have got the One (the Tao) are—

    Heaven which by it is bright and pure;
    Earth rendered thereby firm and sure;
    Spirits with powers by it supplied;
    Valleys kept full throughout their void
    All creatures which through it do live
    Princes and kings who from it get
    The model which to all they give.

    All these are the results of the One (Tao).

2. If Heaven were not thus pure, it soon would rend;
    If Earth were not thus sure, 'twould break and bend;
    Without these powers, the spirits soon would fail;
    If not so filled, the drought would parch each vale;
    Without that life, creatures would pass away;
    Princes and kings, without that moral sway,
    However grand and high, would all decay.

3. Thus it is that dignity finds its (firm) root in its (previous) meanness, and what is lofty finds its stability in the lowness (from which it rises). Hence princes and kings call themselves "Orphans," "Men of small virtue," and as "Carriages without a nave." Is not this an acknowledgment that in their considering themselves mean they see the foundation of their dignity? So it is that in the enumeration of the different parts of a carriage we do not come on what makes it answer the ends of a carriage. They do not wish to show themselves elegant-looking as jade, but (prefer) to be coarse-looking as an (ordinary) stone.

XL
DISPENSING WITH THE USE (OF MEANS)

1. The movement of the Tao
      By contraries proceeds;
    And weakness marks the course
      Of Tao's mighty deeds.

2. All things under Heaven sprang from It as existing (and named); that existence sprang from It as non-existent (and not named).

XLI
SAMENESS AND DIFFERENCE

1. Scholars of the highest class, when they hear about the Tao, earnestly carry it into practice. Scholars of the middle class, when they have heard about it, seem now to keep it and now to lose it. Scholars of the lowest class, when they have heard about it, laugh greatly at it. If it were not (thus) laughed at, it would not be fit to be the Tao.

2. Therefore the sentence-makers have thus expressed themselves:

> The Tao, when brightest seen, seems light to lack;
> Who progress in it makes, seems drawing back;
> Its even way is like a rugged track.
> Its highest virtue from the vale doth rise;
> Its greatest beauty seems to offend the eyes;
> And he has most whose lot the least supplies.
> Its firmest virtue seems but poor and low;
> Its solid truth seems change to undergo;
> Its largest square doth yet no corner show
> A vessel great, it is the slowest made;
> Loud is its sound, but never word it said;
> A semblance great, the shadow of a shade.

3. The Tao is hidden, and has no name; but it is the Tao which is skillful at imparting (to all things what they need) and making them complete.

XLII
THE TRANSFORMATIONS OF THE TAO

1. The Tao produced One; One produced Two; Two produced Three; Three produced All things. All things leave behind them the Obscurity (out of which they have come), and go forward to embrace the Brightness (into which they have emerged), while they are harmonized by the Breath of Vacancy.

2. What men dislike is to be orphans, to have little virtue, to be as carriages without naves; and yet these are the designations which kings and princes use for themselves. So it is that some things are increased by being diminished, and others are diminished by being increased.

3. What other men (thus) teach, I also teach. The violent and strong do not die their natural death. I will make this the basis of my teaching.

XLIII
THE UNIVERSAL USE
(OF THE ACTION IN WEAKNESS OF THE TAO)

1. The softest thing in the world dashes against and overcomes the hardest; that which has no (substantial) existence enters where there is no crevice. I know hereby what advantage belongs to doing nothing (with a purpose).

2. There are few in the world who attain to the teaching without words, and the advantage arising from non-action.

XLIV
CAUTIONS

1. Or fame or life,
        Which do you hold more dear?
    Or life or wealth,
        To which would you adhere?
    Keep life and lose those other things;
    Keep them and lose your life: which brings
        Sorrow and pain more near?

2. Thus we may see,
        Who cleaves to fame
        Rejects what is more great;
    Who loves large stores
        Gives up the richer state.

3. Who is content
    Needs fear no shame.
    Who knows to stop
    Incurs no blame.
    From danger free
    Long live shall he.

XLV
GREAT OR OVERFLOWING VIRTUE

1. Who thinks his great achievements poor
    Shall find his vigor long endure.
    Of greatest fullness, deemed a void,
    Exhaustion ne'er shall stem the tide.
    Do thou what's straight still crooked deem;

Thy greatest art still stupid seem,
And eloquence a stammering scream.

2. Constant action overcomes cold; being still overcomes heat. Purity and stillness give the correct law to all under Heaven.

XLVI
THE MODERATING OF DESIRE OR AMBITION

1. When the Tao prevails in the world, they send back their swift horses to (draw) the dung-carts. When the Tao is disregarded in the world, the war-horses breed in the border lands.

2. There is no guilt greater than to sanction ambition; no calamity greater than to be discontented with one's lot; no fault greater than the wish to be getting. Therefore the sufficiency of contentment is an enduring and unchanging sufficiency.

XLVII
SURVEYING WHAT IS FAR OFF

1. Without going outside his door, one understands (all that takes place) under the sky; without looking out from his window, one sees the Tao of Heaven. The farther that one goes out (from himself), the less he knows.

2. Therefore the sages got their knowledge without traveling; gave their (right) names to things without seeing them; and accomplished their ends without any purpose of doing so.

XLVIII
FORGETTING KNOWLEDGE

1. He who devotes himself to learning (seeks) from day to day to increase (his knowledge); he who devotes himself to the Tao (seeks) from day to day to diminish (his doing).

2. He diminishes it and again diminishes it, till he arrives at doing nothing (on purpose). Having arrived at this point of non-action, there is nothing which he does not do.

3. He who gets as his own all under Heaven does so by giving himself no trouble (with that end). If one take trouble (with that end), he is not equal to getting as his own all under Heaven.

XLIX
THE QUALITY OF INDULGENCE

1. The sage has no invariable mind of his own; he makes the mind of the people his mind.

2. To those who are good (to me), I am good; and to those who are not good (to me), I am also good; and thus (all) get to be good. To those who are sincere (with me), I am sincere; and to those who are not sincere (with me), I am also sincere; and thus (all) get to be sincere.

3. The sage has in the world an appearance of indecision, and keeps his mind in a state of indifference to all. The people all keep their eyes and ears directed to him, and he deals with them all as his children.

L
THE VALUE SET ON LIFE

1. Men come forth and live; they enter (again) and die.

2. Of every ten three are ministers of life (to themselves); and three are ministers of death.

3. There are also three in every ten whose aim is to live, but whose movements tend to the land (or place) of death. And for what reason? Because of their excessive endeavors to perpetuate life.

4. But I have heard that he who is skillful in managing the life entrusted to him for a time travels on the land without having to shun rhinoceros or tiger, and enters a host without having to avoid buff coat or sharp weapon. The rhinoceros finds no place in him into which to thrust its horn, nor the tiger a place in which to fix its claws, nor the weapon a place to admit its point. And for what reason? Because there is in him no place of death.

LI
THE OPERATION (OF THE TAO)
IN NOURISHING THINGS

1. All things are produced by the Tao, and nourished by its outflowing operation. They receive their forms according to the nature of each, and are completed according to the circumstances of their condition. Therefore all things without exception honor the Tao, and exalt its outflowing operation.

2. This honoring of the Tao and exalting of its operation is not the result of any ordination, but always a spontaneous tribute.

3. Thus it is that the Tao produces (all things), nourishes them, brings them to their full growth, nurses them, completes them, matures them, maintains them, and overspreads them.

4. It produces them and makes no claim to the possession of them; it carries them through their processes and does not vaunt its ability in doing so; it brings them to maturity and exercises no control over them; this is called its mysterious operation.

LII
RETURNING TO THE SOURCE

1. (The Tao) which originated all under the sky is to be considered as the mother of them all.

2. When the mother is found, we know what her children should be. When one knows that he is his mother's child, and proceeds to guard (the qualities of) the mother that belong to him, to the end of his life he will be free from all peril.

3. Let him keep his mouth closed, and shut up the portals (of his nostrils), and all his life he will be exempt from laborious exertion. Let him keep his mouth open, and (spend his breath) in the promotion of his affairs, and all his life there will be no safety for him.

4. The perception of what is small is (the secret of) clear-sightedness; the guarding of what is soft and tender is (the secret of) strength.

5. Who uses well his light,
Reverting to its (source so) bright,
Will from his body ward all blight,
And hides the unchanging from men's sight.

LIII
INCREASE OF EVIDENCE

1. If I were suddenly to become known, and (put into a position to) conduct (a government) according to the Great Tao, what I should be most afraid of would be a boastful display.

2. The Great Tao (or Way) is very level and easy; but people love the by-ways.

3. Their court(-yards and buildings) shall be well kept, but their fields shall be ill-cultivated, and their granaries very empty. They shall wear elegant and ornamented robes, carry a sharp sword at their girdle, pamper themselves in eating and drinking, and have a superabundance of property and wealth; such (princes) may be called robbers and boasters. This is contrary to the Tao surely!

LIV
THE CULTIVATION (OF THE TAO),
AND THE OBSERVATION (OF ITS EFFECTS)

1. What (Tao's) skillful planter plants
      Can never be uptorn;
    What his skillful arms enfold,
      From him can ne'er be borne.
    Sons shall bring in lengthening line,
    Sacrifices to his shrine.

2. Tao when nursed within one's self,
      His vigor will make true;
    And where the family it rules
      What riches will accrue!
    The neighborhood where it prevails
      In thriving will abound;
    And when 'tis seen throughout the state,
      Good fortune will be found.
    Employ it the kingdom o'er,
      And men thrive all around.

3. In this way the effect will be seen in the person, by the observation of different cases; in the family; in the neighborhood; in the state; and in the kingdom.

4. How do I know that this effect is sure to hold thus all under the sky? By this (method of observation).

LV
THE MYSTERIOUS CHARM

1. He who has in himself abundantly the attributes (of the Tao) is like an infant. Poisonous insects will not sting him; fierce beasts will not seize him; birds of prey will not strike him.

2. (The infant's) bones are weak and its sinews soft, but yet its grasp is firm. It knows not yet the union of male and female, and yet its virile member may be excited; showing the perfection of its physical essence. All day long it will cry without its throat becoming hoarse; showing the harmony (in its constitution).

3. To him by whom this harmony is known,
   (The secret of) the unchanging (Tao) is shown,
   And in the knowledge wisdom finds its throne.
   All life-increasing arts to evil turn;
   Where the mind makes the vital breath to burn,
   (False) is the strength, (and o'er it we should mourn.)

4. When things have become strong, they (then) become old, which may be said to be contrary to the Tao. Whatever is contrary to the Tao soon ends.

LVI
THE MYSTERIOUS EXCELLENCE

1. He who knows (the Tao) does not (care to) speak (about it); he who is (ever ready to) speak about it does not know it.

2. He (who knows it) will keep his mouth shut and close the portals (of his nostrils). He will blunt his sharp points and unravel the complications of things; he will attemper his brightness, and bring himself into agreement with the obscurity (of others). This is called "the Mysterious Agreement."

3. (Such a one) cannot be treated familiarly or distantly; he is beyond all consideration of profit or injury; of nobility or meanness: he is the noblest man under Heaven.

LVII
THE GENUINE INFLUENCE

1. A state may be ruled by (measures of) correction; weapons of war may be used with crafty dexterity; (but) the kingdom is made one's own (only) by freedom from action and purpose.

2. How do I know that it is so? By these facts: In the kingdom the multiplication of prohibitive enactments increases the poverty of the people; the more implements to add to their profit that the people have, the greater disorder is there in the state and clan; the more acts of crafty dexterity that men possess, the more do strange

contrivances appear; the more display there is of legislation, the more thieves and robbers there are.

3. Therefore a sage has said, "I will do nothing (of purpose), and the people will be transformed of themselves; I will be fond of keeping still, and the people will of themselves become correct. I will take no trouble about it, and the people will of themselves become rich; I will manifest no ambition, and the people will of themselves attain to the primitive simplicity."

LVIII
TRANSFORMATION ACCORDING TO CIRCUMSTANCES

1. The government that seems the most unwise,
    Oft goodness to the people best supplies;
    That which is meddling, touching everything,
    Will work but ill, and disappointment bring.

    Misery! Happiness is to be found by its side! Happiness! Misery lurks beneath it! Who knows what either will come to in the end?

2. Shall we then dispense with correction? The (method of) correction shall by a turn become distortion, and the good in it shall by a turn become evil. The delusion of the people (on this point) has indeed subsisted for a long time.

3. Therefore the sage is (like) a square which cuts no one (with its angles); (like) a corner which injures no one (with its sharpness). He is straightforward, but allows himself no license; he is bright, but does not dazzle.

LIX
GUARDING THE TAO

1. For regulating the human (in our constitution) and rendering the (proper) service to the heavenly, there is nothing like moderation.

2. It is only by this moderation that there is effected an early return (to man's normal state). That early return is what I call the repeated accumulation of the attributes (of the Tao). With that repeated accumulation of those attributes, there comes the subjugation (of every obstacle to such return). Of this subjugation we know not what shall be the limit; and when one knows not what the limit shall be, he may be the ruler of a state.

3. He who possesses the mother of the state may continue long. His case is like that (of the plant) of which we say that its roots are deep and its flower stalks firm—this is the way to secure that its enduring life shall long be seen.

LX
OCCUPYING THE THRONE

1. Governing a great state is like cooking small fish.

2. Let the kingdom be governed according to the Tao, and the manes of the departed will not manifest their spiritual energy. It is not that those manes have not that spiritual energy, but it will not be employed to hurt men. It is not that it could not hurt men, but neither does the ruling sage hurt them.

3. When these two do not injuriously affect each other, their good influences converge in the virtue (of the Tao).

LXI
THE ATTRIBUTE OF HUMILITY

1. What makes a great state is its being (like) a low-lying, down-flowing (stream); it becomes the center to which tend (all the small states) under Heaven.

2. (To illustrate from) the case of all females: the female always overcomes the male by her stillness. Stillness may be considered (a sort of) abasement.

3. Thus it is that a great state, by condescending to small states, gains them for itself; and that small states, by abasing themselves to a great state, win it over to them. In the one case the abasement leads to gaining adherents, in the other case to procuring favor.

4. The great state only wishes to unite men together and nourish them; a small state only wishes to be received by, and to serve, the other. Each gets what it desires, but the great state must learn to abase itself.

LXII
PRACTICING THE TAO

1. Tao has of all things the most honored place.
No treasures give good men so rich a grace;
Bad men it guards, and doth their ill efface.

2. (Its) admirable words can purchase honor; (its) admirable deeds can raise their performer above others. Even men who are not good are not abandoned by it.

3. Therefore when the sovereign occupies his place as the Son of Heaven, and he has appointed his three ducal ministers, though (a prince) were to send in a round symbol-of-rank large enough to fill both the hands, and that as the precursor of the team of horses (in the courtyard), such an offering would not be equal to (a lesson of) this Tao, which one might present on his knees.

4. Why was it that the ancients prized this Tao so much? Was it not because it could be got by seeking for it, and the guilty could escape (from the stain of their guilt) by it? This is the reason why all under Heaven consider it the most valuable thing.

LXIII
THINKING IN THE BEGINNING

1. (It is the way of the Tao) to act without (thinking of) acting; to conduct affairs without (feeling the) trouble of them; to taste without discerning any flavor; to consider what is small as great, and a few as many; and to recompense injury with kindness.

2. (The master of it) anticipates things that are difficult while they are easy, and does things that would become great while they are small. All difficult things in the world are sure to arise from a previous state in which they were easy, and all great things from one in which they were small. Therefore the sage, while he never does what is great, is able on that account to accomplish the greatest things.

3. He who lightly promises is sure to keep but little faith; he who is continually thinking things easy is sure to find them difficult. Therefore the sage sees difficulty even in what seems easy, and so never has any difficulties.

LXIV
GUARDING THE MINUTE

1. That which is at rest is easily kept hold of; before a thing has given indications of its presence, it is easy to take measures against it; that which is brittle is easily broken; that which is very small is easily dispersed. Action should be taken before a thing has made its appearance; order should be secured before disorder has begun.

2. The tree which fills the arms grew from the tiniest sprout; the tower of nine stories rose from a (small) heap of earth; the journey of a thousand *li* commenced with a single step.

3. He who acts (with an ulterior purpose) does harm; he who takes hold of a thing (in the same way) loses his hold. The sage does not act (so), and therefore does no harm; he does not lay hold (so), and therefore does not lose his hold. (But) people in their conduct of affairs are constantly ruining them when they are on the eve of success. If they were careful at the end, as (they should be) at the beginning, they would not so ruin them.

4. Therefore the sage desires what (other men) do not desire, and does not prize things difficult to get; he learns what (other men) do not learn, and turns back to what the multitude of men have passed by. Thus he helps the natural development of all things, and does not dare to act (with an ulterior purpose of his own).

LXV
PURE, UNMIXED EXCELLENCE

1. The ancients who showed their skill in practicing the Tao did so, not to enlighten the people, but rather to make them simple and ignorant.

2. The difficulty in governing the people arises from their having much knowledge. He who (tries to) govern a state by his wisdom is a scourge to it; while he who does not (try to) do so is a blessing.

3. He who knows these two things finds in them also his model and rule. Ability to know this model and rule constitutes what we call the mysterious excellence (of a governor). Deep and far-reaching is such mysterious excellence, showing indeed its possessor as opposite to others, but leading them to a great conformity to him.

LXVI
PUTTING ONE'S SELF LAST

1. That whereby the rivers and seas are able to receive the homage and tribute of all the valley streams, is their skill in being lower than they; it is thus that they are the kings of them all. So it is that the sage (ruler), wishing to be above men, puts himself by his words below them, and, wishing to be before them, places his person behind them.

2. In this way though he has his place above them, men do not feel his weight, nor though he has his place before them, do they feel it an injury to them.

3. Therefore all in the world delight to exalt him and do not weary of him. Because he does not strive, no one finds it possible to strive with him.

LXVII
THREE PRECIOUS THINGS

1. All the world says that, while my Tao is great, it yet appears to be inferior (to other systems of teaching). Now it is just its greatness that makes it seem to be inferior. If it were like any other (system), for long would its smallness have been known!

2. But I have three precious things which I prize and hold fast. The first is gentleness; the second is economy; and the third is shrinking from taking precedence of others.

3. With that gentleness I can be bold; with that economy I can be liberal; shrinking from taking precedence of others, I can become a vessel of the highest honor. Nowadays they give up gentleness and are all for being bold; economy, and are all for being liberal; the hindmost place, and seek only to be foremost — (of all which the end is) death.

4. Gentleness is sure to be victorious even in battle, and firmly to maintain its ground. Heaven will save its possessor, by his (very) gentleness protecting him.

LXVIII
MATCHING HEAVEN

He who in (Tao's) wars has skill
   Assumes no martial port;
He who fights with most good will
   To rage makes no resort.
He who vanquishes yet still
   Keeps from his foes apart;
He whose hests men most fulfill
   Yet humbly plies his art.
Thus we say, "He ne'er contends,
   And therein is his might."
Thus we say, "Men's wills he bends,

That they with him unite."
Thus we say, "Like Heaven's his ends,
    No sage of old more bright."

LXIX
THE USE OF THE MYSTERIOUS (TAO)

1. A master of the art of war has said, "I do not dare to be the host (to commence the war); I prefer to be the guest (to act on the defensive). I do not dare to advance an inch; I prefer to retire a foot." This is called marshalling the ranks where there are no ranks; baring the arms (to fight) where there are no arms to bare; grasping the weapon where there is no weapon to grasp; advancing against the enemy where there is no enemy.

2. There is no calamity greater than lightly engaging in war. To do that is near losing (the gentleness) which is so precious. Thus it is that when opposing weapons are (actually) crossed, he who deplores (the situation) conquers.

LXX
THE DIFFICULTY OF BEING (RIGHTLY) KNOWN

1. My words are very easy to know, and very easy to practice; but there is no one in the world who is able to know and able to practice them.

2. There is an originating and all-comprehending (principle) in my words, and an authoritative law for the things (which I enforce). It is because they do not know these, that men do not know me.

3. They who know me are few, and I am on that account (the more) to be prized. It is thus that the sage wears (a poor garb of) hair cloth, while he carries his (signet of) jade in his bosom.

LXXI
THE DISEASE OF KNOWING

1. To know and yet (think) we do not know is the highest (attainment); not to know (and yet think) we do know is a disease.

2. It is simply by being pained at (the thought of) having this disease that we are preserved from it. The sage has not the disease. He knows the pain that would be inseparable from it, and therefore he does not have it.

LXXII
LOVING ONE'S SELF

1. When the people do not fear what they ought to fear, that which is their great dread will come on them.

2. Let them not thoughtlessly indulge themselves in their ordinary life; let them not act as if weary of what that life depends on.

3. It is by avoiding such indulgence that such weariness does not arise.

4. Therefore the sage knows (these things) of himself, but does not parade (his knowledge); loves, but does not (appear to set a) value on, himself. And thus he puts the latter alternative away and makes choice of the former.

LXXIII
ALLOWING MEN TO TAKE THEIR COURSE

1. He whose boldness appears in his daring (to do wrong, in defiance of the laws) is put to death; he whose boldness appears in his not daring (to do so) lives on. Of these two cases the one appears to be advantageous, and the other to be injurious. But

> When Heaven's anger smites a man,
> Who the cause shall truly scan?

On this account the sage feels a difficulty (as to what to do in the former case).

2. It is the way of Heaven not to strive, and yet it skillfully overcomes; not to speak, and yet it is skillful in obtaining a reply; does not call, and yet men come to it of themselves. Its demonstrations are quiet, and yet its plans are skillful and effective. The meshes of the net of Heaven are large; far apart, but letting nothing escape.

LXXIV
RESTRAINING DELUSION

1. The people do not fear death; to what purpose is it to (try to) frighten them with death? If the people were always in awe of death, and I could always seize those who do wrong, and put them to death, who would dare to do wrong?

2. There is always One who presides over the infliction of death. He who would inflict death in the room of him who so presides over it may be described as hewing wood instead of a great carpenter. Seldom is it that he who undertakes the hewing, instead of the great carpenter, does not cut his own hands!

LXXV
HOW GREEDINESS INJURES

1. The people suffer from famine because of the multitude of taxes consumed by their superiors. It is through this that they suffer famine.

2. The people are difficult to govern because of the (excessive) agency of their superiors (in governing them). It is through this that they are difficult to govern.

3. The people make light of dying because of the greatness of their labors in seeking for the means of living. It is this which makes them think light of dying. Thus it is that to leave the subject of living altogether out of view is better than to set a high value on it.

LXXVI
A WARNING AGAINST (TRUSTING IN) STRENGTH

1. Man at his birth is supple and weak; at his death, firm and strong. (So it is with) all things. Trees and plants, in their early growth, are soft and brittle; at their death, dry and withered.

2. Thus it is that firmness and strength are the concomitants of death; softness and weakness, the concomitants of life.

3. Hence he who (relies on) the strength of his forces does not conquer; and a tree which is strong will fill the out-stretched arms, (and thereby invites the feller.)

4. Therefore the place of what is firm and strong is below, and that of what is soft and weak is above.

LXXVII
THE WAY OF HEAVEN

1. May not the Way (or Tao) of Heaven be compared to the (method of) bending a bow? The (part of the bow) which was high is brought low, and what was low is raised up. (So Heaven) diminishes where there is superabundance, and supplements where there is deficiency.

2. It is the Way of Heaven to diminish superabundance, and to supplement deficiency. It is not so with the way of man. He takes away from those who have not enough to add to his own superabundance.

3. Who can take his own superabundance and therewith serve all under Heaven? Only he who is in possession of the Tao!

4. Therefore the (ruling) sage acts without claiming the results as his; he achieves his merit and does not rest (arrogantly) in it: he does not wish to display his superiority.

LXXVIII
THINGS TO BE BELIEVED

1. There is nothing in the world more soft and weak than water, and yet for attacking things that are firm and strong there is nothing that can take precedence of it; for there is nothing (so effectual) for which it can be changed.

2. Every one in the world knows that the soft overcomes the hard, and the weak the strong, but no one is able to carry it out in practice.

3. Therefore a sage has said,

    > He who accepts his state's reproach,
    > Is hailed therefore its altars' lord;
    > To him who bears men's direful woes
    > They all the name of King accord.

4. Words that are strictly true seem to be paradoxical.

LXXIX
ADHERENCE TO BOND OR COVENANT

1. When a reconciliation is effected (between two parties) after a great animosity, there is sure to be a grudge remaining (in the mind of the one who was wrong). And how can this be beneficial (to the other)?

2. Therefore (to guard against this), the sage keeps the left-hand portion of the record of the engagement, and does not insist on the (speedy) fulfillment of it by the other party. (So), he who has the attributes (of the Tao) regards (only) the conditions of the engagement, while he who has not those attributes regards only the conditions favorable to himself.

3. In the Way of Heaven, there is no partiality of love; it is always on the side of the good man.

LXXX
STANDING ALONE

1. In a little state with a small population, I would so order it, that, though there were individuals with the abilities of ten or a hundred men, there should be no employment of them; I would make the people, while looking on death as a grievous thing, yet not remove elsewhere (to avoid it).

2. Though they had boats and carriages, they should have no occasion to ride in them; though they had buff coats and sharp weapons, they should have no occasion to don or use them.

3. I would make the people return to the use of knotted cords (instead of the written characters).

4. They should think their (coarse) food sweet; their (plain) clothes beautiful; their (poor) dwellings places of rest; and their common (simple) ways sources of enjoyment.

5. There should be a neighboring state within sight, and the voices of the fowls and dogs should be heard all the way from it to us, but I would make the people to old age, even to death, not have any intercourse with it.

LXXXI
THE MANIFESTATION OF SIMPLICITY

1. Sincere words are not fine; fine words are not sincere. Those who are skilled (in the Tao) do not dispute (about it); the disputatious are not skilled in it. Those who know (the Tao) are not extensively learned; the extensively learned do not know it.

2. The sage does not accumulate (for himself). The more that he expends for others, the more does he possess of his own; the more that he gives to others, the more does he have himself.

3. With all the sharpness of the Way of Heaven, it injures not; with all the doing in the way of the sage he does not strive.

Confucian Analects

BOOK I

HSIO R

I

1. The Master said, "Is it not pleasant to learn with a constant perseverance and application?

2. "Is it not delightful to have friends coming from distant quarters?"

3. "Is he not a man of complete virtue, who feels no discomposure though men may take no note of him?"

II

1. The philosopher Yû said, "They are few who, being filial and fraternal, are fond of offending against their superiors. There have been none, who, not liking to offend against their superiors, have been fond of stirring up confusion.

2. "The superior man bends his attention to what is radical. That being established, all practical courses naturally grow up. Filial piety and fraternal submission! Are they not the root of all benevolent actions?"

III

The Master said, "Fine words and an insinuating appearance are seldom associated with true virtue."

IV

The philosopher Tsǎng said, "I daily examine myself on three points: whether, in transacting business for others, I may have been not faithful—whether, in intercourse with friends, I may have been not sincere—whether I may have not mastered and practiced the instructions of my teacher."

V

The Master said, "To rule a country of a thousand chariots, there must be reverent attention to business, and sincerity; economy in expenditure, and love for men; and the employment of the people at the proper seasons."

VI

The Master said, "A youth, when at home, should be filial, and, abroad, respectful to his elders. He should be earnest and truthful. He should overflow in love to all, and cultivate the friendship of the good. When he has time and opportunity, after the performance of these things, he should employ them in polite studies."

VII

Tsze-hsiâ said, "If a man withdraws his mind from the love of beauty, and applies it as sincerely to the love of the virtuous; if, in serving his parents, he can exert his utmost strength; if, in serving his prince, he can devote his life; if, in his intercourse with his friends, his words are sincere: although men say that he has not learned, I will certainly say that he has."

VIII

1. The Master said, "If the scholar be not grave, he will not call forth any veneration, and his learning will not be solid.

2. "Hold faithfulness and sincerity as first principles.

3. "Have no friends not equal to yourself.

4. "When you have faults, do not fear to abandon them."

IX

The philosopher Tsăng said, "Let there be a careful attention to perform the funeral rites to parents, and let them be followed when long gone with the ceremonies of sacrifice—then the virtue of the people will resume its proper excellence."

X

1. Tsze-ch'in asked Tsze-kung, saying, "When our master comes to any country, he does not fail to learn all about its government. Does he ask his information? or is it given to him?"

2. Tsze-kung said, "Our master is benign, upright, courteous, temperate, and complaisant, and thus he gets his information. The

master's mode of asking information! —is it not different from that of other men?"

XI

The Master said, "While a man's father is alive, look at the bent of his will; when his father is dead, look at his conduct. If for three years he does not alter from the way of his father, he may be called filial."

XII

1. The philosopher Yû said, "In practicing the rules of propriety, a natural ease is to be prized. In the ways prescribed by the ancient kings, this is the excellent quality, and in things small and great we follow them.

2. "Yet it is not to be observed in all cases. If one, knowing how such ease should be prized, manifests it, without regulating it by the rules of propriety, this likewise is not to be done."

XIII

The philosopher Yû said, "When agreements are made according to what is right, what is spoken can be made good. When respect is shown according to what is proper, one keeps far from shame and disgrace. When the parties upon whom a man leans are proper persons to be intimate with, he can make them his guides and masters."

XIV

The Master said, "He who aims to be a man of complete virtue in his food does not seek to gratify his appetite, nor in his dwelling place does he seek the appliances of ease; he is earnest in what he is doing, and careful in his speech; he frequents the company of men of principle that he may be rectified: such a person may be said indeed to love to learn."

XV

1. Tsze-kung said, "What do you pronounce concerning the poor man who yet does not flatter, and the rich man who is not proud?" The Master replied, "They will do; but they are not equal to him, who,

though poor, is yet cheerful, and to him, who, though rich, loves the rules of propriety."

2. Tsze-kung replied, "It is said in the Book of Poetry, "As you cut and then file, as you carve and then polish." — The meaning is the same, I apprehend, as that which you have just expressed."

3. The Master said, "With one like Ts'ze, I can begin to talk about the odes. I told him one point, and he knew its proper sequence."

XVI

The Master said, "I will not be afflicted at men's not knowing me; I will be afflicted that I do not know men."

BOOK II

WEI CHĂNG

I

The Master said, "He who exercises government by means of his virtue may be compared to the north polar star, which keeps its place and all the stars turn towards it."

II

The Master said, "In the Book of Poetry are three hundred pieces, but the design of them all may be embraced in one sentence— 'Having no depraved thoughts.'"

III

1. The Master said, "If the people be led by laws, and uniformity sought to be given them by punishments, they will try to avoid the punishment, but have no sense of shame.

2. "If they be led by virtue, and uniformity sought to be given them by the rules of propriety, they will have the sense of shame, and moreover will become good."

IV

1. The Master said, "At fifteen, I had my mind bent on learning.

2. "At thirty, I stood firm.

3. "At forty, I had no doubts.

4. "At fifty, I knew the decrees of Heaven.

5. "At sixty, my ear was an obedient organ for the reception of truth.

6. "At seventy, I could follow what my heart desired, without transgressing what was right."

V

1. Măng Î asked what filial piety was. The Master said, "It is not being disobedient."

2. Soon after, as Fan Ch'ih was driving him, the Master told him, saying, "Măng-sun asked me what filial piety was, and I answered him, 'not being disobedient.'"

3. Fan Ch'ih said, "What did you mean?" The Master replied, "That parents, when alive, be served according to propriety; that, when dead, they should be buried according to propriety; and that they should be sacrificed to according to propriety."

VI

Măng Wû asked what filial piety was. The Master said, "Parents are anxious lest their children should be sick."

VII

Tsze-yû asked what filial piety was. The Master said, "The filial piety of now-a-days means the support of one's parents. But dogs and horses likewise are able to do something in the way of support — without reverence, what is there to distinguish the one support given from the other?"

VIII

Tsze-hsiâ asked what filial piety was. The Master said, "The difficulty is with the countenance. If, when their elders have any troublesome affairs, the young take the toil of them, and if, when the young have wine and food, they set them before their elders, is *this* to be considered filial piety?"

IX

The Master said, "I have talked with Hûi for a whole day, and he has not made any objection to anything I said—as if he were stupid. He has retired, and I have examined his conduct when away from me, and found him able to illustrate my teachings. Hûi! He is not stupid."

X

1. The Master said, "See what a man does.

2. "Mark his motives.

3. "Examine in what things he rests.

4. "How can a man conceal his character?

5. "How can a man conceal his character?"

XI

The Master said, "If a man keeps cherishing his old knowledge, so as continually to be acquiring new, he may be a teacher of others."

XII

The Master said, "The accomplished scholar is not a utensil."

XIII

Tsze-kung asked what constituted the superior man. The Master said, "He acts before he speaks, and afterwards speaks according to his actions."

XIV

The Master said, "The superior man is catholic and no partisan. The mean man is partisan and not catholic."

XV

The Master said, "Learning without thought is labor lost; thought without learning is perilous."

XVI

The Master said, "The study of strange doctrines is injurious indeed!"

XVII

The Master said, "Yû, shall I teach you what knowledge is? When you know a thing, to hold that you know it; and when you do not know a thing, to allow that you do not know it—this is knowledge."

XVII

1. Tsze-chang was learning with a view to official emolument.

2. The Master said, "Hear much and put aside the points of which you stand in doubt, while you speak cautiously at the same time of the others: then you will afford few occasions for blame. See much and put aside the things which seem perilous, while you are cautious at the same time in carrying the others into practice: then you will have few occasions for repentance. When one gives few occasions for blame in his words, and few occasions for repentance in his conduct, he is in the way to get emolument."

XIX

The Duke Âi asked, saying, "What should be done in order to secure the submission of the people?" Confucius replied, "Advance the upright and set aside the crooked, then the people will submit. Advance the crooked and set aside the upright, then the people will not submit."

XX

Chî K'ang asked how to cause the people to reverence their ruler, to be faithful to him, and to go on to nerve themselves to virtue. The Master said, "Let him preside over them with gravity—then they will reverence him. Let him be filial and kind to all—then they will be faithful to him. Let him advance the good and teach the incompetent—then they will eagerly seek to be virtuous."

XXI

1. Someone addressed Confucius, saying, "Sir, why are you not engaged in the government?"

2. The Master said, "What does the Shû-ching say of filial piety?— "You are filial, you discharge your brotherly duties. These qualities are displayed in government." This then also constitutes the exercise of government. Why must there be that—making one be in the government?"

XXII

The Master said, "I do not know how a man without truthfulness is to get on. How can a large carriage be made to go without the cross-bar for yoking the oxen to, or a small carriage without the arrangement for yoking the horses?"

XXIII

1. Tsze-chang asked whether the affairs of ten ages after could be known.

2. Confucius said, "The Yin dynasty followed the regulations of the Hsia: wherein it took from or added to them may be known. The Châu dynasty has followed the regulations of Yin: wherein it took from or added to them may be known. Some other may follow the Châu, but though it should be at the distance of a hundred ages, its affairs may be known."

XXIV

1. The Master said, "For a man to sacrifice to a spirit which does not belong to him is flattery.

2. "To see what is right and not to do it is want of courage."

BOOK III

PÂ YÎH

I

Confucius said of the head of the Chî family, who had eight rows of pantomimes in his area, "If he can bear to do this, what may he not bear to do?"

II

The three families used the *Yung* ode, while the vessels were being removed, at the conclusion of the sacrifice. The Master said, "'Assisting are the princes—the son of Heaven looks profound and grave'—what application can these words have in the hall of the three families?"

III

The Master said, "If a man be without the virtues proper to humanity, what has he to do with the rites of propriety? If a man be without the virtues proper to humanity, what has he to do with music?"

IV

1. Lin Fang asked what was the first thing to be attended to in ceremonies.

2. The Master said, "A great question indeed!

3. "In festive ceremonies, it is better to be sparing than extravagant. In the ceremonies of mourning, it is better that there be deep sorrow than a minute attention to observances."

V

The Master said, "The rude tribes of the east and north have their princes, and are not like the States of our great land which are without them."

VI

The chief of the Chî family was about to sacrifice to the T'âi mountain. The Master said to Zan Yû, "Can you not save him from this?" He answered, "I cannot." Confucius said, "Alas! Will you say that the T'âi mountain is not so discerning as Lin Fang?"

VII

The Master said, "The student of virtue has no contentions. If it be said he cannot avoid them, shall this be in archery? But he bows complaisantly to his competitors; thus he ascends the hall, descends, and exacts the forfeit of drinking. In his contention, he is still the Chün-tsze."

VIII

1. Tsze-hsiâ asked, saying, "What is the meaning of the passage — 'The pretty dimples of her artful smile! The well-defined black and white of her eye! The plain ground for the colors?'"

2. The Master said, "The business of laying on the colors follows (the preparation of) the plain ground."

3. "Ceremonies then are a subsequent thing?" The Master said, "It is Shang who can bring out my meaning. Now I can begin to talk about the odes with him."

IX

The Master said, "I could describe the ceremonies of the Hsiâ dynasty, but Chî cannot sufficiently attest my words. I could describe the ceremonies of the Yin dynasty, but Sung cannot sufficiently attest my words. (They cannot do so) because of the insufficiency of their records and wise men. If those were sufficient, I could adduce them in support of my words."

X

The Master said, "At the great sacrifice, after the pouring out of the libation, I have no wish to look on."

XI

Someone asked the meaning of the great sacrifice. The Master said, "I do not know. He who knew its meaning would find it as easy to govern the kingdom as to look on this"—pointing to his palm.

XII

1. He sacrificed to the dead, as if they were present. He sacrificed to the spirits, as if the spirits were present.

2. The Master said, "I consider my not being present at the sacrifice, as if I did not sacrifice."

XIII

1. Wang-sun Chiâ asked, saying, "What is the meaning of the saying, 'It is better to pay court to the furnace than to the southwest corner?'"

2. The Master said, "Not so. He who offends against Heaven has none to whom he can pray."

XIV

The Master said, "Châu had the advantage of viewing the two past dynasties. How complete and elegant are its regulations! I follow Châu."

XV

The Master, when he entered the grand temple, asked about everything. Someone said, "Who will say that the son of the man of Tsâu knows the rules of propriety! He has entered the grand temple and asks about everything." The Master heard the remark, and said, "This is a rule of propriety."

XVI

The Master said, "In archery it is not going through the leather which is the principal thing—because people's strength is not equal. This was the old way."

XVII

1. Tsze-kung wished to do away with the offering of a sheep connected with the inauguration of the first day of each month.

2. The Master said, "Ts'ze, you love the sheep; I love the ceremony."

XVIII

The Master said, "The full observance of the rules of propriety in serving one's prince is accounted by people to be flattery."

XIX

The Duke Ting asked how a prince should employ his ministers, and how ministers should serve their prince. Confucius replied, "A prince should employ his minister according to the rules of propriety; ministers should serve their prince with faithfulness."

XX

The Master said, "The Kwan Tsü is expressive of enjoyment without being licentious, and of grief without being hurtfully excessive."

XXI

1. The Duke Âi asked Tsâi Wo about the altars of the spirits of the land. Tsâi Wo replied, "The Hsiâ sovereign planted the pine tree about them; the men of the Yin planted the cypress; and the men of the Châu planted the chestnut tree, meaning thereby to cause the people to be in awe."

2. When the Master heard it, he said, "Things that are done, it is needless to speak about; things that have had their course, it is needless to remonstrate about; things that are past, it is needless to blame."

XXII

1. The Master said, "Small indeed was the capacity of Kwan Chung!"

2. Someone said, "Was Kwan Chung parsimonious?" "Kwan," was the reply, "had the *San Kwei*, and his officers performed no double duties; how can he be considered parsimonious?"

3. "Then, did Kwan Chung know the rules of propriety?" The Master said, "The princes of States have a screen intercepting the view at their gates. Kwan had likewise a screen at his gate. The princes of States on any friendly meeting between two of them, had a stand on which to place their inverted cups. Kwan had also such a stand. If Kwan knew the rules of propriety, who does not know them?"

XXIII

The Master instructing the grand music master of Lu said, "How to play music may be known. At the commencement of the piece, all the parts should sound together. As it proceeds, they should be in harmony while severally distinct and flowing without break, and thus on to the conclusion."

XXIV

The border warden at Yi requested to be introduced to the Master, saying, "When men of superior virtue have come to this, I have never been denied the privilege of seeing them." The followers of the sage introduced him, and when he came out from the interview, he said, "My friends, why are you distressed by your master's loss of office? The kingdom has long been without the principles of truth and right; Heaven is going to use your master as a bell with its wooden tongue."

XXV

The Master said of the Shâo that it was perfectly beautiful and also perfectly good. He said of the Wû that it was perfectly beautiful but not perfectly good.

XXVI

The Master said, "High station filled without indulgent generosity; ceremonies performed without reverence; mourning conducted without sorrow—wherewith should I contemplate such ways?"

BOOK IV

LÎ ZĂN

I

The Master said, "It is virtuous manners which constitute the excellence of a neighborhood. If a man in selecting a residence, do not fix on one where such prevail, how can he be wise?"

II

The Master said, "Those who are without virtue cannot abide long either in a condition of poverty and hardship, or in a condition of enjoyment. The virtuous rest in virtue; the wise desire virtue."

III

The Master said, "It is only the (truly) virtuous man, who can love, or who can hate, others."

IV

The Master said, "If the will be set on virtue, there will be no practice of wickedness."

V

1. The Master said, "Riches and honors are what men desire. If it cannot be obtained in the proper way, they should not be held. Poverty and meanness are what men dislike. If it cannot be avoided in the proper way, they should not be avoided.

2. "If a superior man abandon virtue, how can he fulfill the requirements of that name?

3. "The superior man does not, even for the space of a single meal, act contrary to virtue. In moments of haste, he cleaves to it. In seasons of danger, he cleaves to it."

VI

1. The Master said, "I have not seen a person who loved virtue, or one who hated what was not virtuous. He who loved virtue, would esteem nothing above it. He who hated what is not virtuous, would practice virtue in such a way that he would not allow anything that is not virtuous to approach his person.

2. "Is anyone able for one day to apply his strength to virtue? I have not seen the case in which his strength would be insufficient.

3. "Should there possibly be any such case, I have not seen it."

VII

The Master said, "The faults of men are characteristic of the class to which they belong. By observing a man's faults, it may be known that he is virtuous."

VIII

The Master said, "If a man in the morning hear the right way, he may die in the evening without regret."

IX

The Master said, "A scholar, whose mind is set on truth, and who is ashamed of bad clothes and bad food, is not fit to be discoursed with."

X

The Master said, "The superior man, in the world, does not set his mind either for anything, or against anything; what is right he will follow."

XI

The Master said, "The superior man thinks of virtue; the small man thinks of comfort. The superior man thinks of the sanctions of law; the small man thinks of favors which he may receive."

XII

The Master said: "He who acts with a constant view to his own advantage will be much murmured against."

XIII

The Master said, "If a prince is able to govern his kingdom with the complaisance proper to the rules of propriety, what difficulty will he have? If he cannot govern it with that complaisance, what has he to do with the rules of propriety?"

XIV

The Master said, "A man should say, I am not concerned that I have no place, I am concerned how I may fit myself for one. I am not concerned that I am not known, I seek to be worthy to be known."

XV

1. The Master said, "Shăn, my doctrine is that of an all-pervading unity." The disciple Tsăng replied, "Yes."

2. The Master went out, and the other disciples asked, saying, "What do his words mean?" Tsăng said, "The doctrine of our master is to be true to the principles of our nature and the benevolent exercise of them to others—this and nothing more."

XVI

The Master said, "The mind of the superior man is conversant with righteousness; the mind of the mean man is conversant with gain."

XVII

The Master said, "When we see men of worth, we should think of equaling them; when we see men of a contrary character, we should turn inwards and examine ourselves."

XVIII

The Master said, "In serving his parents, a son may remonstrate with them, but gently; when he sees that they do not incline to follow his advice, he shows an increased degree of reverence, but does not abandon his purpose; and should they punish him, he does not allow himself to murmur."

XIX

The Master said, "While his parents are alive, the son may not go abroad to a distance. If he does go abroad, he must have a fixed place to which he goes."

XX

The Master said, "If the son for three years does not alter from the way of his father, he may be called filial."

XXI

The Master said, "The years of parents may by no means not be kept in the memory, as an occasion at once for joy and for fear."

XXII

The Master said, "The reason why the ancients did not readily give utterance to their words, was that they feared lest their actions should not come up to them."

XXIII

The Master said, "The cautious seldom err."

XXIV

The Master said, "The superior man wishes to be slow in his speech and earnest in his conduct."

XXV

The Master said, "Virtue is not left to stand alone. He who practices it will have neighbors."

XXVI

Tsze-yû said, "In serving a prince, frequent remonstrances lead to disgrace. Between friends, frequent reproofs make the friendship distant."

BOOK V

KUNG-YÊ CH'ANG

I

1. The Master said of Kung-yê Ch'ang that he might be wived; although he was put in bonds, he had not been guilty of any crime. Accordingly, he gave him his own daughter to wife.

2. Of Nan Yung he said that if the country were well governed he would not be out of office, and if it were ill-governed, he would escape punishment and disgrace. He gave him the daughter of his own elder brother to wife.

II

The Master said of Tsze-chien, "Of superior virtue indeed is such a man! If there were not virtuous men in Lû, how could this man have acquired this character?"

III

Tsze-kung asked, "What do you say of me, Ts'ze? The Master said, "You are a utensil." "What utensil?" "A gemmed sacrificial utensil."

IV

1. Someone said, "Yung is truly virtuous, but he is not ready with his tongue."

2. The Master said, "What is the good of being ready with the tongue? They who encounter men with smartness of speech for the most part procure themselves hatred. I know not whether he be truly virtuous, but why should he show readiness of the tongue?"

V

The Master was wishing Ch'î-tiâo K'âi to enter on official employment. He replied, "I am not yet able to rest in the assurance of this." The Master was pleased.

VI

The Master said, "My doctrines make no way. I will get upon a raft, and float about on the sea. He that will accompany me will be Yû, I dare say." Tsze-lû hearing this was glad, upon which the Master said, "Yû is fonder of daring than I am. He does not exercise his judgment upon matters."

VII

1. Mang Wu asked about Tsze-lû, whether he was perfectly virtuous. The Master said, "I do not know."

2. He asked again, when the Master replied, "In a kingdom of a thousand chariots, Yû might be employed to manage the military levies, but I do not know whether he be perfectly virtuous."

3. "And what do you say of Ch'iû?" The Master replied, "In a city of a thousand families, or a clan of a hundred chariots, Ch'iû might be employed as governor, but I do not know whether he is perfectly virtuous."

4. "What do you say of Ch'ih?" The Master replied, "With his sash girt and standing in a court, Ch'ih might be employed to converse with the visitors and guests, but I do not know whether he is perfectly virtuous."

VIII

1. The Master said to Tsze-kung, "Which do you consider superior, yourself or Hûi?"

2. Tsze-kung replied, "How dare I compare myself with Hûi? Hûi hears one point and knows all about a subject; I hear one point, and know a second."

3. The Master said, "You are not equal to him. I grant you, you are not equal to him."

IX

1. Tsâi Yü being asleep during the daytime, the Master said, "Rotten wood cannot be carved; a wall of dirty earth will not receive the trowel. This Yü! What is the use of my reproving him?"

2. The Master said, "At first, my way with men was to hear their words, and give them credit for their conduct. Now my way is to hear their

words, and look at their conduct. It is from Yü that I have learned to make this change."

X

The Master said, "I have not seen a firm and unbending man." Someone replied, "There is Shăn Ch'ang." "Ch'ang," said the Master, "is under the influence of his passions; how can he be pronounced firm and unbending?"

XI

Tsze-kung said, "What I do not wish men to do to me, I also wish not to do to men." The Master said, "Ts'ze, you have not attained to that."

XII

Tsze-kung said, "The Master's personal displays of his principles and ordinary descriptions of them may be heard. His discourses about man's nature, and the way of Heaven, cannot be heard."

XIII

When Tsze-lû heard anything, if he had not yet succeeded in carrying it into practice, he was only afraid lest he should hear something else.

XIV

Tsze-kung asked, saying, "On what ground did Kung-wăn get that title of Wăn?" The Master said, "He was of an active nature and yet fond of learning, and he was not ashamed to ask and learn of his inferiors! On these grounds he has been styled Wăn."

XV

The Master said of Tsze-ch'an that he had four of the characteristics of a superior man: in his conduct of himself, he was humble; in serving his superiors, he was respectful; in nourishing the people, he was kind; in ordering the people, he was just.

XVI

The Master said, "Yen P'ing knew well how to maintain friendly intercourse. The acquaintance might be long, but he showed the same respect as at first."

XVII

The Master said, "Tsang Wăn kept a large tortoise in a house, on the capitals of the pillars of which he had hills made, and with representations of duckweed on the small pillars above the beams supporting the rafters. Of what sort was his wisdom?"

XVIII

1. Tsze-chang asked, saying, "The minister Tsze-wăn thrice took office, and manifested no joy in his countenance. Thrice he retired from office, and manifested no displeasure. He made it a point to inform the new minister of the way in which he had conducted the government—what do you say of him?" The Master replied. "He was loyal." "Was he perfectly virtuous?" "I do not know. How can he be pronounced perfectly virtuous?"

2. Tsze-chang proceeded, "When the officer Ch'ûi killed the prince of Ch'i, Ch'ăn Wăn, though he was the owner of forty horses, abandoned them and left the country. Coming to another State, he said, 'They are here like our great officer, Ch'ûi,' and left it. He came to a second State, and with the same observation left it also—what do you say of him?" The Master replied, "He was pure." "Was he perfectly virtuous?" "I do not know. How can he be pronounced perfectly virtuous?"

XIX

Chî Wân thought thrice, and then acted. When the Master was informed of it, he said, "Twice may do."

XX

The Master said, "When good order prevailed in his country, Ning Wû acted the part of a wise man. When his country was in disorder, he acted the part of a stupid man. Others may equal his wisdom, but they cannot equal his stupidity."

XXI

When the Master was in Ch'ăn, he said, "Let me return! Let me return! The little children of my school are ambitious and too hasty. They are accomplished and complete so far, but they do not know how to restrict and shape themselves."

XXII

The Master said, "Po-î and Shû-ch'î did not keep the former wickednesses of men in mind, and hence the resentments directed towards them were few."

XXIII

The Master said, "Who says of Wei-shăng Kâo that he is upright? One begged some vinegar of him, and he begged it of a neighbor and gave it to the man."

XXIV

The Master said, "Fine words, an insinuating appearance, and excessive respect—Tso Ch'iû-ming was ashamed of them. I also am ashamed of them. To conceal resentment against a person, and appear friendly with him—Tso Ch'iû-ming was ashamed of such conduct. I also am ashamed of it."

XXV

1. Yen Yüan and Chî Lû being by his side, the Master said to them, "Come, let each of you tell his wishes."

2. Tsze-lû said, "I should like having chariots and horses, and light fur dresses, to share them with my friends, and though they should spoil them, I would not be displeased."

3. Yen Yüan said, "I should like not to boast of my excellence, nor to make a display of my meritorious deeds."

4. Tsze-lû then said, "I should like, sir, to hear your wishes." The Master said, "They are, in regard to the aged, to give them rest; in regard to friends, to show them sincerity; in regard to the young, to treat them tenderly."

XXVI

The Master said, "It is all over! I have not yet seen one who could perceive his faults, and inwardly accuse himself."

XXVII

The Master said, "In a hamlet of ten families, there may be found one honorable and sincere as I am, but not so fond of learning."

BOOK VI

YUNG YÊY

I

1. The Master said, "There is Yung! He might occupy the place of a prince."

2. Chung-kung asked about Tsze-sang Po-tsze. The Master said, "He may pass. He does not mind small matters."

3. Chung-kung said, "If a man cherish in himself a reverential feeling of the necessity of attention to business, though he may be easy in small matters in his government of the people, that may be allowed. But if he cherish in himself that easy feeling, and also carry it out in his practice, is not such an easy mode of procedure excessive?"

4. The Master said, "Yung's words are right."

II

The Duke Âi asked which of the disciples loved to learn. Confucius replied to him, "There was Yen Hûi; he loved to learn. He did not transfer his anger; he did not repeat a fault. Unfortunately, his appointed time was short and he died; and now there is not such another. I have not yet heard of anyone who loves to learn as he did."

III

1. Tsze-hwâ being employed on a mission to Ch'î, the disciple Zan requested grain for his mother. The Master said, "Give her a *fû*." Yen requested more. "Give her an *yü*," said the Master. Yen gave her five *ping*.

2. The Master said, "When Ch'ih was proceeding to Ch'î, he had fat horses to his carriage, and wore light furs. I have heard that a superior man helps the distressed, but does not add to the wealth of the rich."

3. Yüan Sze being made governor of his town by the Master, he gave him nine hundred measures of grain, but Sze declined them.

4. The Master said, "Do not decline them. May you not give them away in the neighborhoods, hamlets, towns, and villages?"

IV

The Master, speaking of Chung-kung, said, "If the calf of a brindled cow be red and horned, although men may not wish to use it, would the spirits of the mountains and rivers put it aside?"

V

The Master said, "Such was Hûi that for three months there would be nothing in his mind contrary to perfect virtue. The others may attain to this on some days or in some months, but nothing more."

VI

Chi K'ang asked about Chung-yû, whether he was fit to be employed as an officer of government. The Master said, "Yû is a man of decision; what difficulty would he find in being an officer of government?" K'ang asked, "Is Ts'ze fit to be employed as an officer of government?" and was answered, "Ts'ze is a man of intelligence; what difficulty would he find in being an officer of government?" And to the same question about Ch'iû the Master gave the same reply, saying, "Ch'iû is a man of various ability."

VII

The chief of the Chî family sent to ask Min Tsze-ch'ien to be governor of Pî. Min Tsze-ch'ien said, "Decline the offer for me politely. If anyone come again to me with a second invitation, I shall be obliged to go and live on the banks of the Wăn."

VIII

Po-niû being ill, the Master went to ask for him. He took hold of his hand through the window, and said, "It is killing him. It is the appointment of Heaven, alas! That such a man should have such a sickness! That such a man should have such a sickness!"

IX

The Master said, "Admirable indeed was the virtue of Hûi! With a single bamboo dish of rice, a single gourd dish of drink, and living in his mean narrow lane, while others could not have endured the distress, he did not allow his joy to be affected by it. Admirable indeed was the virtue of Hûi!"

X

Yen Ch'iû said, "It is not that I do not delight in your doctrines, but my strength is insufficient." The Master said, "Those whose strength is insufficient give over in the middle of the way but now you limit yourself."

XI

The Master said to Tsze-hsiâ, "Do you be a scholar after the style of the superior man, and not after that of the mean man."

XII

Tsze-yû being governor of Wû-ch'ǎng, the Master said to him, "Have you got good men there?" He answered, "There is Tan-t'âi Mieh-ming, who never in walking takes a shortcut, and never comes to my office, excepting on public business."

XIII

The Master said, "Mǎng Chih-fan does not boast of his merit. Being in the rear on an occasion of flight, when they were about to enter the gate, he whipped up his horse, saying, 'It is not that I dare to be last. My horse would not advance.'"

XIV

The Master said, "Without the specious speech of the litanist T'o and the beauty of the prince Châo of Sung, it is difficult to escape in the present age."

XV

The Master said, "Who can go out but by the door? How is it that men will not walk according to these ways?"

XVI

The Master said, "Where the solid qualities are in excess of accomplishments, we have rusticity; where the accomplishments are in excess of the solid qualities, we have the manners of a clerk.

When the accomplishments and solid qualities are equally blended, we then have the man of virtue."

XVII

The Master said, "Man is born for uprightness. If a man lose his uprightness, and yet live, his escape from death is the effect of mere good fortune."

XVIII

The Master said, "They who know the truth are not equal to those who love it, and they who love it are not equal to those who delight in it."

XIX

The Master said, "To those whose talents are above mediocrity, the highest subjects may be announced. To those who are below mediocrity, the highest subjects may not be announced."

XX

Fan Ch'ih asked what constituted wisdom. The Master said, "To give one's self earnestly to the duties due to men, and, while respecting spiritual beings, to keep aloof from them, may be called wisdom." He asked about perfect virtue. The Master said, "The man of virtue makes the difficulty to be overcome his first business, and success only a subsequent consideration—this may be called perfect virtue."

XXI

The Master said, "The wise find pleasure in water; the virtuous find pleasure in hills. The wise are active; the virtuous are tranquil. The wise are joyful; the virtuous are long-lived."

XXII

The Master said, "Ch'î, by one change, would come to the State of Lû. Lû, by one change, would come to a State where true principles predominated."

XXIII

The Master said, "A cornered vessel without corners. A strange cornered vessel! A strange cornered vessel!"

XXIV

Tsâi Wo asked, saying, "A benevolent man, though it be told him, 'There is a man in the well' will go in after him, I suppose." Confucius said, "Why should he do so? A superior man may be made to go to the well, but he cannot be made to go down into it. He may be imposed upon, but he cannot be fooled."

XXV

The Master said, "The superior man, extensively studying all learning, and keeping himself under the restraint of the rules of propriety, may thus likewise not overstep what is right."

XXVI

The Master having visited Nan-tsze, Tsze-lû was displeased, on which the Master swore, saying, "Wherein I have done improperly, may Heaven reject me, may Heaven reject me!"

XXVII

The Master said, "Perfect is the virtue which is according to the Constant Mean! Rare for a long time has been its practice among the people."

XXVIII

1. Tsze-kung said, "Suppose the case of a man extensively conferring benefits on the people, and able to assist all, what would you say of him? Might he be called perfectly virtuous?" The Master said, "Why speak only of virtue in connection with him? Must he not have the qualities of a sage? Even Yâo and Shun were still solicitous about this.

2. "Now the man of perfect virtue, wishing to be established himself, seeks also to establish others; wishing to be enlarged himself, he seeks also to enlarge others.

3. "To be able to judge of others by what is nigh in ourselves—this may be called the art of virtue."

BOOK VII

SHÛ R

I

The Master said, "A transmitter and not a maker, believing in and loving the ancients, I venture to compare myself with our old P'ang."

II

The Master said, "The silent treasuring up of knowledge; learning without satiety; and instructing others without being wearied: which one of these things belongs to me?"

III

The Master said, "The leaving virtue without proper cultivation; the not thoroughly discussing what is learned; not being able to move towards righteousness of which a knowledge is gained; and not being able to change what is not good: these are the things which occasion me solicitude."

IV

When the Master was unoccupied with business, his manner was easy, and he looked pleased.

V

The Master said, "Extreme is my decay. For a long time, I have not dreamed, as I was wont to do, that I saw the Duke of Châu."

VI

1. The Master said, "Let the will be set on the path of duty.

2. "Let every attainment in what is good be firmly grasped.

3. "Let perfect virtue be accorded with.

4. "Let relaxation and enjoyment be found in the polite arts."

VII

The Master said, "From the man bringing his bundle of dried flesh for my teaching upwards, I have never refused instruction to any one."

VIII

The Master said, "I do not open up the truth to one who is not eager to get knowledge, nor help out anyone who is not anxious to explain himself. When I have presented one corner of a subject to anyone, and he cannot from it learn the other three, I do not repeat my lesson."

IX

1. When the Master was eating by the side of a mourner, he never ate to the full.

2. He did not sing on the same day in which he had been weeping.

X

1. The Master said to Yen Yüan, "When called to office, to undertake its duties; when not so called, to lie retired—it is only I and you who have attained to this."

2. Tsze-lû said, "If you had the conduct of the armies of a great State, whom would you have to act with you?"

3. The Master said, "I would not have him to act with me, who will unarmed attack a tiger, or cross a river without a boat, dying without any regret. My associate must be the man who proceeds to action full of solicitude, who is fond of adjusting his plans, and then carries them into execution."

XI

The Master said, "If the search for riches is sure to be successful, though I should become a groom with whip in hand to get them, I will do so. As the search may not be successful, I will follow after that which I love."

XII

The things in reference to which the Master exercised the greatest caution were—fasting, war, and sickness.

XIII

When the Master was in Ch'î, he heard the Shâo, and for three months did not know the taste of flesh. "I did not think" he said, "that music could have been made so excellent as this."

XIV

1. Yen Yû said, "Is our Master for the ruler of Wei?" Tsze-kung said, "Oh! I will ask him."

2. He went in accordingly, and said, "What sort of men were Po-î and Shû-ch'î?" "They were ancient worthies," said the Master. "Did they have any repinings because of their course?" The Master again replied, "They sought to act virtuously, and they did so; what was there for them to repine about?" On this, Tsze-kung went out and said, "Our Master is not for him."

XV

The Master said, "With coarse rice to eat, with water to drink, and my bended arm for a pillow—I have still joy in the midst of these things. Riches and honors acquired by unrighteousness, are to me as a floating cloud."

XVI

The Master said, "If some years were added to my life, I would give fifty to the study of the Yî, and then I might come to be without great faults."

XVII

The Master's frequent themes of discourse were—the Odes, the History, and the maintenance of the Rules of Propriety. On all these he frequently discoursed.

XVIII

1. The Duke of Sheh asked Tsze-lû about Confucius, and Tsze-lû did not answer him.

2. The Master said, "Why did you not say to him, 'He is simply a man, who in his eager pursuit (of knowledge) forgets his food, who in the joy of its attainment forgets his sorrows, and who does not perceive that old age is coming on?'"

XIX

The Master said, "I am not one who was born in the possession of knowledge; I am one who is fond of antiquity, and earnest in seeking it there."

XX

The subjects on which the Master did not talk, were—extraordinary things, feats of strength, disorder, and spiritual beings.

XXI

The Master said, "When I walk along with two others, they may serve me as my teachers. I will select their good qualities and follow them, their bad qualities and avoid them."

XXII

The Master said, "Heaven produced the virtue that is in me. Hwan T'ui—what can he do to me?"

XXIII

The Master said, "Do you think, my disciples, that I have any concealments? I conceal nothing from you. There is nothing which I do that is not shown to you, my disciples—that is my way."

XXIV

There were four things which the Master taught—letters, ethics, devotion of soul, and truthfulness.

XXV

1. The Master said, "A sage it is not mine to see; could I see a man of real talent and virtue, that would satisfy me."

2. The Master said, "A good man it is not mine to see; could I see a man possessed of constancy, that would satisfy me.

3. "Having not and yet affecting to have, empty and yet affecting to be full, straitened and yet affecting to be at ease—it is difficult with such characteristics to have constancy."

XXVI

The Master angled—but did not use a net. He shot—but not at birds perching.

XXVII

The Master said, "There may be those who act without knowing why. I do not do so. Hearing much and selecting what is good and following it; seeing much and keeping it in memory: this is the second style of knowledge."

XXVIII

1. It was difficult to talk (profitably and reputably) with the people of Hû-hsiang, and a lad of that place having had an interview with the Master, the disciples doubted.

2. The Master said, "I admit people's approach to me without committing myself as to what they may do when they have retired. Why must one be so severe? If a man purify himself to wait upon me, I receive him so purified, without guaranteeing his past conduct."

XXIX

The Master said, "Is virtue a thing remote? I wish to be virtuous, and lo! Virtue is at hand."

XXX

1. The minister of crime of Ch'ăn asked whether the Duke Chao knew propriety, and Confucius said, "He knew propriety."

2. Confucius having retired, the minister bowed to Wû-mâ Ch'î to come forward, and said, "I have heard that the superior man is not a partisan. May the superior man be a partisan also? The prince married a daughter of the house of Wû, of the same surname with himself, and called her 'the elder Tsze of Wû.' If the prince knew propriety, who does not know it?"

3. Wû-mâ Ch'î reported these remarks, and the Master said, "I am fortunate! If I have any errors, people are sure to know them."

XXXI

When the Master was in company with a person who was singing, if he sang well, he would make him repeat the song, while he accompanied it with his own voice.

XXXII

The Master said, "In letters I am perhaps equal to other men, but the character of the superior man, carrying out in his conduct what he professes, is what I have not yet attained to."

XXXIII

The Master said, "The sage and the man of perfect virtue—how dare I rank myself with them? It may simply be said of me, that I strive to become such without satiety, and teach others without weariness." Kung-hsî Hwâ said, "This is just what we, the disciples, cannot imitate you in."

XXXIV

The Master being very sick, Tsze-lû asked leave to pray for him. He said, "May such a thing be done?" Tsze-lû replied, "It may. In the Eulogies it is said, 'Prayer has been made for thee to the spirits of the upper and lower worlds.'" The Master said, "My praying has been for a long time."

XXXV

The Master said, "Extravagance leads to insubordination, and parsimony to meanness. It is better to be mean than to be insubordinate."

XXXVI

The Master said, "The superior man is satisfied and composed; the mean man is always full of distress."

XXXVII

The Master was mild, and yet dignified; majestic, and yet not fierce; respectful, and yet easy.

BOOK VIII

T'ÂI-PO

I

The Master said, "T'âi-po may be said to have reached the highest point of virtuous action. Thrice he declined the kingdom, and the people in ignorance of his motives could not express their approbation of his conduct."

II

1. The Master said, "Respectfulness, without the rules of propriety, becomes laborious bustle; carefulness, without the rules of propriety, becomes timidity; boldness, without the rules of propriety, becomes insubordination; straightforwardness, without the rules of propriety, becomes rudeness.

2. "When those who are in high stations perform well all their duties to their relations, the people are aroused to virtue. When old friends are not neglected by them, the people are preserved from meanness."

III

The philosopher Tsăng being ill, he called to him the disciples of his school, and said, "Uncover my feet, uncover my hands. It is said in the Book of Poetry, 'We should be apprehensive and cautious, as if on the brink of a deep gulf, as if treading on thin ice,' and so have I been. Now and hereafter, I know my escape from all injury to my person, O ye, my little children."

IV

1. The philosopher Tsăng being ill, Măng Chăng went to ask how he was.

2. Tsăng said to him, "When a bird is about to die, its notes are mournful; when a man is about to die, his words are good.

3. "There are three principles of conduct which the man of high rank should consider specially important: that in his deportment and

manner he keep from violence and heedlessness; that in regulating his countenance he keep near to sincerity; and that in his words and tones he keep far from lowness and impropriety. As to such matters as attending to the sacrificial vessels, there are the proper officers for them."

V

The philosopher Tsǎng said, "Gifted with ability, and yet putting questions to those who were not so; possessed of much, and yet putting questions to those possessed of little; having, as though he had not; full, and yet counting himself as empty; offended against, and yet entering into no altercation; formerly I had a friend who pursued this style of conduct."

VI

The philosopher Tsǎng said, "Suppose that there is an individual who can be entrusted with the charge of a young orphan prince, and can be commissioned with authority over a state of a hundred li, and whom no emergency however great can drive from his principles: is such a man a superior man? He is a superior man indeed."

VII

1. The philosopher Tsǎng said, "The officer may not be without breadth of mind and vigorous endurance. His burden is heavy and his course is long.

2. "Perfect virtue is the burden which he considers it is his to sustain — is it not heavy? Only with death does his course stop — is it not long?"

VIII

1. The Master said, "It is by the Odes that the mind is aroused.

2. "It is by the Rules of Propriety that the character is established.

3. "It is from Music that the finish is received."

IX

The Master said, "The people may be made to follow a path of action, but they may not be made to understand it."

X

The Master said, "The man who is fond of daring and is dissatisfied with poverty, will proceed to insubordination. So will the man who is not virtuous, when you carry your dislike of him to an extreme."

XI

The Master said, "Though a man have abilities as admirable as those of the Duke of Châu, yet if he be proud and niggardly, those other things are really not worth being looked at."

XII

The Master said, "It is not easy to find a man who has learned for three years without coming to be good."

XIII

1. The Master said, "With sincere faith he unites the love of learning; holding firm to death, he is perfecting the excellence of his course.

2. "Such a one will not enter a tottering State, nor dwell in a disorganized one. When right principles of government prevail in the kingdom, he will show himself; when they are prostrated, he will keep concealed.

3. "When a country is well-governed, poverty and a mean condition are things to be ashamed of. When a country is ill-governed, riches and honor are things to be ashamed of."

XIV

The Master said, "He who is not in any particular office, has nothing to do with plans for the administration of its duties."

XV

The Master said, "When the music master Chih first entered on his office, the finish of the Kwan Tsü was magnificent—how it filled the ears!"

XVI

The Master said, "Ardent and yet not upright; stupid and yet not attentive; simple and yet not sincere: such persons I do not understand."

XVII

The Master said, "Learn as if you could not reach your object, and were always fearing also lest you should lose it."

XVIII

The Master said, "How majestic was the manner in which Shun and Yü held possession of the empire, as if it were nothing to them!"

XIX

1. The Master said, "Great indeed was Yâo as a sovereign! How majestic was he! It is only Heaven that is grand, and only Yâo corresponded to it. How vast was his virtue! The people could find no name for it.

2. "How majestic was he in the works which he accomplished! How glorious in the elegant regulations which he instituted!"

XX

1. Shun had five ministers, and the empire was well-governed.

2. King Wû said, "I have ten able ministers."

3. Confucius said, "Is not the saying that talents are difficult to find, true? Only when the dynasties of T'ang and Yû met, were they more abundant than in this of Châu, yet there was a woman among them. The able ministers were no more than nine men.

4. "King Wǎn possessed two of the three parts of the empire, and with those he served the dynasty of Yin. The virtue of the house of Châu may be said to have reached the highest point indeed."

XXI

The Master said, "I can find no flaw in the character of Yû. He used himself coarse food and drink, but displayed the utmost filial piety towards the spirits. His ordinary garments were poor, but he displayed the utmost elegance in his sacrificial cap and apron. He lived in a low mean house, but expended all his strength on the ditches and water channels. I can find nothing like a flaw in Yû."

BOOK IX

TSZE HAN

I

The subjects of which the Master seldom spoke were—profitableness, and also the appointments of Heaven, and perfect virtue.

II

1. A man of the village of Tâ-hsiang said, "Great indeed is the philosopher K'ung! His learning is extensive, and yet he does not render his name famous by any particular thing."

2. The Master heard the observation, and said to his disciples, "What shall I practice? Shall I practice charioteering, or shall I practice archery? I will practice charioteering."

III

1. The Master said, "The linen cap is that prescribed by the rules of ceremony, but now a silk one is worn. It is economical, and I follow the common practice.

2. "The rules of ceremony prescribe the bowing below the hall, but now the practice is to bow only after ascending it. That is arrogant. I continue to bow below the hall, though I oppose the common practice."

IV

There were four things from which the Master was entirely free. He had no foregone conclusions, no arbitrary predeterminations, no obstinacy, and no egoism.

V

1. The Master was put in fear in K'wang.

2. He said, "After the death of King Wăn, was not the cause of truth lodged here in me?

3. "If Heaven had wished to let this cause of truth perish, then I, a future mortal, should not have got such a relation to that cause. While Heaven does not let the cause of truth perish, what can the people of K'wang do to me?"

VI

1. A high officer asked Tsze-kung, saying, "May we not say that your Master is a sage? How various is his ability!"

2. Tsze-kung said, "Certainly Heaven has endowed him unlimitedly. He is about a sage. And, moreover, his ability is various."

3. The Master heard of the conversation and said, "Does the high officer know me? When I was young, my condition was low, and therefore I acquired my ability in many things, but they were mean matters. Must the superior man have such variety of ability? He does not need variety of ability."

4. Lâo said, "The Master said, 'Having no official employment, I acquired many arts.'"

VII

The Master said, "Am I indeed possessed of knowledge? I am not knowing. But if a mean person, who appears quite empty-like, ask anything of me, I set it forth from one end to the other, and exhaust it."

VIII

The Master said, "The *făng* bird does not come; the river sends forth no map: it is all over with me!"

IX

When the Master saw a person in a mourning dress, or anyone with the cap and upper and lower garments of full dress, or a blind person, on observing them approaching, though they were younger than himself, he would rise up, and if he had to pass by them, he would do so hastily.

X

1. Yen Yüan, in admiration of the Master's doctrines, sighed and said, "I looked up to them, and they seemed to become more high; I tried

to penetrate them, and they seemed to become more firm; I looked at them before me, and suddenly they seemed to be behind.

2. "The Master, by orderly method, skillfully leads men on. He enlarged my mind with learning, and taught me the restraints of propriety.

3. "When I wish to give over the study of his doctrines, I cannot do so, and having exerted all my ability, there seems something to stand right up before me; but though I wish to follow and lay hold of it, I really find no way to do so."

XI

1. The Master being very ill, Tsze-lû wished the disciples to act as ministers to him.

2. During a remission of his illness, he said, "Long has the conduct of Yû been deceitful! By pretending to have ministers when I have them not, whom should I impose upon? Should I impose upon Heaven?

3. "Moreover, than that I should die in the hands of ministers, is it not better that I should die in the hands of you, my disciples? And though I may not get a great burial, shall I die upon the road?"

XII

Tsze-kung said, "There is a beautiful gem here. Should I lay it up in a case and keep it? or should I seek for a good price and sell it?" The Master said, "Sell it! Sell it! But I would wait for one to offer the price."

XIII

1. The Master was wishing to go and live among the nine wild tribes of the east.

2. Someone said, "They are rude. How can you do such a thing?" The Master said, "If a superior man dwelt among them, what rudeness would there be?"

XIV

The Master said, "I returned from Wei to Lû, and then the music was reformed, and the pieces in the Royal songs and Praise songs all found their proper places."

XV

The Master said, "Abroad, to serve the high ministers and nobles; at home, to serve one's father and elder brothers; in all duties to the dead, not to dare not to exert one's self; and not to be overcome of wine: which one of these things do I attain to?"

XVI

The Master standing by a stream, said, "It passes on just like this, not ceasing day or night!"

XVII

The Master said, "I have not seen one who loves virtue as he loves beauty."

XVIII

The Master said, "The prosecution of learning may be compared to what may happen in raising a mound. If there want but one basket of earth to complete the work, and I stop, the stopping is my own work. It may be compared to throwing down the earth on the level ground. Though but one basketful is thrown at a time, the advancing with it is my own going forward."

XIX

The Master said, "Never flagging when I set forth anything to him — ah! That is Hûi."

XX

The Master said of Yen Yüan, "Alas! I saw his constant advance. I never saw him stop in his progress."

XXI

The Master said, "There are cases in which the blade springs, but the plant does not go on to flower! There are cases where it flowers, but no fruit is subsequently produced!"

XXII

The Master said, "A youth is to be regarded with respect. How do we know that his future will not be equal to our present? If he reach the age of forty or fifty, and has not made himself heard of, then indeed he will not be worth being regarded with respect."

XXIII

The Master said, "Can men refuse to assent to the words of strict admonition? But it is reforming the conduct because of them which is valuable. Can men refuse to be pleased with words of gentle advice? But it is unfolding their aim which is valuable. If a man be pleased with these words, but does not unfold their aim, and assents to those, but does not reform his conduct, I can really do nothing with him."

XXIV

The Master said, "Hold faithfulness and sincerity as first principles. Have no friends not equal to yourself. When you have faults, do not fear to abandon them."

XXV

The Master said, "The commander of the forces of a large state may be carried off, but the will of even a common man cannot be taken from him."

XXVI

1. The Master said, "Dressed himself in a tattered robe quilted with hemp, yet standing by the side of men dressed in furs, and not ashamed—ah! it is Yû who is equal to this!

2. "'He dislikes none, he covets nothing—what can he doubt what is good!'"

3. Tsze-lû kept continually repeating these words of the ode, when the Master said, "Those things are by no means sufficient to constitute (perfect) excellence."

XXVII

The Master said, "When the year becomes cold, then we know how the pine and the cypress are the last to lose their leaves."

XXVIII

The Master said, "The wise are free from perplexities; the virtuous from anxiety; and the bold from fear."

XXIX

The Master said, "There are some with whom we may study in common, but we shall find them unable to go along with us to principles. Perhaps we may go on with them to principles, but we shall find them unable to get established in those along with us. Or if we may get so established along with them, we shall find them unable to weigh occurring events along with us."

XXX

1. How the flowers of the aspen-plum flutter and turn! Do I not think of you? But your house is distant.

2. The Master said, "It is the want of thought about it. How is it distant?"

BOOK X

HSIANG TANG

I

1. Confucius, in his village, looked simple and sincere, and as if he were not able to speak.

2. When he was in the prince's ancestorial temple, or in the court, he spoke minutely on every point, but cautiously.

II

1. When he was waiting at court, in speaking with the great officers of the lower grade, he spake freely, but in a straightforward manner; in speaking with those of the higher grade, he did so blandly, but precisely.

2. When the ruler was present, his manner displayed respectful uneasiness; it was grave, but self-possessed.

III

1. When the prince called him to employ him in the reception of a visitor, his countenance appeared to change, and his legs to move forward with difficulty.

2. He inclined himself to the other officers among whom he stood, moving his left or right arm, as their position required, but keeping the skirts of his robe before and behind evenly adjusted.

3. He hastened forward, with his arms like the wings of a bird.

4. When the guest had retired, he would report to the prince, "The visitor is not turning round anymore."

IV

1. When he entered the palace gate, he seemed to bend his body, as if it were not sufficient to admit him.

2. When he was standing, he did not occupy the middle of the gateway; when he passed in or out, he did not tread upon the threshold.

3. When he was passing the vacant place of the prince, his countenance appeared to change, and his legs to bend under him, and his words came as if he hardly had breath to utter them.

4. He ascended the reception hall, holding up his robe with both his hands, and his body bent; holding in his breath also, as if he dared not breathe.

5. When he came out from the audience, as soon as he had descended one step, he began to relax his countenance, and had a satisfied look. When he had got to the bottom of the steps, he advanced rapidly to his place, with his arms like wings, and on occupying it, his manner still showed respectful uneasiness.

V

1. When he was carrying the scepter of his ruler, he seemed to bend his body, as if he were not able to bear its weight. He did not hold it higher than the position of the hands in making a bow, nor lower than their position in giving anything to another. His countenance seemed to change, and look apprehensive, and he dragged his feet along as if they were held by something to the ground.

2. In presenting the presents with which he was charged, he wore a placid appearance.

3. At his private audience, he looked highly pleased.

VI

1. The superior man did not use a deep purple, or a puce color, in the ornaments of his dress.

2. Even in his undress, he did not wear anything of a red or reddish color.

3. In warm weather, he had a single garment either of coarse or fine texture, but he wore it displayed over an inner garment.

4. Over lamb's fur he wore a garment of black; over fawn's fur one of white; and over fox's fur one of yellow.

5. The fur robe of his undress was long, with the right sleeve short.

6. He required his sleeping dress to be half as long again as his body.

7. When staying at home, he used thick furs of the fox or the badger.

8. When he put off mourning, he wore all the appendages of the girdle.

9. His undergarment, except when it was required to be of the curtain shape, was made of silk cut narrow above and wide below.

10. He did not wear lamb's fur or a black cap, on a visit of condolence.

11. On the first day of the month he put on his court robes, and presented himself at court.

VII

1. When fasting, he thought it necessary to have his clothes brightly clean and made of linen cloth.

2. When fasting, he thought it necessary to change his food, and also to change the place where he commonly sat in the apartment.

VIII

1. He did not dislike to have his rice finely cleaned, nor to have his minced meat cut quite small.

2. He did not eat rice which had been injured by heat or damp and turned sour, nor fish or flesh which was gone. He did not eat what was discolored, or what was of a bad flavor, nor anything which was ill-cooked, or was not in season.

3. He did not eat meat which was not cut properly, nor what was served without its proper sauce.

4. Though there might be a large quantity of meat, he would not allow what he took to exceed the due proportion for the rice. It was only in wine that he laid down no limit for himself, but he did not allow himself to be confused by it.

5. He did not partake of wine and dried meat bought in the market.

6. He was never without ginger when he ate.

7. He did not eat much.

8. When he had been assisting at the prince's sacrifice, he did not keep the flesh which he received overnight. The flesh of his family sacrifice he did not keep over three days. If kept over three days, people could not eat it.

9. When eating, he did not converse. When in bed, he did not speak.

10. Although his food might be coarse rice and vegetable soup, he would offer a little of it in sacrifice with a grave, respectful air.

IX

If his mat was not straight, he did not sit on it.

X

1. When the villagers were drinking together, on those who carried staffs going out, he went out immediately after.

2. When the villagers were going through their ceremonies to drive away pestilential influences, he put on his court robes and stood on the eastern steps.

XI

1. When he was sending complimentary inquiries to any one in another State, he bowed twice as he escorted the messenger away.

2. Chî K'ang having sent him a present of physic, he bowed and received it, saying, "I do not know it. I dare not taste it."

XII

The stable being burned down, when he was at court, on his return he said, "Has any man been hurt?" He did not ask about the horses.

XIII

1. When the prince sent him a gift of cooked meat, he would adjust his mat, first taste it, and then give it away to others. When the prince sent him a gift of undressed meat, he would have it cooked, and offer it to the spirits of his ancestors. When the prince sent him a gift of a living animal, he would keep it alive.

2. When he was in attendance on the prince and joining in the entertainment, the prince only sacrificed. He first tasted everything.

3. When he was ill and the prince came to visit him, he had his head to the east, made his court robes be spread over him, and drew his girdle across them.

4. When the prince's order called him, without waiting for his carriage to be yoked, he went at once.

XIV

When he entered the ancestral temple of the State, he asked about everything.

XV

1. When any of his friends died, if he had no relations who could be depended on for the necessary offices, he would say, "I will bury him."

2. When a friend sent him a present, though it might be a carriage and horses, he did not bow.

3. The only present for which he bowed was that of the flesh of sacrifice.

XVI

1. In bed, he did not lie like a corpse. At home, he did not put on any formal deportment.

2. When he saw anyone in a mourning dress, though it might be an acquaintance, he would change countenance; when he saw anyone wearing the cap of full dress, or a blind person, though he might be in his undress, he would salute them in a ceremonious manner.

3. To any person in mourning he bowed forward to the crossbar of his carriage; he bowed in the same way to anyone bearing the tables of population.

4. When he was at an entertainment where there was an abundance of provisions set before him, he would change countenance and rise up.

5. On a sudden clap of thunder, or a violent wind, he would change countenance.

XVII

1. When he was about to mount his carriage, he would stand straight, holding the cord.

2. When he was in the carriage, he did not turn his head quite round, he did not talk hastily, he did not point with his hands.

XVIII

1. Seeing the countenance, it instantly rises. It flies round, and by and by settles.

2. The Master said, "There is the hen-pheasant on the hill bridge. At its season! At its season!" Tsze-lû made a motion to it. Thrice it smelt him and then rose.

BOOK XI

HSIEN TSIN

I

1. The Master said, "The men of former times, in the matters of ceremonies and music were rustics, it is said, while the men of these latter times, in ceremonies and music, are accomplished gentlemen.

2. "If I have occasion to use those things, I follow the men of former times."

II

1. The Master said, "Of those who were with me in Ch'ăn and Ts'âi, there are none to be found to enter my door."

2. Distinguished for their virtuous principles and practice, there were Yen Yûan, Min Tsze-ch'ien, Zan Po-niû, and Chung-kung; for their ability in speech, Tsâi Wo and Tsze-kung; for their administrative talents, Zan Yû and Chî Lû; for their literary acquirements, Tsze-yû and Tsze-hsiâ.

III

The Master said, "Hûi gives me no assistance. There is nothing that I say in which he does not delight."

IV

The Master said, "Filial indeed is Min Tsze-ch'ien! Other people say nothing of him different from the report of his parents and brothers."

V

Nan Yung was frequently repeating the lines about a white scepter stone. Confucius gave him the daughter of his elder brother to wife.

VI

Chî K'ang asked which of the disciples loved to learn. Confucius replied to him, "There was Yen Hûi; he loved to learn. Unfortunately his appointed time was short, and he died. Now there is no one who loves to learn, as he did."

VII

1. When Yen Yüan died, Yen Lû begged the carriage of the Master to sell and get an outer shell for his son's coffin.

2. The Master said, "Everyone calls his son his son, whether he has talents or has not talents. There was Lî; when he died, he had a coffin but no outer shell. I would not walk on foot to get a shell for him, because, having followed in the rear of the great officers, it was not proper that I should walk on foot."

VIII

When Yen Yüan died, the Master said, "Alas! Heaven is destroying me! Heaven is destroying me!"

IX

1. When Yen Yüan died, the Master bewailed him exceedingly, and the disciples who were with him said, "Master, your grief is excessive?"

2. "Is it excessive?" said he.

3. "If I am not to mourn bitterly for this man, for whom should I mourn?"

X

1. When Yen Yüan died, the disciples wished to give him a great funeral, and the Master said, "You may not do so."

2. The disciples did bury him in great style.

3. The Master said, "Hûi behaved towards me as his father. I have not been able to treat him as my son. The fault is not mine; it belongs to you, O disciples."

XI

Chî Lû asked about serving the spirits of the dead. The Master said, "While you are not able to serve men, how can you serve their spirits?" Chî Lû added, "I venture to ask about death?" He was answered, "While you do not know life, how can you know about death?"

XII

1. The disciple Min was standing by his side, looking bland and precise; Tsze-lû, looking bold and soldierly; Zan Yû and Tsze-kung, with a free and straightforward manner. The Master was pleased.

2. He said, "Yû, there! He will not die a natural death."

XIII

1. Some parties in Lû were going to takedown and rebuild the Long Treasury.

2. Min Tsze-ch'ien said, "Suppose it were to be repaired after its old style—why must it be altered and made anew?"

3. The Master said, "This man seldom speaks; when he does, he is sure to hit the point."

XIV

1. The Master said, "What has the lute of Yû to do in my door?"

2. The other disciples began not to respect Tsze-lû. The Master said, "Yû has ascended to the hall, though he has not yet passed into the inner apartments."

XV

1. Tsze-kung asked which of the two, Shih or Shang, was the superior. The Master said, "Shih goes beyond the due mean, and Shang does not come up to it."

2. "Then," said Tsze-kung, "the superiority is with Shih, I suppose."

3. The Master said, "To go beyond is as wrong as to fall short."

XVI

1. The head of the Chî family was richer than the Duke of Châu had been, and yet Ch'iû collected his imposts for him, and increased his wealth.

2. The Master said, "He is no disciple of mine. My little children, beat the drum and assail him."

XVII

1. Ch'âi is simple.

2. Shǎn is dull.

3. Shih is specious.

4. Yû is coarse.

XVIII

1. The Master said, "There is Hûi! He has nearly attained to perfect virtue. He is often in want.

2. "Ts'ze does not acquiesce in the appointments of Heaven, and his goods are increased by him. Yet his judgments are often correct."

XIX

Tsze-chang asked what were the characteristics of the *good man*. The Master said, "He does not tread in the footsteps of others, but moreover, he does not enter the chamber of the sage."

XX

The Master said, "If, because a man's discourse appears solid and sincere, we allow him to be a good man, is he really a superior man? Or is his gravity only in appearance?"

XXI

Tsze-lû asked whether he should immediately carry into practice what he heard. The Master said, "There are your father and elder brothers to be consulted—why should you act on that principle of immediately carrying into practice what you hear?" Zan Yû asked the same, whether he should immediately carry into practice what he heard, and the Master answered, "Immediately carry into practice what you hear." Kung-hsî Hwâ said, "Yû asked whether he should carry immediately into practice what he heard, and you said, 'There are your father and elder brothers to be consulted.' Ch'iû asked whether he should immediately carry into practice what he heard, and you said, 'Carry it immediately into practice.' I, Ch'ih, am perplexed, and venture to ask you for an explanation." The Master said, "Ch'iû is retiring and slow; therefore, I urged him forward. Yû has more than his own share of energy; therefore I kept him back."

XXII

The Master was put in fear in K'wang and Yen Yüan fell behind. The Master, on his rejoining him, said, "I thought you had died." Hûi replied, "While you were alive, how should I presume to die?"

XXIII

1. Chî Tsze-zan asked whether Chung Yû and Zan Ch'iû could be called great ministers.

2. The Master said, "I thought you would ask about some extraordinary individuals, and you only ask about Yû and Ch'iû!

3. "What is called a great minister, is one who serves his prince according to what is right, and when he finds he cannot do so, retires.

4. "Now, as to Yû and Ch'iû, they may be called ordinary ministers."

5. Tsze-zan said, "Then they will always follow their chief—will they?"

6. The Master said, "In an act of parricide or regicide, they would not follow him."

XXIV

1. Tsze-lû got Tsze-kâo appointed governor of Pî.

2. The Master said, "You are injuring a man's son."

3. Tsze-lû said, "There are (there) common people and officers; there are the altars of the spirits of the land and grain. Why must one read books before he can be considered to have learned?"

4. The Master said, "It is on this account that I hate your glib-tongued people."

XXV

1. Tsze-lû, Tsăng Hsî, Zan Yû, and Kung-hsî Hwâ were sitting by the Master.

2. He said to them, "Though I am a day or so older than you, do not think of that.

3. "From day to day you are saying, 'We are not known.' If some ruler were to know you, what would you like to do?"

4. Tsze-lû hastily and lightly replied, "Suppose the case of a State of ten thousand chariots; let it be straitened between other large States; let it be suffering from invading armies; and to this let there be added

a famine in corn and in all vegetables: if I were entrusted with the government of it, in three years' time I could make the people to be bold, and to recognize the rules of righteous conduct." The Master smiled at him.

5. Turning to Yen Yû, he said, "Ch'iû, what are your wishes?" Ch'iû replied, "Suppose a state of sixty or seventy lî square, or one of fifty or sixty, and let me have the government of it—in three years' time, I could make plenty to abound among the people. As to teaching them the principles of propriety, and music, I must wait for the rise of a superior man to do that."

6. "What are your wishes, Ch'ih," said the Master next to Kung-hsî Hwâ. Ch'ih replied, "I do not say that my ability extends to these things, but I should wish to learn them. At the services of the ancestral temple, and at the audiences of the princes with the sovereign, I should like, dressed in the dark square-made robe and the black linen cap, to act as a small assistant."

7. Last of all, the Master asked Tsăng Hsî, "Tien, what are your wishes?" Tien, pausing as he was playing on his lute, while it was yet twanging, laid the instrument aside, and rose. "My wishes," he said, "are different from the cherished purposes of these three gentlemen." "What harm is there in that?" said the Master. "Do you also, as well as they, speak out your wishes." Tien then said, "In this, the last month of spring, with the dress of the season all complete, along with five or six young men who have assumed the cap, and six or seven boys, I would wash in the Î, enjoy the breeze among the rain altars, and return home singing." The Master heaved a sigh and said, "I give my approval to Tien."

8. The three others having gone out, Tsăng Hsî remained behind, and said, "What do you think of the words of these three friends?" The Master replied, "They simply told each one his wishes."

9. Hsî pursued, "Master, why did you smile at Yû?"

10. He was answered, "The management of a State demands the rules of propriety. His words were not humble; therefore I smiled at him."

11. Hsî again said, "But was it not a State which Ch'iû proposed for himself?" The reply was, "Yes; did you ever see a territory of sixty or seventy lî or one of fifty or sixty, which was not a State?"

12. Once more, Hsî inquired, "And was it not a State which Ch'ih proposed for himself?" The Master again replied, "Yes; who but

princes have to do with ancestral temples, and with audiences but the sovereign? If Ch'ih were to be a small assistant in these services, who could be a great one?"

BOOK XII

YEN YÜAN

I

1. Yen Yüan asked about perfect virtue. The Master said, "To subdue one's self and return to propriety, is perfect virtue. If a man can for one day subdue himself and return to propriety, all under heaven will ascribe perfect virtue to him. Is the practice of perfect virtue from a man himself, or is it from others?"

2. Yen Yüan said, "I beg to ask the steps of that process." The Master replied, "Look not at what is contrary to propriety; listen not to what is contrary to propriety; speak not what is contrary to propriety; make no movement which is contrary to propriety." Yen Yüan then said, "Though I am deficient in intelligence and vigor, I will make it my business to practice this lesson."

II

Chung-kung asked about perfect virtue. The Master said, "It is, when you go abroad, to behave to everyone as if you were receiving a great guest; to employ the people as if you were assisting at a great sacrifice; not to do to others as you would not wish done to yourself; to have no murmuring against you in the country, and none in the family." Chung-kung said, "Though I am deficient in intelligence and vigor, I will make it my business to practice this lesson."

III

1. Sze-mâ Niû asked about perfect virtue.

2. The Master said, "The man of perfect virtue is cautious and slow in his speech."

3. "Cautious and slow in his speech!" said Niû. "Is this what is meant by perfect virtue?" The Master said, "When a man feels the difficulty of doing, can he be other than cautious and slow in speaking?"

IV

1. Sze-mâ Niû asked about the superior man. The Master said, "The superior man has neither anxiety nor fear."

2. "Being without anxiety or fear!" said Niû. "Does this constitute what we call the superior man?"

3. The Master said, "When internal examination discovers nothing wrong, what is there to be anxious about, what is there to fear?"

V

1. Sze-mâ Niû, full of anxiety, said, "Other men all have their brothers, I only have not."

2. Tsze-hsiâ said to him, "There is the following saying which I have heard:

3. "'Death and life have their determined appointment; riches and honors depend upon Heaven.'

4. "Let the superior man never fail reverentially to order his own conduct, and let him be respectful to others and observant of propriety: then all within the four seas will be his brothers. What has the superior man to do with being distressed because he has no brothers?"

VI

Tsze-chang asked what constituted intelligence. The Master said, "He with whom neither slander that gradually soaks into the mind, nor statements that startle like a wound in the flesh, are successful, may be called intelligent indeed. Yea, he with whom neither soaking slander, nor startling statements, are successful, may be called farseeing."

VII

1. Tsze-kung asked about government. The Master said, "The requisites of government are that there be sufficiency of food, sufficiency of military equipment, and the confidence of the people in their ruler."

2. Tsze-kung said, "If it cannot be helped, and one of these must be dispensed with, which of the three should be foregone first?" "The military equipment," said the Master.

3. Tsze-kung again asked, "If it cannot be helped, and one of the remaining two must be dispensed with, which of them should be foregone?" The Master answered, "Part with the food. From of old, death has been the lot of all men; but if the people have no faith in their rulers, there is no standing for the state."

VIII

1. Chî Tsze-ch'ăng said, "In a superior man it is only the substantial qualities which are wanted—why should we seek for ornamental accomplishments?"

2. Tsze-kung said, "Alas! Your words, sir, show you to be a superior man, but four horses cannot overtake the tongue.

3. "Ornament is as substance; substance is as ornament. The hide of a tiger or a leopard stripped of its hair, is like the hide of a dog or a goat stripped of its hair."

IX

1. The Duke Âi inquired of Yû Zo, saying, "The year is one of scarcity, and the returns for expenditure are not sufficient—what is to be done?"

2. Yû Zo replied to him, "Why not simply tithe the people?"

3. "With two tenths, said the duke, "I find it not enough—how could I do with that system of one tenth?"

4. Yû Zo answered, "If the people have plenty, their prince will not be left to want alone. If the people are in want, their prince cannot enjoy plenty alone."

X

1. Tsze-chang having asked how virtue was to be exalted, and delusions to be discovered, the Master said, "Hold faithfulness and sincerity as first principles, and be moving continually to what is right—this is the way to exalt one's virtue.

2. "You love a man and wish him to live; you hate him and wish him to die. Having wished him to live, you also wish him to die. This is a case of delusion.

3. "'It may not be on account of her being rich, yet you come to make a difference.'"

XI

1. The Duke Ching, of Ch'î, asked Confucius about government.

2. Confucius replied, "There is government, when the prince is prince, and the minister is minister; when the father is father, and the son is son."

3. "Good!" said the duke. "If, indeed, the prince be not prince, the minister not minister, the father not father, and the son not son, although I have my revenue, can I enjoy it?"

XII

1. The Master said, "Ah! It is Yû, who could with half a word settle litigations!"

2. Tsze-lû never slept over a promise.

XIII

The Master said, "In hearing litigations, I am like any other body. What is necessary, however, is to cause the people to have no litigations."

XIV

Tsze-chang asked about government. The Master said, "The art of governing is to keep its affairs before the mind without weariness, and to practice them with undeviating consistency."

XV

The Master said, "By extensively studying all learning, and keeping himself under the restraint of the rules of propriety, one may thus likewise not err from what is right."

XVI

The Master said, "The superior man seeks to perfect the admirable qualities of men, and does not seek to perfect their bad qualities. The mean man does the opposite of this."

XVII

Chi K'ang asked Confucius about government. Confucius replied, "To govern means to rectify. If you lead on the people with correctness, who will dare not to be correct?"

XVIII

Chi K'ang, distressed about the number of thieves in the state, inquired of Confucius how to do away with them. Confucius said, "If you, sir, were not covetous, although you should reward them to do it, they would not steal."

XIX

Chi K'ang asked Confucius about government, saying, "What do you say to killing the unprincipled for the good of the principled?" Confucius replied, "Sir, in carrying on your government, why should you use killing at all? Let your evinced desires be for what is good, and the people will be good. The relation between superiors and inferiors is like that between the wind and the grass. The grass must bend when the wind blows across it."

XX

1. Tsze-chang asked, "What must the officer be, who may be said to be distinguished?"

2. The Master said, "What is it you call being distinguished?"

3. Tsze-chang replied, "It is to be heard of through the State, to be heard of throughout his clan."

4. The Master said, "That is notoriety, not distinction.

5. "Now the man of distinction is solid and straightforward, and loves righteousness. He examines people's words, and looks at their countenances. He is anxious to humble himself to others. Such a man will be distinguished in the country; he will be distinguished in his clan.

6. "As to the man of notoriety, he assumes the appearance of virtue, but his actions are opposed to it, and he rests in this character without any doubts about himself. Such a man will be heard of in the country; he will be heard of in the clan."

XXI

1. Fan Ch'ih rambling with the Master under the trees about the rain altars, said, "I venture to ask how to exalt virtue, to correct cherished evil, and to discover delusions."

2. The Master said, "Truly a good question!

3. "If doing what is to be done be made the first business, and success a secondary consideration—is not this the way to exalt virtue? To assail one's own wickedness and not assail that of others—is not this the way to correct cherished evil? For a morning's anger to disregard one's own life, and involve that of his parents—is not this a case of delusion?"

XXII

1. Fan Ch'ih asked about benevolence. The Master said, "It is to love all men." He asked about knowledge. The Master said, "It is to know all men."

2. Fan Ch'ih did not immediately understand these answers.

3. The Master said, "Employ the upright and put aside all the crooked—in this way the crooked can be made to be upright."

4. Fan Ch'ih retired, and, seeing Tsze-hsiâ, he said to him, "A little while ago, I had an interview with our Master, and asked him about knowledge. He said, 'Employ the upright, and put aside all the crooked—in this way, the crooked will be made to be upright.' What did he mean?"

5. Tsze-hsiâ said, "Truly rich is his saying!

6. "Shun, being in possession of the kingdom, selected from among all the people, and employed Kâo-yâo, on which all who were devoid of virtue disappeared. T'ang, being in possession of the kingdom, selected from among all the people, and employed Î Yin, and all who were devoid of virtue disappeared."

XXIII

Tsze-kung asked about friendship. The Master said, "Faithfully admonish your friend, and skillfully lead him on. If you find him impracticable, stop. Do not disgrace yourself."

XXIV

The philosopher Tsăng said, "The superior man on grounds of culture meets with his friends, and by their friendship helps his virtue."

BOOK XIII

TSZE-LÛ

I

1. Tsze-lû asked about government. The Master said, "Go before the people with your example, and be laborious in their affairs."

2. He requested further instruction, and was answered, "Be not weary (in these things)."

II

1. Chung-kung, being chief minister to the Head of the Chî family, asked about government. The Master said, "Employ first the services of your various officers, pardon small faults, and raise to office men of virtue and talents."

2. Chung-kung said, "How shall I know the men of virtue and talent, so that I may raise them to office?" He was answered, "Raise to office those whom you know. As to those whom you do not know, will others neglect them?"

III

1. Tsze-lû said, "The ruler of Wei has been waiting for you, in order with you to administer the government. What will you consider the first thing to be done?"

2. The Master replied, "What is necessary is to rectify names."

3. "So, indeed!" said Tsze-lû. "You are wide of the mark! Why must there be such rectification?"

4. The Master said, "How uncultivated you are, Yû! A superior man, in regard to what he does not know, shows a cautious reserve.

5. "If names be not correct, language is not in accordance with the truth of things. If language be not in accordance with the truth of things, affairs cannot be carried on to success.

6. "When affairs cannot be carried on to success, proprieties and music will not flourish. When proprieties and music do not flourish,

punishments will not be properly awarded. When punishments are not properly awarded, the people do not know how to move hand or foot.

7. "Therefore a superior man considers it necessary that the names he uses may be spoken appropriately, and also that what he speaks may be carried out appropriately. What the superior man requires, is just that in his words there may be nothing incorrect."

IV

1. Fan Ch'ih requested to be taught husbandry. The Master said, "I am not so good for that as an old husbandman." He requested also to be taught gardening, and was answered, "I am not so good for that as an old gardener."

2. Fan Ch'ih having gone out, the Master said, "A small man, indeed, is Fan Hsü!

3. "If a superior loves propriety, the people will not dare not to be reverent. If he loves righteousness, the people will not dare not to submit to his example. If he loves good faith, the people will not dare not to be sincere. Now, when these things obtain, the people from all quarters will come to him, bearing their children on their backs—what need has he of a knowledge of husbandry?"

V

The Master said, "Though a man may be able to recite the three hundred odes, yet if, when entrusted with a governmental charge, he knows not how to act, or if, when sent to any quarter on a mission, he cannot give his replies unassisted, notwithstanding the extent of his learning, of what practical use is it?"

VI

The Master said, "When a prince's personal conduct is correct, his government is effective without the issuing of orders. If his personal conduct is not correct, he may issue orders, but they will not be followed."

VII

The Master said, "The governments of Lû and Wei are brothers."

VIII

The Master said of Ching, a scion of the ducal family of Wei, that he knew the economy of a family well. When he began to have means, he said, "Ha! Here is a collection!" When they were a little increased, he said, "Ha! This is complete!" When he had become rich, he said, "Ha! This is admirable!"

IX

1. When the Master went to Wei, Zan Yû acted as driver of his carriage.

2. The Master observed, "How numerous are the people!"

3. Yû said, "Since they are thus numerous, what more shall be done for them?" "Enrich them," was the reply.

4. "And when they have been enriched, what more shall be done?" The Master said, "Teach them."

X

The Master said, "If there were (any of the princes) who would employ me, in the course of twelve months, I should have done something considerable. In three years, the government would be perfected."

XI

The Master said, "'If good men were to govern a country in succession for a hundred years, they would be able to transform the violently bad, and dispense with capital punishments.' True indeed is this saying!"

XII

The Master said, "If a truly royal ruler were to arise, it would still require a generation, and then virtue would prevail."

XIII

The Master said, "If a minister make his own conduct correct, what difficulty will he have in assisting in government? If he cannot rectify himself, what has he to do with rectifying others?"

XIV

The disciple Zan returning from the court, the Master said to him, "How are you so late?" He replied, "We had government business." The Master said, "It must have been family affairs. If there had been government business, though I am not now in office, I should have been consulted about it."

XV

1. The Duke Ting asked whether there was a single sentence which could make a country prosperous. Confucius replied, "Such an effect cannot be expected from one sentence.

2. "There is a saying, however, which people have: 'To be a prince is difficult; to be a minister is not easy.'

3. "If a ruler knows this—the difficulty of being a prince—may there not be expected from this one sentence the prosperity of his country?"

4. The duke then said, "Is there a single sentence which can ruin a country?" Confucius replied, "Such an effect as that cannot be expected from one sentence. There is, however, the saying which people have: 'I have no pleasure in being a prince, but only in that no one can offer any opposition to what I say!'

5. "If a ruler's words be good, is it not also good that no one oppose them? But if they are not good, and no one opposes them, may there not be expected from this one sentence the ruin of his country?"

XVI

1. The Duke of Sheh asked about government.

2. The Master said, "Good government obtains, when those who are near are made happy, and those who are far off are attracted."

XVII

Tsze-hsiâ, being governor of Chü-fû, asked about government. The Master said, "Do not be desirous to have things done quickly; do not look at small advantages. Desire to have things done quickly prevents their being done thoroughly. Looking at small advantages prevents great affairs from being accomplished."

XVIII

1. The Duke of Sheh informed Confucius, saying, "Among us here there are those who may be styled upright in their conduct. If their father have stolen a sheep, they will bear witness to the fact."

2. Confucius said, "Among us, in our part of the country, those who are upright are different from this. The father conceals the misconduct of the son, and the son conceals the misconduct of the father. Uprightness is to be found in this."

XIX

Fan Ch'ih asked about perfect virtue. The Master said, "It is, in retirement, to be sedately grave; in the management of business, to be reverently attentive; in intercourse with others, to be strictly sincere. Though a man go among rude, uncultivated tribes, these qualities may not be neglected."

XX

1. Tsze-kung asked, saying, "What qualities must a man possess to entitle him to be called an officer?" The Master said, "He who in his conduct of himself maintains a sense of shame, and when sent to any quarter will not disgrace his prince's commission, deserves to be called an officer."

2. Tsze-kung pursued, "I venture to ask who may be placed in the next lower rank?" And he was told, "He whom the circle of his relatives pronounce to be filial, whom his fellow villagers and neighbors pronounce to be fraternal."

3. Again the disciple asked, "I venture to ask about the class still next in order." The Master said, "They are determined to be sincere in what they say, and to carry out what they do. They are obstinate little men. Yet perhaps they may make the next class."

4. Tsze-kung finally inquired, "Of what sort are those of the present day, who engage in government?" The Master said, "Pooh! They are so many pecks and hampers, not worth being taken into account."

XXI

The Master said, "Since I cannot get men pursuing the due medium, to whom I might communicate my instructions, I must find the ardent and the cautiously decided. The ardent will advance and lay hold of truth; the cautiously decided will keep themselves from what is wrong."

XXII

1. The Master said, "The people of the south have a saying: 'A man without constancy cannot be either a wizard or a doctor.' Good!

2. "Inconstant in his virtue, he will be visited with disgrace."

3. The Master said, "This arises simply from not attending to the prognostication."

XXIII

The Master said, "The superior man is affable, but not adulatory; the mean man is adulatory, but not affable."

XXIV

Tsze-kung asked, saying, "What do you say of a man who is loved by all the people of his neighborhood?" The Master replied, "We may not for that accord our approval of him." "And what do you say of him who is hated by all the people of his neighborhood?" The Master said, "We may not for that conclude that he is bad. It is better than either of these cases that the good in the neighborhood love him, and the bad hate him."

XXV

The Master said, "The superior man is easy to serve and difficult to please. If you try to please him in any way which is not accordant with right, he will not be pleased. But in his employment of men, he uses them according to their capacity. The mean man is difficult to serve, and easy to please. If you try to please him, though it be in a way which is not accordant with right, he may be pleased. But in his employment of men, he wishes them to be equal to everything."

XXVI

The Master said, "The superior man has a dignified ease without pride. The mean man has pride without a dignified ease."

XXVII

The Master said, "The firm, the enduring, the simple, and the modest are near to virtue."

XXVIII

Tsze-lû asked, saying, "What qualities must a man possess to entitle him to be called a scholar?" The Master said, "He must be thus — earnest, urgent, and bland: among his friends, earnest and urgent; among his brethren, bland."

XXIX

The Master said, "Let a good man teach the people seven years, and they may then likewise be employed in war."

XXX

The Master said, "To lead an uninstructed people to war, is to throw them away."

BOOK XIV

HSIEN WĂN

I

Hsien asked what was shameful. The Master said, "When good government prevails in a state, to be thinking only of salary; and, when bad government prevails, to be thinking, in the same way, only of salary—this is shameful."

II

1. "When the love of superiority, boasting, resentments, and covetousness are repressed, this may be deemed perfect virtue."

2. The Master said, "This may be regarded as the achievement of what is difficult. But I do not know that it is to be deemed perfect virtue."

III

The Master said, "The scholar who cherishes the love of comfort is not fit to be deemed a scholar."

IV

The Master said, "When good government prevails in a state, language may be lofty and bold, and actions the same. When bad government prevails, the actions may be lofty and bold, but the language may be with some reserve."

V

The Master said, "The virtuous will be sure to speak correctly, but those whose speech is good may not always be virtuous. Men of principle are sure to be bold, but those who are bold may not always be men of principle."

VI

Nan-kung Kwo, submitting an inquiry to Confucius, said, "I was skillful at archery, and Âo could move a boat along upon the land, but neither of them died a natural death. Yü and Chî personally wrought at the toils of husbandry, and they became possessors of the kingdom." The Master made no reply; but when Nan-kung Kwo went out, he said, "A superior man indeed is this! An esteemer of virtue indeed is this!"

VII

The Master said, "Superior men, and yet not always virtuous, there have been, alas! But there never has been a mean man, and, at the same time, virtuous."

VIII

The Master said, "Can there be love which does not lead to strictness with its object? Can there be loyalty which does not lead to the instruction of its object?"

IX

The Master said, "In preparing the governmental notifications, P'î Shǎn first made the rough draught; Shî-shû examined and discussed its contents; Tsze-yü, the manager of Foreign intercourse, then polished the style; and, finally, Tsze-ch'ân of Tung-lî gave it the proper elegance and finish."

X

1. Someone asked about Tsze-ch'ân. The Master said, "He was a kind man."

2. He asked about Tsze-hsî. The Master said, "That man! That man!"

3. He asked about Kwan Chung. "For him," said the Master, "the city of Pien, with three hundred families, was taken from the chief of the Po family, who did not utter a murmuring word, though, to the end of his life, he had only coarse rice to eat."

XI

The Master said, "To be poor without murmuring is difficult. To be rich without being proud is easy."

XII

The Master said, "Măng Kung-ch'o is more than fit to be chief officer in the families of Châo and Wei, but he is not fit to be great officer to either of the States T'ang or Hsieh."

XIII

1. Tsze-lû asked what constituted a complete man. The Master said, "Suppose a man with the knowledge of Tsang Wû-chung, the freedom from covetousness of Kung-ch'o, the bravery of Chwang of Pien, and the varied talents of Zan Ch'iû; add to these the accomplishments of the rules of propriety and music: such a one might be reckoned a complete man."

2. He then added, "But what is the necessity for a complete man of the present day to have all these things? The man, who in the view of gain, thinks of righteousness; who in the view of danger is prepared to give up his life; and who does not forget an old agreement however far back it extends: such a man may be reckoned a complete man."

XIV

1. The Master asked Kung-ming Chiâ about Kung-shû Wăn, saying, "Is it true that your master speaks not, laughs not, and takes not?"

2. Kung-ming Chiâ replied, "This has arisen from the reporters going beyond the truth. My master speaks when it is the time to speak, and so men do not get tired of his speaking. He laughs when there is occasion to be joyful, and so men do not get tired of his laughing. He takes when it is consistent with righteousness to do so, and so men do not get tired of his taking." The Master said, "So! But is it so with him?"

XV

The Master said, "Tsang Wû-chung, keeping possession of Fang, asked of the Duke of Lû to appoint a successor to him in his family. Although it may be said that he was not using force with his sovereign, I believe he was."

XVI

The Master said, "The Duke Wăn of Tsin was crafty and not upright. The Duke Hwan of Ch'î was upright and not crafty."

XVII

1. Tsze-lû said, "The Duke Hwan caused his brother Chiû to be killed, when Shâo Hû died with his master, but Kwan Chung did not die. May not I say that he was wanting in virtue?"

2. The Master said, "The Duke Hwan assembled all the princes together, and that not with weapons of war and chariots: it was all through the influence of Kwan Chung. Whose beneficence was like his? Whose beneficence was like his?"

XVIII

1. Tsze-kung said, "Kwan Chung, I apprehend, was wanting in virtue. When the Duke Hwan caused his brother Chiû to be killed, Kwan Chung was not able to die with him. Moreover, he became prime minister to Hwan."

2. The Master said, "Kwan Chung acted as prime minister to the Duke Hwan, made him leader of all the princes, and united and rectified the whole kingdom. Down to the present day, the people enjoy the gifts which he conferred. But for Kwan Chung, we should now be wearing our hair unbound, and the lappets of our coats buttoning on the left side.

3. "Will you require from him the small fidelity of common men and common women, who would commit suicide in a stream or ditch, no one knowing anything about them?"

XIX

1. The great officer, Hsien, who had been family minister to Kung-shû Wǎn, ascended to the prince's court in company with Wǎn.

2. The Master, having heard of it, said, "He deserved to be considered Wǎn (the accomplished)."

XX

1. The Master was speaking about the unprincipled course of the Duke Ling of Wei, when Ch'î K'ang said, "Since he is of such a character, how is it he does not lose his State?"

2. Confucius said, "The Chung-shû Yü has the superintendence of his guests and of strangers; the litanist, T'o, has the management of his ancestral temple; and Wang-sun Chiâ has the direction of the army and forces: with such officers as these, how should he lose his State?"

XXI

The Master said, "He who speaks without modesty will find it difficult to make his words good."

XXII

1. Chăn Ch'ăng murdered the Duke Chien of Ch'î.

2. Confucius bathed, went to court, and informed the Duke Âi, saying, "Chăn Ch'ăng has slain his sovereign. I beg that you will undertake to punish him."

3. The duke said, "Inform the chiefs of the three families of it."

4. Confucius retired, and said, "Following in the rear of the great officers, I did not dare not to represent such a matter, and my prince says, 'Inform the chiefs of the three families of it.'"

5. He went to the chiefs, and informed them, but they would not act. Confucius then said, "Following in the rear of the great officers, I did not dare not to represent such a matter."

XXIII

Tsze-lû asked how a ruler should be served. The Master said, "Do not impose on him, and, moreover, withstand him to his face."

XXIV

The Master said, "The progress of the superior man is upwards; the progress of the mean man is downwards."

XXV

The Master said, "In ancient times, men learned with a view to their own improvement. Nowadays, men learn with a view to the approbation of others."

XXVI

1. Chü Po-yü sent a messenger with friendly inquiries to Confucius.

2. Confucius sat with him, and questioned him. "What," said he, "is your master engaged in?" The messenger replied, "My master is anxious to make his faults few, but he has not yet succeeded." He then went out, and the Master said, "A messenger indeed! A messenger indeed!"

XXVII

The Master said, "He who is not in any particular office, has nothing to do with plans for the administration of its duties."

XXVIII

The philosopher Tsǎng said, "The superior man, in his thoughts, does not go out of his place."

XXIX

The Master said, "The superior man is modest in his speech, but exceeds in his actions."

XXX

1. The Master said, "The way of the superior man is threefold, but I am not equal to it. Virtuous, he is free from anxieties; wise, he is free from perplexities; bold, he is free from fear.

2. Tsze-kung said, "Master, that is what you yourself say."

XXXI

Tsze-kung was in the habit of comparing men together. The Master said, "Tsze must have reached a high pitch of excellence! Now, I have not leisure for this."

XXXII

The Master said, "I will not be concerned at men's not knowing me; I will be concerned at my own want of ability."

XXXIII

The Master said, "He who does not anticipate attempts to deceive him, nor think beforehand of his not being believed, and yet apprehends these things readily (when they occur) — is he not a man of superior worth?"

XXXIV

1. Wei-shǎng Mâu said to Confucius, "Ch'iû, how is it that you keep roosting about? Is it not that you are an insinuating talker?"

2. Confucius said, "I do not dare to play the part of such a talker, but I hate obstinacy."

XXXV

The Master said, "A horse is called a ch'î, not because of its strength, but because of its other good qualities."

XXXVI

1. Someone said, "What do you say concerning the principle that injury should be recompensed with kindness?"

2. The Master said, "With what then will you recompense kindness?

3. "Recompense injury with justice, and recompense kindness with kindness."

XXXVII

1. The Master said, "Alas! There is no one that knows me."

2. Tsze-kung said, "What do you mean by thus saying—that no one knows you?" The Master replied, "I do not murmur against Heaven. I do not grumble against men. My studies lie low, and my penetration rises high. But there is Heaven—that knows me!"

XXXVIII

1. The Kung-po Liâo, having slandered Tsze-lû to Chî-sun, Tsze-fû Ching-po informed Confucius of it, saying, "Our master is certainly being led astray by the Kung-po Liâo, but I have still power enough left to cut Liâo off, and expose his corpse in the market and in the court."

2. The Master said, "If my principles are to advance, it is so ordered. If they are to fall to the ground, it is so ordered. What can the Kung-po Liâo do where such ordering is concerned?"

XXXIX

1. The Master said, "Some men of worth retire from the world.

2. "Some retire from particular states.

3. "Some retire because of disrespectful looks.

4. "Some retire because of contradictory language."

XL

The Master said, "Those who have done this are seven men."

XLI

Tsze-lû happening to pass the night in Shih-măn, the gatekeeper said to him, "Whom do you come from?" Tsze-lû said, "From Mr. K'ung." "It is he, is it not," said the other, "who knows the impracticable nature of the times and yet will be doing in them?"

XLII

1. The Master was playing, one day, on a musical stone in Wei, when a man, carrying a straw basket, passed the door of the house where Confucius was, and said, "His heart is full who so beats the musical stone."

2. A little while after, he added, "How contemptible is the one-ideaed obstinacy those sounds display! When one is taken no notice of, he has simply at once to give over his wish for public employment. 'Deep water must be crossed with the clothes on; shallow water may be crossed with the clothes held up.'"

3. The Master said, "How determined is he in his purpose! But this is not difficult!"

XLIII

1. Tsze-chang said, "What is meant when the Shû says that Kâo-tsung, while observing the usual imperial mourning, was for three years without speaking?"

2. The Master said, "Why must Kâo-tsung be referred to as an example of this? The ancients all did so. When the sovereign died, the officers all attended to their several duties, taking instructions from the prime minister for three years."

XLIV

The Master said, "When rulers love to observe the rules of propriety, the people respond readily to the calls on them for service."

XLV

Tsze-lû asked what constituted the superior man. The Master said, "The cultivation of himself in reverential carefulness." "And is this all?" said Tsze-lû. "He cultivates himself so as to give rest to others," was the reply. "And is this all?" again asked Tsze-lû. The Master said, "He cultivates himself so as to give rest to all the people. He cultivates himself so as to give rest to all the people: even Yâo and Shun were still solicitous about this."

XLVI

Yüan Zang was squatting on his heels, and so waited the approach of the Master, who said to him, "In youth not humble as befits a junior; in manhood, doing nothing worthy of being handed down; and living on to old age: this is to be a pest." With this he hit him on the shank with his staff.

XLVII

1. A youth of the village of Ch'üeh was employed by Confucius to carry the messages between him and his visitors. Someone asked about him, saying, "I suppose he has made great progress."

2. The Master said, "I observe that he is fond of occupying the seat of a full-grown man; I observe that he walks shoulder to shoulder with his elders. He is not one who is seeking to make progress in learning. He wishes quickly to become a man."

BOOK XV

WEI LING KUNG

I

1. The Duke Ling of Wei asked Confucius about tactics. Confucius replied, "I have heard all about sacrificial vessels, but I have not learned military matters." On this, he took his departure the next day.

2. When he was in Chan, their provisions were exhausted, and his followers became so ill that they were unable to rise.

3. Tsze-lû, with evident dissatisfaction, said, "Has the superior man likewise to endure in this way?" The Master said, "The superior man may indeed have to endure want, but the mean man, when he is in want, gives way to unbridled license."

II

1. The Master said, "Ts'ze, you think, I suppose, that I am one who learns many things and keeps them in memory?"

2. Tsze-kung replied, "Yes—but perhaps it is not so?"

3. "No," was the answer; "I seek a unity all-pervading."

III

The Master said, "Yu, those who know virtue are few."

IV

The Master said, "May not Shun be instanced as having governed efficiently without exertion? What did he do? He did nothing but gravely and reverently occupy his royal seat."

V

1. Tsze-chang asked how a man should conduct himself, so as to be everywhere appreciated.

2. The Master said, "Let his words be sincere and truthful, and his actions honorable and careful—such conduct may be practiced among the rude tribes of the South or the North. If his words be not sincere and truthful and his actions not honorable and careful, will he, with such conduct, be appreciated, even in his neighborhood?

3. "When he is standing, let him see those two things, as it were, fronting him. When he is in a carriage, let him see them attached to the yoke. Then may he subsequently carry them into practice."

4. Tsze-chang wrote these counsels on the end of his sash.

VI

1. The Master said, "Truly straightforward was the historiographer Yü. When good government prevailed in his State, he was like an arrow. When bad government prevailed, he was like an arrow.

2. A superior man indeed is Chü Po-yü! When good government prevails in his state, he is to be found in office. When bad government prevails, he can roll his principles up, and keep them in his breast."

VII

The Master said, "When a man may be spoken with, not to speak to him is to err in reference to the man. When a man may not be spoken with, to speak to him is to err in reference to our words. The wise err neither in regard to their man nor to their words."

VIII

The Master said, "The determined scholar and the man of virtue will not seek to live at the expense of injuring their virtue. They will even sacrifice their lives to preserve their virtue complete."

IX

Tsze-kung asked about the practice of virtue. The Master said, "The mechanic, who wishes to do his work well, must first sharpen his tools. When you are living in any state, take service with the most worthy among its great officers, and make friends of the most virtuous among its scholars."

X

1. Yen Yüan asked how the government of a country should be administered.

~ 318 ~

2. The Master said, "Follow the seasons of Hsiâ.

3. "Ride in the state carriage of Yin.

4. "Wear the ceremonial cap of Châu.

5. "Let the music be the Shâo with its pantomimes.

6. "Banish the songs of Chăng, and keep far from specious talkers. The songs of Chăng are licentious; specious talkers are dangerous."

XI

The Master said, "If a man take no thought about what is distant, he will find sorrow near at hand."

XII

The Master said, "It is all over! I have not seen one who loves virtue as he loves beauty."

XIII

The Master said, "Was not Tsang Wăn like one who had stolen his situation? He knew the virtue and the talents of Hûi of Liû-hsiâ, and yet did not procure that he should stand with him in court."

XIV

The Master said, "He who requires much from himself and little from others, will keep himself from being the object of resentment."

XV

The Master said, "When a man is not in the habit of saying, 'What shall I think of this? What shall I think of this?' I can indeed do nothing with him!"

XVI

The Master said, "When a number of people are together, for a whole day, without their conversation turning on righteousness, and when they are fond of carrying out the suggestions of a small shrewdness—theirs is indeed a hard case."

XVII

The Master said, "The superior man in everything considers righteousness to be essential. He performs it according to the rules of propriety. He brings it forth in humility. He completes it with sincerity. This is indeed a superior man."

XVIII

The Master said, "The superior man is distressed by his want of ability. He is not distressed by men's not knowing him."

XIX

The Master said, "The superior man dislikes the thought of his name not being mentioned after his death."

XX

The Master said, "What the superior man seeks, is in himself. What the mean man seeks, is in others."

XXI

The Master said, "The superior man is dignified, but does not wrangle. He is sociable, but not a partisan."

XXII

The Master said, "The superior man does not promote a man simply on account of his words, nor does he put aside good words because of the man."

XXIII

Tsze-kung asked, saying, "Is there one word which may serve as a rule of practice for all one's life?" The Master said, "Is not reciprocity such a word? What you do not want done to yourself, do not do to others."

XXIV

1. The Master said, "In my dealings with men, whose evil do I blame, whose goodness do I praise, beyond what is proper? If I do sometimes exceed in praise, there must be ground for it in my examination of the individual.

2. "This people supplied the ground why the three dynasties pursued the path of straightforwardness."

XXV

The Master said, "Even in my early days, a historiographer would leave a blank in his text, and he who had a horse would lend him to another to ride. Now, alas! There are no such things."

XXVI

The Master said, "Specious words confound virtue. Want of forbearance in small matters confounds great plans."

XXVII

The Master said, "When the multitude hate a man, it is necessary to examine into the case. When the multitude like a man, it is necessary to examine into the case."

XXVIII

The Master said, "A man can enlarge the principles which he follows; those principles do not enlarge the man."

XXIX

The Master said, "To have faults and not to reform them—this, indeed, should be pronounced having faults."

XXX

The Master said, "I have been the whole day without eating, and the whole night without sleeping—occupied with thinking. It was of no use. The better plan is to learn."

XXXI

The Master said, "The object of the superior man is truth. Food is not his object. There is plowing—even in that there is sometimes want. So with learning—emolument may be found in it. The superior man is anxious lest he should not get truth; he is not anxious lest poverty should come upon him."

XXXII

1. The Master said, "When a man's knowledge is sufficient to attain, and his virtue is not sufficient to enable him to hold, whatever he may have gained, he will lose again.

2. "When his knowledge is sufficient to attain, and he has virtue enough to hold fast, if he cannot govern with dignity, the people will not respect him.

3. "When his knowledge is sufficient to attain, and he has virtue enough to hold fast; when he governs also with dignity, yet if he try to move the people contrary to the rules of propriety: full excellence is not reached."

XXXIII

The Master said, "The superior man cannot be known in little matters; but he may be entrusted with great concerns. The small man may not be entrusted with great concerns, but he may be known in little matters."

XXXIV

The Master said, "Virtue is more to man than either water or fire. I have seen men die from treading on water and fire, but I have never seen a man die from treading the course of virtue."

XXXV

The Master said, "Let every man consider virtue as what devolves on himself. He may not yield the performance of it even to his teacher."

XXXVI

The Master said, "The superior man is correctly firm, and not firm merely."

XXXVII

The Master said, "A minister, in serving his prince, reverently discharges his duties, and makes his emolument a secondary consideration."

XXXVIII

The Master said, "In teaching there should be no distinction of classes."

XXXIX

The Master said, "Those whose courses are different cannot lay plans for one another."

XL

The Master said, "In language it is simply required that it convey the meaning."

XLI

1. The Music-master, Mien, having called upon him, when they came to the steps, the Master said, "Here are the steps." When they came to the mat for the guest to sit upon, he said, "Here is the mat." When all were seated, the Master informed him, saying, "So and so is here; so and so is here."

2. The Music-master, Mien, having gone out, Tsze-chang asked, saying, "Is it the rule to tell those things to the Music-master?"

3. The Master said, "Yes. This is certainly the rule for those who lead the blind."

BOOK XVI

CHÎ SHIH

I

1. The head of the Chî family was going to attack Chwan-yü.

2. Zan Yü and Chî-lû had an interview with Confucius, and said, "Our chief, Chî, is going to commence operations against Chwan-yü."

3. Confucius said, "Ch'iû, is it not you who are in fault here?

4. "Now, in regard to Chwan-yü, long ago, a former king appointed its ruler to preside over the sacrifices to the eastern Măng; moreover, it is in the midst of the territory of our State; and its ruler is a minister in direct connection with the sovereign: What has your chief to do with attacking it?"

5. Zan Yü said, "Our master wishes the thing; neither of us two ministers wishes it."

6. Confucius said, "Ch'iû, there are the words of Châu Zan: 'When he can put forth his ability, he takes his place in the ranks of office; when he finds himself unable to do so, he retires from it. How can he be used as a guide to a blind man, who does not support him when tottering, nor raise him up when fallen?'

7. "And further, you speak wrongly. When a tiger or rhinoceros escapes from his cage; when a tortoise or piece of jade is injured in its repository: whose is the fault?"

8. Zan Yü said, "But at present, Chwan-yü is strong and near to Pî; if our chief do not now take it, it will hereafter be a sorrow to his descendants."

9. Confucius said, "Ch'iû, the superior man hates those declining to say—'I want such and such a thing,' and framing explanations for the conduct.

10. "I have heard that rulers of States and chiefs of families are not troubled lest their people should be few, but are troubled lest they should not keep their several places; that they are not troubled with

fears of poverty, but are troubled with fears of a want of contented repose among the people in their several places. For when the people keep their several places, there will be no poverty; when harmony prevails, there will be no scarcity of people; and when there is such a contented repose, there will be no rebellious upsettings.

11. "So it is. Therefore, if remoter people are not submissive, all the influences of civil culture and virtue are to be cultivated to attract them to be so; and when they have been so attracted, they must be made contented and tranquil.

12. "Now, here are you, Yü and Ch'iû, assisting your chief. Remoter people are not submissive, and, with your help, he cannot attract them to him. In his own territory there are divisions and downfalls, leavings and separations, and, with your help, he cannot preserve it.

13. "And yet he is planning these hostile movements within the State. I am afraid that the sorrow of the Chî-sun family will not be on account of Chwan-yü, but will be found within the screen of their own court."

II

1. Confucius said, "When good government prevails in the empire, ceremonies, music, and punitive military expeditions proceed from the son of Heaven. When bad government prevails in the empire, ceremonies, music, and punitive military expeditions proceed from the princes. When these things proceed from the princes, as a rule, the cases will be few in which they do not lose their power in ten generations. When they proceed from the great officers of the princes, as a rule, the cases will be few in which they do not lose their power in five generations. When the subsidiary ministers of the great officers hold in their grasp the orders of the state, as a rule, the cases will be few in which they do not lose their power in three generations.

2. "When right principles prevail in the kingdom, government will not be in the hands of the great officers.

3. "When right principles prevail in the kingdom, there will be no discussions among the common people."

III

Confucius said, "The revenue of the state has left the ducal house now for five generations. The government has been in the hands of the great officers for four generations. On this account, the descendants of the three Hwan are much reduced."

IV

Confucius said, "There are three friendships which are advantageous, and three which are injurious. Friendship with the upright; friendship with the sincere; and friendship with the man of much observation: these are advantageous. Friendship with the man of specious airs; friendship with the insinuatingly soft; and friendship with the glib-tongued: these are injurious."

V

Confucius said, "There are three things men find enjoyment in which are advantageous, and three things they find enjoyment in which are injurious. To find enjoyment in the discriminating study of ceremonies and music; to find enjoyment in speaking of the goodness of others; to find enjoyment in having many worthy friends: these are advantageous. To find enjoyment in extravagant pleasures; to find enjoyment in idleness and sauntering; to find enjoyment in the pleasures of feasting: these are injurious."

VI

Confucius said, "There are three errors to which they who stand in the presence of a man of virtue and station are liable. They may speak when it does not come to them to speak—this is called rashness. They may not speak when it comes to them to speak—this is called concealment. They may speak without looking at the countenance of their superior—this is called blindness."

VII

Confucius said, "There are three things which the superior man guards against. In youth, when the physical powers are not yet settled, he guards against lust. When he is strong and the physical powers are full of vigor, he guards against quarrelsomeness. When he is old, and the animal powers are decayed, he guards against covetousness."

VIII

1. Confucius said, "There are three things of which the superior man stands in awe. He stands in awe of the ordinances of Heaven. He stands in awe of great men. He stands in awe of the words of sages.

2. "The mean man does not know the ordinances of Heaven, and consequently does not stand in awe of them. He is disrespectful to great men. He makes sport of the words of sages."

IX

Confucius said, "Those who are born with the possession of knowledge are the highest class of men. Those who learn, and so, readily, get possession of knowledge, are the next. Those who are dull and stupid, and yet compass the learning, are another class next to these. As to those who are dull and stupid and yet do not learn — they are the lowest of the people."

X

Confucius said, "The superior man has nine things which are subjects with him of thoughtful consideration. In regard to the use of his eyes, he is anxious to see clearly. In regard to the use of his ears, he is anxious to hear distinctly. In regard to his countenance, he is anxious that it should be benign. In regard to his demeanor, he is anxious that it should be respectful. In regard to his speech, he is anxious that it should be sincere. In regard to his doing of business, he is anxious that it should be reverently careful. In regard to what he doubts about, he is anxious to question others. When he is angry, he thinks of the difficulties (his anger may involve him in). When he sees gain to be got, he thinks of righteousness."

XI

1. Confucius said, "Contemplating good, and pursuing it, as if they could not reach it; contemplating evil, and shrinking from it, as they would from thrusting the hand into boiling water: I have seen such men, as I have heard such words.

2. "Living in retirement to study their aims, and practicing righteousness to carry out their principles: I have heard these words, but I have not seen such men."

XII

1. The duke Ching of Ch'î had a thousand teams, each of four horses, but on the day of his death, the people did not praise him for a single virtue. Po-î and Shû-ch'i died of hunger at the foot of the Shâu-yang mountain, and the people, down to the present time, praise them.

2. "Is not that saying illustrated by this?"

XIII

1. Ch'ăn K'ang asked Po-yü, saying, "Have you heard any lessons from your father different from what we have all heard?"

2. Po-yü replied, "No. He was standing alone once, when I passed below the hall with hasty steps, and said to me, "Have you learned the Odes?" On my replying "Not yet," he added, "If you do not learn the Odes, you will not be fit to converse with." I retired and studied the Odes.

3. "Another day, he was in the same way standing alone, when I passed by below the hall with hasty steps, and said to me, "Have you learned the rules of Propriety?" On my replying "Not yet," he added, "If you do not learn the rules of Propriety, your character cannot be established." I then retired, and learned the rules of Propriety.

4. "I have heard only these two things from him."

5. Ch'ăng K'ang retired, and, quite delighted, said, "I asked one thing, and I have got three things. I have heard about the Odes. I have heard about the rules of Propriety. I have also heard that the superior man maintains a distant reserve towards his son."

XIV

The wife of the prince of a state is called by him *Fû-zan*. She calls herself *Hʃiâo T'ung*. The people of the State call her *Chün Fû-zan*, and, to the people of other States, they call her *K'wa Hʃiâo Chün*. The people of other states also call her *Chün Fû-zan*.

BOOK XVII

YANG HO

I

1. Yang Ho wished to see Confucius, but Confucius would not go to see him. On this, he sent a present of a pig to Confucius, who, having chosen a time when Ho was not at home, went to pay his respects for the gift. He met him, however, on the way.

2. Ho said to Confucius, "Come, let me speak with you." He then asked, "Can he be called benevolent who keeps his jewel in his bosom, and leaves his country to confusion?" Confucius replied, "No." "Can he be called wise, who is anxious to be engaged in public employment, and yet is constantly losing the opportunity of being so?" Confucius again said, "No." "The days and months are passing away; the years do not wait for us." Confucius said, "Right; I will go into office."

II

The Master said, "By nature, men are nearly alike; by practice, they get to be wide apart."

III

The Master said, "There are only the wise of the highest class, and the stupid of the lowest class, who cannot be changed."

IV

1. The Master, having come to Wû-chăng, heard there the sound of stringed instruments and singing.

2. Well pleased and smiling, he said, "Why use an ox knife to kill a fowl?"

3. Tsze-yû replied, "Formerly, Master, I heard you say, 'When the man of high station is well instructed, he loves men; when the man of low station is well instructed, he is easily ruled.'"

4. The Master said, "My disciples, Yen's words are right. What I said was only in sport."

V

1. Kung-shăn Fû-zâo, when he was holding Pî, and in an attitude of rebellion, invited the Master to visit him, who was rather inclined to go.

2. Tsze-lû was displeased, and said, "Indeed, you cannot go! Why must you think of going to see Kung-shăn?"

3. The Master said, "Can it be without some reason that he has invited me? If anyone employ me, may I not make an eastern Chău?"

VI

Tsze-chang asked Confucius about perfect virtue. Confucius said, "To be able to practice five things everywhere under Heaven constitutes perfect virtue." He begged to ask what they were, and was told, "Gravity, generosity of soul, sincerity, earnestness, and kindness. If you are grave, you will not be treated with disrespect. If you are generous, you will win all. If you are sincere, people will repose trust in you. If you are earnest, you will accomplish much. If you are kind, this will enable you to employ the services of others."

VII

1. Pî Hsî inviting him to visit him, the Master was inclined to go.

2. Tsze-lû said, "Master, formerly I have heard you say, 'When a man in his own person is guilty of doing evil, a superior man will not associate with him.' Pî Hsî is in rebellion, holding possession of Chung-mâu; if you go to him, what shall be said?"

3. The Master said, "Yes, I did use these words. But is it not said, that, if a thing be really hard, it may be ground without being made thin? Is it not said, that, if a thing be really white, it may be steeped in a dark fluid without being made black?

4. "Am I a bitter gourd? How can I be hung up out of the way of being eaten?"

VIII

1. The Master said, "Yû, have you heard the six words to which are attached six becloudings?" Yû replied, "I have not."

2. "Sit down, and I will tell them to you.

3. "There is the love of being benevolent without the love of learning—the beclouding here leads to a foolish simplicity. There is the love of knowing without the love of learning—the beclouding here leads to dissipation of mind. There is the love of being sincere without the love of learning—the beclouding here leads to an injurious disregard of consequences. There is the love of straightforwardness without the love of learning—the beclouding here leads to rudeness. There is the love of boldness without the love of learning—the beclouding here leads to insubordination. There is the love of firmness without the love of learning—the beclouding here leads to extravagant conduct."

IX

1. The Master said, "My children, why do you not study the Book of Poetry?

2. "The Odes serve to stimulate the mind.

3. "They may be used for purposes of self-contemplation.

4. "They teach the art of sociability.

5. "They show how to regulate feelings of resentment.

6. "From them you learn the more immediate duty of serving one's father, and the remoter one of serving one's prince.

7. "From them we become largely acquainted with the names of birds, beasts, and plants."

X

The Master said to Po-yü, "Do you give yourself to the Châu-nan and the Shâo-nan. The man who has not studied the Châu-nan and the Shâo-nan is like one who stands with his face right against a wall. Is he not so?"

XI

The Master said, "'It is according to the rules of propriety,' they say. 'It is according to the rules of propriety,' they say. Are gems and silk all that is meant by propriety? 'It is music,' they say. 'It is music,' they say. Are bells and drums all that is meant by music?"

XII

The Master said, "He who puts on an appearance of stern firmness, while inwardly he is weak, is like one of the small, mean people — yea, is he not like the thief who breaks through, or climbs over, a wall?"

XIII

The Master said, "Your good, careful people of the villages are the thieves of virtue."

XIV

The Master said, "To tell, as we go along, what we have heard on the way, is to cast away our virtue."

XV

1. The Master said, "There are those mean creatures! How impossible it is along with them to serve one's prince!

2. "While they have not got their aims, their anxiety is how to get them. When they have got them, their anxiety is lest they should lose them.

3. "When they are anxious lest such things should be lost, there is nothing to which they will not proceed."

XVI

1. The Master said, "Anciently, men had three failings, which now perhaps are not to be found.

2. "The high-mindedness of antiquity showed itself in a disregard of small things; the high-mindedness of the present day shows itself in wild license. The stern dignity of antiquity showed itself in grave reserve; the stern dignity of the present day shows itself in quarrelsome perverseness. The stupidity of antiquity showed itself in straightforwardness; the stupidity of the present day shows itself in sheer deceit."

XVII

The Master said, "Fine words and an insinuating appearance are seldom associated with virtue."

XVIII

The Master said, "I hate the manner in which purple takes away the luster of vermilion. I hate the way in which the songs of Chang confound the music of the Yâ.

I hate those who with their sharp mouths overthrow kingdoms and families."

XIX

1. The Master said, "I would prefer not speaking."

2. Tsze-kung said, "If you, Master, do not speak, what shall we, your disciples, have to record?"

3. The Master said, "Does Heaven speak? The four seasons pursue their courses, and all things are continually being produced, but does Heaven say anything?"

XX

Zû Pei wished to see Confucius, but Confucius declined, on the ground of being sick, to see him. When the bearer of this message went out at the door, (the Master) took his lute and sang to it, in order that Pei might hear him.

XXI

1. Tsâi Wo asked about the three years' mourning for parents, saying that one year was long enough.

2. "If the superior man," said he, "abstains for three years from the observances of propriety, those observances will be quite lost. If for three years he abstains from music, music will be ruined.

3. "Within a year the old grain is exhausted, and the new grain has sprung up, and, in procuring fire by friction, we go through all the changes of wood for that purpose. After a complete year, the mourning may stop."

4. The Master said, "If you were, after a year, to eat good rice, and wear embroidered clothes, would you feel at ease?" "I should," replied Wo.

5. The Master said, "If you can feel at ease, do it. But a superior man, during the whole period of mourning, does not enjoy pleasant food which he may eat, nor derive pleasure from music which he may hear.

He also does not feel at ease, if he is comfortably lodged. Therefore he does not do what you propose. But now you feel at ease and may do it."

6. Tsâi Wo then went out, and the Master said, "This shows Yü's want of virtue. It is not till a child is three years old that it is allowed to leave the arms of its parents. And the three years' mourning is universally observed throughout the empire. Did Yü enjoy the three years' love of his parents?"

XXII

The Master said, "Hard is it to deal with him, who will stuff himself with food the whole day, without applying his mind to anything good! Are there not gamesters and chess players? To be one of these would still be better than doing nothing at all."

XXIII

Tsze-lû said, "Does the superior man esteem valor?" The Master said, "The superior man holds righteousness to be of highest importance. A man in a superior situation, having valor without righteousness, will be guilty of insubordination; one of the lower people having valor without righteousness, will commit robbery."

XXIV

1. Tsze-kung said, "Has the superior man his hatreds also?" The Master said, "He has his hatreds. He hates those who proclaim the evil of others. He hates the man who, being in a low station, slanders his superiors. He hates those who have valor merely, and are unobservant of propriety. He hates those who are forward and determined, and, at the same time, of contracted understanding."

2. The Master then inquired, "Ts'ze, have you also your hatreds?" Tsze-kung replied, "I hate those who pry out matters, and ascribe the knowledge to their wisdom. I hate those who are only not modest, and think that they are valorous. I hate those who make known secrets, and think that they are straightforward."

XXV

The Master said, "Of all people, girls and servants are the most difficult to behave to. If you are familiar with them, they lose their humility. If you maintain a reserve towards them, they are discontented."

XXVI

The Master said, "When a man at forty is the object of dislike, he will always continue what he is."

BOOK XVIII

WEI TSZE

I

1. The viscount of Wei withdrew from the court. The Viscount of Chî became a slave to Châu. Pî-kan remonstrated with him and died.

2. Confucius said, "The Yin dynasty possessed these three men of virtue."

II

Hûi of Liû-hsiâ being chief criminal judge, was thrice dismissed from his office. Someone said to him, "Is it not yet time for you, sir, to leave this?" He replied, "Serving men in an upright way, where shall I go to, and not experience such a thrice-repeated dismissal? If I choose to serve men in a crooked way, what necessity is there for me to leave the country of my parents?"

III

The duke Ching of Ch'î, with reference to the manner in which he should treat Confucius, said, "I cannot treat him as I would the chief of the Chî family. I will treat him in a manner between that accorded to the chief of the Chî, and that given to the chief of the Măng family." He also said, "I am old; I cannot use his doctrines." Confucius took his departure.

IV

The people of Ch'î sent to Lû a present of female musicians, which Chî Hwan received, and for three days no court was held. Confucius took his departure.

V

1. The madman of Ch'û, Chieh-yü, passed by Confucius, singing and saying, "O Făng! O Făng! How is your virtue degenerated! As to the past, reproof is useless; but the future may still be provided

against. Give up your vain pursuit. Give up your vain pursuit. Peril awaits those who now engage in affairs of government."

2. Confucius alighted and wished to converse with him, but Chieh-yü hastened away, so that he could not talk with him.

VI

1. Ch'ang-tsü and Chieh-nî were at work in the field together, when Confucius passed by them, and sent Tsze-lû to inquire for the ford.

2. Ch'ang-tsü said, "Who is he that holds the reins in the carriage there?" Tsze-lû told him, "It is K'ung Ch'iû." "Is it not K'ung Ch'iû of Lû?" asked he. "Yes," was the reply, to which the other rejoined, "He knows the ford."

3. Tsze-lû then inquired of Chieh-nî, who said to him, "Who are you, sir?" He answered, "I am Chung Yü." "Are you not the disciple of K'ung Ch'iû of Lû?" asked the other. "I am," replied he, and then Chieh-nî said to him, "Disorder, like a swelling flood, spreads over the whole empire, and who is he that will change its state for you? Than follow one who merely withdraws from this one and that one, had you not better follow those who have withdrawn from the world altogether?" With this he fell to covering up the seed, and proceeded with his work, without stopping.

4. Tsze-lû went and reported their remarks, when the Master observed with a sigh, "It is impossible to associate with birds and beasts, as if they were the same with us. If I associate not with these people — with mankind — with whom shall I associate? If right principles prevailed through the empire, there would be no use for me to change its state."

VII

1. Tsze-lû, following the Master, happened to fall behind, when he met an old man, carrying across his shoulder on a staff a basket for weeds. Tsze-lû said to him, "Have you seen my master, sir!" The old man replied, "Your four limbs are unaccustomed to toil; you cannot distinguish the five kinds of grain: who is your master?" With this, he planted his staff in the ground, and proceeded to weed.

2. Tsze-lû joined his hands across his breast, and stood before him.

3. The old man kept Tsze-lû to pass the night in his house, killed a fowl, prepared millet, and feasted him. He also introduced to him his two sons.

4. Next day, Tsze-lû went on his way, and reported his adventure. The Master said, "He is a recluse," and sent Tsze-lû back to see him again, but when he got to the place, the old man was gone.

5. Tsze-lû then said to the family, "Not to take office is not righteous. If the relations between old and young may not be neglected, how is it that he sets aside the duties that should be observed between sovereign and minister? Wishing to maintain his personal purity, he allows that great relation to come to confusion. A superior man takes office, and performs the righteous duties belonging to it. As to the failure of right principles to make progress, he is aware of that."

VIII

1. The men who have retired to privacy from the world have been Po-î, Shû-ch'î, Yü-chung, Î-yî, Chû-chang, Hûi of Liû-hsîa, and Shâo-lien.

2. The Master said, "Refusing to surrender their wills, or to submit to any taint in their persons—such, I think, were Po-î and Shû-ch'î.

3. "It may be said of Hûi of Liû-hsîa, and of Shâo-lien, that they surrendered their wills, and submitted to taint in their persons, but their words corresponded with reason, and their actions were such as men are anxious to see. This is all that is to be remarked in them.

4. "It may be said of Yü-chung and Î-yî, that, while they hid themselves in their seclusion, they gave a license to their words; but, in their persons, they succeeded in preserving their purity, and, in their retirement, they acted according to the exigency of the times.

5. "I am different from all these. I have no course for which I am predetermined, and no course against which I am predetermined."

IX

1. The grand music master, Chih, went to Ch'î.

2. Kan, the master of the band at the second meal, went to Ch'û. Liâo, the band master at the third meal, went to Ts'âi. Chüeh, the band master at the fourth meal, went to Ch'in.

3. Fang-shü, the drum master, withdrew to the north of the river.

4. Wû, the master of the hand drum, withdrew to the Han.

5. Yang, the assistant music master, and Hsiang, master of the musical stone, withdrew to an island in the sea.

X

The Duke of Châu addressed his son, the Duke of Lû, saying, "The virtuous prince does not neglect his relations. He does not cause the great ministers to repine at his not employing them. Without some great cause, he does not dismiss from their offices the members of old families. He does not seek in one man talents for every employment."

XI

To Châu belonged the eight officers, Po-tâ, Po-kwô, Chung-tû, Chung-hwû, Shû-yâ, Shû-hsiâ, Chî-sui, and Chî-kwa.

BOOK XIX

TSZE-CHANG

I

Tsze-chang said, "The scholar, trained for public duty, seeing threatening danger, is prepared to sacrifice his life. When the opportunity of gain is presented to him, he thinks of righteousness. In sacrificing, his thoughts are reverential. In mourning, his thoughts are about the grief which he should feel. Such a man commands our approbation indeed."

II

Tsze-chang said, "When a man holds fast to virtue, but without seeking to enlarge it, and believes right principles, but without firm sincerity, what account can be made of his existence or nonexistence?"

III

The disciples of Tsze-hsiâ asked Tsze-chang about the principles that should characterize mutual intercourse. Tsze-chang asked, "What does Tsze-hsiâ say on the subject?" They replied, "Tsze-hsiâ says: 'Associate with those who can advantage you. Put away from you those who cannot do so.'" Tsze-chang observed, "This is different from what I have learned. The superior man honors the talented and virtuous, and bears with all. He praises the good, and pities the incompetent. Am I possessed of great talents and virtue? Who is there among men whom I will not bear with? Am I devoid of talents and virtue? Men will put me away from them. What have we to do with the putting away of others?"

IV

Tsze-hsiâ said, "Even in inferior studies and employments there is something worth being looked at; but if it be attempted to carry them out to what is remote, there is a danger of their proving inapplicable. Therefore, the superior man does not practice them."

V

Tsze-hsiâ said, "He, who from day to day recognizes what he has not yet, and from month to month does not forget what he has attained to, may be said indeed to love to learn."

VI

Tsze-hsiâ said, "There are learning extensively, and having a firm and sincere aim; inquiring with earnestness, and reflecting with self-application: virtue is in such a course."

VII

Tsze-hsiâ said, "Mechanics have their shops to dwell in, in order to accomplish their works. The superior man learns, in order to reach to the utmost of his principles."

VIII

Tsze-hsiâ said, "The mean man is sure to gloss his faults."

IX

Tsze-hsiâ said, "The superior man undergoes three changes. Looked at from a distance, he appears stern; when approached, he is mild; when he is heard to speak, his language is firm and decided."

X

Tsze-hsiâ said, "The superior man, having obtained their confidence, may then impose labors on his people. If he have not gained their confidence, they will think that he is oppressing them. Having obtained the confidence of his prince, one may then remonstrate with him. If he have not gained his confidence, the prince will think that he is vilifying him."

XI

Tsze-hsiâ said, "When a person does not transgress the boundary line in the great virtues, he may pass and repass it in the small virtues."

XII

1. Tsze-yû said, "The disciples and followers of Tsze-hsiâ, in sprinkling and sweeping the ground, in answering and replying, in advancing

and receding, are sufficiently accomplished. But these are only the branches of learning, and they are left ignorant of what is essential. How can they be acknowledged as sufficiently taught?"

2. Tsze-hsiâ heard of the remark and said, "Alas! Yen Yû is wrong. According to the way of the superior man in teaching, what departments are there which he considers of prime importance, and delivers? What are there which he considers of secondary importance, and allows himself to be idle about? But as in the case of plants, which are assorted according to their classes, so he deals with his disciples. How can the way of a superior man be such as to make fools of any of them? Is it not the sage alone, who can unite in one the beginning and the consummation of learning?"

XIII

Tsze-hsiâ said, "The officer, having discharged all his duties, should devote his leisure to learning. The student, having completed his learning, should apply himself to be an officer."

XIV

Tsze-hsiâ said, "Mourning, having been carried to the utmost degree of grief, should stop with that."

XV

Tsze-hsiâ said, "My friend Chang can do things which are hard to be done, but yet he is not perfectly virtuous."

XVI

The philosopher Tsăng said, "How imposing is the manner of Chang! It is difficult along with him to practice virtue."

XVII

The philosopher Tsăng said, "I heard this from our Master: 'Men may not have shown what is in them to the full extent, and yet they will be found to do so, on occasion of mourning for their parents.'"

XVIII

The philosopher Tsăng said, "I have heard this from our Master: 'The filial piety of Măng Chwang, in other matters, was what other men are competent to, but, as seen in his not changing the ministers of his father, nor his father's mode of government, it is difficult to be attained to.'"

XIX

The chief of the Măng family having appointed Yang Fû to be chief criminal judge, the latter consulted the philosopher Tsăng. Tsăng said, "The rulers have failed in their duties, and the people consequently have been disorganized, for a long time. When you have found out the truth of any accusation, be grieved for and pity them, and do not feel joy at your own ability."

XX

Tsze-kung said, "Châu's wickedness was not so great as that name implies. Therefore, the superior man hates to dwell in a low-lying situation, where all the evil of the world will flow in upon him."

XXI

Tsze-kung said, "The faults of the superior man are like the eclipses of the sun and moon. He has his faults, and all men see them; he changes again, and all men look up to him."

XXII

1. Kung-sun Ch'âo of Wei asked Tsze-kung, saying, "From whom did Chung-nî get his learning?"

2. Tsze-kung replied, "The doctrines of Wăn and Wû have not yet fallen to the ground. They are to be found among men. Men of talents and virtue remember the greater principles of them, and others, not possessing such talents and virtue, remember the smaller. Thus, all possess the doctrines of Wăn and Wû. Where could our Master go that he should not have an opportunity of learning them? And yet what necessity was there for his having a regular master?"

XXIII

1. Shû-sun Wû-shû observed to the great officers in the court, saying, "Tsze-kung is superior to Chung-nî."

2. Tsze-fû Ching-po reported the observation to Tsze-kung, who said, "Let me use the comparison of a house and its encompassing wall. My wall only reaches to the shoulders. One may peep over it, and see whatever is valuable in the apartments.

3. "The wall of my Master is several fathoms high. If one does not find the door and enter by it, he cannot see the ancestral temple with its beauties, nor all the officers in their rich array.

4. "But I may assume that they are few who find the door. Was not the observation of the chief only what might have been expected?"

XXIV

Shû-sun Wû-shû having spoken revilingly of Chung-nî, Tsze-kung said, "It is of no use doing so. Chung-nî cannot be reviled. The talents and virtue of other men are hillocks and mounds which may be stepped over. Chung-nî is the sun or moon, which it is not possible to step over. Although a man may wish to cut himself off from the sage, what harm can he do to the sun or moon? He only shows that he does not know his own capacity.

XXV

1. Ch'ăn Tsze-ch'in, addressing Tsze-kung, said, "You are too modest. How can Chung-nî be said to be superior to you?"

2. Tsze-kung said to him, "For one word a man is often deemed to be wise, and for one word he is often deemed to be foolish. We ought to be careful indeed in what we say.

3. "Our Master cannot be attained to, just in the same way as the heavens cannot be gone up to by the steps of a stair.

4. "Were our Master in the position of the ruler of a State or the chief of a Family, we should find verified the description which has been given of a sage's rule: he would plant the people, and forthwith they would be established; he would lead them on, and forthwith they would follow him; he would make them happy, and forthwith multitudes would resort to his dominions; he would stimulate them, and forthwith they would be harmonious. While he lived, he would be glorious. When he died, he would be bitterly lamented. How is it possible for him to be attained to?"

BOOK XX

YÂO YÜEH

I

1. Yâo said, "Oh! you, Shun, the Heaven-determined order of succession now rests in your person. Sincerely hold fast the due Mean. If there shall be distress and want within the four seas, the Heavenly revenue will come to a perpetual end."

2. Shun also used the same language in giving charge to Yü.

3. T'ang said, "I, the child Lî, presume to use a dark-colored victim, and presume to announce to Thee, O most great and sovereign God, that the sinner I dare not pardon, and thy ministers, O God, I do not keep in obscurity. The examination of them is by thy mind, O God. If, in my person, I commit offenses, they are not to be attributed to you, the people of the myriad regions. If you in the myriad regions commit offenses, these offenses must rest on my person."

4. Châu conferred great gifts, and the good were enriched.

5. "Although he has his near relatives, they are not equal to my virtuous men. The people are throwing blame upon me, the One man."

6. He carefully attended to the weights and measures, examined the body of the laws, restored the discarded officers, and the good government of the kingdom took its course.

7. He revived States that had been extinguished, restored families whose line of succession had been broken, and called to office those who had retired into obscurity, so that throughout the kingdom the hearts of the people turned towards him.

8. What he attached chief importance to were the food of the people, the duties of mourning, and sacrifices.

9. By his generosity, he won all. By his sincerity, he made the people repose trust in him. By his earnest activity, his achievements were great. By his justice, all were delighted.

II

1. Tsze-chang asked Confucius, saying, "In what way should a person in authority act in order that he may conduct government properly?" The Master replied, "Let him honor the five excellent, and banish away the four bad things—then may he conduct government properly." Tsze-chang said, "What are meant by the five excellent things?" The Master said, "When the person in authority is beneficent without great expenditure; when he lays tasks on the people without their repining; when he pursues what he desires without being covetous; when he maintains a dignified ease without being proud; when he is majestic without being fierce."

2. Tsze-chang said, "What is meant by being beneficent without great expenditure?" The Master replied, "When the person in authority makes more beneficial to the people the things from which they naturally derive benefit—is not this being beneficent without great expenditure? When he chooses the labors which are proper, and makes them labor on them, who will repine? When his desires are set on benevolent government, and he secures it, who will accuse him of covetousness? Whether he has to do with many people or few, or with things great or small, he does not dare to indicate any disrespect—is not this to maintain a dignified ease without any pride? He adjusts his clothes and cap, and throws a dignity into his looks, so that, thus dignified, he is looked at with awe—is not this to be majestic without being fierce?"

3. Tsze-chang then asked, "What are meant by the four bad things?" The Master said, "To put the people to death without having instructed them—this is called cruelty. To require from them, suddenly, the full tale of work, without having given them warning—this is called oppression. To issue orders as if without urgency, at first, and, when the time comes, to insist on them with severity—this is called injury. And, generally, in the giving pay or rewards to men, to do it in a stingy way—this is called acting the part of a mere official."

III

1. The Master said, "Without recognizing the ordinances of Heaven, it is impossible to be a superior man.

2. "Without an acquaintance with the rules of Propriety, it is impossible for the character to be established.

3. "Without knowing the force of words, it is impossible to know men."

The Great Learning

THE TEXT OF CONFUCIUS

1. What the Great Learning teaches, is — to illustrate illustrious virtue; to renovate the people; and to rest in the highest excellence.

2. The point where to rest being known, the object of pursuit is then determined; and, that being determined, a calm unperturbedness may be attained to. To that calmness there will succeed a tranquil repose. In that repose there may be careful deliberation, and that deliberation will be followed by the attainment of the desired end.

3. Things have their root and their branches. Affairs have their end and their beginning. To know what is first and what is last will lead near to what is taught in the Great Learning.

4. The ancients who wished to illustrate illustrious virtue throughout the kingdom, first ordered well their own states. Wishing to order well their states, they first regulated their families. Wishing to regulate their families, they first cultivated their persons. Wishing to cultivate their persons, they first rectified their hearts. Wishing to rectify their hearts, they first sought to be sincere in their thoughts. Wishing to be sincere in their thoughts, they first extended to the utmost their knowledge. Such extension of knowledge lay in the investigation of things.

5. Things being investigated, knowledge became complete. Their knowledge being complete, their thoughts were sincere. Their thoughts being sincere, their hearts were then rectified. Their hearts being rectified, their persons were cultivated. Their persons being cultivated, their families were regulated. Their families being regulated, their states were rightly governed. Their states being rightly governed, the whole kingdom was made tranquil and happy.

6. From the Son of Heaven down to the mass of the people, all must consider the cultivation of the person the root of everything besides.

7. It cannot be, when the root is neglected, that what should spring from it will be well ordered. It never has been the case that what was of great importance has been slightly cared for, and, at the same time, that what was of slight importance has been greatly cared for.

COMMENTARY OF THE PHILOSOPHER TSŬNG

I

1. In the Announcement to K'ang, it is said, "He was able to make his virtue illustrious."

2. In the T'âi Chiâ, it is said, "He contemplated and studied the illustrious decrees of Heaven."

3. In the Canon of the emperor (Yâo), it is said, "He was able to make illustrious his lofty virtue."

4. These passages all show how those sovereigns made themselves illustrious.

II

1. On the bathing tub of T'ang, the following words were engraved: "If you can one day renovate yourself, do so from day to day. Yea, let there be daily renovation."

2. In the Announcement to K'ang, it is said, "To stir up the new people."

3. In the Book of Poetry, it is said, "Although Châu was an ancient state the ordinance which lighted on it was new."

4. Therefore, the superior man in everything uses his utmost endeavors.

III

1. In the Book of Poetry, it is said, "The royal domain of a thousand lî is where the people rest."

2. In the Book of Poetry, it is said, "The twittering yellow bird rests on a corner of the mound." The Master said, "When it rests, it knows where to rest. Is it possible that a man should not be equal to this bird?"

3. In the Book of Poetry, it is said, "Profound was King Wǎn. With how bright and unceasing a feeling of reverence did he regard his resting places!" As a sovereign, he rested in benevolence. As a minister, he

rested in reverence. As a son, he rested in filial piety. As a father, he rested in kindness. In communication with his subjects, he rested in good faith.

4. In the Book of Poetry, it is said, "Look at that winding course of the Ch'î, with the green bamboos so luxuriant! Here is our elegant and accomplished prince! As we cut and then file; as we chisel and then grind: so has he cultivated himself. How grave is he and dignified! How majestic and distinguished! Our elegant and accomplished prince never can be forgotten." That expression—"As we cut and then file," the work of learning. "As we chisel and then grind," indicates that of self-culture. "How grave is he and dignified!" indicates the feeling of cautious reverence. "How commanding and distinguished!" indicates an awe-inspiring deportment. "Our elegant and accomplished prince never can be forgotten," indicates how, when virtue is complete and excellence extreme, the people cannot forget them.

5. In the Book of Poetry, it is said, "Ah! The former kings are not forgotten." Future princes deem worthy what they deemed worthy, and love what they loved. The common people delight in what delighted them, and are benefited by their beneficial arrangements. It is on this account that the former kings, after they have quitted the world, are not forgotten.

IV

The Master said, "In hearing litigations, I am like any other body. What is necessary is to cause the people to have no litigations." So, those who are devoid of principle find it impossible to carry out their speeches, and a great awe would be struck into men's minds; this is called knowing the root.

V

1. This is called knowing the root.
2. This is called the perfecting of knowledge.

VI

1. What is meant by "making the thoughts sincere," is the allowing no self-deception, as when we hate a bad smell, and as when we love what is beautiful. This is called self-enjoyment. Therefore, the superior man must be watchful over himself when he is alone.

2. There is no evil to which the mean man, dwelling retired, will not proceed, but when he sees a superior man, he instantly tries to disguise himself, concealing his evil, and displaying what is good. The other beholds him, as if he saw his heart and reins—of what use is his disguise? This is an instance of the saying—"What truly is within will be manifested without." Therefore, the superior man must be watchful over himself when he is alone.

3. The disciple Tsăng said, "What ten eyes behold, what ten hands point to, is to be regarded with reverence!"

4. Riches adorn a house, and virtue adorns the person. The mind is expanded, and the body is at ease. Therefore, the superior man must make his thoughts sincere.

VII

1. What is meant by, "The cultivation of the person depends on rectifying the mind may be thus illustrated: If a man be under the influence of passion he will be incorrect in his conduct. He will be the same, if he is under the influence of terror, or under the influence of fond regard, or under that of sorrow and distress.

2. When the mind is not present, we look and do not see; we hear and do not understand; we eat and do not know the taste of what we eat.

3. This is what is meant by saying that the cultivation of the person depends on the rectifying of the mind.

VIII

1. What is meant by "The regulation of one's family depends on the cultivation of his person" is this: men are partial where they feel affection and love; partial where they despise and dislike; partial where they stand in awe and reverence; partial where they feel sorrow and compassion; partial where they are arrogant and rude. Thus it is that there are few men in the world who love and at the same time know the bad qualities of the object of their love, or who hate and yet know the excellences of the object of their hatred.

2. Hence it is said, in the common adage, "A man does not know the wickedness of his son; he does not know the richness of his growing corn."

3. This is what is meant by saying that if the person be not cultivated, a man cannot regulate his family.

IX

1. What is meant by "In order rightly to govern the state, it is necessary first to regulate the family," is this: It is not possible for one to teach others, while he cannot teach his own family. Therefore, the ruler, without going beyond his family, completes the lessons for the state. There is filial piety: therewith the sovereign should be served. There is fraternal submission: therewith elders and superiors should be served. There is kindness: therewith the multitude should be treated.

2. In the Announcement to K'ang, it is said, "Act as if you were watching over an infant." If a mother is really anxious about it, though she may not hit exactly the wants of her infant, she will not be far from doing so. There never has been a girl who learned to bring up a child, that she might afterwards marry.

3. From the loving example of one family a whole state becomes loving, and from its courtesies the whole state becomes courteous while, from the ambition and perverseness of the One man, the whole state may be led to rebellious disorder; such is the nature of the influence. This verifies the saying, "Affairs may be ruined by a single sentence; a kingdom may be settled by its One man."

4. Yâo and Shun led on the kingdom with benevolence and the people followed them. Chieh and Châu led on the kingdom with violence, and people followed them. The orders which these issued were contrary to the practices which they loved, and so the people did not follow them. On this account, the ruler must himself be possessed of the good qualities, and then he may require them in the people. He must not have the bad qualities in himself, and then he may require that they shall not be in the people. Never has there been a man, who, not having reference to his own character and wishes in dealing with others, was able effectually to instruct them.

5. Thus we see how the government of the state depends on the regulation of the family.

6. In the Book of Poetry, it is said, "That peach tree, so delicate and elegant! How luxuriant is its foliage! This girl is going to her husband's house. She will rightly order her household." Let the household be rightly ordered, and then the people of the state may be taught.

7. In the Book of Poetry, it is said, "They can discharge their duties to their elder brothers. They can discharge their duties to their younger

brothers." Let the ruler discharge his duties to his elder and younger brothers, and then he may teach the people of the state.

8. In the Book of Poetry, it is said, "In his deportment there is nothing wrong; he rectifies all the people of the state." Yes; when the ruler, as a father, a son, and a brother, is a model, then the people imitate him.

9. This is what is meant by saying, "The government of his kingdom depends on his regulation of the family."

X

1. What is meant by "The making the whole kingdom peaceful and happy depends on the government of his state," this: When the sovereign behaves to his aged, as the aged should be behaved to, the people become filial; when the sovereign behaves to his elders, as the elders should be behaved to, the people learn brotherly submission; when the sovereign treats compassionately the young and helpless, the people do the same. Thus the ruler has a principle with which, as with a measuring square, he may regulate his conduct.

2. What a man dislikes in his superiors, let him not display in the treatment of his inferiors; what he dislikes in inferiors, let him not display in the service of his superiors; what he hates in those who are before him, let him not therewith precede those who are behind him; what he hates in those who are behind him, let him not bestow on the left; what he hates to receive on the left, let him not bestow on the right: this is what is called "The principle with which, as with a measuring square, to regulate one's conduct."

3. In the Book of Poetry, it is said, "How much to be rejoiced in are these princes, the parents of the people!" When a prince loves what the people love, and hates what the people hate, then is he what is called the parent of the people.

4. In the Book of Poetry, it is said, "Lofty is that southern hill, with its rugged masses of rocks! Greatly distinguished are you, O grand-teacher Yin, the people all look up to you." Rulers of states may not neglect to be careful. If they deviate to a mean selfishness, they will be a disgrace in the kingdom.

5. In the Book of Poetry, it is said, "Before the sovereigns of the Yin dynasty had lost the hearts of the people, they could appear before God. Take warning from the house of Yin. The great decree is

not easily preserved." This shows that, by gaining the people, the kingdom is gained, and, by losing the people, the kingdom is lost.

6. On this account, the ruler will first take pains about his own virtue. Possessing virtue will give him the people. Possessing the people will give the territory. Possessing the territory will give him its wealth. Possessing the wealth, he will have resources for expenditure.

7. Virtue is the root; wealth is the result.

8. If he make the root his secondary object, and the result his primary, he will only wrangle with his people, and teach them rapine.

9. Hence, the accumulation of wealth is the way to scatter the people; and the letting it be scattered among them is the way to collect the people.

10. And hence, the ruler's words going forth contrary to right, will come back to him in the same way, and wealth, gotten by improper ways, will take its departure by the same.

11. In the Announcement to K'ang, it is said, "The decree indeed may not always rest on us"; that is, goodness obtains the decree, and the want of goodness loses it.

12. In the Book of Ch'û, it is said, "The kingdom of Ch'û does not consider that to be valuable. It values, instead, its good men."

13. Duke Wăn's uncle, Fan, said, "Our fugitive does not account that to be precious. What he considers precious is the affection due to his parent."

14. In the Declaration of the Duke of Ch'in, it is said, "Let me have but one minister, plain and sincere, not pretending to other abilities, but with a simple, upright, mind; and possessed of generosity, regarding the talents of others as though he himself possessed them, and, where he finds accomplished and perspicacious men, loving them in his heart more than his mouth expresses, and really showing himself able to bear them and employ them:-such a minister will be able to preserve my sons and grandsons and black-haired people, and benefits likewise to the kingdom may well be looked for from him. But if it be his character, when he finds men of ability, to be jealous and hate them; and, when he finds accomplished and perspicacious men, to oppose them and not allow their advancement, showing himself really not able to bear them: such a minister will not be able

to protect my sons and grandsons and people; and may he not also be pronounced dangerous to the state?"

15. It is only the truly virtuous man who can send away such a man and banish him, driving him out among the barbarous tribes around, determined not to dwell along with him in the Auddle Kingdom. This is in accordance with the saying, "It is only the truly virtuous man who can love or who can hate others."

16. To see men of worth and not be able to raise them to office; to raise them to office, but not to do so quickly: this is disrespectful. To see bad men and not be able to remove them; to remove them, but not to do so to a distance: this is weakness.

17. To love those whom men hate, and to hate those whom men love; this is to outrage the natural feeling of men. Calamities cannot fail to come down on him who does so.

18. Thus we see that the sovereign has a great course to pursue. He must show entire self-devotion and sincerity to attain it, and by pride and extravagance he will fail of it.

19. There is a great course also for the production of wealth. Let the producers be many and the consumers few. Let there be activity in the production, and economy in the expenditure. Then the wealth will always be sufficient.

20. The virtuous ruler, by means of his wealth, makes himself more distinguished. The vicious ruler accumulates wealth, at the expense of his life.

21. Never has there been a case of the sovereign loving benevolence, and the people not loving righteousness. Never has there been a case where the people have loved righteousness, and the affairs of the sovereign have not been carried to completion. And never has there been a case where the wealth in such a state, collected in the treasuries and arsenals, did not continue in the sovereign's possession.

22. The officer Măng Hsien said, "He who keeps horses and a carriage does not look after fowls and pigs. The family which keeps its stores of ice does not rear cattle or sheep. So, the house which possesses a hundred chariots should not keep a minister to look out for imposts that he may lay them on the people. Than to have such a minister, it were better for that house to have one who should rob it of its revenues." This is in accordance with the saying: "In a

state, pecuniary gain is not to be considered to be prosperity, but its prosperity will be found in righteousness."

23. When he who presides over a state or a family makes his revenues his chief business, he must be under the influence of some small, mean man. He may consider this man to be good; but when such a person is employed in the administration of a state or family, calamities from Heaven, and injuries from men, will befall it together, and, though a good man may take his place, he will not be able to remedy the evil. This illustrates again the saying, "In a State, gain is not to be considered prosperity, but its prosperity will be found in righteousness."

The Doctrine of the Mean

THE DOCTRINE OF THE MEAN

I

1. What Heaven has conferred is called *The Nature*; an accordance with this nature is called *The Path* of duty; the regulation of this path is called *Instruction*.

2. The path may not be left for an instant. If it could be left, it would not be the path. On this account, the superior man does not wait till he sees things, to be cautious, nor till he hears things, to be apprehensive.

3. There is nothing more visible than what is secret, and nothing more manifest than what is minute. Therefore the superior man is watchful over himself, when he is alone.

4. While there are no stirrings of pleasure, anger, sorrow, or joy, the mind may be said to be in the state of *Equilibrium*. When those feelings have been stirred, and they act in their due degree, there ensues what may be called the state of *Harmony*. This *Equilibrium* is the great root from which grow all the human actings in the world, and this *Harmony* is the universal path which they all should pursue.

5. Let the states of Equilibrium and Harmony exist in perfection, and a happy order will prevail throughout Heaven and Earth, and all things will be nourished and flourish.

II

1. Chung-nî said, "The superior man embodies the course of the Mean; the mean man acts contrary to the course of the Mean.

2. "The superior man's embodying the course of the Mean is because he is a superior man, and so always maintains the Mean. The mean man's acting contrary to the course of the Mean is because he is a mean man, and has no caution."

III

The Master said, "Perfect is the virtue which is according to the Mean! Rare have they long been among the people, who could practice it!"

IV

1. The Master said, "I know how it is that the path of the Mean is not walked in: The knowing go beyond it, and the stupid do not come up to it. I know how it is that the path of the Mean is not understood: The men of talents and virtue go beyond it, and the worthless do not come up to it.

2. "There is nobody but eats and drinks. But they are few who can distinguish flavors."

V

The Master said, "Alas! How is the path of the Mean untrodden!"

VI

The Master said, "There was Shun: He indeed was greatly wise! Shun loved to question others, and to study their words, though they might be shallow. He concealed what was bad in them and displayed what was good. He took hold of their two extremes, determined the Mean, and employed it in his government of the people. It was by this that he was Shun!"

VII

The Master said, "Men all say, 'We are wise'; but being driven forward and taken in a net, a trap, or a pitfall, they know not how to escape. Men all say, 'We are wise'; but happening to choose the course of the Mean, they are not able to keep it for a round month."

VIII

The Master said "This was the manner of Hûi: he made choice of the Mean, and whenever he got hold of what was good, he clasped it firmly, as if wearing it on his breast, and did not lose it."

IX

The Master said, "The kingdom, its States, and its families, may be perfectly ruled; dignities and emoluments may be declined; naked weapons may be trampled under the feet; but the course of the Mean cannot be attained to."

X

1. Tsze-lû asked about energy.

2. The Master said, "Do you mean the energy of the South, the energy of the North, or the energy which you should cultivate yourself?

3. "To show forbearance and gentleness in teaching others; and not to revenge unreasonable conduct: this is the energy of southern regions, and the good man makes it his study.

4. "To lie under arms; and meet death without regret: this is the energy of northern regions, and the forceful make it their study.

5. "Therefore, the superior man cultivates a friendly harmony, without being weak. How firm is he in his energy! He stands erect in the middle, without inclining to either side. How firm is he in his energy! When good principles prevail in the government of his country, he does not change from what he was in retirement. How firm is he in his energy! When bad principles prevail in the country, he maintains his course to death without changing. How firm is he in his energy!"

XI

1. The Master said, "To live in obscurity, and yet practice wonders, in order to be mentioned with honor in future ages: this is what I do not do.

2. "The good man tries to proceed according to the right path, but when he has gone halfway, he abandons it: I am not able so to stop.

3. "The superior man accords with the course of the Mean. Though he may be all unknown, unregarded by the world, he feels no regret. It is only the sage who is able for this."

XII

1. The way which the superior man pursues, reaches wide and far, and yet is secret.

2. Common men and women, however ignorant, may intermeddle with the knowledge of it; yet in its utmost reaches, there is that which even the sage does not know. Common men and women, however much below the ordinary standard of character, can carry it into practice; yet in its utmost reaches, there is that which even the sage is not able to carry into practice. Great as Heaven and Earth are, men still find some things in them with which to be dissatisfied. Thus it is that, were the superior man to speak of his way in all its greatness, nothing in the world would be found able to embrace it,

and were he to speak of it in its minuteness, nothing in the world would be found able to split it.

3. It is said in the Book of Poetry, "The hawk flies up to Heaven; the fishes leap in the deep." This expresses how this way is seen above and below.

4. The way of the superior man may be found, in its simple elements, in the intercourse of common men and women; but in its utmost reaches, it shines brightly through Heaven and Earth.

XIII

1. The Master said "The path is not far from man. When men try to pursue a course, which is far from the common indications of consciousness, this course cannot be considered the Path.

2. "In the Book of Poetry, it is said, 'In hewing an ax handle, in hewing an ax handle, the pattern is not far off.' We grasp one ax handle to hew the other; and yet, if we look askance from the one to the other, we may consider them as apart. Therefore, the superior man governs men, according to their nature, with what is proper to them, and as soon as they change what is wrong, he stops.

3. "When one cultivates to the utmost the principles of his nature, and exercises them on the principle of reciprocity, he is not far from the Path. What you do not like when done to yourself, do not do to others.

4. "In the way of the superior man there are four things, to not one of which have I as yet attained. To serve my father, as I would require my son to serve me: to this I have not attained; to serve my prince as I would require my minister to serve me: to this I have not attained; to serve my elder brother as I would require my younger brother to serve me: to this I have not attained; to set the example in behaving to a friend, as I would require him to behave to me: to this I have not attained. Earnest in practicing the ordinary virtues, and careful in speaking about them, if, in his practice, he has anything defective, the superior man dares not but exert himself; and if, in his words, he has any excess, he dares not allow himself such license. Thus his words have respect to his actions, and his actions have respect to his words; is it not just an entire sincerity which marks the superior man?"

XIV

1. The superior man does what is proper to the station in which he is; he does not desire to go beyond this.

2. In a position of wealth and honor, he does what is proper to a position of wealth and honor. In a poor and low position, he does what is proper to a poor and low position. Situated among barbarous tribes, he does what is proper to a situation among barbarous tribes. In a position of sorrow and difficulty, he does what is proper to a position of sorrow and difficulty. The superior man can find himself in no situation in which he is not himself.

3. In a high situation, he does not treat with contempt his inferiors. In a low situation, he does not court the favor of his superiors. He rectifies himself, and seeks for nothing from others, so that he has no dissatisfactions. He does not murmur against Heaven, nor grumble against men.

4. Thus it is that the superior man is quiet and calm, waiting for the appointments of Heaven, while the mean man walks in dangerous paths, looking for lucky occurrences.

5. The Master said, "In archery we have something like the way of the superior man. When the archer misses the center of the target, he turns round and seeks for the cause of his failure in himself."

XV

1. The way of the superior man may be compared to what takes place in traveling, when to go to a distance we must first traverse the space that is near, and in ascending a height, when we must begin from the lower ground.

2. It is said in the Book of Poetry, "Happy union with wife and children is like the music of lutes and harps. When there is concord among brethren, the harmony is delightful and enduring. Thus may you regulate your family, and enjoy the pleasure of your wife and children."

3. The Master said, "In such a state of things, parents have entire complacence!"

XVI

1. The Master said, "How abundantly do spiritual beings display the powers that belong to them!

2. "We look for them, but do not see them; we listen to, but do not hear them; yet they enter into all things, and there is nothing without them.

3. "They cause all the people in the kingdom to fast and purify themselves, and array themselves in their richest dresses, in order to attend at their sacrifices. Then, like overflowing water, they seem to be over the heads, and on the right and left of their worshippers.

4. "It is said in the Book of Poetry, 'The approaches of the spirits, you cannot surmise; and can you treat them with indifference?'

5. "Such is the manifestness of what is minute! Such is the impossibility of repressing the outgoings of sincerity!"

XVII

1. The Master said, "How greatly filial was Shun! His virtue was that of a sage; his dignity was the throne; his riches were all within the four seas. He offered his sacrifices in his ancestral temple, and his descendants preserved the sacrifices to himself.

2. "Therefore having such great virtue, it could not but be that he should obtain the throne, that he should obtain those riches, that he should obtain his fame, that he should attain to his long life.

3. "Thus it is that Heaven, in the production of things, is sure to be bountiful to them, according to their qualities. Hence the tree that is flourishing, it nourishes, while that which is ready to fall, it overthrows.

4. "In the Book of Poetry, it is said, 'The admirable amiable prince displayed conspicuously his excelling virtue, adjusting his people, and adjusting his officers. Therefore, he received from Heaven his emoluments of dignity. It protected him, assisted him, decreed him the throne; sending from Heaven these favors, as it were repeatedly.'

5. "We may say therefore that he who is greatly virtuous will be sure to receive the appointment of Heaven."

XVIII

1. The Master said, "It is only King Wăn of whom it can be said that he had no cause for grief! His father was King Chî, and his son was King Wû. His father laid the foundations of his dignity, and his son transmitted it.

2. "King Wû continued the enterprise of King T'âi, King Chî, and King Wăn. He once buckled on his armor, and got possession of the kingdom. He did not lose the distinguished personal reputation which he had throughout the kingdom. His dignity was the royal throne. His riches were the possession of all within the four seas. He offered his sacrifices in his ancestral temple, and his descendants maintained the sacrifices to himself.

3. "It was in his old age that King Wû received the appointment to the throne, and the Duke of Châu completed the virtuous course of Wăn and Wû. He carried up the title of king to T'âi and Chî, and sacrificed to all the former dukes above them with the royal ceremonies. And this rule he extended to the princes of the kingdom, the great officers, the scholars, and the common people. If the father were a great officer and the son a scholar, then the burial was that due to a great officer, and the sacrifice that due to a scholar. If the father were a scholar and the son a great officer, then the burial was that due to a scholar, and the sacrifice that due to a great officer. The one year's mourning was made to extend only to the great officers, but the three years' mourning extended to the Son of Heaven. In the mourning for a father or mother, he allowed no difference between the noble and the mean.

XIX

1. The Master said, "How far-extending was the filial piety of King Wû and the Duke of Châu!

2. "Now filial piety is seen in the skillful carrying out of the wishes of our forefathers, and the skillful carrying forward of their undertakings.

3. "In spring and autumn, they repaired and beautified the temple halls of their fathers, set forth their ancestral vessels, displayed their various robes, and presented the offerings of the several seasons.

4. "By means of the ceremonies of the ancestral temple, they distinguished the royal kindred according to their order of descent. By ordering the parties present according to their rank, they

distinguished the more noble and the less. By the arrangement of the services, they made a distinction of talents and worth. In the ceremony of general pledging, the inferiors presented the cup to their superiors, and thus something was given the lowest to do. At the concluding feast, places were given according to the hair, and thus was made the distinction of years.

5. "They occupied the places of their forefathers, practiced their ceremonies, and performed their music. They reverenced those whom they honored, and loved those whom they regarded with affection. Thus they served the dead as they would have served them alive; they served the departed as they would have served them had they been continued among them.

6. "By the ceremonies of the sacrifices to Heaven and Earth they served God, and by the ceremonies of the ancestral temple they sacrificed to their ancestors. He who understands the ceremonies of the sacrifices to Heaven and Earth, and the meaning of the several sacrifices to ancestors, would find the government of a kingdom as easy as to look into his palm!"

XX

1. The Duke Âi asked about government.

2. The Master said, "The government of Wăn and Wû is displayed in the records, the tablets of wood and bamboo. Let there be the men and the government will flourish; but without the men, their government decays and ceases.

3. "With the right men the growth of government is rapid, just as vegetation is rapid in the earth; and, moreover, their government might be called an easily-growing rush.

4. "Therefore the administration of government lies in getting proper men. Such men are to be got by means of the ruler's own character. That character is to be cultivated by his treading in the ways of duty. And the treading those ways of duty is to be cultivated by the cherishing of benevolence.

5. "Benevolence is the characteristic element of humanity, and the great exercise of it is in loving relatives. Righteousness is the accordance of actions with what is right, and the great exercise of it is in honoring the worthy. The decreasing measures of the love due to relatives,

and the steps in the honor due to the worthy, are produced by the principle of propriety.

6. "When those in inferior situations do not possess the confidence of their superiors, they cannot retain the government of the people.

7. "Hence the sovereign may not neglect the cultivation of his own character. Wishing to cultivate his character, he may not neglect to serve his parents. In order to serve his parents, he may not neglect to acquire knowledge of men. In order to know men, he may not dispense with a knowledge of Heaven.

8. "The duties of universal obligation are five and the virtues wherewith they are practiced are three. The duties are those between sovereign and minister, between father and son, between husband and wife, between elder brother and younger, and those belonging to the intercourse of friends. Those five are the duties of universal obligation. Knowledge, magnanimity, and energy, these three, are the virtues universally binding. And the means by which they carry the duties into practice is singleness.

9. "Some are born with the knowledge of those duties; some know them by study; and some acquire the knowledge after a painful feeling of their ignorance. But the knowledge being possessed, it comes to the same thing. Some practice them with a natural ease; some from a desire for their advantages; and some by strenuous effort. But the achievement being made, it comes to the same thing."

10. The Master said, "To be fond of learning is to be near to knowledge. To practice with vigor is to be near to magnanimity. To possess the feeling of shame is to be near to energy.

11. "He who knows these three things knows how to cultivate his own character. Knowing how to cultivate his own character, he knows how to govern other men. Knowing how to govern other men, he knows how to govern the kingdom with all its States and families.

12. "All who have the government of the kingdom with its States and families have nine standard rules to follow—viz., the cultivation of their own characters; the honoring of men of virtue and talents; affection towards their relatives; respect towards the great ministers; kind and considerate treatment of the whole body of officers; dealing with the mass of the people as children; encouraging the resort of all classes of artisans; indulgent treatment of men from a distance; and the kindly cherishing of the princes of the States.

13. "By the ruler's cultivation of his own character, the duties of universal obligation are set forth. By honoring men of virtue and talents, he is preserved from errors of judgment. By showing affection to his relatives, there is no grumbling nor resentment among his uncles and brethren. By respecting the great ministers, he is kept from errors in the practice of government. By kind and considerate treatment of the whole body of officers, they are led to make the most grateful return for his courtesies. By dealing with the mass of the people as his children, they are led to exhort one another to what is good. By encouraging the resort of all classes of artisans, his resources for expenditure are rendered ample. By indulgent treatment of men from a distance, they are brought to resort to him from all quarters. And by kindly cherishing the princes of the States, the whole kingdom is brought to revere him.

14. "Self-adjustment and purification, with careful regulation of his dress, and the not making a movement contrary to the rules of propriety, this is the way for a ruler to cultivate his person. Discarding slanderers, and keeping himself from the seductions of beauty; making light of riches, and giving honor to virtue—this is the way for him to encourage men of worth and talents. Giving them places of honor and large emolument, and sharing with them in their likes and dislikes; this is the way for him to encourage his relatives to love him. Giving them numerous officers to discharge their orders and commissions: this is the way for him to encourage the great ministers. According to them a generous confidence, and making their emoluments large: this is the way to encourage the body of officers. Employing them only at the proper times, and making the imposts light: this is the way to encourage the people. By daily examinations and monthly trials, and by making their rations in accordance with their labors: this is the way to encourage the classes of artisans. To escort them on their departure and meet them on their coming; to commend the good among them, and show compassion to the incompetent: this is the way to treat indulgently men from a distance. To restore families whose line of succession has been broken, and to revive States that have been extinguished; to reduce to order States that are in confusion, and support those which are in peril; to have fixed times for their own reception at court, and the reception of their envoys; to send them away after liberal treatment, and welcome their coming with small contributions: this is the way to cherish the princes of the States.

15. "All who have the government of the kingdom with its States and families have the above nine standard rules. And the means by which they are carried into practice is singleness.

16. "In all things success depends on previous preparation, and without such previous preparation there is sure to be failure. If what is to be spoken be previously determined, there will be no stumbling. If affairs be previously determined, there will be no difficulty with them. If one's actions have been previously determined, there will be no sorrow in connection with them. If principles of conduct have been previously determined, the practice of them will be inexhaustible.

17. "When those in inferior situations do not obtain the confidence of the sovereign, they cannot succeed in governing the people. There is a way to obtain the confidence of the sovereign—if one is not trusted by his friends, he will not get the confidence of his sovereign. There is a way to being trusted by one's friends—if one is not obedient to his parents, he will not be true to friends. There is a way to being obedient to one's parents—if one, on turning his thoughts in upon himself, finds a want of sincerity, he will not be obedient to his parents. There is a way to the attainment of sincerity in one's self—if a man do not understand what is good, he will not attain sincerity in himself.

18. "Sincerity is the way of Heaven. The attainment of sincerity is the way of men. He who possesses sincerity is he who, without an effort, hits what is right, and apprehends, without the exercise of thought— he is the sage who naturally and easily embodies the right way. He who attains to sincerity is he who chooses what is good, and firmly holds it fast.

19. "To this attainment there are requisite the extensive study of what is good, accurate inquiry about it, careful reflection on it, the clear discrimination of it, and the earnest practice of it.

20. "The superior man, while there is anything he has not studied, or while in what he has studied there is anything he cannot understand, will not intermit his labor. While there is anything he has not inquired about, or anything in what he has inquired about which he does not know, he will not intermit his labor. While there is anything which he has not reflected on, or anything in what he has reflected on which he does not apprehend, he will not intermit his labor. While there is anything which he has not discriminated or his discrimination is not clear, he will not intermit his labor. If there be anything which

he has not practiced, or his practice fails in earnestness, he will not intermit his labor. If another man succeed by one effort, he will use a hundred efforts. If another man succeed by ten efforts, he will use a thousand.

21. "Let a man proceed in this way, and, though dull, he will surely become intelligent; though weak, he will surely become strong."

XXI

When we have intelligence resulting from sincerity, this condition is to be ascribed to nature; when we have sincerity resulting from intelligence, this condition is to be ascribed to instruction. But given the sincerity, and there shall be the intelligence; given the intelligence, and there shall be the sincerity.

XXII

It is only he who is possessed of the most complete sincerity that can exist under Heaven, who can give its full development to his nature. Able to give its full development to his own nature, he can do the same to the nature of other men. Able to give its full development to the nature of other men, he can give their full development to the natures of animals and things. Able to give their full development to the natures of creatures and things, he can assist the transforming and nourishing powers of Heaven and Earth. Able to assist the transforming and nourishing powers of Heaven and Earth, he may with Heaven and Earth form a ternion.

XXIII

Next to the above is he who cultivates to the utmost the shoots of goodness in him. From those he can attain to the possession of sincerity. This sincerity becomes apparent. From being apparent, it becomes manifest. From being manifest, it becomes brilliant. Brilliant, it affects others. Affecting others, they are changed by it. Changed by it, they are transformed. It is only he who is possessed of the most complete sincerity that can exist under Heaven, who can transform.

XXIV

It is characteristic of the most entire sincerity to be able to foreknow. When a nation or family is about to flourish, there are sure to be happy omens; and when it is about to perish, there are sure to be unlucky omens. Such events are seen in the milfoil and tortoise, and affect the movements of the four limbs. When calamity or happiness is about to come, the good shall certainly be foreknown by him, and the evil also. Therefore the individual possessed of the most complete sincerity is like a spirit.

XXV

1. Sincerity is that whereby self-completion is effected, and its way is that by which man must direct himself.

2. Sincerity is the end and beginning of things; without sincerity there would be nothing. On this account, the superior man regards the attainment of sincerity as the most excellent thing.

3. The possessor of sincerity does not merely accomplish the self-completion of himself. With this quality he completes other men and things also. The completing himself shows his perfect virtue. The completing other men and things shows his knowledge. But these are virtues belonging to the nature, and this is the way by which a union is effected of the external and internal. Therefore, whenever he—the entirely sincere man—employs them—that is, these virtues—their action will be right.

XXVI

1. Hence to entire sincerity there belongs ceaselessness.

2. Not ceasing, it continues long. Continuing long, it evidences itself.

3. Evidencing itself, it reaches far. Reaching far, it becomes large and substantial. Large and substantial, it becomes high and brilliant.

4. Large and substantial—this is how it contains all things. High and brilliant—this is how it overspreads all things. Reaching far and continuing long—this is how it perfects all things.

5. So large and substantial, the individual possessing it is the co-equal of Earth. So high and brilliant, it makes him the co-equal of Heaven. So far-reaching and long-continuing, it makes him infinite.

6. Such being its nature, without any display, it becomes manifested; without any movement, it produces changes; and without any effort, it accomplishes its ends.

7. The way of Heaven and Earth may be completely declared in one sentence. They are without any doubleness, and so they produce things in a manner that is unfathomable.

8. The way of Heaven and Earth is large and substantial, high and brilliant, far-reaching and long-enduring.

9. The Heaven now before us is only this bright shining spot; but when viewed in its inexhaustible extent, the sun, moon, stars, and constellations of the zodiac are suspended in it, and all things are overspread by it. The Earth before us is but a handful of soil; but when regarded in its breadth and thickness, it sustains mountains like the Hwâ and the Yo, without feeling their weight, and contains the rivers and seas, without their leaking away. The mountain now before us appears only a stone; but when contemplated in all the vastness of its size, we see how the grass and trees are produced on it, and birds and beasts dwell on it, and precious things which men treasure up are found on it. The water now before us appears but a ladleful; yet extending our view to its unfathomable depths, the largest tortoises, iguanas, iguanodons, dragons, fishes, and turtles, are produced in it, articles of value and sources of wealth abound in it.

10. It is said in the Book of Poetry, "The ordinances of Heaven, how profound are they and unceasing!" The meaning is, that it is thus that Heaven is Heaven. And again, "How illustrious was it, the singleness of the virtue of King Wăn!" indicating that it was thus that King Wăn was what he was. Singleness likewise is unceasing.

XXVII

1. How great is the path proper to the Sage!

2. Like overflowing water, it sends forth and nourishes all things, and rises up to the height of Heaven.

3. All-complete is its greatness! It embraces the three hundred rules of ceremony, and the three thousand rules of demeanor.

4. It waits for the proper man, and then it is trodden.

5. Hence it is said, "Only by perfect virtue can the perfect path, in all its courses, be made a fact."

6. Therefore, the superior man honors his virtuous nature, and maintains constant inquiry and study, seeking to carry it out to its breadth and greatness, so as to omit none of the more exquisite and

minute points which it embraces, and to raise it to its greatest height and brilliancy, so as to pursue the course of the Mean. He cherishes his old knowledge, and is continually acquiring new. He exerts an honest, generous earnestness, in the esteem and practice of all propriety.

7. Thus, when occupying a high situation he is not proud, and in a low situation he is not insubordinate. When the kingdom is well governed, he is sure by his words to rise; and when it is ill governed, he is sure by his silence to command forbearance to himself. Is not this what we find in the Book of Poetry—"Intelligent is he and prudent, and so preserves his person?"

XXVIII

1. The Master said, "Let a man who is ignorant be fond of using his own judgment; let a man without rank be fond of assuming a directing power to himself; let a man who is living in the present age go back to the ways of antiquity—on the persons of all who act thus calamities will be sure to come."

2. To no one but the Son of Heaven does it belong to order ceremonies, to fix the measures, and to determine the written characters.

3. Now over the kingdom, carriages have all wheels of the same size; all writing is with the same characters; and for conduct there are the same rules.

4. One may occupy the throne, but if he have not the proper virtue, he may not dare to make ceremonies or music. One may have the virtue, but if he does not occupy the throne, he may not presume to make ceremonies or music.

5. The Master said, "I may describe the ceremonies of the Hsiâ dynasty, but Chî cannot sufficiently attest my words. I have learned the ceremonies of the Yin dynasty, and in Sung they still continue. I have learned the ceremonies of Châu, which are now used, and I follow Châu."

XXIX

1. He who attains to the sovereignty of the kingdom, having those three important things, shall be able to effect that there shall be few errors under his government.

2. However excellent may have been the regulations of those of former times, they cannot be attested. Not being attested, they cannot command credence, and not being credited, the people would not follow them. However excellent might be the regulations made by one in an inferior situation, he is not in a position to be honored. Unhonored, he cannot command credence, and not being credited, the people would not follow his rules.

3. Therefore the institutions of the Ruler are rooted in his own character and conduct, and sufficient attestation of them is given by the masses of the people. He examines them by comparison with those of the three kings, and finds them without mistake. He sets them up before Heaven and Earth, and finds nothing in them contrary to their mode of operation. He presents himself with them before spiritual beings, and no doubts about them arise. He is prepared to wait for the rise of a sage a hundred ages after, and has no misgivings.

4. His presenting himself with his institutions before spiritual beings, without any doubts arising about them, shows that he knows Heaven. His being prepared, without any misgivings, to wait for the rise of a sage a hundred ages after, shows that he knows men.

5. Such being the case, the movements of such a ruler, illustrating his institutions, constitute an example to the world for ages. His acts are for ages a law to the kingdom. His words are for ages a lesson to the kingdom. Those who are far from him look longingly for him; and those who are near him are never wearied with him.

6. It is said in the Book of Poetry — "Not disliked there, not tired of here, from day to day and night tonight, will they perpetuate their praise." Never has there been a ruler, who did not realize this description, that obtained an early renown throughout the kingdom.

XXX

1. Chung-nî handed down the doctrines of Yâo and Shun, as if they had been his ancestors, and elegantly displayed the regulations of Wăn and Wû, taking them as his model. Above, he harmonized with the times of Heaven, and below, he was conformed to the water and land.

2. He may be compared to Heaven and Earth in their supporting and containing, their overshadowing and curtaining, all things. He may

be compared to the four seasons in their alternating progress, and to the sun and moon in their successive shining.

3. All things are nourished together without their injuring one another. The courses of the seasons, and of the sun and moon, are pursued without any collision among them. The smaller energies are like river currents; the greater energies are seen in mighty transformations. It is this which makes Heaven and Earth so great.

XXXI

1. It is only he, possessed of all sagely qualities that can exist under Heaven, who shows himself quick in apprehension, clear in discernment, of far-reaching intelligence, and all-embracing knowledge, fitted to exercise rule; magnanimous, generous, benign, and mild, fitted to exercise forbearance; impulsive, energetic, firm, and enduring, fitted to maintain a firm hold; self-adjusted, grave, never swerving from the Mean, and correct, fitted to command reverence; accomplished, distinctive, concentrative, and searching, fitted to exercise discrimination.

2. All-embracing is he and vast, deep and active as a fountain, sending forth in their due season his virtues.

3. All-embracing and vast, he is like Heaven. Deep and active as a fountain, he is like the abyss. He is seen, and the people all reverence him; he speaks, and the people all believe him; he acts, and the people all are pleased with him.

4. Therefore his fame overspreads the Middle Kingdom, and extends to all barbarous tribes. Wherever ships and carriages reach; wherever the strength of man penetrates; wherever the heavens overshadow and the earth sustains; wherever the sun and moon shine; wherever frosts and dews fall: all who have blood and breath unfeignedly honor and love him. Hence it is said—"He is the equal of Heaven."

XXXII

1. It is only the individual possessed of the most entire sincerity that can exist under Heaven, who can adjust the great invariable relations of mankind, establish the great fundamental virtues of humanity, and know the transforming and nurturing operations of Heaven and Earth—shall this individual have any being or anything beyond himself on which he depends?

2. Call him man in his ideal, how earnest is he! Call him an abyss, how deep is he! Call him Heaven, how vast is he!

3. Who can know him, but he who is indeed quick in apprehension, clear in discernment, of far-reaching intelligence, and all-embracing knowledge, possessing all Heavenly virtue?

XXXIII

1. It is said in the Book of Poetry, "Over her embroidered robe she puts a plain single garment," intimating a dislike to the display of the elegance of the former. Just so, it is the way of the superior man to prefer the concealment of his virtue, while it daily becomes more illustrious, and it is the way of the mean man to seek notoriety, while he daily goes more and more to ruin. It is characteristic of the superior man, appearing insipid, yet never to produce satiety; while showing a simple negligence, yet to have his accomplishments recognized; while seemingly plain, yet to be discriminating. He knows how what is distant lies in what is near. He knows where the wind proceeds from. He knows how what is minute becomes manifested. Such a one, we may be sure, will enter into virtue.

2. It is said in the Book of Poetry, "Although the fish sink and lie at the bottom, it is still quite clearly seen." Therefore the superior man examines his heart, that there may be nothing wrong there, and that he may have no cause for dissatisfaction with himself. That wherein the superior man cannot be equaled is simply this; his work which other men cannot see.

3. It is said in the Book of Poetry, "Looked at in your apartment, be there free from shame as being exposed to the light of Heaven." Therefore, the superior man, even when he is not moving, has a feeling of reverence, and while he speaks not, he has the feeling of truthfulness.

4. It is said in the Book of Poetry, "In silence is the offering presented, and the spirit approached to; there is not the slightest contention." Therefore the superior man does not use rewards, and the people are stimulated to virtue. He does not show anger, and the people are awed more than by hatchets and battle-axes.

5. It is said in the Book of Poetry, "What needs no display is virtue. All the princes imitate it." Therefore, the superior man being sincere

and reverential, the whole world is conducted to a state of happy tranquility.

6. It is said in the Book of Poetry, "I regard with pleasure your brilliant virtue, making no great display of itself in sounds and appearances." The Master said, "Among the appliances to transform the people, sound and appearances are but trivial influences. It is said in another ode, 'His Virtue is light as a hair.' Still, a hair will admit of comparison as to its size. 'The doings of the supreme Heaven have neither sound nor smell.' That is perfect virtue."

The Works of Mencius

BOOK I
KING HÛI OF LIANG

PART I

I

BENVOLENCE AND RIGHTEOUSNESS MENCIUS'S ONLY TOPICS
WITH THE PRINCES OF HIS TIME; AND THE ONLY PRINCIPLES
WHICH CAN MAKE A COUNTRY PROSPEROUS.

1. Mencius went to see King Hûi of Liang.

2. The king said, "Venerable sir, since you have not counted it far to come here, a distance of a thousand lî, may I presume that you are provided with counsels to profit my kingdom?"

3. Mencius replied, "Why must your Majesty use that word 'profit'? What I am provided with, are counsels to benevolence and righteousness, and these are my only topics.

4. "If your Majesty say, 'What is to be done to profit my kingdom?' the great officers will say, 'What is to be done to profit our families?' and the inferior officers and the common people will say, 'What is to be done to profit our persons?' Superiors and inferiors will try to snatch this profit the one from the other, and the kingdom will be endangered. In the kingdom of ten thousand chariots, the murderer of his sovereign shall be the chief of a family of a thousand chariots. In the kingdom of a thousand chariots, the murderer of his prince shall be the chief of a family of a hundred chariots. To have a thousand in ten thousand, and a hundred in a thousand, cannot be said not to be a large allotment, but if righteousness be put last, and profit be put first, they will not be satisfied without snatching all.

5. "There never has been a benevolent man who neglected his parents. There never has been a righteous man who made his sovereign an after consideration.

6. "Let your Majesty also say, 'Benevolence and righteousness, and let these be your only themes.' Why must you use that word—'profit'?"

II

RULERS MUST SHARE THEIR PLEASURES WITH THE PEOPLE. THEY CAN ONLY BE HAPPY WHEN THEY RULE OVER HAPPY SUBJECTS.

1. Mencius, another day, saw King Hûi of Liang. The king went and stood with him by a pond, and, looking round at the large geese and deer, said, "Do wise and good princes also find pleasure in these things?"

2. Mencius replied, "Being wise and good, they have pleasure in these things. If they are not wise and good, though they have these things, they do not find pleasure.

3. "It is said in the Book of Poetry,

> He measured out and commenced his marvelous tower;
> He measured it out and planned it.
> The people addressed themselves to it,
> And in less than a day completed it.
> When he measured and began it, he said to them—
> Be not so earnest:
> But the multitudes came as if they had been his children.
> The king was in his marvelous park;
> The does reposed about,
> The does so sleek and fat:
> And the white birds came glistening.
> The king was by his marvelous pond;
> How full was it of fishes leaping about!

"King Wăn used the strength of the people to make his tower and his pond, and yet the people rejoiced to do the work, calling the tower 'the marvelous tower,' calling the pond 'the marvelous pond,' and rejoicing that he had his large deer, his fishes, and turtles. The ancients caused the people to have pleasure as well as themselves, and therefore they could enjoy it.

4. "In the Declaration of T'ang it is said, 'O sun, when wilt thou expire? We will die together with thee.' The people wished for Chieh's death, though they should die with him. Although he had towers, ponds, birds, and animals, how could he have pleasure alone?"

III

HALF MEASURES ARE OF LITTLE USE. THE GREAT PRINCIPLES OF ROYAL GOVERNMENT MUST BE FAITHFULLY AND IN THEIR SPIRIT CARRIED OUT.

1. King Hûi of Liang said, "Small as my virtue is, in the government of my kingdom, I do indeed exert my mind to the utmost. If the year be bad on the inside of the river, I remove as many of the people as I can to the east of the river, and convey grain to the country in the inside. When the year is bad on the east of the river, I act on the same plan. On examining the government of the neighboring kingdoms, I do not find that there is any prince who exerts his mind as I do. And yet the people of the neighboring kingdoms do not decrease, nor do my people increase. How is this?"

2. Mencius replied, "Your majesty is fond of war; let me take an illustration from war. The soldiers move forward to the sound of the drums; and after their weapons have been crossed, on one side they throw away their coats of mail, trail their arms behind them, and run. Some run a hundred paces and stop; some run fifty paces and stop. What would you think if those who run fifty paces were to laugh at those who run a hundred paces?" The king said, "They should not do so. Though they did not run a hundred paces, yet they also ran away." "Since your Majesty knows this," replied Mencius, "you need not hope that your people will become more numerous than those of the neighboring kingdoms.

3. "If the seasons of husbandry be not interfered with, the grain will be more than can be eaten. If close nets are not allowed to enter the pools and ponds, the fishes and turtles will be more than can be consumed. If the axes and bills enter the hills and forests only at the proper time, the wood will be more than can be used. When the grain and fish and turtles are more than can be eaten, and there is more wood than can be used, this enables the people to nourish their living and mourn for their dead, without any feeling against any. This condition, in which the people nourish their living and bury their dead without any feeling against any, is the first step of royal government.

4. "Let mulberry trees be planted about the homesteads with their five *mâu*, and persons of fifty years may be clothed with silk. In keeping fowls, pigs, dogs, and swine, let not their times of breeding

be neglected, and persons of seventy years may eat flesh. Let there not be taken away the time that is proper for the cultivation of the farm with its hundred *mâu*, and the family of several mouths that is supported by it shall not suffer from hunger. Let careful attention be paid to education in schools, inculcating in it especially the filial and fraternal duties, and gray-haired men will not be seen upon the roads, carrying burdens on their backs or on their heads. It never has been that the ruler of a State, where such results were seen—persons of seventy wearing silk and eating flesh, and the black-haired people suffering neither from hunger nor cold—did not attain to the royal dignity.

5. "Your dogs and swine eat the food of men, and you do not make any restrictive arrangements. There are people dying from famine on the roads, and you do not issue the stores of your granaries for them. When people die, you say, 'It is not owing to me; it is owing to the year.' In what does this differ from stabbing a man and killing him, and then saying, 'It was not I; it was the weapon'? Let your Majesty cease to lay the blame on the year, and instantly from all the nation the people will come to you."

IV

A CONTINUATION OF THE FORMER CHAPTER, CARRYING ON THE APPEAL, IN THE LAST PARAGRAPH, ON THE CHARACTER OF KING HÛI'S OWN GOVERNMENT.

1. King Hûi of Liang said, "I wish quietly to receive your instructions."

2. Mencius replied, "Is there any difference between killing a man with a stick and with a sword?" The king said, "There is no difference!"

3. "Is there any difference between doing it with a sword and with the style of government?" "There is no difference," was the reply.

4. Mencius then said, "In your kitchen there is fat meat; in your stables there are fat horses. But your people have the look of hunger, and on the wilds there are those who have died of famine. This is leading on beasts to devour men.

5. "Beasts devour one another, and men hate them for doing so. When a prince, being the parent of his people, administers his government so as to be chargeable with leading on beasts to devour men, where is his parental relation to the people?"

6. Chung-nî said, "Was he not without posterity who first made wooden images to bury with the dead? So he said, because that man made the semblances of men, and used them for that purpose: what shall be thought of him who causes his people to die of hunger?"

V

HOW A RULER MAY BEST TAKE SATISFACTION FOR LOSSES
WHICH HE HAS SUSTAINED. THAT BENEVOLENT
GOVERNMENT WILL RAISE HIM HIGH ABOVE HIS ENEMIES.

1. King Hûi of Liang said, "There was not in the nation a stronger State than Tsin, as you, venerable Sir, know. But since it descended to me, on the east we have been defeated by Ch'î, and then my eldest son perished; on the west we have lost seven hundred lî of territory to Ch'in; and on the south we have sustained disgrace at the hands of Ch'û. I have brought shame on my departed predecessors, and wish on their account to wipe it away, once for all. What course is to be pursued to accomplish this?"

2. Mencius replied, "With a territory which is only a hundred lî square, it is possible to attain to the royal dignity.

3. "If Your Majesty will indeed dispense a benevolent government to the people, being sparing in the use of punishments and fines, and making the taxes and levies light, so causing that the fields shall be plowed deep, and the weeding of them be carefully attended to, and that the strong-bodied, during their days of leisure, shall cultivate their filial piety, fraternal respectfulness, sincerity, and truthfulness, serving thereby, at home, their fathers and elder brothers, and, abroad, their elders and superiors—you will then have a people who can be employed, with sticks which they have prepared, to oppose the strong mail and sharp weapons of the troops of Ch'in and Ch'û.

4. "The rulers of those States rob their people of their time, so that they cannot plow and weed their fields, in order to support their parents. Their parents suffer from cold and hunger. Brothers, wives, and children are separated and scattered abroad.

5. "Those rulers, as it were, drive their people into pit-falls, or drown them. Your Majesty will go to punish them. In such a case, who will oppose your Majesty?

6. "In accordance with this is the saying, 'The benevolent has no enemy.' I beg your Majesty not to doubt what I say."

VI

DISAPPOINTMENT OF MENCIUS WITH THE KING HSIANG; BY WHOM THE TORN NATION MAY BE UNITED UNDER ONE SWAY.

1. Mencius went to see the king Hsiang of Liang.

2. On coming out from the interview, he said to some persons, "When I looked at him from a distance, he did not appear like a sovereign; when I drew near to him, I saw nothing venerable about him. Abruptly he asked me, 'How can the kingdom be settled?' I replied, 'It will be settled by being united under one sway.'

3. " 'Who can so unite it?'

4. "I replied, 'He who has no pleasure in killing men can so unite it.'

5. " 'Who can give it to him?'

6. "I replied, 'All the people of the nation will unanimously give it to him. Does your Majesty understand the way of the growing grain? During the seventh and eighth months, when drought prevails, the plants become dry. Then the clouds collect densely in the heavens, they send down torrents of rain, and the grain erects itself, as if by a shoot. When it does so, who can keep it back? Now among the shepherds of men throughout the nation, there is not one who does not find pleasure in killing men. If there were one who did not find pleasure in killing men, all the people in the nation would look towards him with outstretched necks. Such being indeed the case, the people would flock to him, as water flows downwards with a rush, which no one can repress.'"

VII

LOVING AND PROTECTING THE PEOPLE IS THE CHARACTERISTIC OF ROYAL GOVERNMENT, AND THE SURE PATH TO THE ROYAL DIGNITY.

1. The king Hsüan of Ch'î asked, saying, "May I be informed by you of the transactions of Hwan of Ch'î, and Wăn of Tsin?"

2. Mencius replied, "There were none of the disciples of Chung-nî who spoke about the affairs of Hwan and Wăn, and therefore they have not been transmitted to these after-ages; your servant has not heard them. If you will have me speak, let it be about royal government."

3. The king said, "What virtue must there be in order to attain to royal sway?" Mencius answered, "The love and protection of the people;

with this there is no power which can prevent a ruler from attaining to it."

4. The king asked again, "Is such a one as I competent to love and protect the people?" Mencius said, "Yes." "How do you know that I am competent for that?" "I heard the following incident from Hû Ho: 'The king,' said he, 'was sitting aloft in the hall, when a man appeared, leading an ox past the lower part of it. The king saw him, and asked, Where is the ox going? The man replied, We are going to consecrate a bell with its blood. The king said, Let it go. I cannot bear its frightened appearance, as if it were an innocent person going to the place of death. The man answered, Shall we then omit the consecration of the bell? The king said, How can that be omitted? Change it for a sheep.' I do not know whether this incident really occurred."

5. The king replied, "It did," and then Mencius said, "The heart seen in this is sufficient to carry you to the royal sway. The people all supposed that your Majesty grudged the animal, but your servant knows surely, that it was your Majesty's not being able to bear the sight, which made you do as you did."

6. The king said, "You are right. And yet there really was an appearance of what the people condemned. But though Ch'î be a small and narrow State, how should I grudge one ox? Indeed it was because I could not bear its frightened appearance, as if it were an innocent person going to the place of death, that therefore I changed it for a sheep."

7. Mencius pursued, "Let not your Majesty deem it strange that the people should think you were grudging the animal. When you changed a large one for a small, how should they know the true reason? If you felt pained by its being led without guilt to the place of death, what was there to choose between an ox and a sheep?" The king laughed and said, "What really was my mind in the matter? I did not grudge the expense of it, and changed it for a sheep! There was reason in the people's saying that I grudged it."

8. "There is no harm in their saying so," said Mencius. "Your conduct was an artifice of benevolence. You saw the ox, and had not seen the sheep. So is the superior man affected towards animals, that, having seen them alive, he cannot bear to see them die; having heard their dying cries, he cannot bear to eat their flesh. Therefore he keeps away from his slaughter-house and cook-room."

9. The king was pleased, and said, "It is said in the Book of Poetry, 'The minds of others, I am able by reflection to measure'—this is verified, my Master, in your discovery of my motive. I indeed did the thing, but when I turned my thoughts inward, and examined into it, I could not discover my own mind. When you, Master, spoke those words, the movements of compassion began to work in my mind. How is it that this heart has in it what is equal to the royal sway?"

10. Mencius replied, "Suppose a man were to make this statement to your Majesty: 'My strength is sufficient to lift three thousand catties, but it is not sufficient to lift one feather; my eyesight is sharp enough to examine the point of an autumn hair, but I do not see a wagon-load of faggots'—would your Majesty allow what he said?" "No," was the answer, on which Mencius proceeded, "Now here is kindness sufficient to reach to animals, and no benefits are extended from it to the people. How is this? Is an exception to be made here? The truth is, the feather is not lifted , because strength is not used; the wagon-load of firewood is not seen, because the eyesight is not used; and the people are not loved and protected, because kindness is not employed. Therefore your Majesty's not exercising the royal sway, is because you do not do it, not because you are not able to do it."

11. The king asked, "How may the difference between the not doing a thing, and the not being able to do it, be represented?" Mencius replied, "In such a thing as taking the T'âi mountain under your arm, and leaping over the north sea with it, if you say to people: 'I am not able to do it,' that is a real case of not being able. In such a matter as breaking off a branch from a tree at the order of a superior, if you say to people: 'I am not able to do it,' that is a case of not doing it, it is not a case of not being able to do it. Therefore your Majesty's not exercising the royal sway, is not such a case as that of taking the T'âi mountain under your arm, and leaping over the north sea with it. Your Majesty's not exercising the royal sway is a case like that of breaking off a branch from a tree.

12. "Treat with the reverence due to age the elders in your own family, so that the elders in the families of others shall be similarly treated; treat with the kindness due to youth the young in your own family, so that the young in the families of others shall be similarly treated: do this, and the kingdom may be made to go round in your palm. It is said in the Book of Poetry, 'His example affected his wife. It reached to his brothers, and his family of the State was governed

by it.' The language shows how king Wăn simply took his kindly heart, and exercised it towards those parties. Therefore the carrying out his kindness of heart by a prince will suffice for the love and protection of all within the four seas, and if he do not carry it out, he will not be able to protect his wife and children. The way in which the ancients came greatly to surpass other men, was no other but this: simply that they knew well how to carry out, so as to affect others, what they themselves did. Now your kindness is sufficient to reach to animals, and no benefits are extended from it to reach the people. How is this? Is an exception to be made here?

13. "By weighing, we know what things are light, and what heavy. By measuring, we know what things are long, and what short. The relations of all things may be thus determined, and it is of the greatest importance to estimate the motions of the mind. I beg your Majesty to measure it.

14. "You collect your equipments of war, endanger your soldiers and officers, and excite the resentment of the other princes; do these things cause you pleasure in your mind?"

15. The king replied, "No. How should I derive pleasure from these things? My object in them is to seek for what I greatly desire."

16. Mencius said, "May I hear from you what it is that you greatly desire?" The king laughed and did not speak. Mencius resumed, "Are you led to desire it, because you have not enough of rich and sweet food for your mouth? Or because you have not enough of light and warm clothing for your body? Or because you have not enough of beautifully colored objects to delight your eyes? Or because you have not voices and tones enough to please your ears? Or because you have not enough of attendants and favorites to stand before you and receive your orders? Your Majesty's various officers are sufficient to supply you with those things. How can your Majesty be led to entertain such a desire on account of them?" "No," said the king; "my desire is not on account of them." Mencius added, "Then, what your Majesty greatly desires may be known. You wish to enlarge your territories, to have Ch'in and Ch'û wait at your court, to rule the Middle Kingdom, and to attract to you the barbarous tribes that surround it. But doing what you do to seek for what you desire is like climbing a tree to seek for fish."

17. The king said, "Is it so bad as that?" "It is even worse," was the reply. "If you climb a tree to seek for fish, although you do not get

the fish, you will not suffer any subsequent calamity. But doing what you do to seek for what you desire, doing it moreover with all your heart, you will assuredly afterwards meet with calamities." The king asked, "May I hear from you the proof of that?" Mencius said, "If the people of Tsâu should fight with the people of Ch'û, which of them does your Majesty think would conquer?" "The people of Ch'û would conquer." "Yes; and so it is certain that a small country cannot contend with a great, that few cannot contend with many, that the weak cannot contend with the strong. The territory within the four seas embraces nine divisions, each of a thousand lî square. All Ch'î together is but one of them. If with one part you try to subdue the other eight, what is the difference between that and Tsâu's contending with Ch'û? For, with such a desire, you must turn back to the proper course for its attainment.

18. "Now if your Majesty will institute a government whose action shall be benevolent, this will cause all the officers in the kingdom to wish to stand in your Majesty's court, and all the farmers to wish to plow in your Majesty's fields, and all the merchants, both traveling and stationary, to wish to store their goods in your Majesty's market-places, and all traveling strangers to wish to make their tours on your Majesty's roads, and all throughout the kingdom who feel aggrieved by their rulers to wish to come and complain to your Majesty. And when they are so bent, who will be able to keep them back?"

19. The king said, "I am stupid, and not able to advance to this. I wish you, my Master, to assist my intentions. Teach me clearly; although I am deficient in intelligence and vigor, I will essay and try to carry your instructions into effect."

20. Mencius replied, "They are only men of education, who, without a certain livelihood, are able to maintain a fixed heart. As to the people, if they have not a certain livelihood, it follows that they will not have a fixed heart. And if they have not a fixed heart, there is nothing which they will not do, in the way of self-abandonment, of moral deflection, of depravity, and of wild license. When they thus have been involved in crime, to follow them up and punish them; this is to entrap the people. How can such a thing as entrapping the people be done under the rule of a benevolent man?

21. "Therefore an intelligent ruler will regulate the livelihood of the people, so as to make sure that, for those above them, they shall have sufficient wherewith to serve their parents, and, for those below

them, sufficient wherewith to support their wives and children; that in good years they shall always be abundantly satisfied, and that in bad years they shall escape the danger of perishing. After this he may urge them, and they will proceed to what is good, for in this case the people will follow after it with ease.

22. "Now, the livelihood of the people is so regulated, that, above, they have not sufficient wherewith to serve their parents, and, below, they have not sufficient wherewith to support their wives and children. Notwithstanding good years, their lives are continually embittered, and, in bad years, they do not escape perishing. In such circumstances they only try to save themselves from death, and are afraid they will not succeed. What leisure have they to cultivate propriety and righteousness?

23. "If your Majesty wishes to effect this regulation of the livelihood of the people, why not turn to that which is the essential step to it?

24. "Let mulberry-trees be planted about the homesteads with their five *mâu*, and persons of fifty years may be clothed with silk. In keeping fowls, pigs, dogs, and swine, let not their times of breeding be neglected, and persons of seventy years may eat flesh. Let there not be taken away the time that is proper for the cultivation of the farm with its hundred *mâu*, and the family of eight mouths that is supported by it shall not suffer from hunger. Let careful attention be paid to education in schools—the inculcation in it especially of the filial and fraternal duties, and gray-haired men will not be seen upon the roads, carrying burdens on their backs or on their heads. It never has been that the ruler of a State where such results were seen—the old wearing silk and eating flesh, and the black-haired people suffering neither from hunger nor cold—did not attain to the royal dignity."

KING HÛI OF LIANG

PART II

I

HOW THE LOVE OF MUSIC MAY BE MADE SUBSERVIENT TO GOOD
GOVERNMENT, AND TO A PRINCE'S OWN ADVANCEMENT.

1. Chwang Pâo, seeing Mencius, said to him, "I had an interview with the king. His Majesty told me that he loved music, and I was not prepared with anything to reply to him. What do you pronounce about that love of music?" Mencius replied, "If the king's love of music were very great, the kingdom of Ch'î would be near to a state of good government!"

2. Another day, Mencius, having an interview with the king, said, "Your Majesty, I have heard, told the officer Chwang, that you love music—was it so?" The king changed color, and said, "I am unable to love the music of the ancient sovereigns; I only love the music that suits the manners of the present age."

3. Mencius said, "If your Majesty's love of music were very great, Ch'î would be near to a state of good government! The music of the present day is just like the music of antiquity, as regards effecting that."

4. The king said, "May I hear from you the proof of that?" Mencius asked, "Which is the more pleasant, to enjoy music by yourself alone, or to enjoy it with others?" "To enjoy it with others," was the reply. "And which is the more pleasant, to enjoy music with a few, or to enjoy it with many?" "To enjoy it with many."

5. Mencius proceeded, "Your servant begs to explain what I have said about music to your Majesty.

6. "Now, your Majesty is having music here. The people hear the noise of your bells and drums, and the notes of your fifes and pipes, and they all, with aching heads, knit their brows, and say to one another, 'That's how our king likes his music! But why does he reduce us

to this extremity of distress? Fathers and sons cannot see one another. Elder brothers and younger brothers, wives and children, are separated and scattered abroad.' Now, your Majesty is hunting here. The people hear the noise of your carriages and horses, and see the beauty of your plumes and streamers, and they all, with aching heads, knit their brows, and say to one another, 'That's how our king likes his hunting! But why does he reduce us to this extremity of distress? Fathers and sons cannot see one another. Elder brothers and younger brothers, wives and children, are separated and scattered abroad.' Their feeling thus is from no other reason but that you do not allow the people to have pleasure as well as yourself.

7. "Now, your Majesty is having music here. The people hear the noise of your bells and drums, and the notes of your fifes and pipes, and they all, delighted, and with joyful looks, say to one another, 'That sounds as if our king were free from all sickness! If he were not, how could he enjoy this music?' Now, your Majesty is hunting here. The people hear the noise of your carriages and horses, and see the beauty of your plumes and streamers, and they all, delighted, and with joyful looks, say to one another, 'That looks as if our king were free from all sickness! If he were not, how could he enjoy this hunting?' Their feeling thus is from no other reason but that you cause them to have their pleasure as you have yours.

8. "If your Majesty now will make pleasure a thing common to the people and yourself, the royal sway awaits you."

II

HOW A RULER MUST NOT INDULGE HIS LOVE FOR PARKS AND HUNTING TO THE DISCOMFORT OF HIS PEOPLE.

1. The king Hsüan of Ch'î asked, "Was it so, that the park of King Wăn contained seventy square lî?" Mencius replied, "It is so in the records."

2. "Was it so large as that?" exclaimed the king. "The people," said Mencius, "still looked on it as small." The king added, "My park contains only forty square lî, and the people still look on it as large. How is this?" "The park of King Wăn," was the reply, "contained seventy square lî, but the grass-cutters and fuel-gatherers had the privilege of entrance into it; so also had the catchers of pheasants

and hares. He shared it with the people, and was it not with reason that they looked on it as small?

3. "When I first arrived at the borders of your kingdom, I inquired about the great prohibitory regulations, before I would venture to enter it; and I heard, that inside the barrier-gates there was a park of forty square lî, and that he who killed a deer in it, was held guilty of the same crime as if he had killed a man. Thus those forty square lî are a pitfall in the middle of the kingdom. Is it not with reason that the people look upon them as large?"

III

HOW FRIENDLY INTERCOURSE WITH NEIGHBORING KINGDOMS MAY BE MAINTAINED, AND THE LOVE OF VALOR MADE SUBSERVIENT TO THE GOOD OF THE PEOPLE, AND THE GLORY OF THE PRINCE.

1. The king Hsüan of Ch'î asked, saying, "Is there any way to regulate one's maintenance of intercourse with neighboring kingdoms?" Mencius replied, "There is. But it requires a perfectly virtuous prince to be able, with a great country, to serve a small one—as, for instance, T'ăng served Ko, and King Wăn served the Kwan barbarians. And it requires a wise prince to be able, with a small country, to serve a large one—as the king T'âi served the Hsün-yü, and Kâu-ch'îen served Wû.

2. "He who with a great State serves a small one, delights in Heaven. He who with a small State serves a large one, stands in awe of Heaven. He who delights in Heaven, will affect with his love and protection the whole kingdom. He who stands in awe of Heaven, will affect with his love and protection his own kingdom.

3. "It is said in the Book of Poetry, 'I fear the Majesty of Heaven, and will thus preserve its favoring decree.'"

4. The king said, "A great saying! But I have an infirmity—I love valor."

5. "I beg your Majesty," was the reply, "not to love small valor. If a man brandishes his sword, looks fiercely, and says, "How dare he withstand me?"—this is the valor of a common man, who can be the opponent only of a single individual. I beg your Majesty to greaten it.

6. "It is said in the Book of Poetry,

The king blazed with anger,
And he marshaled his hosts,
To stop the march to Chü,
To consolidate the prosperity of Châu,
To meet the expectations of the nation.

This was the valor of King Wăn. King Wăn, in one burst of his anger, gave repose to all the people of the kingdom.

7. "In the Book of History it is said, 'Heaven having produced the inferior people, made for them rulers and teachers, with the purpose that they should be assisting to God, and therefore distinguished them throughout the four quarters of the land. Whoever are offenders, and whoever are innocent, here am I to deal with them. How dare any under heaven give indulgence to their refractory wills?' There was one man pursuing a violent and disorderly course in the kingdom, and King Wû was ashamed of it. This was the valor of King Wû. He also, by one display of his anger, gave repose to all the people of the kingdom.

8. "Let now your Majesty also, in one burst of anger, give repose to all the people of the kingdom. The people are only afraid that your Majesty does not love valor."

IV

A RULER'S PROSPERITY DEPENDS ON HIS EXERCISING A RESTRAINT UPON HIMSELF, AND SYMPATHIZING WITH THE PEOPLE IN THEIR JOYS AND SORROWS.

1. The king Hsüan of Ch'î had an interview with Mencius in the Snow palace, and said to him, "Do men of talents and worth likewise find pleasure in these things?" Mencius replied, "They do; and if people generally are not able to enjoy themselves, they condemn their superiors.

2. "For them, when they cannot enjoy themselves, to condemn their superiors is wrong, but when the superiors of the people do not make enjoyment a thing common to the people and themselves, they also do wrong.

3. "When a ruler rejoices in the joy of his people, they also rejoice in his joy; when he grieves at the sorrow of his people, they also grieve at his sorrow. A sympathy of joy will pervade the kingdom; a sympathy

of sorrow will do the same: in such a state of things, it cannot be but that the ruler attain to the royal dignity.

4. "Formerly, the duke Ching of Ch'î asked the minister Yen, saying, 'I wish to pay a visit of inspection to Chwǎn-fû, and Châo-wû, and then to bend my course southward along the shore, till I come to Lang-yê. What shall I do that my tour may be fit to be compared with the visits of inspection made by the ancient sovereigns?"

5. "The minister Yen replied, 'An excellent inquiry! When the Son of Heaven visited the princes, it was called a tour of inspection, that is, be surveyed the States under their care. When the princes attended at the court of the Son of Heaven, it was called a report of office, that is, they reported their administration of their offices. Thus, neither of the proceedings was without a purpose. And moreover, in the spring they examined the plowing, and supplied any deficiency of seed; in the autumn they examined the reaping, and supplied any deficiency of yield. There is the saying of the Hsiâ dynasty: If our king do not take his ramble, what will become of our happiness? If our king do not make his excursion, what will become of our help? That ramble, and that excursion, were a pattern to the princes.

6. "'Now, the state of things is different. A host marches in attendance on the ruler, and stores of provisions are consumed. The hungry are deprived of their food, and there is no rest for those who are called to toil. Maledictions are uttered by one to another with eyes askance, and the people proceed to the commission of wickedness. Thus the royal ordinances are violated, and the people are oppressed, and the supplies of food and drink flow away like water. The rulers yield themselves to the current, or they urge their way against it; they are wild; they are utterly lost: these things proceed to the grief of the inferior princes.

7. "'Descending along with the current, and forgetting to return, is what I call yielding to it. Pressing up against it, and forgetting to return, is what I call urging their way against it. Pursuing the chase without satiety is what I call being wild. Delighting in wine without satiety is what I call being lost.

8. "'The ancient sovereigns had no pleasures to which they gave themselves as on the flowing stream; no doings which might be so characterized as wild and lost.

9. "'It is for you, my prince, to pursue your course.'"

10. "The duke Ching was pleased. He issued a proclamation throughout his State, and went out and occupied a shed in the borders. From that time he began to open his granaries to supply the wants of the people, and calling the Grand music-master, he said to him—'Make for me music to suit a prince and his minister pleased with each other.' And it was then that the Chî-shâo and Chio-shâo were made, in the words to which it was said, 'Is it a fault to restrain one's prince?' He who restrains his prince loves his prince."

V

TRUE ROYAL GOVERNMENT WILL ASSUREDLY RAISE TO THE
SUPREME DIGNITY, AND NEITHER GREED OF WEALTH, NOR LOVE
OF WOMAN, NEED INTERFERE WITH ITS EXERCISE.

1. The king Hsüan of Ch'î said, "People all tell me to pull down and remove the Hall of Distinction. Shall I pull it down, or stop the movement for that object?"

2. Mencius replied, "The Hall of Distinction is a Hall appropriate to the sovereigns. If your Majesty wishes to practice the true royal government, then do not pull it down."

3. The king said, "May I hear from you what the true royal government is?" "Formerly," was the reply, "King Wăn's government of Ch'î was as follows: The husbandmen cultivated for the government one-ninth of the land; the descendants of officers were salaried; at the passes and in the markets, strangers were inspected, but goods were not taxed: there were no prohibitions respecting the ponds and weirs; the wives and children of criminals were not involved in their guilt. There were the old and wifeless, or widowers; the old and husbandless, or widows; the old and childless, or solitaries; the young and fatherless, or orphans: these four classes are the most destitute of the people, and have none to whom they can tell their wants, and king Wăn, in the institution of his government with its benevolent action, made them the first objects of his regard, as it is said in the Book of Poetry,

   The rich may get through life well;
   But alas! for the miserable and solitary!"

4. The king said, "O excellent words!" Mencius said, "Since your Majesty deems them excellent, why do you not practice them?" "I have an infirmity," said the king; "I am fond of wealth." The reply

was, "Formerly, Kung-lîu was fond of wealth. It is said in the Book of Poetry,

> He reared his ricks, and filled his granaries,
> He tied up dried provisions and grain,
> In bottomless bags, and sacks,
> That he might gather his people together, and glorify his State.
> With bows and arrows all-displayed,
> With shields, and spears, and battle-axes, large and small,
> He commenced his march.

In this way those who remained in their old seat had their ricks and granaries, and those who marched had their bags of provisions. It was not till after this that he thought he could begin his march. If your Majesty loves wealth, give the people power to gratify the same feeling, and what difficulty will there be in your attaining the royal sway?"

5. The king said, "I have an infirmity; I am fond of beauty." The reply was, "Formerly, King T'âi was fond of beauty, and loved his wife. It is said in the Book of Poetry,

> Kû-kung T'an-fû
> Came in the morning, galloping his horse,
> By the banks of the western waters,
> As far as the foot of Ch'î hill,
> Along with the lady of Chiang;
> They came and together chose the site for their settlement.

At that time, in the seclusion of the house, there were no dissatisfied women, and abroad, there were no unmarried men. If your Majesty loves beauty, let the people be able to gratify the same feeling, and what difficulty will there be in your attaining the royal sway?"

VI

BRINGING HOME HIS BAD GOVERNMENT TO THE KING OF CH'Î.

1. Mencius said to the king Hsüan of Ch'î, "Suppose that one of your Majesty's ministers were to entrust his wife and children to the care of his friend, while he himself went into Ch'û to travel, and that, on his return, he should find that the friend had let his wife and children suffer from cold and hunger—how ought he to deal with him?" The king said, "He should cast him off."

2.	Mencius proceeded, "Suppose that the chief criminal judge could not regulate the officers under him, how would you deal with him?" The king said, "Dismiss him."

3.	Mencius again said, "If within the four borders of your kingdom there is not good government, what is to be done?" The king looked to the right and left, and spoke of other matters.

VII

THE CARE TO BE EMPLOYED BY A PRINCE IN THE EMPLOYMENT OF MINISTERS; AND THEIR RELATION TO HIMSELF AND THE STABILITY OF THE KINGDOM.

1.	Mencius, having an interview with the king Hsüan of Ch'î, said to him, "When men speak of 'an ancient kingdom,' it is not meant thereby that it has lofty trees in it, but that it has ministers sprung from families which have been noted in it for generations. Your Majesty has no intimate ministers even. Those whom you advanced yesterday are gone today, and you do not know it."

2.	The king said, "How shall I know that they have not ability, and so avoid employing them at all?"

3.	The reply was, "The ruler of a State advances to office men of talents and virtue only as a matter of necessity. Since he will thereby cause the low to overstep the honorable, and distant to overstep his near relatives, ought he to do so but with caution?

4.	"When all those about you say, 'This is a man of talents and worth,' you may not therefore believe it. When your great officers all say, 'This is a man of talents and virtue,' neither may you for that believe it. When all the people say, 'This is a man of talents and virtue,' then examine into the case, and when you find that the man is such, employ him. When all those about you say, 'This man won't do,' don't listen to them. When all your great officers say, 'This man won't do,' don't listen to them. When the people all say, 'This man won't do,' then examine into the case, and when you find that the man won't do, send him away.

5.	"When all those about you say, 'This man deserves death,' don't listen to them. When all your great officers say, 'This man deserves death,' don't listen to them. When the people all say, 'This man deserves death,' then inquire into the case, and when you see that the man deserves death, put him to death. In accordance with this we have the saying, 'The people killed him.'

6. "You must act in this way in order to be the parent of the people."

VIII

KILLING A SOVEREIGN IS NOT NECESSARILY REBELLION OR MURDER.

1. The king Hsüan of Ch'î asked, saying, "Was it so, that T'ăng banished Chieh, and that King Wû smote Châu?" Mencius replied, "It is so in the records."

2. The king said, "May a minister then put his sovereign to death?"

3. Mencius said, "He who outrages the benevolence proper to his nature, is called a robber; he who outrages righteousness, is called a ruffian. The robber and ruffian we call a mere fellow. I have heard of the cutting off of the fellow Châu, but I have not heard of the putting a sovereign to death, in his case."

IX

THE ABSURDITY OF A RULER'S NOT ACTING ACCORDING TO THE COUNSEL OF THE MEN OF TALENTS AND VIRTUE, WHOM HE CALLS TO AID IN HIS GOVERNMENT, BUT REQUIRING THEM TO FOLLOW HIS WAYS.

1. Mencius, having an interview with the king Hsüan of Ch'î, said to him, "If you are going to build a large mansion, you will surely cause the Master of the workmen to look out for large trees, and when he has found such large trees, you will be glad, thinking that they will answer for the intended object. Should the workmen hew them so as to make them too small, then your Majesty will be angry, thinking that they will not answer for the purpose. Now, a man spends his youth in learning the principles of right government, and, being grown up to vigor, he wishes to put them in practice—if your Majesty says to him, 'For the present put aside what you have learned, and follow me,' what shall we say?

2. "Here now you have a gem unwrought, in the stone. Although it may be worth 240,000 taels, you will surely employ a lapidary to cut and polish it. But when you come to the government of the State, then you say, 'For the present put aside what you have learned, and

follow me.' How is it that you herein act so differently from your conduct in calling in the lapidary to cut the gem?"

X

THE DISPOSAL OF KINGDOMS RESTS WITH THE MINDS OF THE PEOPLE.

1. The people of Ch'î attacked Yen, and conquered it.

2. The king Hsüan asked, saying, "Some tell me not to take possession of it for myself, and some tell me to take possession of it. For a kingdom of ten thousand chariots, attacking another of ten thousand chariots, to complete the conquest of it in fifty days, is an achievement beyond mere human strength. If I do not take possession of it, calamities from Heaven will surely come upon me. What do you say to my taking possession of it?"

3. Mencius replied, "If the people of Yen will be pleased with your taking possession of it, then do so. Among the ancients there was one who acted on this principle, namely King Wû. If the people of Yen will not be pleased with your taking possession of it, then do not do so. Among the ancients there was one who acted on this principle, namely King Wăn.

4. "When, with all the strength of your country of ten thousand chariots, you attacked another country of ten thousand chariots, and the people brought baskets of rice and vessels of congee, to meet your Majesty's host, was there any other reason for this but that they hoped to escape out of fire and water? If you make the water more deep and the fire more fierce, they will in like manner make another revolution."

XI

AMBITION AND AVARICE ONLY MAKE ENEMIES AND BRING DISASTERS. SAFETY AND PROSPERITY LIE IN A BENEVOLENT GOVERNMENT.

1. The people of Ch'î, having smitten Yen, took possession of it, and upon this, the princes of the various States deliberated together, and resolved to deliver Yen from their power. The king Hsüan said to Mencius, "The princes have formed many plans to attack me: how shall I prepare myself for them?" Mencius replied, "I have heard of one who with seventy lî exercised all the functions of government

throughout the kingdom. That was T'ăng. I have never heard of a prince with a thousand lî standing in fear of others."

2. "It is said in the Book of History, As soon as T'ăng began his work of executing justice, he commenced with Ko. The whole kingdom had confidence in him. When he pursued his work in the east, the rude tribes on the west murmured. So did those on the north, when he was engaged in the south. Their cry was—'Why does he put us last?' Thus, the people looked to him, as we look in a time of great drought to the clouds and rainbows. The frequenters of the markets stopped not. The husbandmen made no change in their operations. While he punished their rulers, he consoled the people. His progress was like the falling of opportune rain, and the people were delighted. It is said again in the Book of History, 'We have waited for our prince long; the prince's coming will be our reviving!'

3. "Now the ruler of Yen was tyrannizing over his people, and your Majesty went and punished him. The people supposed that you were going to deliver them out of the water and the fire, and brought baskets of rice and vessels of congee, to meet your Majesty's host. But you have slain their fathers and elder brothers, and put their sons and younger brothers in confinement. You have pulled down the ancestral temple of the State, and are removing to Ch'î its precious vessels. How can such a course be deemed proper? The rest of the kingdom is indeed jealously afraid of the strength of Ch'î; and now, when with a doubled territory you do not put in practice a benevolent government—it is this which sets the arms of the kingdom in in motion.

4. "If your Majesty will make haste to issue an ordinance, restoring your captives, old and young, stopping the removal of the precious vessels, and saying that, after consulting with the people of Yen, you will appoint them a ruler, and withdraw from the country—in this way you may still be able to stop the threatened attack."

XII

THE AFFECTIONS OF THE PEOPLE CAN ONLY BE SECURED THROUGH A BENEVOLENT GOVERNMENT. AS THEY ARE DEALT WITH BY THEIR SUPERIORS, SO WILL THEY DEAL BY THEM.

1. There had been a brush between Tsâu and Lû, when the duke Mû asked Mencius, saying, "Of my officers there were killed thirty-three men, and none of the people would die in their defense. Though I sentenced them to death for their conduct, it is impossible to put such a multitude to death. If I do not put them to death, then there is the crime unpunished of their looking angrily on at the death of their officers, and not saving them. How is the exigency of the case to be met?"

2. Mencius replied, "In calamitous years and years of famine, the old and weak of your people, who have been found lying in the ditches and water-channels, and the able-bodied who have been scattered about to the four quarters, have amounted to several thousands. All the while, your granaries, O prince, have been stored with grain, and your treasuries and arsenals have been full, and not one of your officers has told you of the distress. Thus negligent have the superiors in your State been, and cruel to their inferiors. The philosopher Tsang said, 'Beware, beware. What proceeds from you, will return to you again.' Now at length the people have paid back the conduct of their officers to them. Do not you, O prince, blame them.

3. "If you will put in practice a benevolent government, this people will love you and all above them, and will die for their officers."

XIII

A PRINCE SHOULD DEPEND ON HIMSELF, AND NOT RELY ON, OR TRY TO PROPITIATE, OTHER POWERS.

1. The duke Wăn of T'ăng asked Mencius, saying, "T'ăng is a small kingdom, and lies between Ch'î and Ch'û. Shall I serve Ch'î? Or shall I serve Ch'û?"

2. Mencius replied, "This plan which you propose is beyond me. If you will have me counsel you, there is one thing I can suggest. Dig deeper your moats; build higher your walls; guard them as well as your people. In case of attack, be prepared to die in your defense, and have the people so that they will not leave you—this is a proper course.

XIV

A PRINCE, THREATENED BY HIS NEIGHBORS, WILL FIND HIS BEST DEFENSE AND CONSOLATION IN DOING WHAT IS GOOD AND RIGHT.

1. The duke Wăn of T'ăng asked Mencius, saying, "The people of Ch'î are going to fortify Hsieh. The movement occasions me great alarm. What is the proper course for me to take in the case?"

2. Mencius replied, "Formerly, when King T'âi dwelt in Pin, the barbarians of the north were continually making incursions upon it. He therefore left it, went to the foot of mount Ch'î, and there took up his residence. He did not take that situation, as having selected it. It was a matter of necessity with him.

3. "If you do good, among your descendants, in after generations, there shall be one who will attain to the royal dignity. A prince lays the foundation of the inheritance, and hands down the beginning which he has made, doing what may be continued by his successors. As to the accomplishment of the great result, that is with Heaven. What is that Ch'î to you, O prince? Be strong to do good. That is all your business."

XV

TWO COURSES OPEN TO A PRINCE PRESSED BY HIS ENEMIES — FLIGHT OR DEATH.

1. The duke Wăn of T'ăng asked Mencius, saying, "T'ăng is a small State. Though I do my utmost to serve those large kingdoms on either side of it, we cannot escape suffering from them. What course shall I take that we may do so?" Mencius replied, "Formerly, when King T'âi dwelt in Pin, the barbarians of the north were constantly making incursions upon it. He served them with skins and silks, and still he suffered from them. He served them with dogs and horses, and still he suffered from them. He served them with pearls and gems, and still he suffered from them. Seeing this, he assembled the old men, and announced to them, saying, 'What the barbarians want is my territory. I have heard this—that a ruler does not injure his people with that wherewith he nourishes them. My children, why should you be troubled about having no prince? I will leave this.' Accordingly, he left Pin, crossed the mountain Liang, built a town at the foot of mount Ch'î, and dwelt there. The people of Pin said, 'He

is a benevolent man. We must not lose him.' Those who followed him looked like crowds hastening to market.

2. "On the other hand, some say, 'The kingdom is a thing to be kept from generation to generation. One individual cannot undertake to dispose of it in his own person. Let him be prepared to die for it. Let him not quit it.'

3. "I ask you, prince, to make your election between these two courses."

XVI

A MAN'S WAY IN LIFE IS ORDERED BY HEAVEN.
THE INSTRUMENTALITY OF OTHER MEN IS ONLY SUBORDINATE.

1. The duke P'ing of Lû was about to leave his palace, when his favorite, one Tsang Ts'ang, made a request to him, saying, "On other days, when you have gone out, you have given instructions to the officers as to where you were going. But now, the horses have been put to the carriage, and the officers do not yet know where you are going. I venture to ask." The duke said, "I am going to see the scholar Măng." "How is this?" said the other. "That you demean yourself, prince, in paying the honor of the first visit to a common man, is, I suppose, because you think that he is a man of talents and virtue. By such men the rules of ceremonial proprieties and right are observed. But on the occasion of this Măng's second mourning, his observances exceeded those of the former. Do not go to see him, my prince." The duke said, "I will not."

2. The officer Yo-chăng entered the court, and had an audience. He said, "Prince, why have you not gone to see Măng K'o?" the duke said, "One told me that, on the occasion of the scholar Măng's second mourning, his observances exceeded those of the former. It is on that account that I have not gone to see him." "How is this!" answered Yo-chăng. "By what you call 'exceeding,' you mean, I suppose, that, on the first occasion, he used the rites appropriate to a scholar, and, on the second, those appropriate to a great officer; that he first used three tripods, and afterwards five tripods." The duke said, "No; I refer to the greater excellence of the coffin, the shell, the grave-clothes, and the shroud." Yo-chăng said, "That cannot be called 'exceeding.' That was the difference between being poor and being rich."

3. After this, Yo-chăng saw Mencius, and said to him, "I told the prince about you, and he was consequently coming to see you, when one of his favorites, named Tsang Ts'ang, stopped him, and therefore he did not come according to his purpose." Mencius said, "A man's advancement is effected, it may be, by others, and the stopping him is, it may be, from the efforts of others. But to advance a man or to stop his advance is really beyond the power of other men. My not finding in the prince of Lû a ruler who would confide in me, and put my counsels into practice, is from Heaven. How could that scion of the Tsang family cause me not to find the ruler that would suit me?"

BOOK II

KUNG-SUN CH'ÂU

PART I

I

WHILE MENCIUS WISHED TO SEE A TRUE ROYAL GOVERNMENT
AND SWAY IN THE KINGDOM, AND COULD EASILY HAVE REALIZED
IT, FROM THE PECULIAR CIRCUMSTANCES OF THE TIME, HE
WOULD NOT, TO DO SO, HAVE HAD RECOURSE TO ANY WAYS
INCONSISTENT WITH ITS IDEAS.

1. Kung-sun Ch'âu asked Mencius, saying, "Master, if you were to obtain the ordering of the government in Ch'î, could you promise yourself to accomplish anew such results as those realized by Kwan Chung and Yen?"

2. Mencius said, "You are indeed a true man of Ch'î. You know about Kwan Chung and Yen, and nothing more.

3. "Someone asked Tsăng Hsî, saying, 'Sir, to which do you give the superiority, to yourself or to Tsze-lû?' Tsăng Hsî looked uneasy, and said, 'He was an object of veneration to my grandfather.' 'Then,' pursued the other, 'Do you give the superiority to yourself or to Kwan Chung?' Tsăng Hsî, flushed with anger and displeased, said, 'How dare you compare me with Kwan Chung? Considering how entirely Kwan Chung possessed the confidence of his prince, how long he enjoyed the direction of the government of the State, and how low, after all, was what he accomplished—how is it that you liken me to him?'

4. "Thus," concluded Mencius, "Tsăng Hsî would not play Kwan Chung, and is it what you desire for me that I should do so?"

5. Kung-sun Ch'âu said, "Kwan Chung raised his prince to be the leader of all the other princes, and Yen made his prince illustrious, and do you still think it would not be enough for you to do what they did?"

6. Mencius answered, "To raise Ch'î to the royal dignity would be as easy as it is to turn round the hand."

7. "So!" returned the other. "The perplexity of your disciple is hereby very much increased. There was King Wăn, moreover, with all the virtue which belonged to him; and who did not die till he had reached a hundred years: and still his influence had not penetrated throughout the kingdom. It required King Wû and the duke of Châu to continue his course, before that influence greatly prevailed. Now you say that the royal dignity might be so easily obtained: is King Wăn then not a sufficient object for imitation?"

8. Mencius said, "How can King Wăn be matched? From T'ăng to Wû-ting there had appeared six or seven worthy and sage sovereigns. The kingdom had been attached to Yin for a long time, and this length of time made a change difficult. Wû-ting had all the princes coming to his court, and possessed the kingdom as if it had been a thing which he moved round in his palm. Then, Châu was removed from Wû-ting by no great interval of time. There were still remaining some of the ancient families and of the old manners, of the influence also which had emanated from the earlier sovereigns, and of their good government. Moreover, there were the viscount of Wei and his second son, their Royal Highnesses Pî-kan and the viscount of Ch'î, and Kâo-ko, all men of ability and virtue, who gave their joint assistance to Châu in his government. In consequence of these things, it took a long time for him to lose the throne. There was not a foot of ground which he did not possess. There was not one of all the people who was not his subject. So it was on his side, and king Wăn at his beginning had only a territory of one hundred square lî. On all these accounts, it was difficult for him immediately to attain to the royal dignity.

9. "The people of Ch'î have a saying—'A man may have wisdom and discernment, but that is not like embracing the favorable opportunity. A man may have instruments of husbandry, but that is not like waiting for the farming seasons.' The present time is one in which the royal dignity may be easily attained.

10. "In the flourishing periods of the Hsiâ, Yin, and Châu dynasties, the royal domain did not exceed a thousand lî, and Ch'î embraces so much territory. Cocks crow and dogs bark to one another, all the way to the four borders of the State: so Ch'î possesses the people. No change is needed for the enlarging of its territory: no change

is needed for the collecting of a population. If its ruler will put in practice a benevolent government, no power will be able to prevent his becoming sovereign.

11. "Moreover, never was there a time farther removed than the present from the rise of a true sovereign: never was there a time when the sufferings of the people from tyrannical government were more intense than the present. The hungry readily partake of any food, and the thirsty of any drink.

12. "Confucius said, 'The flowing progress of virtue is more rapid than the transmission of royal orders by stages and couriers.'

13. "At the present time, in a country of ten thousand chariots, let benevolent government be put in practice, and the people will be delighted with it, as if they were relieved from hanging by the heels. With half the merit of the ancients, double their achievements is sure to be realized. It is only at this time that such could be the case."

II

THAT MENCIUS HAD ATTAINED TO AN UNPERTURBED MIND; THAT THE MEANS BY WHICH HE HAD DONE SO WAS HIS KNOWLEDGE OF WORDS AND THE NOURISHMENT OF HIS PASSION-NATURE; AND THAT IN THIS HE WAS A FOLLOWER OF CONFUCIUS.

1. Kung-sun Ch'âu asked Mencius, saying, "Master, if you were to be appointed a high noble and the prime minister of Ch'î, so as to be able to carry your principles into practice, though you should thereupon raise the ruler to the headship of all the other princes, or even to the royal dignity, it would not be to be wondered at. In such a position would your mind be perturbed or not?" Mencius replied, "No. At forty, I attained to an unperturbed mind."

2. Ch'âu said, "Since it is so with you, my Master, you are far beyond Mang Pan." "The mere attainment," said Mencius, "is not difficult. The scholar Kâo had attained to an unperturbed mind at an earlier period of life than I did."

3. Ch'âu asked, "Is there any way to an unperturbed mind?" The answer was, "Yes.

4. "Pî-kung Yû had this way of nourishing his valor: He did not flinch from any strokes at his body. He did not turn his eyes aside from any thrusts at them. He considered that the slightest push from anyone

was the same as if he were beaten before the crowds in the market-place, and that what he would not receive from a common man in his loose large garments of hair, neither should he receive from a prince of ten thousand chariots. He viewed stabbing a prince of ten thousand chariots just as stabbing a fellow dressed in cloth of hair. He feared not any of all the princes. A bad word addressed to him be always returned.

5. "Măng Shih-shê had this way of nourishing his valor: He said, 'I look upon not conquering and conquering in the same way. To measure the enemy and then advance; to calculate the chances of victory and then engage: this is to stand in awe of the opposing force. How can I make certain of conquering? I can only rise superior to all fear.'

6. "Măng Shih-shê resembled the philosopher Tsăng. Pî-kung Yû resembled Tsze-hsiâ. I do not know to the valor of which of the two the superiority should be ascribed, but yet Măng Shih-shê attended to what was of the greater importance.

7. "Formerly, the philosopher Tsăng said to Tsze-hsiang, 'Do you love valor? I heard an account of great valor from the Master. It speaks thus: "If, on self-examination, I find that I am not upright, shall I not be in fear even of a poor man in his loose garments of hair-cloth? If, on self-examination, I find that I am upright, I will go forward against thousands and tens of thousands."'

8. "Yet, what Măng Shih-shê maintained, being merely his physical energy, was after all inferior to what the philosopher Tsang maintained, which was indeed of the most importance."

9. Kung-sun Ch'âu said, "May I venture to ask an explanation from you, Master, of how you maintain an unperturbed mind, and how the philosopher Kâo does the same?" Mencius answered, "Kâo says, 'What is not attained in words is not to be sought for in the mind; what produces dissatisfaction in the mind, is not to be helped by passion-effort.' This last—when there is unrest in the mind, not to seek for relief from passion-effort, may be conceded. But not to seek in the mind for what is not attained in words cannot be conceded. The will is the leader of the passion-nature. The passion-nature pervades and animates the body. The will is first and chief, and the passion-nature is subordinate to it. Therefore I say, Maintain firm the will, and do no violence to the passion-nature."

10. Ch'âu observed, "Since you say, 'The will is chief, and the passion-nature is subordinate,' how do you also say, 'Maintain firm the will, and do no violence to the passion-nature?'" Mencius replied, "When it is the will alone which is active, it moves the passion-nature. When it is the passion-nature alone which is active, it moves the will. For instance now, in the case of a man falling or running, that is from the passion-nature, and yet it moves the mind."

11. "I venture to ask," said Ch'âu again, "wherein you, Master, surpass Kâo." Mencius told him, "I understand words. I am skillful in nourishing my vast, flowing passion-nature."

12. Ch'âu pursued, "I venture to ask what you mean by your vast, flowing passion-nature!" The reply was, "It is difficult to describe it.

13. "This is the passion-nature: It is exceedingly great, and exceedingly strong. Being nourished by rectitude, and sustaining no injury, it fills up all between heaven and earth.

14. "This is the passion-nature: It is the mate and assistant of righteousness and reason. Without it, man is in a state of starvation.

15. "It is produced by the accumulation of righteous deeds; it is not to be obtained by incidental acts of righteousness. If the mind does not feel complacency in the conduct, the nature becomes starved. I therefore said, 'Kâo has never understood righteousness, because he makes it something external.'

16. "There must be the constant practice of this righteousness, but without the object of thereby nourishing the passion-nature. Let not the mind forget its work, but let there be no assisting the growth of that nature. Let us not be like the man of Sung. There was a man of Sung, who was grieved that his growing corn was not longer, and so he pulled it up. Having done this, he returned home, looking very stupid, and said to his people, 'I am tired today. I have been helping the corn to grow long.' His son ran to look at it, and found the corn all withered. There are few in the world, who do not deal with their passion-nature, as if they were assisting the corn to grow long. Some indeed consider it of no benefit to them, and let it alone: they do not weed their corn. They who assist it to grow long, pull out their corn. What they do is not only of no benefit to the nature, but it also injures it."

17. Kung-sun Ch'âu further asked, "What do you mean by saying that you understand whatever words you hear?" Mencius replied, "When

words are one-sided, I know how the mind of the speaker is clouded over. When words are extravagant, I know how the mind is fallen and sunk. When words are all-depraved, I know how the mind has departed from principle. When words are evasive, I know how the mind is at its wit's end. These evils growing in the mind, do injury to government, and, displayed in the government, are hurtful to the conduct of affairs. When a Sage shall again arise, he will certainly follow my words."

18. On this Ch'âu observed, "Tsâi Wo and Tsze-kung were skillful in speaking. Zǎn Niû, the disciple Min, and Yen Yüan, while their words were good, were distinguished for their virtuous conduct. Confucius united the qualities of the disciples in himself, but still he said, 'In the matter of speeches, I am not competent.' Then, Master, have you attained to be a Sage?"

19. Mencius said, "Oh! what words are these? Formerly Tsze-kung asked Confucius, saying, 'Master, are you a Sage?' Confucius answered him, 'A Sage is what I cannot rise to. I learn without satiety, and teach without being tired.' Tsze-kung said, 'You learn without satiety: that shows your wisdom. You teach without being tired: that shows your benevolence. Benevolent and wise: Master, you are a Sage.' Now, since Confucius would not allow himself to be regarded as a Sage, what words were those?"

20. Ch'âu said, "Formerly, I once heard this: Tsze-hsiâ, Tsze-yû, and Tsze-chang had each one member of the Sage. Zǎn Niû, the disciple Min, and Yen Yüan had all the members, but in small proportions. I venture to ask, with which of these are you pleased to rank yourself?"

21. Mencius replied, "Let us drop speaking about these, if you please."

22. Ch'âu then asked, "What do you say of Po-î and Î Yin?" "Their ways were different from mine," said Mencius. "Not to serve a prince whom he did not esteem, nor command a people whom he did not approve; in a time of good government to take office, and on the occurrence of confusion to retire: this was the way of Po-î. To say, 'Whom may I not serve? My serving him makes him my ruler. What people may I not command? My commanding them makes them my people.' In a time of good government to take office, and when disorder prevailed, also to take office: that was the way of Î Yin. When it was proper to go into office, then to go into it; when it was proper to keep retired from office, then to keep retired from it; when it was proper to continue in it long, then to continue in it long—when

it was proper to withdraw from it quickly, then to withdraw quickly: that was the way of Confucius. These were all sages of antiquity, and I have not attained to do what they did. But what I wish to do is to learn to be like Confucius."

23. Ch'âu said, "Comparing Po-î and Î Yin with Confucius, are they to be placed in the same rank?" Mencius replied, "No. Since there were living men until now, there never was another Confucius."

24. Ch'âu said, "Then, did they have any points of agreement with him?" The reply was, "Yes. If they had been sovereigns over a hundred lî of territory, they would, all of them, have brought all the princes to attend in their court, and have obtained the throne. And none of them, in order to obtain the throne, would have committed one act of unrighteousness, or put to death one innocent person. In those things they agreed with him."

25. Ch'âu said, "I venture to ask wherein he differed from them." Mencius replied, "Tsâi Wo, Tsze-kung, and Yû Zo had wisdom sufficient to know the sage. Even had they been ranking themselves low, they would not have demeaned themselves to flatter their favorite.

26. "Now, Tsâi Wo said, 'According to my view of our Master, he was far superior to Yâo and Shun.'

27. "Tsze-kung said, 'By viewing the ceremonial ordinances of a prince, we know the character of his government. By hearing his music, we know the character of his virtue. After the lapse of a hundred ages I can arrange, according to their merits, the kings of a hundred ages — not one of them can escape me. From the birth of mankind till now, there has never been another like our Master.'

28. "Yû Zo said, 'Is it only among men that it is so? There is the Ch'î-lin among quadrupeds, the Făng-hăng among birds, the T'âi mountain among mounds and ant-hills, and rivers and seas among rain-pools. Though different in degree, they are the same in kind. So the sages among mankind are also the same in kind. But they stand out from their fellows, and rise above the level, and from the birth of mankind till now, there never has been one so complete as Confucius.'"

III

THE DIFFERENCE BETWEEN A CHIEFTAIN OF THE PRINCES AND A SOVEREIGN OF THE KINGDOM; AND BETWEEN SUBMISSION SECURED BY FORCE AND THAT PRODUCED BY VIRTUE.

1. Mencius said, "He who, using force, makes a pretense to benevolence is the leader of the princes. A leader of the princes requires a large kingdom. He who, using virtue, practices benevolence is the sovereign of the kingdom. To become the sovereign of the kingdom, a prince need not wait for a large kingdom. T'ăng did it with only seventy lî, and King Wăn with only a hundred.

2. "When one by force subdues men, they do not submit to him in heart. They submit, because their strength is not adequate to resist. When one subdues men by virtue, in their hearts' core they are pleased, and sincerely submit, as was the case with the seventy disciples in their submission to Confucius. What is said in the Book of Poetry,

> From the west, from the east,
> From the south, from the north,
> There was not one who thought of refusing submission,

is an illustration of this."

IV

GLORY IS THE SURE RESULT OF BENEVOLENT GOVERNMENT, CALAMITY AND HAPPINESS ARE MEN'S OWN SEEKING.

1. Mencius said, "Benevolence brings glory to a prince, and the opposite of it brings disgrace. For the princes of the present day to hate disgrace and yet to live complacently doing what is not benevolent, is like hating moisture and yet living in a low situation.

2. "If a prince hates disgrace, the best course for him to pursue, is to esteem virtue and honor virtuous scholars, giving the worthiest among them places of dignity, and the able offices of trust. When throughout his kingdom there is leisure and rest from external troubles, let him, taking advantage of such a season, clearly digest the principles of his government with its legal sanctions, and then even great kingdoms will be constrained to stand in awe of him.

3. "It is said in the Book of Poetry,

> Before the heavens were dark with rain,
> I gathered the bark from the roots of the mulberry trees,
> And wove it closely to form the window and door of my nest;
> Now, I thought, ye people below,
> Perhaps ye will not dare to insult me.

Confucius said, 'Did not he who made this ode understand the way of governing?' If a prince is able rightly to govern his kingdom, who will dare to insult him?

4. "But now the princes take advantage of the time when throughout their kingdoms there is leisure and rest from external troubles, to abandon themselves to pleasure and indolent indifference—they in fact seek for calamities for themselves.

5. "Calamity and happiness in all cases are men's own seeking.

6. "This is illustrated by what is said in the Book of Poetry—

> Be always studious to be in harmony with the ordinances of God,
> So you will certainly get for yourself much happiness;

and by the passage of the Tâi Chiah—'When Heaven sends down calamities, it is still possible to escape from them; when we occasion the calamities ourselves, it is not possible any longer to live.'"

V

VARIOUS POINTS OF TRUE ROYAL GOVERNMENT NEGLECTED BY THE PRINCES OF MENCIUS'S TIME, ATTENTION TO WHICH WOULD SURELY CARRY ANY ONE OF THEM TO THE ROYAL THRONE.

1. Mencius said, "If a ruler give honor to men of talents and virtue and employ the able, so that offices shall all be filled by individuals of distinction and mark—then all the scholars of the kingdom will be pleased, and wish to stand in his court.

2. "If, in the market-place of his capital, he levy a ground-rent on the shops but do not tax the goods, or enforce the proper regulations without levying a ground-rent—then all the traders of the kingdom will be pleased, and wish to store their goods in his market-place.

3. "If, at his frontier-passes, there be an inspection of persons, but no taxes charged on goods or other articles, then all the travelers of the kingdom will be pleased, and wish to make their tours on his roads.

4. "If he require that the husbandmen give their mutual aid to cultivate the public field, and exact no other taxes from them—then all the husbandmen of the kingdom will be pleased, and wish to plow in his fields.

5. "If from the occupiers of the shops in his market-place he do not exact the fine of the individual idler, or of the hamlet's quota of cloth,

then all the people of the kingdom will be pleased, and wish to come and be his people.

6. "If a ruler can truly practice these five things, then the people in the neighboring kingdoms will look up to him as a parent. From the first birth of mankind till now, never has anyone led children to attack their parent, and succeeded in his design. Thus, such a ruler will not have an enemy in all the kingdom, and he who has no enemy in the kingdom is the minister of Heaven. Never has there been a ruler in such a case who did not attain to the royal dignity."

VI

THAT BENEVOLENCE, RIGHTEOUSNESS, PROPRIETY, AND KNOWLEDGE BELONG TO MAN AS NATURALLY AS HIS FOUR LIMBS, AND MAY EASILY BE EXERCISED.

1. Mencius said, "All men have a mind which cannot bear to see the sufferings of others.

2. "The ancient kings had this commiserating mind, and they, as a matter of course, had likewise a commiserating government. When with a commiserating mind was practiced a commiserating government, to rule the kingdom was as easy a matter as to make anything go round in the palm.

3. "When I say that all men have a mind which cannot bear to see the sufferings of others, my meaning may be illustrated thus: even nowadays, if men suddenly see a child about to fall into a well, they will without exception experience a feeling of alarm and distress. They will feel so, not as a ground on which they may gain the favor of the child's parents, nor as a ground on which they may seek the praise of their neighbors and friends, nor from a dislike to the reputation of having been unmoved by such a thing.

4. "From this case we may perceive that the feeling of commiseration is essential to man, that the feeling of shame and dislike is essential to man, that the feeling of modesty and complaisance is essential to man, and that the feeling of approving and disapproving is essential to man.

5. "The feeling of commiseration is the principle of benevolence. The feeling of shame and dislike is the principle of righteousness. The feeling of modesty and complaisance is the principle of propriety.

The feeling of approving and disapproving is the principle of knowledge.

6. "Men have these four principles just as they have their four limbs. When men, having these four principles, yet say of themselves that they cannot develop them, they play the thief with themselves, and he who says of his prince that he cannot develop them plays the thief with his prince.

7. "Since all men have these four principles in themselves, let them know to give them all their development and completion, and the issue will be like that of fire which has begun to burn, or that of a spring which has begun to find vent. Let them have their complete development, and they will suffice to love and protect all within the four seas. Let them be denied that development, and they will not suffice for a man to serve his parents with."

VII

AN EXHORTATION TO BENEVOLENCE FROM THE DISGRACE WHICH MUST ATTEND THE WANT OF IT, LIKE THE DISGRACE OF A MAN WHO DOES NOT KNOW HIS PROFESSION.

1. Mencius said, "Is the arrow-maker less benevolent than the maker of armor of defense? And yet, the arrow-maker's only fear is lest men should not be hurt, and the armor-maker's only fear is lest men should be hurt. So it is with the priest and the coffin-maker. The choice of a profession, therefore, is a thing in which great caution is required.

2. "Confucius said, 'It is virtuous manners which constitute the excellence of a neighborhood. If a man, in selecting a residence, do not fix on one where such prevail, how can he be wise?' Now, benevolence is the most honorable dignity conferred by Heaven, and the quiet home in which man should dwell. Since no one can hinder us from being so, if yet we are not benevolent—this is being not wise.

3. "From the want of benevolence and the want of wisdom will ensue the entire absence of propriety and righteousness—he who is in such a case must be the servant of other men. To be the servant of men and yet ashamed of such servitude, is like a bowmaker's being ashamed to make bows, or an arrow-maker's being ashamed to make arrows.

4. "If he be ashamed of his case, his best course is to practice benevolence.

5. "The man who would be benevolent is like the archer. The archer adjusts himself and then shoots. If he misses, he does not murmur against those who surpass himself. He simply turns round and seeks the cause of his failure in himself."

VIII

HOW SAGES AND WORTHIES DELIGHTED IN WHAT IS GOOD.

1. Mencius said, "When anyone told Tsze-lû that he had a fault, he rejoiced.

2. "When Yü heard good words, he bowed to the speaker.

3. "The great Shun had a still greater delight in what was good. He regarded virtue as the common property of himself and others, giving up his own way to follow that of others, and delighting to learn from others to practice what was good.

4. "From the time when he plowed and sowed, exercised the potter's art, and was a fisherman, to the time when he became emperor, he was continually learning from others.

5. "To take example from others to practice virtue, is to help them in the same practice. Therefore, there is no attribute of the superior man greater than his helping men to practice virtue."

IX

PICTURES OF PO-î AND HÛI OF LIÛ-HSIÂ, AND MENCIUS'S JUDGMENT CONCERNING THEM.

1. Mencius said, "Po-î would not serve a prince whom he did not approve, nor associate with a friend whom he did not esteem. He would not stand in a bad prince's court, nor speak with a bad man. To stand in a bad prince's court, or to speak with a bad man, would have been to him the same as to sit with his court robes and court cap amid mire and ashes. Pursuing the examination of his dislike to what was evil, we find that he thought it necessary, if he happened to be standing with a villager whose cap was not rightly adjusted, to leave him with a high air, as if he were going to be defiled. Therefore, although some of the princes made application to him with very proper messages, he would not receive their gifts. He would not

receive their gifts, counting it inconsistent with his purity to go to them.

2. "Hûi of Liû-hsiâ was not ashamed to serve an impure prince, nor did he think it low to be an inferior officer. When advanced to employment, he did not conceal his virtue, but made it a point to carry out his principles. When neglected and left without office, he did not murmur. When straitened by poverty, he did not grieve. Accordingly, he had a saying, 'You are you, and I am I. Although you stand by my side with breast and aims bare, or with your body naked, how can you defile me?' Therefore, self-possessed, he companied with men indifferently, at the same time not losing himself. When he wished to leave, if pressed to remain in office, he would remain. He would remain in office, when pressed to do so, not counting it required by his purity to go away."

3. Mencius said, "Po-î was narrow-minded, and Hûi of Liû-hsiâ was wanting in self-respect. The superior man will not manifest either narrow-mindedness, or the want of self-respect."

KUNG-SUN CH'ÂU

PART II

I

1. Mencius said, "Opportunities of time vouchsafed by Heaven are not equal to advantages of situation afforded by the Earth, and advantages of situation afforded by the Earth are not equal to the union arising from the accord of Men.

2. "There is a city, with an inner wall of three lî in circumference, and an outer wall of seven. The enemy surround and attack it, but they are not able to take it. Now, to surround and attack it, there must have been vouchsafed to them by Heaven the opportunity of time, and in such case their not taking it is because opportunities of time vouchsafed by Heaven are not equal to advantages of situation afforded by the Earth.

3. "There is a city, whose walls are distinguished for their height, and whose moats are distinguished for their depth, where the arms of its defenders, offensive and defensive, are distinguished for their strength and sharpness, and the stores of rice and other grain are very large. Yet it is obliged to be given up and abandoned. This is because advantages of situation afforded by the Earth are not equal to the union arising from the accord of Men.

4. "In accordance with these principles it is said, 'A people is bounded in, not by the limits of dykes and borders; a State is secured, not by the strengths of mountains and rivers; the kingdom is overawed, not by the sharpness and strength of arms.' He who finds the proper course has many to assist him. He who loses the proper course has few to assist him. When this—the being assisted by few—reaches its extreme point, his own relations revolt from the prince. When the

being assisted by many reaches its highest point, the whole kingdom becomes obedient to the prince.

5.   "When one to whom the whole kingdom is prepared to be obedient, attacks those from whom their own relations revolt, what must be the result? Therefore, the true ruler will prefer not to fight; but if he do fight, he must overcome."

II

HOW MENCIUS CONSIDERED THAT IT WAS SLIGHTING HIM FOR A PRINCE TO CALL HIM BY MESSENGERS TO GO TO SEE HIM, AND THE SHIFTS HE WAS PUT TO TO GET THIS UNDERSTOOD.

1.   As Mencius was about to go to court to see the king, the king sent a person to him with this message—"I was wishing to come and see you. But I have got a cold, and may not expose myself to the wind. In the morning I will hold my court. I do not know whether you will give me the opportunity of seeing you then." Mencius replied, "Unfortunately, I am unwell, and not able to go to the court."

2.   Next day, he went out to pay a visit of condolence to someone of the Tung-kwŏh family, when Kung-sun Ch'âu said to him, "Yesterday, you declined going to the court on the ground of being unwell, and today you are going to pay a visit of condolence. May this not be regarded as improper?" "Yesterday," said Mencius, "I was unwell; today, I am better: why should I not pay this visit?"

3.   In the meantime, the king sent a messenger to inquire about his sickness, and also a physician. Măng Chung replied to them, "Yesterday, when the king's order came, he was feeling a little unwell, and could not go to the court. Today he was a little better, and hastened to go to court. I do not know whether he can have reached it by this time or not." Having said this, he sent several men to look for Mencius on the way, and say to him, "I beg that, before you return home, you will go to the court."

4.   On this, Mencius felt himself compelled to go to Ching Ch'âu's, and there stop the night. Mr. Ching said to him, "In the family, there is the relation of father and son; abroad, there is the relation of prince and minister. These are the two great relations among men. Between father and son the ruling principle is kindness. Between prince and minister the ruling principle is respect. I have seen the respect of the king to you, Sir, but I have not seen in what way you show respect

to him." Mencius replied, "Oh! what words are these? Among the people of Ch'î there is no one who speaks to the king about benevolence and righteousness. Are they thus silent because they do not think that benevolence and righteousness are admirable? No, but in their hearts they say, 'This man is not fit to be spoken with about benevolence and righteousness.' Thus they manifest a disrespect than which there can be none greater. I do not dare to set forth before the king any but the ways of Yâo and Shun. There is therefore no man of Ch'î who respects the king so much as I do."

5. Mr. Ching said, "Not so. That was not what I meant. In the Book of Rites it is said, 'When a father calls, the answer must be without a moment's hesitation. When the prince's order calls, the carriage must not be waited for.' You were certainly going to the court, but when you heard the king's order, then you did not carry your purpose out. This does seem as if it were not in accordance with that rule of propriety."

6. Mencius answered him, "How can you give that meaning to my conduct? The philosopher Tsǎng said, 'The wealth of Tsin and Ch'û cannot be equaled. Let their rulers have their wealth: I have my benevolence. Let them have their nobility: I have my righteousness. Wherein should I be dissatisfied as inferior to them?' Now shall we say that these sentiments are not right? Seeing that the philosopher Tsǎng spoke them, there is in them, I apprehend, a real principle. In the kingdom there are three things universally acknowledged to be honorable. Nobility is one of them; age is one of them; virtue is one of them. In courts, nobility holds the first place of the three; in villages, age holds the first place; and for helping one's generation and presiding over the people, the other two are not equal to virtue. How can the possession of only one of these be presumed on to despise one who possesses the other two?

7. "Therefore a prince who is to accomplish great deeds will certainly have ministers whom he does not call to go to him. When he wishes to consult with them, he goes to them. The prince who does not honor the virtuous, and delight in their ways of doing, to this extent, is not worth having to do with.

8. "Accordingly, there was the behaviour of T'ǎng to Î Yin: he first learned of him, and then employed him as his minister; and so without difficulty he became sovereign. There was the behavior of the duke Hwǎn to Kwan Chung: he first learned of him, and then

employed him as his minister; and so without difficulty he became chief of all the princes.

9. "Now throughout the kingdom, the territories of the princes are of equal extent, and in their achievements they are on a level. Not one of them is able to exceed the others. This is from no other reason, but that they love to make ministers of those whom they teach, and do not love to make ministers of those by whom they might be taught."

10. "So did T'ăng behave to Î Yin, and the duke Hwăn to Kwan Chung, that they would not venture to call them to go to them. If Kwan Chung might not be called to him by his prince, how much less may he be called, who would not play the part of Kwan Chung!"

III

By what principles Mencius was guided in declining or accepting the gifts of princes.

1. Ch'ăn Tsin asked Mencius, saying, "Formerly, when you were in Ch'î, the king sent you a present of 2,400 taels of fine silver, and you refused to accept it. When you were in Sung, 1,680 taels were sent to you, which you accepted; and when you were in Hsieh, 1,200 taels were sent, which you likewise accepted. If your declining to accept the gift in the first case was right, your accepting it in the latter cases was wrong. If your accepting it in the latter cases was right, your declining to do so in the first case was wrong. You must accept, Master, one of these alternatives."

2. Mencius said, "I did right in all the cases.

3. "When I was in Sung, I was about to take a long journey. Travelers must be provided with what is necessary for their expenses. The prince's message was, 'A present against traveling-expenses.' Why should I have declined the gift?

4. "When I was in Hsieh, I was apprehensive for my safety, and taking measures for my protection. The message was, 'I have heard that you are taking measures to protect yourself, and send this to help you in procuring arms.' Why should I have declined the gift?

5. "But when I was in Ch'î, I had no occasion for money. To send a man a gift when he has no occasion for it, is to bribe him. How is it possible that a superior man should be taken with a bribe?"

IV

HOW MENCIUS BROUGHT CONVICTION OF THEIR FAULTS
HOME TO THE KING AND AN OFFICER OF CH'î.

1. Mencius having gone to P'ing-lû, addressed the governor of it, saying, "If one of your spearmen should lose his place in the ranks three times in one day, would you, Sir, put him to death or not?" "I would not wait for three times to do so," was the reply.

2. Mencius said, "Well then, you, Sir, have likewise lost your place in the ranks many times. In bad calamitous years, and years of famine, the old and feeble of your people, who have been found lying in the ditches and water-channels, and the able-bodied, who have been scattered about to the four quarters, have amounted to several thousand." The governor replied, "That is a state of things in which it does not belong to me Chü-hsin to act."

3. "Here," said Mencius, "is a man who receives charge of the cattle and sheep of another, and undertakes to feed them for him—of course he must search for pasture-ground and grass for them. If, after searching for those, he cannot find them, will he return his charge to the owner? Or will he stand by and see them die?" "Herein," said the officer, "I am guilty."

4. Another day, Mencius had an audience of the king, and said to him, "Of the governors of your Majesty's cities I am acquainted with five, but the only one of them who knows his faults is K'ung Chü-hsin." He then repeated the conversation to the king, who said, "In this matter, I am the guilty one."

V

THE FREEDOM BELONGING TO MENCIUS IN RELATION TO
THE MEASURES OF THE KING OF CH'î FROM HIS PARTICULAR
POSITION, AS UNSALARIED.

1. Mencius said to Ch'î Wâ, "There seemed to be reason in your declining the governorship of Ling-ch'iû, and requesting to be appointed chief criminal judge, because the latter office would afford you the opportunity of speaking your views. Now several months have elapsed, and have you yet found nothing of which you might speak?"

2. On this, Ch'î Wâ remonstrated on some matter with the king, and, his counsel not being taken, resigned his office and went away.

3. The people of Ch'î said, "In the course which he marked out for Ch'î Wâ he did well, but we do not know as to the course which he pursues for himself."

4. His disciple Kung-tû told him these remarks.

5. Mencius said, "I have heard that he who is in charge of an office, when he is prevented from fulfilling its duties, ought to take his departure, and that he on whom is the responsibility of giving his opinion, when he finds his words unattended to, ought to do the same. But I am in charge of no office; on me devolves no duty of speaking out my opinion: may not I therefore act freely and without any constraint, either in going forward or in retiring?"

VI

MENCIUS'S BEHAVIOR WITH AN UNWORTHY ASSOCIATE.

1. Mencius, occupying the position of a high dignitary in Ch'î, went on a mission of condolence to T'ăng. The king also sent Wang Hwăn, the governor of Kâ, as assistant-commissioner. Wang Hwăn, morning and evening, waited upon Mencius, who, during all the way to T'ăng and back, never spoke to him about the business of their mission.

2. Kung-sun Ch'âu said to Mencius, "The position of a high dignitary of Ch'î is not a small one; the road from Ch'î to T'ăng is not short. How was it that during all the way there and back, you never spoke to Hwăn about the matters of your mission?" Mencius replied, "There were the proper officers who attended to them. What occasion had I to speak to him about them?"

VII

THAT ONE OUGHT TO DO HIS UTMOST IN THE BURIAL OF HIS
PARENTS — ILLUSTRATED BY MENCIUS'S BURIAL OF HIS MOTHER.

1. Mencius went from Ch'î to Lû to bury his mother. On his return to Ch'î, he stopped at Ying, where Ch'ung Yü begged to put a question to him, and said, "Formerly, in ignorance of my incompetency, you employed me to superintend the making of the coffin. As you were then pressed by the urgency of the business, I did not venture to

put any question to you. Now, however, I wish to take the liberty to submit the matter. The wood of the coffin, it appeared to me, was too good."

2. Mencius replied, "Anciently, there was no rule for the size of either the inner or the outer coffin. In middle antiquity, the inner coffin was made seven inches thick, and the outer one the same. This was done by all, from the sovereign to the common people, and not simply for the beauty of the appearance, but because they thus satisfied the natural feelings of their hearts.

3. "If prevented by statutory regulations from making their coffins in this way, men cannot have the feeling of pleasure. If they have not the money to make them in this way, they cannot have the feeling of pleasure. When they were not prevented, and had the money, the ancients all used this style. Why should I alone not do so?

4. "And moreover, is there no satisfaction to the natural feelings of a man, in preventing the earth from getting near to the bodies of his dead?

5. "I have heard that the superior man will not for all the world be niggardly to his parents."

VIII

DESERVED PUNISHMENT MAY NOT BE INFLICTED BUT BY PROPER AUTHORITY. A STATE OR NATION MAY ONLY BE SMITTEN BY THE MINISTER OF HEAVEN.

1. Shǎn T'ung, on his own impulse, asked Mencius, saying, "May Yen be smitten?" Mencius replied, "It may. Tsze-k'wâi had no right to give Yen to another man, and Tsze-chih had no right to receive Yen from Tsze-k'wâi. Suppose there were an officer here, with whom you, Sir, were pleased, and that, without informing the king, you were privately to give to him your salary and rank; and suppose that this officer, also without the king's orders, were privately to receive them from you—would such a transaction be allowable? And where is the difference between the case of Yen and this?"

2. The people of Ch'î smote Yen. Someone asked Mencius, saying, "Is it really the case that you advised Ch'î to smite Yen?" He replied, "No. Shǎn T'ung asked me whether Yen might be smitten, and I answered him, "It may." They accordingly went and smote it. If he had asked me—'Who may smite it?' I would have answered him,

'He who is the minister of Heaven may smite it.' Suppose the case of a murderer, and that one asks me—'May this man be put to death?' I will answer him—'He may.' If he ask me—'Who may put him to death?' I will answer him, 'The chief criminal judge may put him to death.' But now with one Yen to smite another Yen: how should I have advised this?"

IX

HOW MENCIUS BEAT DOWN THE ATTEMPT TO ARGUE
IN EXCUSE OF ERRORS AND MISCONDUCT.

1. The people of Yen having rebelled, the king of Ch'î said, "I feel very much ashamed when I think of Mencius."

2. Ch'ăn Chiâ said to him, "Let not your Majesty be grieved. Whether does your Majesty consider yourself or Châu-kung the more benevolent and wise?" The king replied, "Oh! what words are those?" "The duke of Châu," said Chiâ, "appointed Kwan-shû to oversee the heir of Yin, but Kwan-shû with the power of the Yin State rebelled. If knowing that this would happen he appointed Kwan-shû, he was deficient in benevolence. If he appointed him, not knowing that it would happen, he was deficient in knowledge. If the duke of Châu was not completely benevolent and wise, how much less can your Majesty be expected to be so! I beg to go and see Mencius, and relieve your Majesty from that feeling."

3. Ch'ăn Chiâ accordingly saw Mencius, and asked him, saying, "What kind of man was the duke of Châu?" "An ancient sage," was the reply. "Is it the fact, that he appointed Kwan-shû to oversee the heir of Yin, and that Kwan-shû with the State of Yin rebelled?" "It is." "Did the duke of Châu know that he would rebel, and purposely appoint him to that office?" Mencius said, "He did not know." "Then, though a sage, he still fell into error?" "The duke of Châu," answered Mencius, "was the younger brother. Kwan-shû was his elder brother. Was not the error of Châu-kung in accordance with what is right?

4. "Moreover, when the superior men of old had errors, they reformed them. The superior men of the present time, when they have errors, persist in them. The errors of the superior men of old were like eclipses of the sun and moon. All the people witnessed them, and when they had reformed them, all the people looked up to them with their former admiration. But do the superior men of the present

day only persist in their errors? They go on to apologize for them likewise."

X

MENCIUS IN LEAVING A COUNTRY OR REMAINING IN IT WAS NOT INFLUENCED BY PECUNIARY CONSIDERATIONS, BUT BY THE OPPORTUNITY DENIED OR ACCORDED TO HIM OF CARRYING HIS PRINCIPLES INTO PRACTICE.

1. Mencius gave up his office, and made arrangements for returning to his native State.

2. The king came to visit him, and said, "Formerly, I wished to see you, but in vain. Then, I got the opportunity of being by your side, and all my court joyed exceedingly along with me. Now again you abandon me, and are returning home. I do not know if hereafter I may expect to have another opportunity of seeing you." Mencius replied, "I dare not request permission to visit you at any particular time, but, indeed, it is what I desire."

3. Another day, the king said to the officer Shih, "I wish to give Mencius a house, somewhere in the middle of the kingdom, and to support his disciples with an allowance of 10,000 *chung*, that all the officers and the people may have such an example to reverence and imitate. Had you not better tell him this for me?"

4. Shih took advantage to convey this message by means of the disciple Ch'ăn, who reported his words to Mencius.

5. Mencius said, "Yes; but how should the officer Shih know that the thing could not be? Suppose that I wanted to be rich, having formerly declined 100,000 *chung*, would my now accepting 10,000 be the conduct of one desiring riches?

6. "Chî-sun said, 'A strange man was Tsze-shû Î. He pushed himself into the service of government. His prince declining to employ him, he had to retire indeed, but he again schemed that his son or younger brother should be made a high officer. Who indeed is there of men but wishes for riches and honor? But he only, among the seekers of these, tried to monopolize the conspicuous mound.

7. "'Of old time, the market-dealers exchanged the articles which they had for others which they had not, and simply had certain officers to keep order among them. It happened that there was a mean fellow,

who made it a point to look out for a conspicuous mound, and get up upon it. Thence he looked right and left, to catch in his net the whole gain of the market. The people all thought his conduct mean, and therefore they proceeded to lay a tax upon his wares. The taxing of traders took its rise from this mean fellow.'"

XI

HOW MENCIUS REPELLED A MAN, WHO, OFFICIOUSLY AND ON HIS OWN IMPULSE, TRIED TO DETAIN HIM IN CH'Î.

1. Mencius, having taken his leave of Ch'î, was passing the night in Châu.

2. A person who wished to detain him on behalf of the king, came and sat down, and began to speak to him. Mencius gave him no answer, but leant upon his stool and slept.

3. The visitor was displeased, and said, "I passed the night in careful vigil, before I would venture to speak to you, and you, Master, sleep and do not listen to me. Allow me to request that I may not again presume to see you." Mencius replied, "Sit down, and I will explain the case clearly to you. Formerly, if the duke Mû had not kept a person by the side of Tsze-sze, he could not have induced Tsze-sze to remain with him. If Hsieh Liû and Shǎn Hsiang had not had a remembrancer by the side of the duke Mû, he would not have been able to make them feel at home and remain with him.

4. "You anxiously form plans with reference to me, but you do not treat me as Tsze-sze was treated. Is it you, Sir, who cut me? Or is it I who cut you?

XII

HOW MENCIUS EXPLAINED HIS SEEMING TO LINGER IN CH'Î, AFTER HE HAD RESIGNED HIS OFFICE, AND LEFT THE COURT.

1. When Mencius had left Ch'î, Yin Shih spoke about him to others, saying, "If he did not know that the king could not be made a T'ǎng or a Wû, that showed his want of intelligence. If he knew that he could not be made such, and came notwithstanding, that shows he was seeking his own benefit. He came a thousand lî to wait on the king; because he did not find in him a ruler to suit him, he took his leave, but how dilatory and lingering was his departure, stopping

three nights before he quitted Châu! I am dissatisfied on account of this."

2. The disciple Kâo informed Mencius of these remarks.

3. Mencius said, "How should Yin Shih know me! When I came a thousand lî to wait on the king, it was what I desired to do. When I went away because I did not find in him a ruler to suit me, was that what I desired to do? I felt myself constrained to do it.

4. "When I stopped three nights before I quitted Châu, in my own mind I still considered my departure speedy. I was hoping that the king might change. If the king had changed, he would certainly have recalled me.

5. "When I quitted Châu, and the king had not sent after me, then, and not till then, was my mind resolutely bent on returning to Tsâu. But, notwithstanding that, how can it be said that I give up the king? The king, after all, is one who may be made to do what is good. If he were to use me, would it be for the happiness of the people of Ch'î only? It would be for the happiness of the people of the whole kingdom. I am hoping that the king will change. I am daily hoping for this.

6. "Am I like one of your little-minded people? They will remonstrate with their prince, and on their remonstrance not being accepted, they get angry; and, with their passion displayed in their countenance, they take their leave, and travel with all their strength for a whole day, before they will stop for the night."

7. When Yin Shih heard this explanation, he said, "I am indeed a small man."

XIII

MENCIUS'S GRIEF AT NOT FINDING AN OPPORTUNITY TO DO THE GOOD WHICH HE COULD.

1. When Mencius left Ch'î, Ch'ung Yü questioned him upon the way, saying, "Master, you look like one who carries an air of dissatisfaction in his countenance. But formerly I heard you say—'The superior man does not murmur against Heaven, nor grudge against men.'"

2. Mencius said, "That was one time, and this is another.

3. "It is a rule that a true royal sovereign should arise in the course of five hundred years, and that during that time there should be men illustrious in their generation.

4. "From the commencement of the Châu dynasty till now, more than seven hundred years have elapsed. Judging numerically, the date is past. Examining the character of the present time, we might expect the rise of such individuals in it.

5. "But Heaven does not yet wish that the kingdom should enjoy tranquility and good order. If it wished this, who is there besides me to bring it about? How should I be otherwise than dissatisfied?"

XIV

THE REASON MENCIUS'S HOLDING AN HONORARY OFFICE
IN CH'Î WITHOUT SALARY, THAT HE WISHED TO BE FREE IN
HIS MOVEMENTS.

1. When Mencius left Ch'î, he dwelt in Hsiû. There Kung-sun Ch'âu asked him, saying, "Was it the way of the ancients to hold office without receiving salary?"

2. Mencius replied, "No; when I first saw the king in Ch'ung, it was my intention, on retiring from the interview, to go away. Because I did not wish to change this intention, I declined to receive any salary.

3. "Immediately after, there came orders for the collection of troops, when it would have been improper for me to beg permission to leave. But to remain so long in Ch'î was not my purpose."

BOOK III

T'ĂNG WĂN KUNG

PART I

I

How all men by developing their natural goodness may become equal to the ancient sages.

1. When the prince, afterwards Duke Wăn of T'ăng, had to go to Ch'û, he went by way of Sung, and visited Mencius.

2. Mencius discoursed to him how the nature of man is good, and when speaking, always made laudatory reference to Yâo and Shun.

3. When the prince was returning from Ch'û, he again visited Mencius. Mencius said to him, "Prince, do you doubt my words? The path is one, and only one.

4. "Ch'ăng Chi'en said to Duke King of Ch'î, 'They were men. I am a man. Why should I stand in awe of them?' Yen Yüan said, 'What kind of man was Shun? What kind of man am I? He who exerts himself will also become such as he was.' Kung-Ming Î said, 'King Wăn is my teacher. How should the duke of Châu deceive me by those words?'

5. "Now, T'ăng, taking its length with its breadth, will amount, I suppose, to fifty lî. It is small, but still sufficient to make a good State. It is said in the Book of History, 'If medicine do not raise a commotion in the patient, his disease will not be cured by it.'"

II

How Mencius advised the duke of T'ăng to conduct the mourning for his father.

1. When the duke Ting of T'ăng died, the prince said to Yen Yû, "Formerly, Mencius spoke with me in Sung, and in my mind I have never forgotten his words. Now, alas! This great duty to my father

devolves upon me; I wish to send you to ask the advice of Mencius, and then to proceed to its various services."

2. Zăn Yû accordingly proceeded to Tsâu, and consulted Mencius. Mencius said, "Is this not good? In discharging the funeral duties to parents, men indeed feel constrained to do their utmost. The philosopher Tsăng said, 'When parents are alive, they should be served according to propriety; when they are dead, they should be buried according to propriety; and they should be sacrificed to according to propriety: this may be called filial piety.' The ceremonies to be observed by the princes I have not learned, but I have heard these points: that the three years' mourning, the garment of coarse cloth with its lower edge even, and the eating of congee, were equally prescribed by the three dynasties, and binding on all, from the sovereign to the mass of the people."

3. Zăn Yû reported the execution of his commission, and the prince determined that the three years' mourning should be observed. His aged relatives, and the body of the officers, did not wish that it should be so, and said, "The former princes of Lû, that kingdom which we honor, have, none of them, observed this practice, neither have any of our own former princes observed it. For you to act contrary to their example is not proper. Moreover, the History says—'In the observances of mourning and sacrifice, ancestors are to be followed,' meaning that they received those things from a proper source to hand them down."

4. The prince said again to Zăn Yû, "Hitherto, I have not given myself to the pursuit of learning, but have found my pleasure in horsemanship and sword-exercise, and now I don't come up to the wishes of my aged relatives and the officers. I am afraid I may not be able to discharge my duty in the great business that I have entered on; do you again consult Mencius for me." On this, Zăn Yû went again to Tsâu, and consulted Mencius. Mencius said, "It is so, but he may not seek a remedy in others, but only in himself. Confucius said, 'When a prince dies, his successor entrusts the administration to the prime minister. He sips the congee. His face is of a deep black. He approaches the place of mourning, and weeps. Of all the officers and inferior ministers there is not one who will presume not to join in the lamentation, he setting them this example. What the superior loves, his inferiors will be found to love exceedingly. The relation between superiors and inferiors is like that between the wind and

grass. The grass must bend when the wind blows upon it.' The business depends on the prince."

5. Zǎn Yû returned with this answer to his commission, and the prince said, "It is so. The matter does indeed depend on me." So for five months he dwelt in the shed, without issuing an order or a caution. All the officers and his relatives said, "He may be said to understand the ceremonies." When the time of interment arrived, they came from all quarters of the State to witness it. Those who had come from other States to condole with him, were greatly pleased with the deep dejection of his countenance and the mournfulness of his wailing and weeping.

III

MENCIUS'S COUNSELS TO THE DUKE OF T'ĂNG FOR THE GOVERNMENT OF THE KINGDOM. AGRICULTURE AND EDUCATION ARE THE CHIEF THINGS THAT MUST BE ATTENDED TO, AND THE FIRST AS AN ESSENTIAL PREPARATION FOR THE SECOND.

1. The duke Wǎn of T'ǎng asked Mencius about the proper way of governing a kingdom.

2. Mencius said, "The business of the people may not be remissly attended to. It is said in the Book of Poetry,

> In the daylight go and gather the grass,
> And at night twist your ropes;
> Then get up quickly on the roofs;
> Soon must we begin sowing again the grain.

3. "The way of the people is this: If they have a certain livelihood, they will have a fixed heart; if they have not a certain livelihood, they have not a fixed heart. If they have not a fixed heart, there is nothing which they will not do in the way of self-abandonment, of moral deflection, of depravity, and of wild license. When they have thus been involved in crime, to follow them up and punish them: this is to entrap the people. How can such a thing as entrapping the people be done under the rule of a benevolent man?

4. "Therefore, a ruler who is endowed with talents and virtue will be gravely complaisant and economical, showing a respectful politeness to his ministers, and taking from the people only in accordance with regulated limits.

5. "Yang Hû said, 'He who seeks to be rich will not be benevolent. He who wishes to be benevolent will not be rich.'

6. "The sovereign of the Hsiâ dynasty enacted the fifty *mâu* allotment, and the payment of a tax. The founder of the Yin enacted the seventy *mâu* allotment, and the system of mutual aid. The founder of the Châu enacted the hundred *mâu* allotment, and the share system. In reality, what was paid in all these was a tithe. The share system means mutual division. The aid system means mutual dependence.

7. "Lung said, 'For regulating the lands, there is no better system than that of mutual aid, and none which is not better than that of taxing. By the tax system, the regular amount was fixed by taking the average of several years. In good years, when the grain lies about in abundance, much might be taken without its being oppressive, and the actual exaction would be small. But in bad years, the produce being not sufficient to repay the manuring of the fields, this system still requires the taking of the full amount. When the parent of the people causes the people to wear looks of distress, and, after the whole year's toil, yet not to be able to nourish their parents, so that they proceed to borrowing to increase their means, till the old people and children are found lying in the ditches and water-channels: where, in such a case, is his parental relation to the people?'

8. "As to the system of hereditary salaries, that is already observed in T'ăng.

9. "It is said in the Book of Poetry,

> May the rain come down on our public field,
> And then upon our private fields!

It is only in the system of mutual aid that there is a public field, and from this passage we perceive that even in the Châu dynasty this system has been recognized.

10. "Establish *hsiang*, *hsü*, *hsio*, and *hsiâo* — all those educational institutions — for the instruction of the people. The name *hsiang* indicates nourishing as its object; *hsiâo*, indicates teaching; and *hsü* indicates archery. By the Hsiâ dynasty the name *hsiâo* was used; by the Yin, that of *hsü*; and by the Châu, that of *hsiang*. As to the *hsio*, they belonged to the three dynasties, and by that name. The object of them all is to illustrate the human relations. When those are thus illustrated by superiors, kindly feeling will prevail among the inferior people below.

11. "Should a real sovereign arise, he will certainly come and take an example from you; and thus you will be the teacher of the true sovereign.

12. "It is said in the Book of Poetry,

> Although Châu was an old country,
> It received a new destiny.

That is said with reference to King Wăn. Do you practice those things with vigor, and you also will by them make new your kingdom."

13. The duke afterwards sent Pî Chan to consult Mencius about the nine-squares system of dividing the land. Mencius said to him, "Since your prince, wishing to put in practice a benevolent government, has made choice of you and put you into this employment, you must exert yourself to the utmost. Now, the first thing towards a benevolent government must be to lay down the boundaries. If the boundaries be not defined correctly, the division of the land into squares will not be equal, and the produce available for salaries will not be evenly distributed. On this account, oppressive rulers and impure ministers are sure to neglect this defining of the boundaries. When the boundaries have been defined correctly, the division of the fields and the regulation of allowances may be determined by you, sitting at your ease.

14. "Although the territory of T'ăng is narrow and small, yet there must be in it men of a superior grade, and there must be in it country-men. If there were not men of a superior grade, there would be none to rule the country-men. If there were not country-men, there would be none to support the men of superior grade.

15. "I would ask you, in the remoter districts, observing the nine-squares division, to reserve one division to be cultivated on the system of mutual aid, and in the more central parts of the kingdom, to make the people pay for themselves a tenth part of their produce.

16. "From the highest officers down to the lowest, each one must have his holy field, consisting of fifty *mâu*.

17. "Let the supernumerary males have their twenty-five *mâu*.

18. "On occasions of death, or removal from one dwelling to another, there will be no quitting the district. In the fields of a district, those who belong to the same nine squares render all friendly offices to one another in their going out and coming in, aid one another in

keeping watch and ward, and sustain one another in sickness. Thus the people are brought to live in affection and harmony.

19. "A square lî covers nine squares of land, which nine squares contain nine hundred *mâu*. The central square is the public field, and eight families, each having its private hundred *mâu*, cultivate in common the public field. And not till the public work is finished, may they presume to attend to their private affairs. This is the way by which the country-men are distinguished from those of a superior grade.

20. "Those are the great outlines of the system. Happily to modify and adapt it depends on the prince and you."

IV

MENCIUS'S REFUTATION OF THE DOCTRINE THAT THE RULER
OUGHT TO LABOR AT HUSBANDRY WITH HIS OWN HANDS.
HE VINDICATES THE PROPRIETY OF THE DIVISION OF LABOR,
AND OF A LETTERED CLASS CONDUCTING GOVERNMENT.

1. There came from Ch'û to T'ǎng one Hsü Hsing, who gave out that he acted according to the words of Shǎn-nǎng. Coming right to his gate, he addressed the duke Wǎn, saying, "A man of a distant region, I have heard that you, Prince, are practicing a benevolent government, and I wish to receive a site for a house, and to become one of your people." The duke Wǎn gave him a dwelling-place. His disciples, amounting to several tens, all wore clothes of haircloth, and made sandals of hemp and wove mats for a living.

2. At the same time, Ch'an Hsiang, a disciple of Ch'ǎn Liang, and his younger brother, Hsin, with their plow-handles and shares on their backs, came from Sung to T'ǎng, saying, "We have heard that you, Prince, are putting into practice the government of the ancient sages, showing that you are likewise a sage. We wish to become the subjects of a sage."

3. When Ch'ǎn Hsiang saw Hsü Hsing, he was greatly pleased with him, and, abandoning entirely whatever he had learned, became his disciple. Having an interview with Mencius, he related to him with approbation the words of Hsü Hsing to the following effect: 'The prince of T'ǎng is indeed a worthy prince. He has not yet heard, however, the real doctrines of antiquity. Now, wise and able princes should cultivate the ground equally and along with their people, and eat the fruit of their labor. They should prepare their own

meals, morning and evening, while at the same time they carry on their government. But now, the prince of T'ăng has his granaries, treasuries, and arsenals, which is an oppressing of the people to nourish himself. How can he be deemed a real worthy prince?"

4. Mencius said, "I suppose that Hsü Hsing sows grain and eats the produce. Is it not so?" "It is so," was the answer. "I suppose also he weaves cloth, and wears his own manufacture. Is it not so?" "No. Hsü wears clothes of haircloth." "Does he wear a cap?" "He wears a cap." "What kind of cap?" "A plain cap." "Is it woven by himself?" "No. He gets it in exchange for grain." "Why does Hsü not weave it himself?" "That would injure his husbandry." "Does Hsü cook his food in boilers and earthenware pans, and does he plow with an iron share?" "Yes." "Does he make those articles himself?" "No. He gets them in exchange for grain."

5. Mencius then said, "The getting those various articles in exchange for grain, is not oppressive to the potter and the founder, and the potter and the founder in their turn, in exchanging their various articles for grain, are not oppressive to the husbandman. How should such a thing be supposed? And moreover, why does not Hsü act the potter and founder, supplying himself with the articles which he uses solely from his own establishment? Why does he go confusedly dealing and exchanging with the handicraftsmen? Why does he not spare himself so much trouble?" Ch'ăn Hsiang replied, "The business of the handicraftsman can by no means be carried on along with the business of husbandry."

6. Mencius resumed, "Then, is it the government of the kingdom which alone can be carried on along with the practice of husbandry? Great men have their proper business, and little men have their proper business. Moreover, in the case of any single individual, whatever articles he can require are ready to his hand, being produced by the various handicraftsmen: if he must first make them for his own use, this way of doing would keep all the people running about upon the roads. Hence, there is the saying, 'Some labor with their minds, and some labor with their strength. Those who labor with their minds govern others; those who labor with their strength are governed by others. Those who are governed by others support them; those who govern others are supported by them.' This is a principle universally recognized.

7. "In the time of Yâo, when the world had not yet been perfectly reduced to order, the vast waters, flowing out of their channels, made a universal inundation. Vegetation was luxuriant, and birds and beasts swarmed. The various kinds of grain could not be grown. The birds and beasts pressed upon men. The paths marked by the feet of beasts and prints of birds crossed one another throughout the Middle Kingdom. To Yâo alone this caused anxious sorrow. He raised Shun to office, and measures to regulate the disorder were set forth. Shun committed to Yî the direction of the fire to be employed, and Yî set fire to, and consumed, the forests and vegetation on the mountains and in the marshes, so that the birds and beasts fled away to hide themselves. Yü separated the nine streams, cleared the courses of the Tsî and T'â, and led them all to the sea. He opened a vent also for the Zû and Han, and regulated the course of the Hwâ'i and Sze, so that they all flowed into the Chiang. When this was done, it became possible for the people of the Middle Kingdom to cultivate the ground and get food for themselves. During that time, Yü was eight years away from his home, and though he thrice passed the door of it, he did not enter. Although he had wished to cultivate the ground, could he have done so?"

8. "The Minister of Agriculture taught the people to sow and reap, cultivating the five kinds of grain. When the five kinds of grain were brought to maturity, the people all obtained a subsistence. But men possess a moral nature; and if they are well fed, warmly clad, and comfortably lodged, without being taught at the same time, they become almost like the beasts. This was a subject of anxious solicitude to the sage Shun, and he appointed Hsieh to be the Minister of Instruction, to teach the relations of humanity: how, between father and son, there should be affection; between sovereign and minister, righteousness; between husband and wife, attention to their separate functions; between old and young, a proper order; and between friends, fidelity. The high meritorious sovereign said to him, 'Encourage them; lead them on; rectify them; straighten them; help them; give them wings: thus causing them to become possessors of themselves. Then follow this up by stimulating them, and conferring benefits on them.' When the sages were exercising their solicitude for the people in this way, had they leisure to cultivate the ground?

9. "What Yâo felt giving him anxiety was the not getting Shun. What Shun felt giving him anxiety was the not getting Yü and Kâo Yâo.

But he whose anxiety is about his hundred *mâu* not being properly cultivated, is a mere husbandman.

10. "The imparting by a man to others of his wealth, is called 'kindness.' The teaching others what is good, is called 'the exercise of fidelity.' The finding a man who shall benefit the kingdom, is called 'benevolence.' Hence to give the throne to another man would be easy; to find a man who shall benefit the kingdom is difficult.

11. "Confucius said, 'Great indeed was Yâo as a sovereign. It is only Heaven that is great, and only Yâo corresponded to it. How vast was his virtue! The people could find no name for it. Princely indeed was Shun! How majestic was he, having possession of the kingdom, and yet seeming as if it were nothing to him!' In their governing the kingdom, were there no subjects on which Yâo and Shun employed their minds? There were subjects, only they did not employ their minds on the cultivation of the ground.

12. "I have heard of men using the doctrines of our great land to change barbarians, but I have never yet heard of any being changed by barbarians. Ch'an Liang was a native of Ch'û. Pleased with the doctrines of Châu-kung and Chung-nî, he came northwards to the Middle Kingdom and studied them. Among the scholars of the northern regions, there was perhaps no one who excelled him. He was what you call a scholar of high and distinguished qualities. You and your brother followed him some tens of years, and when your master died, you forthwith turned away from him.

13. "Formerly, when Confucius died, after three years had elapsed, his disciples collected their baggage, and prepared to return to their several homes. But on entering to take their leave of Tsze-kung, as they looked towards one another, they wailed, till they all lost their voices. After this they returned to their homes, but Tsze-kung went back, and built a house for himself on the altar-ground, where he lived alone other three years, before he returned home. On another occasion, Tsze-hsiâ, Tsze-chang, and Tsze-yû, thinking that Yû Zo resembled the sage, wished to render to him the same observances which they had rendered to Confucius. They tried to force the disciple Tsăng to join with them, but he said, 'This may not be done. What has been washed in the waters of the Chiang and Han, and bleached in the autumn sun: how glistening is it! Nothing can be added to it.'

14. "Now here is this shrike-tongued barbarian of the south, whose doctrines are not those of the ancient kings. You turn away from your master and become his disciple. Your conduct is different indeed from that of the philosopher Tsăng.

15. "I have heard of birds leaving dark valleys to remove to lofty trees, but I have not heard of their descending from lofty trees to enter into dark valleys.

16. "In the Praise-songs of Lû it is said,

> He smote the barbarians of the west and the north,
> He punished Ching and Shû."

Thus Châu-kung would be sure to smite them, and you become their disciple again; it appears that your change is not good."

17. Ch'ăn Hsiang said, "If Hsü's doctrines were followed, then there would not be two prices in the market, nor any deceit in the kingdom. If a boy of five cubits were sent to the market, no one would impose on him; linen and silk of the same length would be of the same price. So it would be with bundles of hemp and silk, being of the same weight; with the different kinds of grain, being the same in quantity; and with shoes which were of the same size."

18. Mencius replied, "It is the nature of things to be of unequal quality. Some are twice, some five times, some ten times, some a hundred times, some a thousand times, some ten thousand times as valuable as others. If you reduce them all to the same standard, that must throw the kingdom into confusion. If large shoes and small shoes were of the same price, who would make them? For people to follow the doctrines of Hsü, would be for them to lead one another on to practice deceit. How can they avail for the government of a State?"

V

HOW MENCIUS CONVINCED A MOHIST OF HIS ERROR,
THAT ALL MEN WERE TO BE LOVED EQUALLY, WITHOUT
DIFFERENCE OF DEGREE.

1. The Mohist, Î Chih, sought, through Hsü Pî, to see Mencius. Mencius said, "I indeed wish to see him, but at present I am still unwell. When I am better, I will myself go and see him. He need not come here again."

2. Next day, Î Chih again sought to see Mencius. Mencius said, "Today I am able to see him. But if I do not correct his errors, the true principles will not be fully evident. Let me first correct him. I have heard that this Î is a Mohist. Now Mo considers that in the regulation of funeral matters a spare simplicity should be the rule. Î thinks with Mo's doctrines to change the customs of the kingdom—how does he regard them as if they were wrong, and not honor them? Notwithstanding his views, Î buried his parents in a sumptuous manner, and so he served them in the way which his doctrines discountenance."

3. The disciple Hsü informed Î of these remarks. Î said, "Even according to the principles of the learned, we find that the ancients acted towards the people 'as if they were watching over an infant.' What does this expression mean? To me it sounds that we are to love all without difference of degree; but the manifestation of love must begin with our parents." Hsü reported this reply to Mencius, who said, "Now, does Î really think that a man's affection for the child of his brother is merely like his affection for the infant of a neighbor? What is to be approved in that expression is simply this: that if an infant crawling about is likely to fall into a well, it is no crime in the infant. Moreover, Heaven gives birth to creatures in such a way that they have one root, and Î makes them to have two roots. This is the cause of his error.

4. "And, in the most ancient times, there were some who did not inter their parents. When their parents died, they took them up and threw them into some water-channel. Afterwards, when passing by them, they saw foxes and wildcats devouring them, and flies and gnats biting at them. The perspiration started out upon their foreheads, and they looked away, unable to bear the sight. It was not on account of other people that this perspiration flowed. The emotions of their hearts affected their faces and eyes, and instantly they went home, and came back with baskets and spades and covered the bodies. If the covering them thus was indeed right, you may see that the filial son and virtuous man, in interring in a handsome manner their parents, act according to a proper rule."

5. The disciple Hsü informed Î of what Mencius had said. Î was thoughtful for a short time, and then said, "He has instructed me."

T'ĂNG WĂN KUNG

PART II

I

How Mencius defended the dignity of reserve by which he regulated his intercourse with the princes of his time.

1. Ch'ăn Tâi said to Mencius, "In not going to wait upon any of the princes, you seem to me to be standing on a small point. If now you were once to wait upon them, the result might be so great that you would make one of them sovereign, or, if smaller, that you would make one of them chief of all the other princes. Moreover, the History says, 'By bending only one cubit, you make eight cubits straight.' It appears to me like a thing which might be done."

2. Mencius said, "Formerly, the duke Ching of Ch'î, once when he was hunting, called his forester to him by a flag. The forester would not come, and the duke was going to kill him. With reference to this incident, Confucius said, 'The determined officer never forgets that his end may be in a ditch or a stream; the brave officer never forgets that he may lose his head.' What was it in the forester that Confucius thus approved? He approved his not going to the duke, when summoned by the article which was not appropriate to him. If one go to see the princes without waiting to be invited, what can be thought of him?

3. "Moreover, that sentence, 'By bending only one cubit, you make eight cubits straight,' is spoken with reference to the gain that may be got. If gain be the object, then, if it can be got by bending eight cubits to make one cubit straight, may we likewise do that?

4. "Formerly, the officer Châo Chien made Wang Liang act as charioteer for his favorite Hsî, when, in the course of a whole day, they did not get a single bird. The favorite Hsî reported this result, saying, 'He is the poorest charioteer in the world.' Someone told this to Wang Liang, who said, 'I beg leave to try again.' By dint of pressing, this was accorded to him, when in one morning they got

ten birds. The favorite, reporting this result, said, 'He is the best charioteer in the world.' Chien said, 'I will make him always drive your chariot for you.' When he told Wang Liang so, however, Liang refused, saying, 'I drove for him, strictly observing the proper rules for driving, and in the whole day he did not get one bird. I drove for him so as deceitfully to intercept the birds, and in one morning he got ten. It is said in the Book of Poetry,

> There is no failure in the management of their horses;
> The arrows are discharged surely, like the blows of an axe.

I am not accustomed to drive for a mean man. I beg leave to decline the office.'

5. "Thus this charioteer even was ashamed to bend improperly to the will of such an archer. Though, by bending to it, they would have caught birds and animals sufficient to form a hill, he would not do so. If I were to bend my principles and follow those princes, of what kind would my conduct be? And you are wrong. Never has a man who has bent himself been able to make others straight."

II

MENCIUS'S CONCEPTION OF THE GREAT MAN.

1. Ching Ch'un said to Mencius, "Are not Kung-sun Yen and Chang Î really great men? Let them once be angry, and all the princes are afraid. Let them live quietly, and the flames of trouble are extinguished throughout the kingdom."

2. Mencius said, "How can such men be great men? Have you not read the Ritual Usages? 'At the capping of a young man, his father admonishes him. At the marrying away of a young woman, her mother admonishes her, accompanying her to the door on her leaving, and cautioning her with these words, "You are going to your home. You must be respectful; you must be careful. Do not disobey your husband."' Thus, to look upon compliance as their correct course is the rule for women.

3. "To dwell in the wide house of the world, to stand in the correct seat of the world, and to walk in the great path of the world; when he obtains his desire for office, to practice his principles for the good of the people; and when that desire is disappointed, to practice them alone; to be above the power of riches and honors to make dissipated, of poverty and mean condition to make swerve from principle, and

of power and force to make bend: these characteristics constitute the great man."

III

OFFICE IS TO BE EAGERLY DESIRED, AND YET IT MAY NOT BE SOUGHT BUT BY ITS PROPER PATH.

1. Châu Hsiâo asked Mencius, saying, "Did superior men of old time take office?" Mencius replied, "They did. The Record says, 'If Confucius was three months without being employed by some ruler, he looked anxious and unhappy. When he passed from the boundary of a State, he was sure to carry with him his proper gift of introduction.' Kung-ming Î said, 'Among the ancients, if an officer was three months unemployed by a ruler, he was condoled with.'"

2. Hsiâo said, "Did not this condoling, on being three months unemployed by a ruler, show a too great urgency?"

3. Mencius answered, "The loss of his place to an officer is like the loss of his State to a prince. It is said in the Book of Rites, 'A prince plows himself, and is assisted by the people, to supply the millet for sacrifice. His wife keeps silkworms, and unwinds their cocoons, to make the garments for sacrifice.' If the victims be not perfect, the millet not pure, and the dress not complete, he does not presume to sacrifice. 'And the scholar who, out of office, has no holy field, in the same way, does not sacrifice. The victims for slaughter, the vessels, and the garments, not being all complete, he does not presume to sacrifice, and then neither may he dare to feel happy.' Is there not here sufficient ground also for condolence?"

4. Hsiâo again asked, "What was the meaning of Confucius's always carrying his proper gift of introduction with him, when he passed over the boundaries of the State where he had been?"

5. "An officer's being in office," was the reply, "is like the plowing of a husbandman. Does a husbandman part with his plow, because he goes from one State to another?"

6. Hsiâo pursued, "The kingdom of Tsin is one, as well as others, of official employments, but I have not heard of anyone being thus earnest about being in office. If there should be this urge why does a superior man make any difficulty about taking it?" Mencius answered, "When a son is born, what is desired for him is that he may have a wife; when a daughter is born, what is desired for her is

that she may have a husband. This feeling of the parents is possessed by all men. If the young people, without waiting for the orders of their parents, and the arrangements of the go-betweens, shall bore holes to steal a sight of each other, or get over the wall to be with each other, then their parents and all other people will despise them. The ancients did indeed always desire to be in office, but they also hated being so by any improper way. To seek office by an improper way is of a class with young people's boring holes."

IV

THE LABORER IS WORTHY OF HIS HIRE, AND THERE IS NO LABORER SO WORTHY AS THE SCHOLAR WHO INSTRUCTS MEN IN VIRTUE.

1. P'ăng Kăng asked Mencius, saying, "Is it not an extravagant procedure to go from one prince to another and live upon them, followed by several tens of carriages, and attended by several hundred men?" Mencius replied, "If there be not a proper ground for taking it, a single bamboo-cup of rice may not be received from a man. If there be such a proper ground, then Shun's receiving the kingdom from Yâo is not to be considered excessive. Do you think it was excessive?"

2. Kăng said, "No. But for a scholar performing no service to receive his support notwithstanding is improper."

3. Mencius answered, "If you do not have an intercommunication of the productions of labor, and an interchange of men's services, so that one from his overplus may supply the deficiency of another, then husbandmen will have a superfluity of grain, and women will have a superfluity of cloth. If you have such an interchange, carpenters and carriagewrights may all get their food from you. Here now is a man, who, at home, is filial, and abroad, respectful to his elders; who watches over the principles of the ancient kings, awaiting the rise of future learners: and yet you will refuse to support him. How is it that you give honor to the carpenter and carriage-wright, and slight him who practices benevolence and righteousness?"

4. P'ăng Kăng said, "The aim of the carpenter and carriagewright is by their trades to seek for a living. Is it also the aim of the superior man in his practice of principles thereby to seek for a living?" "What have you to do," returned Mencius, "with his purpose? He is of service to you. He deserves to be supported, and should be supported.

And let me ask—Do you remunerate a man's intention, or do you remunerate his service?" To this Kǎng replied, "I remunerate his intention."

5. Mencius said, "There is a man here, who breaks your tiles, and draws unsightly figures on your walls—his purpose may be thereby to seek for his living, but will you indeed remunerate him?" "No," said Kǎng; and Mencius then concluded, "That being the case, it is not the purpose which you remunerate, but the work done."

V

THE PRINCE WHO WILL SET HIMSELF TO PRACTICE A BENEVOLENT GOVERNMENT ON THE PRINCIPLES OF THE ANCIENT KINGS HAS NONE TO FEAR.

1. Wan Chang asked Mencius, saying, "Sung is a small State. Its ruler is now setting about to practice the true royal government, and Ch'î and Ch'û hate and attack him. What in this case is to be done?"

2. Mencius replied, "When T'ăng dwelt in Po, he adjoined to the State of Ko, the chief of which was living in a dissolute state and neglecting his proper sacrifices. T'ăng sent messengers to inquire why he did not sacrifice. He replied, 'I have no means of supplying the necessary victims.' On this, T'ăng caused oxen and sheep to be sent to him, but he ate them, and still continued not to sacrifice. T'ăng again sent messengers to ask him the same question as before, when he replied, 'I have no means of obtaining the necessary millet.' On this, T'ăng sent the mass of the people of Po to go and till the ground for him, while the old and feeble carried their food to them. The chief of Ko led his people to intercept those who were thus charged with wine, cooked rice, millet, and paddy, and took their stores from them, while they killed those who refused to give them up. There was a boy who had some millet and flesh for the laborers, who was thus slain and robbed. What is said in the Book of History, 'The chief of Ko behaved as an enemy to the provision-carriers,' has reference to this.

3. "Because of his murder of this boy, T'ăng proceeded to punish him. All within the four seas said, 'It is not because he desires the riches of the kingdom, but to avenge a common man and woman.'

4. "When T'ăng began his work of executing justice, he commenced with Ko, and though he made eleven punitive expeditions, he had not an enemy in the kingdom. When he pursued his work in the east, the

rude tribes in the west murmured. So did those on the north, when he was engaged in the south. Their cry was — 'Why does he make us last?' Thus, the people's longing for him was like their longing for rain in a time of great drought. The frequenters of the markets stopped not. Those engaged in weeding in the fields made no change in their operations. While he punished their rulers, he consoled the people. His progress was like the falling of opportune rain, and the people were delighted. It is said in the Book of History, 'We have waited for our prince. When our prince comes, we may escape from the punishments under which we suffer.'

5. "There being some who would not become the subjects of Châu, King Wû proceeded to punish them on the east. He gave tranquility to their people, who welcomed him with baskets full of their black and yellow silks, saying — 'From henceforth we shall serve the sovereign of our dynasty of Châu, that we may be made happy by him.' So they joined themselves, as subjects, to the great city of Châu. Thus, the men of station of Shang took baskets full of black and yellow silks to meet the men of station of Châu, and the lower classes of the one met those of the other with baskets of rice and vessels of congee. Wû saved the people from the midst of fire and water, seizing only their oppressors, and destroying them.

6. "In the Great Declaration it is said, 'My power shall be put forth, and, invading the territories of Shang, I will seize the oppressor. I will put him to death to punish him: so shall the greatness of my work appear, more glorious than that of T'ăng.'

7. "Sung is not, as you say, practicing true royal government, and so forth. If it were practicing royal government, all within the four seas would be lifting up their heads, and looking for its prince, wishing to have him for their sovereign. Great as Ch'î and Ch'û are, what would there be to fear from them?"

VI

The influence of example and association. The importance of having virtuous men about a sovereign's person.

1. Mencius said to Tâi Pû-shang, "I see that you are desiring your king to be virtuous, and will plainly tell you how he may be made so. Suppose that there is a great officer of Ch'û here, who wishes his son to learn the speech of Ch'î. Will he in that case employ a man of Ch'î

THE WORKS OF MENCIUS

as his tutor, or a man of Ch'û?" "He will employ a man of Ch'î to teach him," said Pû-shang. Mencius went on, "If but one man of Ch'î be teaching him, and there be a multitude of men of Ch'û continually shouting out about him, although his father beat him every day, wishing him to learn the speech of Ch'î, it will be impossible for him to do so. But in the same way, if he were to be taken and placed for several years in Chang or Yo, though his father should beat him, wishing him to speak the language of Ch'û, it would be impossible for him to do so.

2. "You supposed that Hsieh Chü-châu was a scholar of virtue, and you have got him placed in attendance on the king. Suppose that all in attendance on the king, old and young, high and low, were Hsieh Chü-châus, whom would the king have to do evil with? And suppose that all in attendance on the king, old and young, high and low, are not Hsieh Chü-châus, whom will the king have to do good with? What can one Hsieh Chü-châu do alone for the king of Sung?"

VII

MENCIUS DEFENDS HIS NOT GOING TO SEE THE PRINCES BY THE
EXAMPLE AND MAXIMS OF THE ANCIENTS.

1. Kung-sun Châu asked Mencius, saying, "What is the point of righteousness involved in your not going to see the princes?" Mencius replied, "Among the ancients, if one had not been a minister in a State, he did not go to see the sovereign.

2. "Twan Kan-mû leaped over his wall to avoid the prince. Hsieh Liû shut his door, and would not admit the prince. These two, however, carried their scrupulosity to excess. When a prince is urgent, it is not improper to see him.

3. "Yang Ho wished to get Confucius to go to see him, but disliked doing so by any want of propriety. As it is the rule, therefore, that when a great officer sends a gift to a scholar, if the latter be not at home to receive it, he must go to the officer's to pay his respects, Yang Ho watched when Confucius was out, and sent him a roasted pig. Confucius, in his turn, watched when Ho was out, and went to pay his respects to him. At that time, Yang Ho had taken the initiative—how could Confucius decline going to see him?

4. "Tsăng-tsze said, 'They who shrug up their shoulders, and laugh in a flattering way, toil harder than the summer laborer in the

fields.' Tsze-lû said, 'There are those who talk with people with whom they have no great community of feeling. If you look at their countenances, they are full of blushes. I do not desire to know such persons.' By considering these remarks, the spirit which the superior man nourishes may be known."

VIII

WHAT IS WRONG SHOULD BE PUT AN END TO AT ONCE,
WITHOUT RESERVE AND WITHOUT DELAY.

1. Tâi Ying-chih said to Mencius, "I am not able at present and immediately to do with the levying of a tithe only, and abolishing the duties charged at the passes and in the markets. With your leave I will lighten, however, both the tax and the duties, until next year, and will then make an end of them. What do you think of such a course?"

2. Mencius said, "Here is a man, who every day appropriates some of his neighbor's strayed fowls. Someone says to him, 'Such is not the way of a good man'; and he replies, 'With your leave I will diminish my appropriations, and will take only one fowl a month, until next year, when I will make an end of the practice.'

3. "If you know that the thing is unrighteous, then use all despatch in putting an end to it: why wait till next year?"

IX

MENCIUS DEFENDS HIMSELF AGAINST THE CHARGE OF BEING
FOND OF DISPUTING. WHAT LED TO HIS APPEARING TO BE SO
WAS THE NECESSITY OF THE TIME.

1. The disciple Kung-tû said to Mencius, "Master, the people beyond our school all speak of you as being fond of disputing. I venture to ask whether it be so." Mencius replied, "Indeed, I am not fond of disputing, but I am compelled to do it.

2. "A long time has elapsed since this world of men received its being, and there has been along its history now a period of good order, and now a period of confusion.

3. "In the time of Yâo, the waters, flowing out of their channels, inundated the Middle Kingdom. Snakes and dragons occupied it, and the people had no place where they could settle themselves. In the low grounds they made nests for themselves on the trees or

raised platforms, and in the high grounds they made caves. It is said in the Book of History, 'The waters in their wild course warned me.' Those 'waters in their wild course' were the waters of the great inundation.

4. "Shun employed Yü to reduce the waters to order. Yü dug open their obstructed channels, and conducted them to the sea. He drove away the snakes and dragons, and forced them into the grassy marshes. On this, the waters pursued their course through the country, even the waters of the Chiang, the Hwâi, the Ho, and the Han, and the dangers and obstructions which they had occasioned were removed. The birds and beasts which had injured the people also disappeared, and after this men found the plains available for them, and occupied them.

5. "After the death of Yâo and Shun, the principles that mark sages fell into decay. Oppressive sovereigns arose one after another, who pulled down houses to make ponds and lakes, so that the people knew not where they could rest in quiet; they threw fields out of cultivation to form gardens and parks, so that the people could not get clothes and food. Afterwards, corrupt speakings and oppressive deeds became more rife; gardens and parks, ponds and lakes, thickets and marshes became more numerous, and birds and beasts swarmed. By the time of the tyrant Châu, the kingdom was again in a state of great confusion.

6. "Châu-kung assisted King Wû, and destroyed Châu. He smote Yen, and after three years put its sovereign to death. He drove Fei-lien to a corner by the sea, and slew him. The States which he extinguished amounted to fifty. He drove far away also the tigers, leopards, rhinoceroses, and elephants — and all the people were greatly delighted. It is said in the Book of History, 'Great and splendid were the plans of King Wăn! Greatly were they carried out by the energy of King Wû! They are for the assistance and instruction of us who are of an after day. They are all in principle correct, and deficient in nothing.'

7. "Again the world fell into decay, and principles faded away. Perverse speakings and oppressive deeds waxed rife again. There were instances of ministers who murdered their sovereigns, and of sons who murdered their fathers.

8. "Confucius was afraid, and made the 'Spring and Autumn.' What the 'Spring and Autumn' contains are matters proper to the sovereign.

On this account Confucius said, 'Yes! It is the Spring and Autumn which will make men know me, and it is the Spring and Autumn which will make men condemn me.'

9. "Once more, sage sovereigns cease to arise, and the princes of the States give the reins to their lusts. Unemployed scholars indulge in unreasonable discussions. The words of Yang Chû and Mo Tî fill the country. If you listen to people's discourses throughout it, you will find that they have adopted the views either of Yang or of Mo. Now, Yang's principle is—'each one for himself,' which does not acknowledge the claims of the sovereign. Mo's principle is—'to love all equally,' which does not acknowledge the peculiar affection due to a father. But to acknowledge neither king nor father is to be in the state of a beast. Kung-ming Î said, 'In their kitchens, there is fat meat. In their stables, there are fat horses. But their people have the look of hunger, and on the wilds there are those who have died of famine. This is leading on beasts to devour men.' If the principles of Yang and Mo be not stopped, and the principles of Confucius not set forth, then those perverse speakings will delude the people, and stop up the path of benevolence and righteousness. When benevolence and righteousness are stopped up, beasts will be led on to devour men, and men will devour one another.

10. "I am alarmed by these things, and address myself to the defense of the doctrines of the former sages, and to oppose Yang and Mo. I drive away their licentious expressions, so that such perverse speakers may not be able to show themselves. Their delusions spring up in men's minds, and do injury to their practice of affairs. Shown in their practice of affairs, they are pernicious to their government. When sages shall rise up again, they will not change my words.

11. "In former times, Yü repressed the vast waters of the inundation, and the country was reduced to order. Châu-kung's achievements extended even to the barbarous tribes of the east and north, and he drove away all ferocious animals, and the people enjoyed repose. Confucius completed the 'Spring and Autumn,' and rebellious ministers and villainous sons were struck with terror.

12. "It is said in the Book of Poetry,

> He smote the barbarians of the west and the north;
> He punished Ching and Shû
> And no one dared to resist us.

These father-deniers and king-deniers would have been smitten by Châu-kung.

13. "I also wish to rectify men's hearts, and to put an end to those perverse doctrines, to oppose their one-sided actions and banish away their licentious expressions—and thus to carry on the work of the three sages. Do I do so because I am fond of disputing? I am compelled to do it.

14. "Whoever is able to oppose Yang and Mo is a disciple of the sages."

X

THE MAN WHO WILL AVOID ALL ASSOCIATION WITH,
AND OBLIGATION TO, THOSE OF WHOM HE DOES NOT APPROVE,
MUST NEEDS GO OUT OF THE WORLD.

1. K'wang Chang said to Mencius, "Is not Ch'ǎn Chung a man of true self-denying purity? He was living in Wû-ling, and for three days was without food, till he could neither hear nor see. Over a well there grew a plum-tree, the fruit of which had been more than half eaten by worms. He crawled to it, and tried to eat some of the fruit, when, after swallowing three mouthfuls, he recovered his sight and hearing."

2. Mencius replied, "Among the scholars of Ch'î, I must regard Chung as the thumb among the fingers. But still, where is the self-denying purity he pretends to? To carry out the principles which he holds, one must become an earthworm, for so only can it be done.

3. "Now, an earthworm eats the dry mold above, and drinks the yellow spring below. Was the house in which Chung dwells built by a Po-î? Or was it built by a robber like Chih? Was the millet which he eats planted by a Po-î? Or was it planted by a robber like Chih? These are things which cannot be known."

4. "But," said Chang, "what does that matter? He himself weaves sandals of hemp, and his wife twists and dresses threads of hemp to sell or exchange them."

5. Mencius rejoined, "Chung belongs to an ancient and noble family of Ch'î. His elder brother Tâi received from Kâ a revenue of 10,000 *chung*, but he considered his brother's emolument to be unrighteous, and would not eat of it, and in the same way he considered his brother's house to be unrighteous, and would not dwell in it. Avoiding

his brother and leaving his mother, he went and dwelt in Wû-ling. One day afterwards, he returned to their house, when it happened that someone sent his brother a present of a live goose. He, knitting his eyebrows, said, 'What are you going to use that cackling thing for?' By-and-by his mother killed the goose, and gave him some of it to eat. Just then his brother came into the house, and said, 'It is the flesh of that cackling thing,' upon which he went out and vomited it.

6. "Thus, what his mother gave him he would not eat, but what his wife gives him he eats. He will not dwell in his brother's house, but he dwells in Wû-ling. How can he in such circumstances complete the style of life which he professes? With such principles as Chung holds, a man must be an earthworm, and then he can carry them out."

BOOK IV

LÎ LÂU

PART I

I

THERE IS AN ART OF GOVERNMENT, AS WELL AS A WISH TO
GOVERN WELL, TO BE LEARNED FROM THE EXAMPLE AND
PRINCIPLES OF THE ANCIENT KINGS, AND WHICH REQUIRES TO BE
STUDIED AND PRACTICED BY RULERS AND THEIR MINISTERS.

1. Mencius said, "The power of vision of Lî Lâu, and skill of hand of Kung-shû, without the compass and square, could not form squares and circles. The acute ear of the music-master K'wang, without the pitch-tubes, could not determine correctly the five notes. The principles of Yâo and Shun, without a benevolent government, could not secure the tranquil order of the kingdom.

2. "There are now princes who have benevolent hearts and a reputation for benevolence, while yet the people do not receive any benefits from them, nor will they leave any example to future ages—all because they do not put into practice the ways of the ancient kings.

3. "Hence we have the saying: 'Virtue alone is not sufficient for the exercise of government; laws alone cannot carry themselves into practice.'

4. "It is said in the Book of Poetry,

   Without transgression, without forgetfulness,
   Following the ancient statutes.

   Never has anyone fallen into error, who followed the laws of the ancient kings.

5. "When the sages had used the vigor of their eyes, they called in to their aid the compass, the square, the level, and the line, to make things square, round, level, and straight: the use of the instruments is inexhaustible. When they had used their power of hearing to

the utmost, they called in the pitch-tubes to their aid to determine the five notes: the use of those tubes is inexhaustible. When they had exerted to the utmost the thoughts of their hearts, they called in to their aid a government that could not endure to witness the sufferings of men: and their benevolence overspread the kingdom.

6. "Hence we have the saying: 'To raise a thing high, we must begin from the top of a mound or a hill; to dig to a great depth, we must commence in the low ground of a stream or a marsh.' Can he be pronounced wise, who, in the exercise of government, does not proceed according to the ways of the former kings?

7. "Therefore only the benevolent ought to be in high stations. When a man destitute of benevolence is in a high station, he thereby disseminates his wickedness among all below him.

8. "When the prince has no principles by which he examines his administration, and his ministers have no laws by which they keep themselves in the discharge of their duties, then in the court obedience is not paid to principle, and in the office obedience is not paid to rule. Superiors violate the laws of righteousness, and inferiors violate the penal laws. It is only by a fortunate chance that a State in such a case is preserved.

9. "Therefore it is said, 'It is not the exterior and interior walls being incomplete, and the supply of weapons offensive and defensive not being large, which constitutes the calamity of a kingdom. It is not the cultivable area not being extended, and stores and wealth not being accumulated, which occasions the ruin of a State.' When superiors do not observe the rules of propriety, and inferiors do not learn, then seditious people spring up, and that State will perish in no time.

10. "It is said in the Book of Poetry,

> When such an overthrow of Châu is being produced by Heaven,
> Be not ye so much at your ease!

11. "'At your ease'—that is, dilatory.

12. "And so dilatory may those officers be deemed, who serve their prince without righteousness, who take office and retire from it without regard to propriety, and who in their words disown the ways of the ancient kings.

13. "Therefore it is said, 'To urge one's sovereign to difficult achievements may be called showing respect for him. To set before him what is

good and repress his perversities may be called showing reverence for him. He who does not do these things, saying to himself—My sovereign is incompetent to this, may be said to play the thief with him.'"

II

A CONTINUATION OF THE LAST CHAPTER—THAT YÂO AND SHUN
ARE THE PERFECT MODELS OF SOVEREIGNS AND MINISTERS,
AND THE CONSEQUENCES OF NOT IMITATING THEM.

1. Mencius said, "The compass and square produce perfect circles and squares. By the sages, the human relations are perfectly exhibited.

2. "He who as a sovereign would perfectly discharge the duties of a sovereign, and he who as a minister would perfectly discharge the duties of a minister, have only to imitate—the one Yâo, and the other Shun. He who does not serve his sovereign as Shun served Yâo, does not respect his sovereign; and he who does not rule his people as Yâo ruled his, injures his people.

3. "Confucius said, 'There are but two courses, which can be pursued, that of virtue and its opposite.'

4. "A ruler who carries the oppression of his people to the highest pitch, will himself be slain, and his kingdom will perish. If one stop short of the highest pitch, his life will notwithstanding be in danger, and his kingdom will be weakened. He will be styled 'The Dark,' or 'The Cruel,' and though he may have filial sons and affectionate grandsons, they will not be able in a hundred generations to change the designation.

5. "This is what is intended in the words of the Book of Poetry,

> The beacon of Yin is not remote,
> It is in the time of the (last) sovereign of Hsiâ."

III

THE IMPORTANCE TO ALL, AND SPECIFICALLY TO RULERS,
OF EXERCISING BENEVOLENCE.

1. Mencius said, "It was by benevolence that the three dynasties gained the throne, and by not being benevolent that they lost it.

2. "It is by the same means that the decaying and flourishing, the preservation and perishing, of States are determined.

3. "If the sovereign be not benevolent, he cannot preserve the throne from passing from him. If the Head of a State be not benevolent, he cannot preserve his rule. If a high noble or great officer be not benevolent, he cannot preserve his ancestral temple. If a scholar or common man be not benevolent, be cannot preserve his four limbs.

4. "Now they hate death and ruin, and yet delight in being not benevolent—this is like hating to be drunk, and yet being strong to drink wine!"

IV

WITH WHAT MEASURE A MAN METES IT WILL BE MEASURED TO HIM AGAIN, AND CONSEQUENTLY BEFORE A MAN DEALS WITH OTHERS, EXPECTING THEM TO BE AFFECTED BY HIM, HE SHOULD FIRST DEAL WITH HIMSELF.

1. Mencius said, "If a man love others, and no responsive attachment is shown to him, let him turn inwards and examine his own benevolence. If he is trying to rule others, and his government is unsuccessful, let him turn inwards and examine his wisdom. If he treats others politely, and they do not return his politeness, let him turn inwards and examine his own feeling of respect.

2. "When we do not, by what we do, realize what we desire, we must turn inwards, and examine ourselves in every point. When a man's person is correct, the whole kingdom will turn to him with recognition and submission.

3. "It is said in the Book of Poetry,

> Be always studious to be in harmony with the ordinances of God,
> And you will obtain much happiness."

V

PERSONAL CHARACTER IS NECESSARY TO ALL GOOD INFLUENCE.

Mencius said, "People have this common saying—'The kingdom, the State, the family.' The root of the kingdom is in the State. The root of the State is in the family. The root of the family is in the person of its Head."

VI

THE IMPORTANCE TO A RULER OF SECURING THE ESTEEM AND
SUBMISSION OF THE GREAT HOUSES.

Mencius said, "The administration of government is not difficult—it
lies in not offending the great families. He whom the great families
affect, will be affected by the whole State; and he whom any one
State affects, will be affected by the whole kingdom. When this is
the case, such a one's virtue and teachings will spread over all within
the four seas like the rush of water."

VII

HOW THE SUBJECTION OF ONE STATE TO ANOTHER IS
DETERMINED AT DIFFERENT TIMES. A PRINCE'S ONLY SECURITY
FOR SAFETY AND PROSPERITY IS IN BEING BENEVOLENT.

1. Mencius said, "When right government prevails in the kingdom,
   princes of little virtue are submissive to those of great, and those of
   little worth to those of great. When bad government prevails in the
   kingdom, princes of small power are submissive to those of great,
   and the weak to the strong. Both these cases are the rule of Heaven.
   They who accord with Heaven are preserved, and they who rebel
   against Heaven perish.

2. "The duke Ching of Ch'î said, 'Not to be able to command others,
   and at the same time to refuse to receive their commands, is to cut
   one's self off from all intercourse with others.' His tears flowed forth
   while he gave his daughter to be married to the prince of Wû.

3. "Now the small States imitate the large, and yet are ashamed to
   receive their commands. This is like a scholar's being ashamed to
   receive the commands of his master.

4. "For a prince who is ashamed of this, the best plan is to imitate King
   Wăn. Let one imitate King Wăn, and in five years, if his State be
   large, or in seven years, if it be small, he will be sure to give laws to
   the kingdom.

5. "It is said in the Book of Poetry,

   > The descendants of the sovereigns of the Shang dynasty,
   > Are in number more than hundreds of thousands,
   > But, God having passed His decree,

> They are all submissive to Châu.
> They are submissive to Châu,
> Because the decree of Heaven is not unchanging.
> The officers of Yin, admirable and alert,
> Pour out the libations, and assist in the capital of Châu.

Confucius said, 'As against so benevolent a sovereign, they could not be deemed a multitude.' Thus, if the prince of a state love benevolence, he will have no opponent in all the kingdom.

6. "Now they wish to have no opponent in all the kingdom, but they do not seek to attain this by being benevolent. This is like a man laying hold of a heated substance, and not having first dipped it in water. It is said in the Book of Poetry,

> Who can take up a heated substance,
> Without first dipping it (in water)?"

VIII

THAT A PRINCE IS THE AGENT OF HIS OWN RUIN BY HIS VICIOUS WAYS AND REFUSING TO BE COUNSELED.

1. Mencius said, "How is it possible to speak with those princes who are not benevolent? Their perils they count safety, their calamities they count profitable, and they have pleasure in the things by which they perish. If it were possible to talk with them who so violate benevolence, how could we have such destruction of States and ruin of Families?

2. "There was a boy singing,

> When the water of the Ts'ang-lang is clear,
> It does to wash the strings of my cap;
> When the water of the Ts'ang-lang is muddy,
> It does to wash my feet.

3. "Confucius said, 'Hear what he sings, my children. When clear, then he will wash his cap-strings; and when muddy, he will wash his feet with it. This different application is brought by the water on itself.'

4. "A man must first despise himself, and then others will despise him. A family must first destroy itself, and then others will destroy it. A State must first smite itself, and then others will smite it.

5. "This is illustrated in the passage of the T'âi Chiâ, 'When Heaven sends down calamities, it is still possible to escape them. When we

occasion the calamities ourselves, it is not possible any longer to live.'"

IX

ONLY BY BEING BENEVOLENT CAN A PRINCE RAISE HIMSELF
TO BE SOVEREIGN, OR EVEN AVOID RUIN.

1. Mencius said, "Chieh and Châu's losing the throne, arose from their losing the people, and to lose the people means to lose their hearts. There is a way to get the kingdom: get the people, and the kingdom is got. There is a way to get the people: get their hearts, and the people are got. There is a way to get their hearts: it is simply to collect for them what they like, and not to lay on them what they dislike.

2. "The people turn to a benevolent rule as water flows downwards, and as wild beasts fly to the wilderness.

3. "Accordingly, as the otter aids the deep waters, driving the fish into them, and the hawk aids the thickets, driving the little birds to them, so Chieh and Châu aided T'ăng and Wû, driving the people to them.

4. "If among the present rulers of the kingdom, there were one who loved benevolence, all the other princes would aid him, by driving the people to him. Although he wished not to become sovereign, he could not avoid becoming so.

5. "The case of one of the present princes wishing to become sovereign is like the having to seek for mugwort three years old, to cure a seven years' sickness. If it have not been kept in store, the patient may all his life not get it. If the princes do not set their wills on benevolence, all their days will be in sorrow and disgrace, and they will be involved in death and ruin.

6. "This is illustrated by what is said in the Book of Poetry,

> How otherwise can you improve the kingdom?
> You will only with it go to ruin."

X

A WARNING TO THE VIOLENTLY EVIL, AND THE WEAKLY EVIL.

1. Mencius said, "With those who do violence to themselves, it is impossible to speak. With those who throw themselves away, it is impossible to do anything. To disown in his conversation propriety

and righteousness, is what we mean by doing violence to one's self. To say—'I am not able to dwell in benevolence or pursue the path of righteousness,' is what we mean by throwing one's self away.

2. "Benevolence is the tranquil habitation of man, and righteousness is his straight path.

3. "Alas for them, who leave the tranquil dwelling empty and do not reside in it, and who abandon the right path and do not pursue it?"

XI

THE TRANQUIL PROSPERITY OF THE KINGDOM DEPENDS ON THE DISCHARGE OF THE COMMON RELATIONS OF LIFE.

Mencius said, "The path of duty lies in what is near, and men seek for it in what is remote. The work of duty lies in what is easy, and men seek for it in what is difficult. If each man would love his parents and show the due respect to his elders, the whole land would enjoy tranquility."

XII

THE GREAT WORK OF MEN SHOULD BE TO STRIVE TO ATTAIN PERFECT SINCERITY.

1. Mencius said, "When those occupying inferior situations do not obtain the confidence of the sovereign, they cannot succeed in governing the people. There is a way to obtain the confidence of the sovereign: if one is not trusted by his friends, he will not obtain the confidence of his sovereign. There is a way of being trusted by one's friends: if one do not serve his parents so as to make them pleased, he will not be trusted by his friends. There is a way to make one's parents pleased: if one, on turning his thoughts inwards, finds a want of sincerity, he will not give pleasure to his parents. There is a way to the attainment of sincerity in one's self: if a man do not understand what is good, he will not attain sincerity in himself.

2. "Therefore, sincerity is the way of Heaven. To think how to be sincere is the way of man.

3. "Never has there been one possessed of complete sincerity, who did not move others. Never has there been one who had not sincerity who was able to move others."

XIII

THE INFLUENCE OF GOVERNMENT LIKE THAT OF KING WĂN.

1. Mencius said, "Po-Î, that he might avoid Châ'u, was dwelling on the coast of the northern sea. When he heard of the rise of King Wăn, he roused himself, and said, 'Why should I not go and follow him? I have heard that the chief of the West knows well how to nourish the old.' T'âi-kung, that he might avoid Châu, was dwelling on the coast of the eastern sea. When he heard of the rise of King Wăn, he roused himself, and said, 'Why should I not go and follow him? I have heard that the chief of the West knows well how to nourish the old.'

2. "Those two old men were the greatest old men of the kingdom. When they came to follow King Wăn, it was the fathers of the kingdom coming to follow him. When the fathers of the kingdom joined him, how could the sons go to any other?

3. "Were any of the princes to practice the government of King Wăn, within seven years he would be sure to be giving laws to the kingdom."

XIV

AGAINST THE MINISTERS OF HIS TIME, WHO PURSUED THEIR WARLIKE AND OTHER SCHEMES, REGARDLESS OF THE HAPPINESS OF THE PEOPLE.

1. Mencius said, "Ch'iû acted as chief officer to the head of the Chî family, whose evil ways he was unable to change, while he exacted from the people double the grain formerly paid. Confucius said, 'He is no disciple of mine. Little children, beat the drum and assail him.'

2. "Looking at the subject from this case, we perceive that when a prince was not practicing benevolent government, all his ministers who enriched him were rejected by Confucius: how much more would he have rejected those who are vehement to fight for their prince! When contentions about territory are the ground on which they fight, they slaughter men till the fields are filled with them. When some struggle for a city is the ground on which they fight, they slaughter men till the city is filled with them. This is what is called 'leading on the land to devour human flesh.' Death is not enough for such a crime.

3. "Therefore, those who are skillful to fight should suffer the highest punishment. Next to them should be punished those who unite some princes in leagues against others; and next to them, those who take in grassy commons, imposing the cultivation of the ground on the people."

XV

THE PUPIL OF THE EYE THE INDEX OF THE HEART.

1. Mencius said, "Of all the parts of a man's body there is none more excellent than the pupil of the eye. The pupil cannot be used to hide a man's wickedness. If within the breast all be correct, the pupil is bright. If within the breast all be not correct, the pupil is dull.

2. "Listen to a man's words and look at the pupil of his eye. How can a man conceal his character?"

XVI

DEEDS, NOT WORDS OR MANNERS, NECESSARY TO PROVE MENTAL QUALITIES.

Mencius said, "The respectful do not despise others. The economical do not plunder others. The prince who treats men with despite and plunders them, is only afraid that they may not prove obedient to him: how can he be regarded as respectful or economical? How can respectfulness and economy be made out of tones of the voice, and a smiling manner?"

XVII

HELP — EFFECTUAL HELP — CAN BE GIVEN TO THE WORLD ONLY IN HARMONY WITH RIGHT AND PROPRIETY.

1. Shun-yü K'wan said, "Is it the rule that males and females shall not allow their hands to touch in giving or receiving anything?" Mencius replied, "It is the rule." K'wan asked, "If a man's sister-in-law be drowning, shall he rescue her with his hand?" Mencius said, "He who would not so rescue the drowning woman is a wolf. For males and females not to allow their hands to touch in giving and receiving is the general rule; when a sister-in-law is drowning, to rescue her with the hand is a peculiar exigency."

2. K'wan said, "The whole kingdom is drowning. How strange it is that you will not rescue it!"

3. Mencius answered, "A drowning kingdom must be rescued with right principles, as a drowning sister-in-law has to be rescued with the hand. Do you wish me to rescue the kingdom with my hand?"

XVIII

HOW A FATHER MAY NOT HIMSELF TEACH HIS SON.

1. Kung-sun Ch'âu said, "Why is it that the superior man does not himself teach his son?"

2. Mencius replied, "The circumstances of the case forbid its being done. The teacher must inculcate what is correct. When he inculcates what is correct, and his lessons are not practiced, he follows them up with being angry. When he follows them up with being angry, then, contrary to what should be, he is offended with his son. At the same time, the pupil says, 'My master inculcates on me what is correct, and he himself does not proceed in a correct path.' The result of this is, that father and son are offended with each other. When father and son come to be offended with each other, the case is evil.

3. "The ancients exchanged sons, and one taught the son of another.

4. "Between father and son, there should be no reproving admonitions to what is good. Such reproofs lead to alienation, and than alienation there is nothing more inauspicious."

XIX

THE RIGHT MANNER OF SERVING PARENTS, AND THE IMPORTANCE OF WATCHING OVER ONE'S SELF, IN ORDER TO DO SO.

1. Mencius said, "Of services, which is the greatest? The service of parents is the greatest. Of charges, which is the greatest? The charge of one's self is the greatest. That those who do not fail to keep themselves are able to serve their parents is what I have heard. But I have never heard of any, who, having failed to keep themselves, were able notwithstanding to serve their parents.

2. "There are many services, but the service of parents is the root of all others. There are many charges, but the charge of one's self is the root of all others.

3. "The philosopher Tsăng, in nourishing Tsăng Hsî, was always sure to have wine and flesh provided. And when they were being removed, he would ask respectfully to whom he should give what was left. If his father asked whether there was anything left, he was sure to say, 'There is.' After the death of Tsăng Hsî, when Tsăng Yüan came to nourish Tsăng-tsze, he was always sure to have wine and flesh provided. But when the things were being removed, he did not ask to whom he should give what was left, and if his father asked whether there was anything left, he would answer 'No'—intending to bring them in again. This was what is called—'nourishing the mouth and body.' We may call Tsăng-tsze's practice—'nourishing the will.'

4. "To serve one's parents as Tsăng-tsze served his, may be accepted as flial piety."

XX

A TRULY GREAT MINISTER WILL BE SEEN IN HIS DIRECTING HIS EFFORTS, NOT TO CORRECTION OF MATTERS IN DETAIL, BUT OF THE SOVEREIGN'S CHARACTER.

Mencius said, "It is not enough to remonstrate with a sovereign on account of the mal-employment of ministers, nor to blame errors of government. It is only the great man who can rectify what is wrong in the sovereign's mind. Let the prince be benevolent, and all his acts will be benevolent. Let the prince be righteous, and all his acts will be righteous. Let the prince be correct, and everything will be correct. Once rectify the ruler, and the kingdom will be firmly settled."

XXI

PRAISE AND BLAME ARE NOT ALWAYS ACCORDING TO DESERT.

Mencius said, "There are cases of praise which could not be expected, and of reproach when the parties have been seeking to be perfect."

XXII

THE BENEFIT OF REPROOF.

Mencius said, "Men's being ready with their tongues arises simply from their not having been reproved."

XXIII

BE NOT MANY MASTERS.

Mencius said, "The evil of men is that they like to be teachers of others."

XXIV

HOW MENCIUS REPROVED YO-CHĂNG FOR ASSOCIATING WITH AN UNWORTHY PERSON, AND BEING REMISS IN WAITING ON HIMSELF.

1. The disciple Yo-chăng went in the train of Tsze-âo to Ch'î.

2. He came to see Mencius, who said to him, "Are you also come to see me?" Yo-chăng replied, "Master, why do you speak such words?" "How many days have you been here?" asked Mencius. "I came yesterday." "Yesterday! Is it not with reason then that I thus speak?" "My lodging-house was not arranged." "Have you heard that a scholar's lodging-house must be arranged before he visit his elder?"

3. Yo-chăng said, "I have done wrong."

XXV

A FURTHER AND MORE DIRECT REPROOF OF YO-CHĂNG.

Mencius, addressing the disciple Yo-chăng, said to him, "Your coming here in the train of Tsze-âo was only because of the food and the drink. I could not have thought that you, having learned the doctrine of the ancients, would have acted with a view to eating and drinking."

XXVI

SHUN'S EXTRAORDINARY WAY OF CONTRACTING MARRIAGE JUSTIFIED BY THE MOTIVE.

1. Mencius said, "There are three things which are unfilial, and to have no posterity is the greatest of them.

2. "Shun married without informing his parents because of this—lest he should have no posterity. Superior men consider that his doing so was the same as if he had informed them."

XXVII

FILIAL PIETY AND FRATERNAL OBEDIENCE IN THEIR RELATION TO
BENEVOLENCE, RIGHTEOUSNESS, WISDOM, PROPRIETY, AND MUSIC.

1. Mencius said, "The richest fruit of benevolence is this—the service of one's parents. The richest fruit of righteousness is this—the obeying one's elder brothers.

2. "The richest fruit of wisdom is this—the knowing those two things, and not departing from them. The richest fruit of propriety is this— the ordering and adorning those two things. The richest fruit of music is this—the rejoicing in those two things. When they are rejoiced in, they grow. Growing, how can they be repressed? When they come to this state that they cannot be repressed, then unconsciously the feet begin to dance and the hands to move."

XXVIII

HOW SHUN VALUED AND EXEMPLIFIED FILIAL PIETY.

1. Mencius said, "Suppose the case of the whole kingdom turning in great delight to an individual to submit to him. To regard the whole kingdom thus turning to him in great delight but as a bundle of grass—only Shun was capable of this. He considered that if one could not get the hearts of his parents he could not be considered a man, and that if he could not get to an entire accord with his parents, he could not be considered a son.

2. "By Shun's completely fulfilling everything by which a parent could be served, Kû-sâu was brought to find delight in what was good. When Kû-sâu was brought to find that delight, the whole kingdom was transformed. When Kû-sâu was brought to find that delight, all fathers and sons in the kingdom were established in their respective duties. This is called great filial piety."

LÎ LÂU

PART II

I

THE AGREEMENT OF SAGES NOT AFFECTED BY PLACE OR TIME.

1. Mencius said, "Shun was born in Chû-fǎng, removed to Fû-hsiâ, and died in Ming-t'iâo—a man near the wild tribes on the east.

2. "King Wǎn was born in Châu by mount Ch'î, and died in Pî-ying—a man near the wild tribes on the west.

3. "Those regions were distant from one another more than a thousand lî, and the age of the one sage was posterior to that of the other more than a thousand years. But when they got their wish, and carried their principles into practice throughout the Middle Kingdom, it was like uniting the two halves of a seal.

4. "When we examine those sages, both the earlier and the later, their principles are found to be the same."

II

GOOD GOVERNMENT LIES IN EQUAL MEASURES FOR THE GENERAL GOOD, NOT IN ACTS OF FAVOR TO INDIVIDUALS.

1. When Tsze-ch'an was chief minister of the State of Chǎng, he would convey people across the Chan and Wei in his own carriage.

2. Mencius said, "It was kind, but showed that he did not understand the practice of government.

3. "When in the eleventh month of the year the foot-bridges are completed, and the carriage-bridges in the twelfth month, the people have not the trouble of wading.

4. "Let a governor conduct his rule on principles of equal justice, and, when he goes abroad, he may cause people to be removed out of his path. But how can he convey everybody across the rivers?

5. "It follows that if a governor will try to please everybody, he will find the days not sufficient for his work."

III

WHAT TREATMENT SOVEREIGNS GIVE TO THEIR MINISTERS WILL BE RETURNED TO THEM BY A CORRESPONDING BEHAVIOR.

1. Mencius said to the king Hsüan of Ch'i, "When the prince regards his ministers as his hands and feet, his ministers regard their prince as their belly and heart; when he regards them as his dogs and horses, they regard him as another man; when he regards them as the ground or as grass, they regard him as a robber and an enemy."

2. The king said, "According to the rules of propriety, a minister wears mourning when he has left the service of a prince. How must a prince behave that his old ministers may thus go into mourning?"

3. Mencius replied, "The admonitions of a minister having been followed, and his advice listened to, so that blessings have descended on the people, if for some cause he leaves the country, the prince sends an escort to conduct him beyond the boundaries. He also anticipates with recommendatory intimations his arrival in the country to which he is proceeding. When he has been gone three years and does not return, only then at length does he take back his fields and residence. This treatment is what is called a 'thrice-repeated display of consideration.' When a prince acts thus, mourning will be worn on leaving his service.

4. "Nowadays, the remonstrances of a minister are not followed, and his advice is not listened to, so that no blessings descend on the people. When for any cause he leaves the country, the prince tries to seize him and hold him a prisoner. He also pushes him to extremity in the country to which he has gone, and on the very day of his departure, takes back his fields and residence. This treatment shows him to be what we call 'a robber and an enemy.' What mourning can be worn for a robber and an enemy?"

IV

PROMPT ACTION IS NECESSARY AT THE RIGHT TIME.

Mencius said, "When scholars are put to death without any crime, the great officers may leave the country. When the people are slaughtered without any crime, the scholars may remove."

V

THE INFLUENCE OF THE RULER'S EXAMPLE.

Mencius said, "If the sovereign be benevolent, all will be benevolent. If the sovereign be righteous, all will be righteous."

VI

THE GREAT MAN MAKES NO MISTAKES IN MATTERS OF PROPRIETY AND RIGHTEOUSNESS.

Mencius said, "Acts of propriety which are not really proper, and acts of righteousness which are not really righteous, the great man does not do."

VII

WHAT DUTIES ARE DUE FROM, AND MUST BE RENEDERED BY, THE VIRTUOUS AND TALENTED.

Mencius said, "Those who keep the Mean, train up those who do not, and those who have abilities, train up those who have not, and hence men rejoice in having fathers and elder brothers who are possessed of virtue and talent. If they who keep the Mean spurn those who do not, and they who have abilities spurn those who have not, then the space between them—those so gifted and the ungifted—will not admit an inch."

VIII

CLEAR DISCRIMINATION OF WHAT IS WRONG AND RIGHT MUST PRECEDE VIGOROUS RIGHT-DOING.

Mencius said, "Men must be decided on what they will not do, and then they are able to act with vigor in what they ought to do."

IX

EVIL SPEAKING IS SURE TO BRING WITH IT EVIL CONSEQUENCES.

Mencius said, "What future misery have they and ought they to endure, who talk of what is not good in others!"

X

THAT CONFUCIUS KEPT THE MEAN.

Mencius said, "Chung-nî did not do extraordinary things."

XI

WHAT IS RIGHT IS THE SUPREME PURSUIT OF THE GREAT MAN.

Mencius said, "The great man does not think beforehand of his words that they may be sincere, nor of his actions that they may be resolute—he simply speaks and does what is right."

XII

A MAN IS GREAT BECAUSE HE IS CHILDLIKE.

Mencius said, "The great man is he who does not lose his child's-heart."

XIII

FILIAL PIETY SEEN IN THE OBSEQUIES OF PARENTS.

Mencius said, "The nourishment of parents when living is not sufficient to be accounted the great thing. It is only in the performing their obsequies when dead that we have what can be considered the great thing."

XIV

THE VALUE OF LEARNING THOROUGHLY IN-WROUGHT INTO THE MIND.

Mencius said, "The superior man makes his advances in what he is learning with deep earnestness and by the proper course, wishing to get hold of it as in himself. Having got hold of it in himself, he abides in it calmly and firmly. Abiding in it calmly and firmly, he reposes a deep reliance on it. Reposing a deep reliance on it, he seizes it on the left and right, meeting everywhere with it as a fountain from which things flow. It is on this account that the superior man wishes to get hold of what he is learning as in himself."

XV

[CONTINUING THE PREVIOUS CHAPTER.]

Mencius said, "In learning extensively and discussing minutely what is learned, the object of the superior man is that he may be able to go back and set forth in brief what is essential."

XVI

[CONTINUING THE PREVIOUS CHAPTER.]

Mencius said, "Never has he who would by his excellence subdue men been able to subdue them. Let a prince seek by his excellence to nourish men, and he will be able to subdue the whole kingdom. It is impossible that anyone should become ruler of the people to whom they have not yielded the subjection of the heart."

XVII

[CONTINUING THE PREVIOUS CHAPTER.]

Mencius said, "Words which are not true are inauspicious, and the words which are most truly obnoxious to the name of inauspicious, are those which throw into the shade men of talents and virtue."

XVIII

HOW MENCIUS EXPLAINED CONFUCIUS'S PRAISE OF WATER.

1. The disciple Hsü said, "Chung-nî often praised water, saying, 'O water! O water!' What did he find in water to praise?"

2. Mencius replied, "There is a spring of water; how it gushes out! It rests not day nor night. It fills up every hole, and then advances, flowing onto the four seas. Such is water having a spring! It was this which he found in it to praise.

3. "But suppose that the water has no spring. In the seventh and eighth when the rain falls abundantly, the channels in the fields are all filled, but their being dried up again may be expected in a short time. So a superior man is ashamed of a reputation beyond his merits."

XIX

WHEREBY SAGES ARE DISTINGUISHED FROM OTHER MEN —
ILLUSTRATED IN SHUN.

1. Mencius said, "That whereby man differs from the lower animals is but small. The mass of people cast it away, while superior men preserve it.

2. "Shun clearly understood the multitude of things, and closely observed the relations of humanity. He walked along the path of benevolence and righteousness; he did not need to pursue benevolence and righteousness."

XX

THE SAME SUBJECT — ILLUSTRATED IN
YÜ, T'ĂNG, WĂN, WÛ, AND CHÂU-KUNG.

1. Mencius said, "Yü hated the pleasant wine, and loved good words.

2. "T'ăng held fast the Mean, and employed men of talents and virtue without regard to where they came from.

3. "King Wăn looked on the people as he would on a man who was wounded, and he looked towards the right path as if he could not see it.

4. "King Wû did not slight the near, and did not forget the distant.

5. "The duke of Châu desired to unite in himself the virtues of those kings, those founders of the three dynasties, that he might display in his practice the four things which they did. If he saw anything in them not suited to his time, he looked up and thought about it, from daytime into the night, and when he was fortunate enough to master the difficulty, he sat waiting for the morning."

XXI

THE SAME SUBJECT — ILLUSTRATED IN CONFUCIUS.

1. Mencius said, "The traces of sovereign rule were extinguished, and the royal odes ceased to be made. When those odes ceased to be made, then the Ch'un Ch'iû was produced.

2. "The Shang of Tsin, the Tâo-wû of Ch'û, and the Ch'un Ch'iû of Lû were books of the same character.

3. "The subject of the Ch'un Ch'iû was the affairs of Hwan of Chî and Wǎn of Tsin, and its style was the historical. Confucius said, "Its righteous decisions I ventured to make.'"

XXII

THE SAME SUBJECT — ILLUSTRATED IN MENCIUS HIMSELF.

1. Mencius said, "The influence of a sovereign sage terminates in the fifth generation. The influence of a mere sage does the same.

2. "Although I could not be a disciple of Confucius himself, I have endeavoured to cultivate my virtue by means of others who were."

XXIII

FIRST JUDGMENTS ARE NOT ALWAYS CORRECT. IMPULSES MUST BE WEIGHED IN THE BALANCE OF REASON, AND WHAT REASON DICTATES MUST BE FOLLOWED.

Mencius said, "When it appears proper to take a thing, and afterwards not proper, to take it is contrary to moderation. When it appears proper to give a thing and afterwards not proper, to give it is contrary to kindness. When it appears proper to sacrifice one's life, and afterwards not proper, to sacrifice it is contrary to bravery."

XXIV

THE IMPORTANCE OF BEING CAREFUL OF WHOM WE MAKE FRIENDS.

1. P'ang Mǎng learned archery of Î. When he had acquired completely all the science of Î, he thought that in all the kingdom only Î was superior to himself, and so he slew him. Mencius said, "In this case Î also was to blame. Kung-ming Î indeed said, 'It would appear as if he were not to be blamed,' but he thereby only meant that his blame was slight. How can he be held without any blame?"

2. "The people of Chǎng sent Tsze-cho Yü to make a stealthy attack on Wei, which sent Yü-kung Sze to pursue him. Tsze-cho Yü said, 'Today I feel unwell, so that I cannot hold my bow. I am a dead man!' At the same time he asked his driver, 'Who is it that is pursuing me?' The driver said, 'It is Yü-kung Sze,' on which, he exclaimed, 'I shall live.' The driver said, 'Yü-kung Sze is the best archer of Wei, what do you mean by saying "I shall live?"' Yü replied, 'Yü-kung Sze learned archery from Yin-kung T'o, who again learned

it from me. Now, Yin-kung T'o is an upright man, and the friends of his selection must be upright also.' When Yü-kung Sze came up, he said, 'Master, why are you not holding your bow?' Yü answered him, 'Today I am feeling unwell, and cannot hold my bow.' On this Sze said, 'I learned archery from Yin-kung T'o, who again learned it from you. I cannot bear to injure you with your own science. The business of today, however, is the prince's business, which I dare not neglect.' He then took his arrows, knocked off their steel points against the carriage-wheel, discharged four of them, and returned."

XXV

IT IS ONLY MORAL BEAUTY THAT IS TRULY EXCELLENT AND ACCEPTABLE.

1. Mencius said, "If the lady Hsî had been covered with a filthy headdress, all people would have stopped their noses in passing her.

2. "Though a man may be wicked, yet if he adjust his thoughts, fast, and bathe, he may sacrifice to God."

XXVI

HOW KNOWLEDGE OUGHT TO BE PURSUED BY THE CAREFUL STUDY OF PHENOMENA.

1. Mencius said, "All who speak about the natures of things, have in fact only their phenomena to reason from, and the value of a phenomenon is in its being natural.

2. "What I dislike in your wise men is their boring out their conclusions. If those wise men would only act as Yü did when he conveyed away the waters, there would be nothing to dislike in their wisdom. The manner in which Yü conveyed away the waters was by doing what gave him no trouble. If your wise men would also do that which gave them no trouble, their knowledge would also be great.

3. "There is heaven so high; there are the stars so distant. If we have investigated their phenomena, we may, while sitting in our places, go back to the solstice of a thousand years ago."

XXVII

HOW MENCIUS WOULD NOT IMITATE OTHERS
IN PAYING COURT TO A FAVORITE.

1. The officer Kung-hang having on hand the funeral of one of his sons, the Master of the Right went to condole with him. When this noble entered the door, some called him to them and spoke with him, and some went to his place and spoke with him.

2. Mencius did not speak with him, so that he was displeased, and said, "All the gentlemen have spoken with me. There is only Mencius who does not speak to me, thereby slighting me."

3. Mencius having heard of this remark, said, "According to the prescribed rules, in the court, individuals may not change their places to speak with one another, nor may they pass from their ranks to bow to one another. I was wishing to observe this rule, and Tsze-âo understands it that I was slighting him: is not this strange?"

XXVIII

HOW THE SUPERIOR MAN IS DISTINGUISHED BY THE CULTIVATION
OF MORAL EXCELLENCE, AND IS PLACED THEREBY BEYOND THE
REACH OF CALAMITY.

1. Mencius said, "That whereby the superior man is distinguished from other men is what he preserves in his heart—namely, benevolence and propriety.

2. "The benevolent man loves others. The man of propriety shows respect to others.

3. "He who loves others is constantly loved by them. He who respects others is constantly respected by them.

4. "Here is a man, who treats me in a perverse and unreasonable manner. The superior man in such a case will turn round upon himself—'I must have been wanting in benevolence; I must have been wanting in propriety—how should this have happened to me?'

5. "He examines himself, and is specially benevolent. He turns round upon himself, and is specially observant of propriety. The perversity and unreasonableness of the other, however, are still the same. The superior man will again turn round on himself—'I must have been failing to do my utmost.'

6. "He turns round upon himself, and proceeds to do his utmost, but still the perversity and unreasonableness of the other are repeated. On this the superior man says, 'This is a man utterly lost indeed! Since he conducts himself so, what is there to choose between him and a brute? Why should I go to contend with a brute?'

7. "Thus it is that the superior man has a lifelong anxiety and not one morning's calamity. As to what is matter of anxiety to him, that indeed he has. He says, 'Shun was a man, and I also am a man. But Shun became an example to all the kingdom, and his conduct was worthy to be handed down to after ages, while I am nothing better than a villager.' This indeed is the proper matter of anxiety to him. And in what way is he anxious about it? Just that he may be like Shun: then only will he stop. As to what the superior man would feel to be a calamity, there is no such thing. He does nothing which is not according to propriety. If there should befall him one morning's calamity, the superior man does not account it a calamity."

XXIX

A RECONCILING PRINCIPLE WILL BE FOUND TO UNDERLIE THE OUTWARDLY DIFFERENT CONDUCT OF GREAT AND GOOD MEN — IN HONOR OF YEN HÛI, WITH A REFERENCE TO MENCIUS HIMSELF.

1. Yü and Chî, in an age when the world was being brought back to order, thrice passed their doors without entering them. Confucius praised them.

2. The disciple Yen, in an age of disorder, dwelt in a mean narrow lane, having his single bamboo-cup of rice, and his single gourd-dish of water; other men could not have endured the distress, but he did not allow his joy to be affected by it. Confucius praised him.

3. Mencius said, "Yü, Chî, and Yen Hûi agreed in the principle of their conduct.

4. "Yü thought that if anyone in the kingdom were drowned, it was as if he drowned him. Chî thought that if anyone in the kingdom suffered hunger, it was as if he famished him. It was on this account that they were so earnest.

5. "If Yü and Chî, and Yen-tsze, had exchanged places, each would have done what the other did.

6. "Here now in the same apartment with you are people fighting: you ought to part them. Though you part them with your cap simply tied over your unbound hair, your conduct will be allowable.

7. "If the fighting be only in the village or neighborhood, if you go to put an end to it with your cap tied over your hair unbound, you will be in error. Although you should shut your door in such a case, your conduct would be allowable."

XXX

HOW MENCIUS EXPLAINED HIS FRIENDLY INTERCOURSE WITH A MAN CHARGED WITH BEING UNFILIAL.

1. The disciple Kung-tû said, "Throughout the whole kingdom everybody pronounces K'wang Chang unfilial. But you, Master, keep company with him, and moreover treat him with politeness. I venture to ask why you do so."

2. Mencius replied, "There are five things which are pronounced in the common usage of the age to be unfilial. The first is laziness in the use of one's four limbs, without attending to the nourishment of his parents. The second is gambling and chess-playing, and being fond of wine, without attending to the nourishment of his parents. The third is being fond of goods and money, and selfishly attached to his wife and children, without attending to the nourishment of his parents. The fourth is following the desires of one's ears and eyes, so as to bring his parents to disgrace. The fifth is being fond of bravery, fighting and quarreling so as to endanger his parents. Is Chang guilty of any one of these things?

3. "Now between Chang and his father there arose disagreement, he, the son, reproving his father, to urge him to what was good.

4. "To urge one another to what is good by reproofs is the way of friends. But such urging between father and son is the greatest injury to the kindness, which should prevail between them.

5. "Moreover, did not Chang wish to have in his family the relationships of husband and wife, child and mother? But because he had offended his father, and was not permitted to approach him, he sent away his wife, and drove forth his son, and all his life receives no cherishing attention from them. He settled it in his mind that if he did not act in this way, his would be one of the greatest of crimes. Such and nothing more is the case of Chang."

XXXI

HOW MENCIUS EXPLAINED THE DIFFERENT CONDUCT OF
TSĂNG-TSZE AND OF TSZE-SZE IN SIMILAR CIRCUMSTANCES.

1. When the philosopher Tsăng dwelt in Wû-ch'ăng, there came a band
    from Yüeh to plunder it. Someone said to him, "The plunderers are
    coming: why not leave this?" Tsăng on this left the city, saying to
    the man in charge of the house, "Do not lodge any persons in my
    house, lest they break and injure the plants and trees." When the
    plunderers withdrew, he sent word to him, saying, "Repair the walls
    of my house. I am about to return." When the plunderers retired, the
    philosopher Tsăng returned accordingly. His disciples said, "Since
    our master was treated with so much sincerity and respect, for him
    to be the first to go away on the arrival of the plunderers, so as to be
    observed by the people, and then to return on their retiring, appears
    to us to be improper." Ch'an-yû Hsing said, "You do not understand
    this matter. Formerly, when Ch'an-yû was exposed to the outbreak
    of the grass-carriers, there were seventy disciples in our master's
    following, and none of them took part in the matter."

2. When Tsze-sze was living in Wei, there came a band from Ch'î to
    plunder. Someone said to him, "The plunderers are coming—why
    not leave this?" Tsze-sze said, "If I go away, whom will the prince
    have to guard the State with?"

3. Mencius said, "The philosophers Tsăng and Tsze-sze agreed in the
    principle of their conduct. Tsăng was a teacher—in the place of a
    father or elder brother. Tsze-sze was a minister—in a meaner place.
    If the philosophers Tsăng and Tsze-sze had exchanged places the
    one would have done what the other did."

XXXII

SAGES ARE JUST LIKE OTHER MEN.

The officer Ch'û said to Mencius, "Master, the king sent persons to
spy out whether you were really different from other men." Mencius
said, "How should I be different from other men? Yâo and Shun
were just the same as other men."

XXXIII

THE DISGRACEFUL MEANS WHICH SOME MEN TAKE TO SEEK FOR THEIR LIVING, AND FOR WEALTH.

1. A man of Ch'î had a wife and a concubine, and lived together with them in his house. When their husband went out, he would get himself well filled with wine and flesh, and then return, and, on his wife's asking him with whom he ate and drank, they were sure to be all wealthy and honorable people. The wife informed the concubine, saying, "When our good man goes out, he is sure to come back having partaken plentifully of wine and flesh. I asked with whom he ate and drank, and they are all, it seems, wealthy and honorable people. And yet no people of distinction ever come here. I will spy out where our good man goes." Accordingly, she got up early in the morning, and privately followed wherever her husband went. Throughout the whole city, there was no one who stood or talked with him. At last, he came to those who were sacrificing among the tombs beyond the outer wall on the east, and begged what they had over. Not being satisfied, he looked about, and went to another party—and this was the way in which he got himself satiated. His wife returned, and informed the concubine, saying, "It was to our husband that we looked up in hopeful contemplation, with whom our lot is cast for life—and now these are his ways!" On this, along with the concubine she reviled their husband, and they wept together in the middle hall. In the meantime the husband, knowing nothing of all this, came in with a jaunty air, carrying himself proudly to his wife and concubine.

2. In the view of a superior man, as to the ways by which men seek for riches, honors, gain, and advancement, there are few of their wives and concubines who would not be ashamed and weep together on account of them.

BOOK V

WAN CHANG

PART I

I

1. Wan Chang asked Mencius, saying, "When Shun went into the fields, he cried out and wept towards the pitying heavens. Why did he cry out and weep?" Mencius replied, "He was dissatisfied, and full of earnest desire."

2. Wan Chang said, "When his parents love him, a son rejoices and forgets them not. When his parents hate him, though they punish him, he does not murmur. Was Shun then murmuring against his parents?" Mencius answered, "Ch'ang Hsî asked Kung-ming Kâo, saying, 'As to Shun's going into the fields, I have received your instructions, but I do not know about his weeping and crying out to the pitying heavens and to his parents.' Kung-ming Kâo answered him, 'You do not understand that matter.' Now, Kung-ming Kâo supposed that the heart of the filial son could not be so free of sorrow. Shun would say, 'I exert my strength to cultivate the fields, but I am thereby only discharging my office as a son. What can there be in me that my parents do not love me?'

3. "The Tî caused his own children, nine sons and two daughters, the various officers, oxen and sheep, storehouses and granaries, all to be prepared, to serve Shun amid the channeled fields. Of the scholars of the kingdom there were multitudes who flocked to him. The sovereign designed that Shun should superintend the kingdom along with him, and then to transfer it to him entirely. But because his parents were not in accord with him, he felt like a poor man who has nowhere to turn to.

4. "To be delighted in by all the scholars of the kingdom, is what men desire, but it was not sufficient to remove the sorrow of Shun. The possession of beauty is what men desire, and Shun had for his wives the two daughters of the Tî, but this was not sufficient to remove his sorrow. Riches are what men desire, and the kingdom was the rich property of Shun, but this was not sufficient to remove his sorrow. Honors are what men desire, and Shun had the dignity of being sovereign, but this was not sufficient to remove his sorrow. The reason why the being the object of men's delight, with the possession of beauty, riches, and honors were not sufficient to remove his sorrow, was that it could be removed only by his getting his parents to be in accord with him.

5. "The desire of the child is towards his father and mother. When he becomes conscious of the attractions of beauty, his desire is towards young and beautiful women. When he comes to have a wife and children, his desire is towards them. When he obtains office, his desire is towards his sovereign: if he cannot get the regard of his sovereign, he burns within. But the man of great filial piety, to the end of his life, has his desire towards his parents. In the great Shun I see the case of one whose desire at fifty year's was towards them."

II

DEFENSE OF SHUN AGAINST THE CHARGES OF VIOLATING THE PROPER RULE IN THE WAY OF HIS MARRYING, AND OF HYPOCRISY IN HIS CONDUCT TO HIS BROTHER.

1. Wan Chang asked Mencius, saying, "It is said in the Book of Poetry,

In marrying a wife, how ought a man to proceed?
He must inform his parents.

If the rule be indeed as here expressed, no man ought to have illustrated it so well as Shun. How was it that Shun's marriage took place without his informing his parents?" Mencius replied, "If he had informed them, he would not have been able to marry. That male and female should dwell together, is the greatest of human relations. If Shun had informed his parents, he must have made void this greatest of human relations, thereby incurring their resentment. On this account, he did not inform them!"

2. Wan Chang said, "As to Shun's marrying without informing his parents, I have heard your instructions; but how was it that the

Tî Yâo gave him his daughters as wives without informing Shun's parents?" Mencius said, "The Tî also knew that if he informed them, he could not marry his daughters to him."

3. Wan Chang said, "His parents set Shun to repair a granary, to which, the ladder having been removed, Kû-sâu set fire. They also made him dig a well. He got out, but they, not knowing that, proceeded to cover him up. Hsiang said, 'Of the scheme to cover up the city-forming prince, the merit is all mine. Let my parents have his oxen and sheep. Let them have his storehouses and granaries. His shield and spear shall be mine. His lute shall be mine. His bow shall be mine. His two wives I shall make attend for me to my bed.' Hsiang then went away into Shun's palace, and there was Shun on his couch playing on his lute. Hsiang said, 'I am come simply because I was thinking anxiously about you.' At the same time, he blushed deeply. Shun said to him, 'There are all my officers: do you undertake the government of them for me.' I do not know whether Shun was ignorant of Hsiang's wishing to kill him." Mencius answered, "How could he be ignorant of that? But when Hsiang was sorrowful, he was also sorrowful; when Hsiang was joyful, he was also joyful."

4. Chang said, "In that case, then, did not Shun rejoice hypocritically?" Mencius replied, "No. Formerly, someone sent a present of a live fish to Tsze-ch'an of Chăng. Tsze-ch'an ordered his pond-keeper to keep it in the pond, but that officer cooked it, and reported the execution of his commission, saying, 'When I first let it go, it embarrassed. In a little while, it seemed to be somewhat at ease, then it swam away joyfully.' Tsze-ch'an observed, 'It had got into its element! It had got into its element!' The pond-keeper then went out and said, 'Who calls Tsze-ch'an a wise man? After I had cooked and eaten the fish, he says, "It had got into its element! It had got into its element!"' Thus a superior man may be imposed on by what seems to be as it ought to be, but he cannot be entrapped by what is contrary to right principle. Hsiang came in the way in which the love of his elder brother would have made him come; therefore Shun sincerely believed him, and rejoiced. What hypocrisy was there?"

III

EXPLANATION AND DEFENSE OF SHUN'S CONDUCT IN THE CASE OF HIS WICKED BROTHER HSIANG — HOW HE BOTH DISTINGUISHED HIM, AND KEPT HIM UNDER RESTRAINT.

1. Wan Chang said, "Hsiang made it his daily business to slay Shun. When Shun was made sovereign, how was it that he only banished him?" Mencius said, "He raised him to be a prince. Some supposed that it was banishing him?"

2. Wan Chang said, "Shun banished the superintendent of works to Yû-châu; he sent away Hwan-tâu to the mountain Ch'ung; he slew the prince of San-miâo in San-wei; and he imprisoned Kwân on the mountain Yü. When the crimes of those four were thus punished, the whole kingdom acquiesced: it was a cutting off of men who were destitute of benevolence. But Hsiang was of all men the most destitute of benevolence, and Shun raised him to be the prince of Yû-pî—of what crimes had the people of Yû-pî been guilty? Does a benevolent man really act thus? In the case of other men, he cut them off; in the case of his brother, he raised him to be a prince." Mencius replied, "A benevolent man does not lay up anger, nor cherish resentment against his brother, but only regards him with affection and love. Regarding him with affection, he wishes him to be honorable: regarding him with love, he wishes him to be rich. The appointment of Hsiang to be the prince of Yû-pî was to enrich and ennoble him. If while Shun himself was sovereign, his brother had been a common man, could he have been said to regard him with affection and love?"

3. Wan Chang said, "I venture to ask what you mean by saying that some supposed that it was a banishing of Hsiang?" Mencius replied, "Hsiang could do nothing in his State. The Son of Heaven appointed an officer to administer its government, and to pay over its revenues to him. This treatment of him led to its being said that he was banished. How indeed could he be allowed the means of oppressing the people? Nevertheless, Shun wished to be continually seeing him, and by this arrangement, he came incessantly to court, as is signified in that expression—'He did not wait for the rendering of tribute, or affairs of government, to receive the prince of Yû-pî.'"

IV

EXPLANATION OF SHUN'S CONDUCT WITH REFERENCE TO THE SOVEREIGN YÂO, AND HIS FATHER KÛ-SÂU.

1. Hsien-ch'iû Măng asked Mencius, saying, "There is the saying, 'A scholar of complete virtue may not be employed as a minister by his sovereign, nor treated as a son by his father. Shun stood with his face to the south, and Yâo, at the head of all the princes, appeared before

him at court with his face to the north. Kû-sâu also did the same. When Shun saw Kû-sâu, his countenance became discomposed. Confucius said, At this time, in what a perilous condition was the kingdom! Its state was indeed unsettled.' I do not know whether what is here said really took place." Mencius replied, "No. These are not the words of a superior man. They are the sayings of an uncultivated person of the east of Ch'î. When Yâo was old, Shun was associated with him in the government. It is said in the Canon of Yâo, 'After twenty and eight years, the Highly Meritorious one deceased. The people acted as if they were mourning for a father or mother for three years, and up to the borders of the four seas every sound of music was hushed.' Confucius said, 'There are not two suns in the sky, nor two sovereigns over the people.' Shun having been sovereign, and, moreover, leading on all the princes to observe the three years' mourning for Yâo, there would have been in this case two sovereigns."

2. Hsien-ch'iû Măng said, "On the point of Shun's not treating Yâo as a minister, I have received your instructions. But it is said in the Book of Poetry,

> Under the whole heaven,
> Every spot is the sovereign's ground;
> To the borders of the land,
> Every individual is the sovereign's minister;

—and Shun had become sovereign. I venture to ask how it was that Kû-sâu was not one of his ministers." Mencius answered, "That ode is not to be understood in that way: it speaks of being laboriously engaged in the sovereign's business, so as not to be able to nourish one's parents, as if the author said, 'This is all the sovereign's business, and how is it that I alone am supposed to have ability, and am made to toil in it?' Therefore, those who explain the odes, may not insist on one term so as to do violence to a sentence, nor on a sentence so as to do violence to the general scope. They must try with their thoughts to meet that scope, and then we shall apprehend it. If we simply take single sentences, there is that in the ode called 'The Milky Way'—

> Of the black-haired people of the remnant of Châu,
> There is not half a one left.

If it had been really as thus expressed, then not an individual of the people of Châu was left.

3. "Of all which a filial son can attain to, there is nothing greater than his honoring his parents. And of what can be attained to in the honoring one's parents, there is nothing greater than the nourishing them with the whole kingdom. Kû-sâu was the father of the sovereign—this was the height of honor. Shun nourished him with the whole kingdom—this was the height of nourishing. In this was verified the sentiment in the Book of Poetry,

> Ever cherishing filial thoughts,
> Those filial thoughts became an example to after ages.

4. "It is said in the Book of History, 'Reverently performing his duties, he waited on Kû-sâu, and was full of veneration and awe. Kû-sâu also believed him and conformed to virtue.' This is the true case of the scholar of complete virtue not being treated as a son by his father."

V

HOW SHUN GOT THE THRONE BY THE GIFT OF HEAVEN. VOX POPULI VOX DEI.

1. Wan Chang said, "Was it the case that Yâo gave the throne to Shun?" Mencius said, "No. The sovereign cannot give the throne to another."

2. "Yes—but Shun had the throne. Who gave it to him?" "Heaven gave it to him," was the answer.

3. "'Heaven gave it to him'—did Heaven confer its appointment on him with specific injunctions?"

4. Mencius replied, "No. Heaven does not speak. It simply showed its will by his personal conduct and his conduct of affairs."

5. "'It showed its will by his personal conduct and his conduct of affairs'—how was this?" Mencius's answer was, "The sovereign can present a man to Heaven, but he cannot make Heaven give that man the throne. A prince can present a man to the sovereign, but he cannot cause the sovereign to make that man a prince. A great officer can present a man to his prince, but he cannot cause the prince to make that man a great officer. Yâo presented Shun to Heaven, and Heaven accepted him. He presented him to the people, and the people accepted him. Therefore I say, 'Heaven does not speak. It simply indicated its will by his personal conduct and his conduct of affairs.'"

6. Chang said, "I presume to ask how it was that Yâo presented Shun to Heaven, and Heaven accepted him; and that he exhibited him to the people, and the people accepted him." Mencius replied, "He caused him to preside over the sacrifices, and all the spirits were well pleased with them—thus Heaven accepted him. He caused him to preside over the conduct of affairs, and affairs were well administered, so that the people reposed under him—thus the people accepted him. Heaven gave the throne to him. The people gave it to him. Therefore I said, 'The sovereign cannot give the throne to another.'

7. "Shun assisted Yâo in the government for twenty and eight years—this was more than man could have done, and was from Heaven. After the death of Yâo, when the three years' mourning was completed, Shun withdrew from the son of Yâo to the south of South river. The princes of the kingdom, however, repairing to court, went not to the son of Yâo, but they went to Shun. Litigants went not to the son of Yâo, but they went to Shun. Singers sang not the son of Yâo, but they sang Shun. Therefore I said, 'Heaven gave him the throne.' It was after these things that he went to the Middle Kingdom, and occupied the seat of the Son of Heaven. If he had, before these things, taken up his residence in the palace of Yâo, and had applied pressure to the son of Yâo, it would have been an act of usurpation, and not the gift of Heaven.

8. "This sentiment is expressed in the words of The Great Declaration—'Heaven sees according as my people see; Heaven hears according as my people hear.'"

VI

HOW THE THRONE DESCENDED FROM YÜ TO HIS SON, AND NOT TO HIS MINISTER YÎ; THAT YÜ WAS NOT TO BE CONSIDERED ON THAT ACCOUNT AS INFERIOR IN VIRTUE TO YÂO AND SHUN.

1. Wan Chang asked Mencius, saying, "People say, 'When the disposal of the kingdom came to Yü, his virtue was inferior to that of Yâo and Shun, and he transmitted it not to the worthiest but to his son.' Was it so?" Mencius replied, "No; it was not so. When Heaven gave the kingdom to the worthiest, it was given to the worthiest. When Heaven gave it to the son of the preceding sovereign, it was given to him. Shun presented Yü to Heaven. Seventeen years elapsed, and Shun died. When the three years' mourning was expired, Yü withdrew from the son of Shun to Yang-ch'ăng. The people of

the kingdom followed him just as after the death of Yâo, instead of following his son, they had followed Shun. Yü presented Yî to Heaven. Seven years elapsed, and Yü died. When the three years' mourning was expired, Yî withdrew from the son of Yü to the north of mount Ch'î. The princes, repairing to court, went not to Yî, but they went to Ch'î. Litigants did not go to Yî, but they went to Ch'î, saying, 'He is the son of our sovereign'; the singers did not sing Yî, but they sang Ch'î, saying, 'He is the son of our sovereign.'

2. "That Tan-chû was not equal to his father, and Shun's son not equal to his; that Shun assisted Yâo, and Yü assisted Shun, for many years, conferring benefits on the people for a long time; that thus the length of time during which Shun, Yü, and Yî assisted in the government was so different; that Ch'î was able, as a man of talents and virtue, reverently to pursue the same course as Yü; that Yî assisted Yü only for a few years, and had not long conferred benefits on the people; that the periods of service of the three were so different; and that the sons were one superior, and the other superior: all this was from Heaven, and what could not be brought about by man. That which is done without man's doing is from Heaven. That which happens without man's causing is from the ordinance of Heaven.

3. "In the case of a private individual obtaining the throne, there must be in him virtue equal to that of Shun or Yü; and moreover there must be the presenting of him to Heaven by the preceding sovereign. It was on this account that Confucius did not obtain the throne.

4. "When the kingdom is possessed by natural succession, the sovereign who is displaced by Heaven must be like Chieh or Châu. It was on this account that Yî, Î Yin, and Châu-kung did not obtain the throne.

5. "Î Yin assisted T'ăng so that he became sovereign over the kingdom. After the demise of T'ăng, T'âi-ting having died before he could be appointed sovereign, Wâ'i-ping reigned two years, and Chung-zin four. T'âi-chiâ was then turning upside down the statutes of T'ăng, when Î Yin placed him in T'ung for three years. There T'âi-chiâ repented of his errors, was contrite, and reformed himself. In T'ung he came to dwell in benevolence and walk in righteousness, during those threee years, listening to the lessons given to him by Î Yin. Then Î Yin again returned with him to Po.

6. "Châu-kung not getting the throne was like the case of Yî and the throne of Hsiâ, or like that of Î Yin and the throne of Yin.

7. "Confucius said, 'T'ăng and Yü resigned the throne to their worthy ministers. The sovereign of Hsiâ and those of Yin and Châu transmitted it to their sons. The principle of righteousness was the same in all the cases.'"

VII

VINDICATION OF Î YIN FROM THE CHARGE OF INTRODUCING HIMSELF TO THE SERVICE OF T'ĂNG BY AN UNWORTHY ARTIFICE.

1. Wan Chang asked Mencius, saying, "People say that Î Yin sought an introduction to T'ăng by his knowledge of cookery. Was it so?"

2. Mencius replied, "No, it was not so. Î Yin was a farmer in the lands of the prince of Hsin, delighting in the principles of Yâo and Shun. In any matter contrary to the righteousness which they prescribed, or contrary to their principles, though he had been offered the throne, he would not have regarded it; though there had been yoked for him a thousand teams of horses, he would not have looked at them. In any matter contrary to the righteousness which they prescribed, or contrary to their principles, he would neither have given nor taken a single straw.

3. "T'ăng sent persons with presents of silk to entreat him to enter his service. With an air of indifference and self-satisfaction he said, 'What can I do with those silks with which T'ăng invites me? Is it not best for me to abide in the channeled fields, and so delight myself with the principles of Yâo and Shun?'

4. "T'ăng thrice sent messengers to invite him. After this, with the change of resolution displayed in his countenance, he spoke in a different style—'Instead of abiding in the channeled fields and thereby delighting myself with the principles of Yâo and Shun, had I not better make this prince a prince like Yâo or Shun, and this people like the people of Yâo or Shun? Had I not better in my own person see these things for myself?

5. "'Heaven's plan in the production of mankind is this: that they who are first informed should instruct those who are later in being informed, and they who first apprehend principles should instruct those who are slower to do so. I am one of Heaven's people who have first apprehended—I will take these principles and instruct this people in them. If I do not instruct them, who will do so?'

6. "He thought that among all the people of the kingdom, even the private men and women, if there were any who did not enjoy such benefits as Yâo and Shun conferred, it was as if he himself pushed them into a ditch. He took upon himself the heavy charge of the kingdom in this way, and therefore he went to T'ǎng, and pressed upon him the subject of attacking Hsiâ and saving the people.

7. "I have not heard of one who bent himself, and at the same time made others straight—how much less could one disgrace himself, and thereby rectify the whole kingdom? The actions of the sages have been different. Some have kept remote from court, and some have drawn near to it; some have left their offices, and some have not done so: that to which those different courses all agree is simply the keeping of their persons pure.

8. "I have heard that Î Yin sought an introduction to T'ǎng by the doctrines of Yâo and Shun. I have not heard that he did so by his knowledge of cookery.

9. "In the 'Instructions of Î,' it is said, 'Heaven destroying Chieh commenced attacking him in the palace of Mû. I commenced in Po.'"

VIII

VINDICATION OF CONFUCIUS FROM THE CHARGE OF LODGING
WITH UNWORTHY CHARACTERS.

1. Wan Chang asked Mencius, saying, "Some say that Confucius, when he was in Wei, lived with the ulcer-doctor, and when he was in Ch'î, with the attendant, Ch'î Hwan—was it so?" Mencius replied, "No; it was not so. Those are the inventions of men fond of strange things.

2. "When he was in Wei, he lived with Yen Ch'âu-yû. The wives of the officer Mî and Tsze-lû were sisters, and Mî told Tsze-lû, 'If Confucius will lodge with me, he may attain to the dignity of a high noble of Wei.' Tsze-lû informed Confucius of this, and he said, 'That is as ordered by Heaven.' Confucius went into office according to propriety, and retired from it according to righteousness. In regard to his obtaining office or not obtaining it, he said, 'That is as ordered.' But if he had lodged with the attendant Chî Hwan, that would neither have been according to righteousness, nor any ordering of Heaven.

3. "When Confucius, being dissatisfied in Lû and Wei, had left those States, he met with the attempt of Hwan, the Master of the Horse, of Sung, to intercept and kill him. He assumed, however, the dress of a common man, and passed by Sung. At that time, though he was in circumstances of distress, he lodged with the city-master Ch'ǎng, who was then a minister of Châu, the marquis of Ch'ǎn.

4. "I have heard that the characters of ministers about court may be discerned from those whom they entertain, and those of stranger officers, from those with whom they lodge. If Confucius had lodged with the ulcer-doctor, and with the attendant Chî Hwan, how could he have been Confucius?"

IX

VINDICATION OF PÂI-LÎ HSÎ FROM THE CHARGE OF SELLING
HIMSELF AS A STEP TO HIS ADVANCEMENT.

1. Wan Chang asked Mencius, "Some say that Pâi-lî Hsî sold himself to a cattle-keeper of Ch'in for the skins of five rams, and fed his oxen, in order to find an introduction to the duke Mû of Ch'in—was this the case?" Mencius said, "No; it was not so. This story was invented by men fond of strange things.

2. "Pâi-lî Hsî was a man of Yü. The people of Tsin, by the inducement of a round piece of jade from Ch'ûi-chî, and four horses of the Ch'ü breed, borrowed a passage through Yü to attack Kwo. On that occasion, Kung Chih-ch'î remonstrated against granting their request, and Pâi-lî Hsî did not remonstrate.

3. "When he knew that the duke of Yü was not to be remonstrated with, and, leaving that State, went to Ch'in, he had reached the age of seventy. If by that time he did not know that it would be a mean thing to seek an introduction to the duke Mû of Ch'in by feeding oxen, could he be called wise? But not remonstrating where it was of no use to remonstrate, could he be said not to be wise? Knowing that the duke of Yü would be ruined, and leaving him before that event, he cannot be said not to have been wise. Being then advanced in Ch'in, he knew that the duke Mû was one with whom he would enjoy a field for action, and became minister to him—could he, acting thus, be said not to be wise? Having become chief minister of Ch'in, he made his prince distinguished throughout the kingdom, and worthy of being handed down to future ages—could he have

done this, if he had not been a man of talents and virtue? As to selling himself in order to accomplish all the aims of his prince, even a villager who had a regard for himself would not do such a thing; and shall we say that a man of talents and virtue did it?"

WAN CHANG

PART II

I

HOW CONFUCIUS DIFFERED FROM AND WAS SUPERIOR
TO ALL OTHER SAGES.

1.   Mencius said, "Po-î would not allow his eyes to look on a bad sight, nor his ears to listen to a bad sound. He would not serve a prince whom he did not approve, nor command a people whom he did not esteem. In a time of good government he took office, and on the occurrence of confusion he retired. He could not bear to dwell either in a court from which a lawless government emanated, or among lawless people. He considered his being in the same place with a villager, as if he were to sit amid mud and coals with his court robes and court cap. In the time of Châu he dwelt on the shores of the North sea, waiting the purification of the kingdom. Therefore when men now hear the character of Po-î, the corrupt become pure, and the weak acquire determination.

2.   "Î Yin said, 'Whom may I not serve? My serving him makes him my sovereign. What people may I not command? My commanding them makes them my people.' In a time of good government he took office, and when confusion prevailed, he also took office. He said, 'Heaven's plan in the production of mankind is this: that they who are first informed should instruct those who are later in being informed, and they who first apprehend principles should instruct those who are slower in doing so. I am the one of Heaven's people who has first apprehended—I will take these principles and instruct the people in them.' He thought that among all the people of the kingdom, even the common men and women, if there were any who did not share in the enjoyment of such benefits as Yâo and Shun conferred, it was as if he himself pushed them into a ditch—for he took upon himself the heavy charge of the kingdom.

3. "Hûi of Liû-hsiâ was not ashamed to serve an impure prince, nor did he think it low to be an inferior officer. When advanced to employment, he did not conceal his virtue, but made it a point to carry out his principles. When dismissed and left without office, he did not murmur. When straitened by poverty, he did not grieve. When thrown into the company of village people, he was quite at ease and could not bear to leave them. He had a saying, 'You are you, and I am I. Although you stand by my side with breast and arms bare, or with your body naked, how can you defile me?' Therefore when men now hear the character of Hûi of Liü-hsiâ, the mean become generous, and the niggardly become liberal.

4. "When Confucius was leaving Ch'î, he strained off with his hand the water in which his rice was being rinsed, took the rice, and went away. When he left Lû, he said, 'I will set out by-and-by'—it was right he should leave the country of his parents in this way. When it was proper to go away quickly, he did so; when it was proper to delay, he did so; when it was proper to keep in retirement, he did so; when it was proper to go into office, he did so: this was Confucius."

5. Mencius said, "Po-î among the sages was the pure one; Î Yin was the one most inclined to take office; Hûi of Liû-hsiâ was the accommodating one; and Confucius was the timeous one.

6. "In Confucius we have what is called a complete concert. A complete concert is when the large bell proclaims the commencement of the music, and the ringing stone proclaims its close. The metal sound commences the blended harmony of all the instruments, and the winding up with the stone terminates that blended harmony. The commencing that harmony is the work of wisdom. The terminating it is the work of sageness.

7. "As a comparison for wisdom, we may liken it to skill, and as a comparison for sageness, we may liken it to strength—as in the case of shooting at a mark a hundred paces distant. That you reach it is owing to your strength, but that you hit the mark is not owing to your strength."

II

THE ARRANGEMENT OF DIGNITIES AND EMOLUMENTS
ACCORDING TO THE DYNASTY OF CHÂU.

1. Pêi-kung Î asked Mencius, saying, "What was the arrangement of dignities and emoluments determined by the House of Châu?"

2. Mencius replied, "The particulars of that arrangement cannot be learned, for the princes, disliking them as injurious to themselves, have all made away with the records of them. Still I have learned the general outline of them.

3. "The Son of Heaven constituted one dignity; the Kung one; the Hâu one; the Pâi one; and the Tsze and the Nan each one of equal rank: altogether making five degrees of rank. The ruler again constituted one dignity; the chief minister one; the great officers one; the scholars of the first class one; those of the middle class one; and those of the lowest class one: altogether making six degrees of dignity.

4. "To the Son of Heaven there was allotted a territory of a thousand lî square. A Kung and a Hâu had each a hundred lî square. A Pâi had seventy lî, and a Tsze and a Nan had each fifty lî. The assignments altogether were of four amounts. Where the territory did not amount to fifty lî, the chief could not have access himself to the Son of Heaven. His land was attached to some Hâu-ship, and was called a *fû-yung*.

5. "The chief ministers of the Son of Heaven received an amount of territory equal to that of a Hâu; a great officer received as much as a Pâi; and a scholar of the first class as much as a Tsze or a Nan.

6. "In a great State, where the territory was a hundred lî square, the ruler had ten times as much income as his chief ministers; a chief minister four times as much as a great officer; a great officer twice as much as a scholar of the first class; a scholar of the first class twice as much as one of the middle; a scholar of the middle class twice as much as one of the lowest; the scholars of the lowest class, and such of the common people as were employed about the government offices, had for their emolument as much as was equal to what they would have made by tilling the fields.

7. "In a State of the next order, where the territory was seventy lî square, the ruler had ten times as much revenue as his chief minister; a chief minister three times as much as a great officer; a great officer

twice as much as a scholar of the first class; a scholar of the first class twice as much as one of the middle; a scholar of the middle class twice as much as one of the lowest; the scholars of the lowest class, and such of the common people as were employed about the government offices, had for their emolument as much as was equal to what they would have made by tilling the fields.

8. "In a small State, where the territory was fifty lî square, the ruler had ten times as much revenue as his chief minister; a chief minister had twice as much as a great officer; a great officer twice as much as a scholar of the highest class; a scholar of the highest class twice as much as one of the middle; a scholar of the middle class twice as much as one of the lowest; scholars of the lowest class, and such of the common people as were employed about the government offices, had the same emolument—as much, namely, as was equal to what they would have made by tilling the fields.

9. "As to those who tilled the fields, each husbandman received a hundred *mâu*. When those *mâu* were manured, the best husbandmen of the highest class supported nine individuals, and those ranking next to them supported eight. The best husbandmen of the second class supported seven individuals, and those ranking next to them supported six; while husbandmen of the lowest class only supported five. The salaries of the common people who were employed about the government offices were regulated according to these differences."

III

FRIENDSHIP MUST HAVE REFERENCE TO THE VIRTUE OF THE FRIEND. THERE MAY BE NO ASSUMPTION ON THE GROUND OF ONE'S OWN ADVANTAGES.

1. Wan Chang asked Mencius, saying, "I venture to ask the principles of friendship." Mencius replied, "Friendship should be maintained without any presumption on the ground of one's superior age, or station, or the circumstances of his relatives. Friendship with a man is friendship with his virtue, and does not admit of assumptions of superiority.

2. "There was Măng Hsien, chief of a family of a hundred chariots. He had five friends, namely, Yŏ-chăng Chiû, Mû Chung, and three others whose names I have forgotten. With those five men Hsien maintained a friendship, because they thought nothing about his

family. If they had thought about his family, he would not have maintained his friendship with them.

3. "Not only has the chief of a family of a hundred chariots acted thus. The same thing was exemplified by the sovereign of a small State. The duke Hûi of Pî said, "I treat Tsze-sze as my Teacher, and Yen Pan as my Friend. As to Wang Shun and Ch'ang Hsî, they serve me."

4. "Not only has the sovereign of a small State acted thus. The same thing has been exemplified by the sovereign of a large State. There was the duke P'ing of Tsin with Hâi T'ăng: when T'ăng told him to come into his house, he came; when he told him to be seated, he sat; when he told him to eat, he ate. There might only be coarse rice and soup of vegetables, but he always ate his fill, not daring to do otherwise. Here, however, he stopped, and went no farther. He did not call him to share any of Heaven's places, or to govern any of Heaven's offices, or to partake of any of Heaven's emoluments. His conduct was but a scholar's honoring virtue and talents, not the honoring them proper to a king or a duke.

5. "Shun went up to court and saw the sovereign, who lodged him as his son-in-law in the second palace. The sovereign also enjoyed there Shun's hospitality. Alternately he was host and guest. Here was the sovereign maintaining friendship with a private man.

6. "Respect shown by inferiors to superiors is called giving to the noble the observance due to rank. Respect shown by superiors to inferiors is called giving honor to talents and virtue. The rightness in each case is the same."

IV

HOW MENCIUS DEFENDED THE ACCEPTING PRESENTS FROM THE PRINCES, OPPRESSORS OF THE PEOPLE.

1. Wan Chang asked Mencius, saying, "I venture to ask what feeling of the mind is expressed in the presents of friendship?" Mencius replied, "The feeling of respect."

2. "How is it," pursued Chang, "that the declining a present is accounted disrespectful?" The answer was, "When one of honorable rank presents a gift, to say in the mind, 'Was the way in which he got this righteous or not? I must know this before I can receive it'—this is deemed disrespectful, and therefore presents are not declined."

3. Wan Chang asked again, "When one does not take on him in so many express words to refuse the gift, but having declined it in his heart, saying, 'It was taken by him unrighteously from the people,' and then assigns some other reason for not receiving it—is not this a proper course?" Mencius said, "When the donor offers it on a ground of reason, and his manner of doing so is according to propriety—in such a case Confucius would have received it."

4. Wan Chang said, "Here now is one who stops and robs people outside the gates of the city. He offers his gift on a ground of reason, and does so in a manner according to propriety—would the reception of it so acquired by robbery be proper?" Mencius replied, "It would not be proper. in 'The Announcement to Kang' it is said, 'When men kill others, and roll over their bodies to take their property, being reckless and fearless of death, among all the people there are none but detest them'—thus, such characters are to be put to death, without waiting to give them warning. Yin received this rule from Hsiâ and Châu received it from Yin. It cannot be questioned, and to the present day is clearly acknowledged. How can the grift of a robber be received?"

5. Chang said, "The princes of the present day take from their people just as a robber despoils his victim. Yet if they put a good face of propriety on their gifts, then the superior man receives them. I venture to ask how you explain this." Mencius answered, "Do you think that, if there should arise a truly royal sovereign, he would collect the princes of the present day, and put them all to death? Or would he admonish them, and then, on their not changing their ways, put them to death? Indeed, to call every one who takes what does not properly belong to him a robber, is pushing a point of resemblance to the utmost, and insisting on the most refined idea of righteousness. When Confucius was in office in Lû, the people struggled together for the game taken in hunting, and he also did the same. If that struggling for the captured game was proper, how much more may the gifts of the princes be received!"

6. Chang urged, "Then are we to suppose that when Confucius held office, it was not with the view to carry his doctrines into practice?" "It was with that view," Mencius replied, and Chang rejoined, "If the practice of his doctrines was his business, what had he to do with that struggling for the captured game?" Mencius said, "Confucius first rectified his vessels of sacrifice according to the registers, and

did not fill them so rectified with food gathered from every quarter." "But why did he not go away?" "He wished to make a trial of carrying his doctrines into practice. When that trial was sufficient to show that they could be practiced and they were still not practiced, then he went away, and thus it was that he never completed in any State a residence of three years.

7. "Confucius took office when he saw that the practice of his doctrines was likely; he took office when his reception was proper; he took office when he was supported by the State. In the case of his relation to Chî Hwan, he took office, seeing that the practice of his doctrines was likely. With the duke Ling of Wei he took office, because his reception was proper. With the duke Hsiâo of Wei he took office, because he was maintained by the State."

V

HOW OFFICE MAY BE TAKEN ON ACCOUNT OF POVERTY, BUT ONLY ON CERTAIN CONDITIONS.

1. Mencius said, "Office is not sought on account of poverty, yet there are times when one seeks office on that account. Marriage is not entered into for the sake of being attended to by the wife, yet there are times when one marries on that account.

2. "He who takes office on account of his poverty must decline an honorable situation and occupy a low one; he must decline riches and prefer to be poor.

3. "What office will be in harmony with this declining an honorable situation and occupying a low one, this declining riches and preferring to be poor? Such a one as that of guarding the gates, or beating the watchman's stick.

4. "Confucius was once keeper of stores, and he then said, 'My calculations must be all right. That is all I have to care about.' He was once in charge of the public fields, and he then said, 'The oxen and sheep must be fat and strong, and superior. That is all I have to care about.'

5. "When one is in a low situation, to speak of high matters is a crime. When a scholar stands in a prince's court, and his principles are not carried into practice, it is a shame to him."

VI

HOW A SCHOLAR MAY NOT BECOME A DEPENDENT BY ACCEPTING
PAY WITHOUT OFFICE, AND HOW THE REPEATED PRESENTS OF A
PRINCE TO A SCHOLAR MUST BE MADE.

1. Wan Chang said, "What is the reason that a scholar does not accept a stated support from a prince?" Mencius replied, "He does not presume to do so. When a prince loses his State, and then accepts a stated support from another prince, this is in accordance with propriety. But for a scholar to accept such support from any of the princes is not in accordance with propriety."

2. Wan Chang said, "If the prince send him a present of grain, for instance, does he accept it?" "He accepts it," answered Mencius. "On what principle of righteousness does he accept it?" "Why—the prince ought to assist the people in their necessities."

3. Chang pursued, "Why is it that the scholar will thus accept the prince's help, but will not accept his pay?" The answer was, "He does not presume to do so." "I venture to ask why he does not presume to do so." "Even the keepers of the gates, with their watchmen's sticks, have their regular offices for which they can take their support from the prince. He who without a regular office should receive the pay of the prince must be deemed disrespectful."

4. Chang asked, "If the prince sends a scholar a present, he accepts it—I do not know whether this present may be constantly repeated." Mencius answered, "There was the conduct of the duke Mû to Tsze-sze—he made frequent inquiries after Tsze-sze's health, and sent him frequent presents of cooked meat. Tsze-sze was displeased; and at length, having motioned to the messenger to go outside the great door, he bowed his head to the ground with his face to the north, did obeisance twice, and declined the gift, saying, 'From this time forth I shall know that the prince supports me as a dog or a horse.' And so from that time a servant was no more sent with the presents. When a prince professes to be pleased with a man of talents and virtue, and can neither promote him to office, nor support him in the proper way, can he be said to be pleased with him?"

5. Chang said, "I venture to ask how the sovereign of a State, when he wishes to support a superior man, must proceed, that he may be said to do so in the proper way?" Mencius answered, "At first, the present must be offered with the prince's commission, and the

scholar, making obeisance twice with his head bowed to the ground, will receive it. But after this the storekeeper will continue to send grain, and the master of the kitchen to send meat, presenting it as if without the prince's express commission. Tsze-sze considered that the meat from the prince's caldron, giving him the annoyance of constantly doing obeisance, was not the way to support a superior man.

6. "There was Yâo's conduct to Shun: He caused his nine sons to serve him, and gave him his two daughters in marriage; he caused the various officers, oxen and sheep, storehouses and granaries, all to be prepared to support Shun amid the channeled fields, and then he raised him to the most exalted situation. From this we have the expression — 'The honoring of virtue and talents proper to a king or a duke.'"

VII

WHY A SCHOLAR SHOULD DECLINE GOING TO SEE THE PRINCES,
WHEN CALLED BY THEM.

1. Wan Chang said, "I venture to ask what principle of righteousness is involved in a scholar's not going to see the princes?" Mencius replied, "A scholar residing in the city is called 'a minister of the market-place and well,' and one residing in the country is called 'a minister of the grass and plants.' In both cases he is a common man, and it is the rule of propriety that common men, who have not presented the introductory present and become ministers, should not presume to have interviews with the prince."

2. Wan Chang said, "If a common man is called to perform any service, he goes and performs it — how is it that a scholar, when the prince, wishing to see him, calls him to his presence, refuses to go?" Mencius replied, "It is right to go and perform the service; it would not be right to go and see the prince.

3. "And," added Mencius, "on what account is it that the prince wishes to see the scholar?" "Because of his extensive information, or because of his talents and virtue," was the reply. "If because of his extensive information," said Mencius, "such a person is a teacher, and the sovereign would not call him — how much less may any of the princes do so? If because of his talents and virtue, then I have

not heard of anyone wishing to see a person with those qualities, and calling him to his presence.

4. "During the frequent interviews of the duke Mû with Tsze-sze, he one day said to him, 'Anciently, princes of a thousand chariots have yet been on terms of friendship with scholars—what do you think of such an intercourse?' Tsze-sze was displeased, and said, 'The ancients have said, "The scholar should be served": how should they have merely said that he should be made a friend of?' When Tsze-sze was thus displeased, did he not say within himself—'With regard to our stations, you are sovereign, and I am subject. How can I presume to be on terms of friendship with my sovereign! With regard to our virtue, you ought to make me your master. How can you be on terms of friendship with me?' Thus, when a ruler of a thousand chariots sought to be on terms of friendship with a scholar, he could not obtain his wish: how much less could he call him to his presence!

5. "The duke Ching of Ch'î, once, when he was hunting, called his forester to him by a flag. The forester would not come, and the duke was going to kill him. With reference to this incident, Confucius said, 'The determined officer never forgets that his end may be in a ditch or a stream; the brave officer never forgets that he may lose his head.' What was it in the forester that Confucius thus approved? He approved his not going to the duke, when summoned by the article which was not appropriate to him."

6. Chang said, "May I ask with what a forester should be summoned?" Mencius replied, "With a skin cap. A common man should be summoned with a plain banner; a scholar who has taken office, with one having dragons embroidered on it; and a great officer, with one having feathers suspended from the top of the staff.

7. "When the forester was summoned with the article appropriate to the summoning of a great officer, he would have died rather than presume to go. If a common man were summoned with the article appropriate to the summoning of a scholar, how could he presume to go? How much more may we expect this refusal to go, when a man of talents and virtue is summoned in a way which is inappropriate to his character!

8. "When a prince wishes to see a man of talents and virtue, and does not take the proper course to get his wish, it is as if he wished him to enter his palace, and shut the door against him. Now, righteousness

is the way, and propriety is the door, but it is only the superior man who can follow this way, and go out and in by this door. It is said in the Book of Poetry,

> The way to Châu is level like a whetstone,
> And straight as an arrow.
> The officers tread it,
> And the lower people see it."

9. Wan Chang said, "When Confucius received the prince's message calling him, he went without waiting for his carriage. Doing so, did Confucius do wrong?" Mencius replied, "Confucius was in office, and had to observe its appropriate duties. And moreover, he was summoned on the business of his office."

VIII

THE REALIZATION OF THE GREATEST ADVANTAGES OF FRIENDSHIP, AND THAT IT IS DEPENDENT ON ONE'S SELF.

1. Mencius said to Wan Chang, "The scholar whose virtue is most distinguished in a village shall make friends of all the virtuous scholars in the village. The scholar whose virtue is most distinguished throughout a State shall make friends of all the virtuous scholars of that State. The scholar whose virtue is most distinguished throughout the kingdom shall make friends of all the virtuous scholars of the kingdom.

2. "When a scholar feels that his friendship with all the virtuous scholars of the kingdom is not sufficient to satisfy him, he proceeds to ascend to consider the men of antiquity. He repeats their poems, and reads their books, and as he does not know what they were as men, to ascertain this, he considers their history. This is to ascend and make friends of the men of antiquity."

IX

THE DUTIES OF THE DIFFERENT CLASSES OH HIGH MINISTERS.

1. The king Hsüan of Ch'î asked about the office of high ministers. Mencius said, "Which high ministers is your Majesty asking about?" "Are there differences among them?" inquired the king. "There are" was the reply. "There are the high ministers who are noble and relatives of the prince, and there are those who are of a different surname." The king said, "I beg to ask about the high ministers who

are noble and relatives of the prince." Mencius answered, "If the prince have great faults, they ought to remonstrate with him, and if he do not listen to them after they have done so again and again, they ought to dethrone him."

2. The king on this looked moved, and changed countenance.

3. Mencius said, "Let not your Majesty be offended. You asked me, and I dare not answer but according to truth."

4. The king's countenance became composed, and he then begged to ask about high ministers who were of a different surname from the prince. Mencius said, "When the prince has faults, they ought to remonstrate with him; and if he do not listen to them after they have done this again and again, they ought to leave the State."

BOOK VI

KÂO TSZE

PART I

I

THAT BENEVOLENCE AND RIGHTEOUSNESS ARE NO UNNATURAL
PRODUCTS OF HUMAN NATURE.

1. The philosopher Kâo said, "Man's nature is like the ch'î-willow, and righteousness is like a cup or a bowl. The fashioning benevolence and righteousness out of man's nature is like the making cups and bowls from the ch'î-willow."

2. Mencius replied, "Can you, leaving untouched the nature of the willow, make with it cups and bowls? You must do violence and injury to the willow, before you can make cups and bowls with it. If you must do violence and injury to the willow in order to make cups and bowls with it, on your principles you must in the same way do violence and injury to humanity in order to fashion from it benevolence and righteousness! Your words, alas, would certainly lead all men on to reckon benevolence and righteousness to be calamities."

II

MAN'S NATURE IS NOT INDIFFERENT TO GOOD AND EVIL.
ITS PROPER TENDENCY IS TO GOOD.

1. The philosopher Kâo said, "Man's nature is like water whirling round in a corner. Open a passage for it to the east, and it will flow to the east; open a passage for it to the west, and it will flow to the west. Man's nature is indifferent to good and evil, just as the water is indifferent to the east and west."

2. Mencius replied, "Water indeed will flow indifferently to the east or west, but will it flow indifferently up or down? The tendency of man's nature to good is like the tendency of water to flow downwards.

There are none but have this tendency to good, just as all water flows downwards.

3. "Now by striking water and causing it to leap up, you may make it go over your forehead, and, by damming and leading it you may force it up a hill—but are such movements according to the nature of water? It is the force applied which causes them. When men are made to do what is not good, their nature is dealt with in this way."

III

THE NATURE IS NOT TO BE CONFOUNDED WITH THE PHENOMENA OF LIFE.

1. The philosopher Kâo said, "Life is what we call nature."

2. Mencius asked him, "Do you say that by nature you mean life, just as you say that white is white?" "Yes, I do," was the reply. Mencius added, "Is the whiteness of a white feather like that of white snow, and the whiteness of white snow like that of white jade?" Kâo again said, "Yes."

3. "Very well," pursued Mencius. "Is the nature of a dog like the nature of an ox, and the nature of an ox like the nature of a man?"

IV

THAT THE BENEVOLENT AFFECTIONS AND THE DISCRIMINATIONS OF WHAT IS RIGHT ARE EQUALLY INTERNAL.

1. The philosopher Kâo said, "To enjoy food and delight in colors is nature. Benevolence is internal and not external; righteousness is external and not internal."

2. Mencius asked him, "What is the ground of your saying that benevolence is internal and righteousness external?" He replied, "There is a man older than I, and I give honor to his age. It is not that there is first in me a principle of such reverence to age. It is just as when there is a white man, and I consider him white; according as he is so externally to me. On this account, I pronounce of righteousness that it is external."

3. Mencius said, "There is no difference between our pronouncing a white horse to be white and our pronouncing a white man to be white. But is there no difference between the regard with which we acknowledge the age of an old horse and that with which we

acknowledge the age of an old man? And what is it which is called righteousness? The fact of a man's being old? Or the fact of our giving honor to his age?"

4. Kâo said, "There is my younger brother—I love him. But the younger brother of a man of Ch'in I do not love: that is, the feeling is determined by myself, and therefore I say that benevolence is internal. On the other hand, I give honor to an old man of Ch'û, and I also give honor to an old man of my own people: that is, the feeling is determined by the age, and therefore I say that righteousness is external."

5. Mencius answered him, "Our enjoyment of meat roasted by a man of Ch'in does not differ from our enjoyment of meat roasted by ourselves. Thus, what you insist on takes place also in the case of such things, and will you say likewise that our enjoyment of a roast is external?"

V

THE SAME SUBJECT—THE DISCRIMINATIONS OF WHAT IS RIGHT ARE FROM WITHIN.

1. The disciple Măng Chî asked Kung-tû, saying, "On what ground is it said that righteousness is internal?"

2. Kung-tû replied, "We therein act out our feeling of respect, and therefore it is said to be internal."

3. The other objected, "Suppose the case of a villager older than your elder brother by one year, to which of them would you show the greater respect?" "To my brother," was the reply. "But for which of them would you first pour out wine at a feast?" "For the villager." Măng Chî argued, "Now your feeling of reverence rests on the one, and now the honor due to age is rendered to the other—this is certainly determined by what is without, and does not proceed from within."

4. Kung-tû was unable to reply, and told the conversation to Mencius. Mencius said, "You should ask him, 'Which do you respect most— your uncle, or your younger brother?' He will answer, 'My uncle.' Ask him again, 'If your younger brother be personating a dead ancestor, to which do you show the greater respect—to him or to your uncle?' He will say, 'To my younger brother.' You can go on, 'But where is the respect due, as you said, to your uncle?' He will

reply to this, 'I show the respect to my younger brother, because of the position which he occupies,' and you can likewise say, 'So my respect to the villager is because of the position which he occupies. Ordinarily, my respect is rendered to my elder brother; for a brief season, on occasion, it is rendered to the villager.'"

5. Măng Chî heard this and observed, "When respect is due to my uncle, I respect him, and when respect is due to my younger brother, I respect him—the thing is certainly determined by what is without, and does not proceed from within." Kung-tû replied, "In winter we drink things hot, in summer we drink things cold; and so, on your principle, eating and drinking also depend on what is external!"

VI

EXPLANATION OF MENCIUS'S OWN DOCTRINE
THAT MAN'S NATURE IS GOOD.

1. The disciple Kung-tû said, "The philosopher Kâo says, 'Man's nature is neither good nor bad.'

2. "Some say, 'Man's nature may be made to practice good, and it may be made to practice evil, and accordingly, under Wăn and Wû, the people loved what was good, while under Yû and Lî, they loved what was cruel.'

3. "Some say, 'The nature of some is good, and the nature of others is bad.' Hence it was that under such a sovereign as Yâo there yet appeared Hsiang; that with such a father as Kû-sâu there yet appeared Shun; and that with Châu for their sovereign, and the son of their elder brother besides, there were found Ch'î, the viscount of Wei, and the prince Pî-Kan.

4. "And now you say, 'The nature is good.' Then are all those wrong?"

5. Mencius said, "From the feelings proper to it, it is constituted for the practice of what is good. This is what I mean in saying that the nature is good.

6. "If men do what is not good, the blame cannot be imputed to their natural powers.

7. "The feeling of commiseration belongs to all men; so does that of shame and dislike; and that of reverence and respect; and that of approving and disapproving. The feeling of commiseration implies the principle of benevolence; that of shame and dislike, the principle

of righteousness; that of reverence and respect, the principle of propriety; and that of approving and disapproving, the principle of knowledge. Benevolence, righteousness, propriety, and knowledge are not infused into us from without. We are certainly furnished with them. And a different view is simply owing to want of reflection. Hence it is said, 'Seek and you will find them. Neglect and you will lose them.' Men differ from one another in regard to them—some as much again as others, some five times as much, and some to an incalculable amount: it is because they cannot carry out fully their natural powers.

8. "It is said in the Book of Poetry,

> Heaven in producing mankind,
> Gave them their various faculties and relations with their
>   specific laws.
> These are the invariable rules of nature for all to hold,
> And all love this admirable virtue.

Confucius said, 'The maker of this ode knew indeed the principle of our nature!' We may thus see that every faculty and relation must have its law, and since there are invariable rules for all to hold, they consequently love this admirable virtue."

VII

ALL MEN ARE THE SAME IN MIND—SAGES AND OTHERS.
IT FOLLOWS THAT THE NATURE OF ALL MEN, LIKE THAT
OF THE SAGES, IS GOOD.

1. Mencius said, "In good years the children of the people are most of them good, while in bad years the most of them abandon themselves to evil. It is not owing to any difference of their natural powers conferred by Heaven that they are thus different. The abandonment is owing to the circumstances through which they allow their minds to be ensnared and drowned in evil.

2. "There now is barley. Let it be sown and covered up; the ground being the same, and the time of sowing likewise the same, it grows rapidly up, and, when the full time is come, it is all found to be ripe. Although there may be inequalities of produce, that is owing to the difference of the soil, as rich or poor, to the unequal nourishment afforded by the rains and dews, and to the different ways in which man has performed his business in reference to it.

3. "Thus all things which are the same in kind are like to one another—why should we doubt in regard to man, as if he were a solitary exception to this? The sage and we are the same in kind.

4. "In accordance with this the scholar Lung said, 'If a man make hempen sandals without knowing the size of people's feet, yet I know that he will not make them like baskets.' Sandals are all like one another, because all men's feet are like one another.

5. "So with the mouth and flavors—all mouths have the same relishes. Yî-yâ only apprehended before me what my mouth relishes. Suppose that his mouth in its relish for flavors differed from that of other men, as is the case with dogs or horses which are not the same in kind with us, why should all men be found following Yî-yâ in their relishes? In the matter of tastes all the people model themselves after Yî-yâ; that is, the mouths of all men are like one another.

6. "And so also it is with the ear. In the matter of sounds, the whole people model themselves after the music-master K'wang; that is, the ears of all men are like one another.

7. "And so also it is with the eye. In the case of Tsze-tû, there is no man but would recognize that he was beautiful. Anyone who would not recognize the beauty of Tsze-tû must have no eyes.

8. "Therefore I say—Men's mouths agree in having the same relishes; their ears agree in enjoying the same sounds; their eyes agree in recognizing the same beauty: shall their minds alone be without that which the similarly approve? What is it then of which they similarly approve? It is, I say, the principles of our nature, and the determinations of righteousness. The sages only apprehended before me that of which my mind approves along with other men. Therefore the principles of our nature and the determinations of righteousness are agreeable to my mind, just as the flesh of grass and grain-fed animals is agreeable to my mouth."

VIII

HOW IT IS THAT THE NATURE PROPERLY GOOD COMES TO APPEAR AS IF IT WERE NOT SO—FROM NOT RECEIVING ITS PROPER NOURISHMENT.

1. Mencius said, "The trees of the Niû mountain were once beautiful. Being situated, however, in the borders of a large State, they were hewn down with axes and bills—and could they retain their beauty?

Still through the activity of the vegetative life day and night, and the nourishing influence of the rain and dew, they were not without buds and sprouts springing forth, but then came the cattle and goats and browsed upon them. To these things is owing the bare and stripped appearance of the mountain, and when people now see it, they think it was never finely wooded. But is this the nature of the mountain?

2. "And so also of what properly belongs to man—shall it be said that the mind of any man was without benevolence and righteousness? The way in which a man loses his proper goodness of mind is like the way in which the trees are denuded by axes and bills. Hewn down day after day, can it—the mind—retain its beauty? But there is a development of its life day and night, and in the calm air of the morning, just between night and day, the mind feels in a degree those desires and aversions which are proper to humanity, but the feeling is not strong, and it is fettered and destroyed by what takes place during the day. This fettering taking place again and again, the restorative influence of the night is not sufficient to preserve the proper goodness of the mind; and when this proves insufficient for that purpose, the nature becomes not much different from that of the irrational animals, and when people now see it, they think that it never had those powers which I assert. But does this condition represent the feelings proper to humanity?

3. "Therefore, if it receive its proper nourishment, there is nothing which will not grow. If it lose its proper nourishment, there is nothing which will not decay away.

4. "Confucius said, 'Hold it fast, and it remains with you. Let it go, and you lose it. Its outgoing and incoming cannot be defined as to time or place.' It is the mind of which this is said!"

IX

ILLUSTRATES THE LAST CHAPTER. HOW THE KING OF CH'Î'S WANT OF WISDOM WAS OWING TO NEGLECT AND BAD ASSOCIATIONS.

1. Mencius said, "It is not to be wondered at that the king is not wise!

2. "Suppose the case of the most easily growing thing in the world—if you let it have one day's genial heat, and then expose it for ten days to cold, it will not be able to grow. It is but seldom that I have an audience of the king, and when I retire, there come all those who act

upon him like the cold. Though I succeed in bringing out some buds of goodness, of what avail is it?

3. "Now chess-playing is but a small art, but without his whole mind being given, and his will bent, to it, a man cannot succeed at it. Chess Ch'iû is the best chess-player in all the kingdom. Suppose that he is teaching two men to play. The one gives to the subject his whole mind and bends to it all his will, doing nothing but listening to Chess Ch'iû. The other, although he seems to be listening to him, has his whole mind running on a swan which he thinks is approaching, and wishes to bend his bow, adjust the string to the arrow, and shoot it. Although he is learning along with the other, he does not come up to him. Why? Because his intelligence is not equal? Not so."

X

THAT IT IS PROPER TO MAN'S NATURE TO LOVE RIGHTEOUSNESS MORE THAN LIFE, AND HOW IT IS THAT MANY ACT AS IF IT WERE NOT SO.

1. Mencius said, "I like fish, and I also like bear's paws. If I cannot have the two together, I will let the fish go, and take the bear's paws. So, I like life, and I also like righteousness. If I cannot keep the two together, I will let life go, and choose righteousness.

2. "I like life indeed, but there is that which I like more than life, and therefore, I will not seek to possess it by any improper ways. I dislike death indeed, but there is that which I dislike more than death, and therefore there are occasions when I will not avoid danger.

3. "If among the things which man likes there were nothing which he liked more than life, why should he not use every means by which he could preserve it? If among the things which man dislikes there were nothing which he disliked more than death, why should he not do everything by which he could avoid danger?

4. "There are cases when men by a certain course might preserve life, and they do not employ it; when by certain things they might avoid danger, and they will not do them.

5. "Therefore, men have that which they like more than life, and that which they dislike more than death. They are not men of distinguished talents and virtue only who have this mental nature. All men have it; what belongs to such men is simply that they do not lose it.

6. "Here are a small basket of rice and a platter of soup, and the case is one in which the getting them will preserve life, and the want of them will be death—if they are offered with an insulting voice, even a tramper will not receive them, or if you first tread upon them, even a beggar will not stoop to take them.

7. "And yet a man will accept of ten thousand *chung*, without any consideration of propriety or righteousness. What can the ten thousand *chung* add to him? When he takes them, is it not that he may obtain beautiful mansions, that he may secure the services of wives and concubines, or that the poor and needy of his acquaintance may be helped by him?

8. "In the former case the offered bounty was not received, though it would have saved from death, and now the emolument is taken for the sake of beautiful mansions. The bounty that would have preserved from death was not received, and the emolument is taken to get the service of wives and concubines. The bounty that would have saved from death was not received, and the emolument is taken that one's poor and needy acquaintance may be helped by him. Was it then not possible likewise to decline this? This is a case of what is called—'Losing the proper nature of one's mind.'"

XI

HOW MEN HAVING LOST THE PROPER QUALITIES OF THEIR
NATURE SHOULD SEEK TO RECOVER THEM.

1. Mencius said, "Benevolence is man's mind, and righteousness is man's path.

2. "How lamentable is it to neglect the path and not pursue it, to lose this mind and not know to seek it again!

3. "When men's fowls and dogs are lost, they know to seek for them again, but they lose their mind, and do not know to seek for it.

4. "The great end of learning is nothing else but to seek for the lost mind."

XII

HOW MEN ARE SENSIBLE OF BODILY, AND NOT OF
MENTAL OR MORAL, DEFECTS.

1. Mencius said, "Here is a man whose fourth finger is bent and cannot be stretched out straight. It is not painful, nor does it incommode his

business, and yet if there be anyone who can make it straight, he will not think the way from Ch'in to Ch'û far to go to him; because his finger is not like the finger of other people.

2. "When a man's finger is not like those of other people, he knows to feel dissatisfied, but if his mind be not like that of other people, he does not know to feel dissatisfaction. This is called—'Ignorance of the relative importance of things.'"

XIII

MEN'S EXTREME WANT OF THOUGHT IN REGARD TO THE
CULTIVATION OF THEMSELVES.

Mencius said, "Anybody who wishes to cultivate the *t'ung* or the *tsze*, which may be grasped with both hands, perhaps with one, knows by what means to nourish them. In the case of their own persons, men do not know by what means to nourish them. Is it to be supposed that their regard of their own persons is inferior to their regard for a *t'ung* or *tsze*? Their want of reflection is extreme."

XIV

THE ATTENTION GIVEN BY MEN TO THE NOURISHMENT OF THE
DIFFERENT PARTS OF THEIR NATURE MUST BE REGULATED BY
THE RELATIVE IMPORTANCE OF THOSE PARTS.

1. Mencius said, "There is no part of himself which a man does not love, and as he loves all, so he must nourish all. There is not an inch of skin which he does not love, and so there is not an inch of skin which he will not nourish. For examining whether his way of nourishing be good or not, what other rule is there but this, that he determine by reflecting on himself where it should be applied?

2. "Some parts of the body are noble, and some ignoble; some great, and some small. The great must not be injured for the small, nor the noble for the ignoble. He who nourishes the little belonging to him is a little man, and he who nourishes the great is a great man.

3. "Here is a plantation-keeper, who neglects his *wû* and *chiâ*, and cultivates his sour jujube-trees—he is a poor plantation-keeper.

4. "He who nourishes one of his fingers, neglecting his shoulders or his back, without knowing that he is doing so, is a man who resembles a hurried wolf.

5. "A man who only eats and drinks is counted mean by others — because he nourishes what is little to the neglect of what is great.

6. "If a man, fond of his eating and drinking, were not to neglect what is of more importance, how should his mouth and belly be considered as no more than an inch of skin?"

XV

HOW SOME ARE GREAT MEN, LORDS OF REASON, AND SOME ARE LITTLE MEN, SLAVES OF SENSE.

1. The disciple Kung-tû said, "All are equally men, but some are great men, and some are little men — how is this?" Mencius replied, "Those who follow that part of themselves which is great are great men; those who follow that part which is little are little men."

2. Kung-tû pursued, "All are equally men, but some follow that part of themselves which is great, and some follow that part which is little — how is this?" Mencius answered, "The senses of hearing and seeing do not think, and are obscured by external things. When one thing comes into contact with another, as a matter of course it leads it away. To the mind belongs the office of thinking. By thinking, it gets the right view of things; by neglecting to think, it fails to do this. These — the senses and the mind — are what Heaven has given to us. Let a man first stand fast in the supremacy of the nobler part of his constitution, and the inferior part will not be able to take it from him. It is simply this which makes the great man."

XVI

THERE IS A NOBILITY THAT IS OF HEAVEN, AND A NOBILITY THAT IS OF MAN. THE NEGLECT OF THE FORMER LEADS TO THE LOSS OF THE LATTER.

1. Mencius said, "There is a nobility of Heaven, and there is a nobility of man. Benevolence, righteousness, self-consecration, and fidelity, with unwearied joy in these virtues — these constitute the nobility of Heaven. To be a *kung*, a *ch'ing*, or a *tâ-fû* — this constitutes the nobility of man.

2. "The men of antiquity cultivated their nobility of Heaven, and the nobility of man came to them in its train.

3. "The men of the present day cultivate their nobility of Heaven in order to seek for the nobility of man, and when they have obtained that, they throw away the other: their delusion is extreme. The issue is simply this, that they must lose that nobility of man as well."

XVII

THE TRUE HONOR WHICH MEN SHOULD DESIRE.

1. Mencius said, "To desire to be honored is the common mind of men. And all men have in themselves that which is truly honorable. Only they do not think of it.

2. "The honor which men confer is not good honor. Those whom Châo the Great ennobles he can make mean again.

3. "It is said in the Book of Poetry,

He has filled us with his wine,
He has satiated us with his goodness.

'Satiated us with his goodness,' that is, satiated us with benevolence and righteousness, and he who is so satiated, consequently, does not wish for the fat meat and fine millet of men. A good reputation and far-reaching praise fall to him, and he does not desire the elegant embroidered garments of men."

XVIII

IT IS NECESSARY TO PRACTICE BENEVOLENCE WITH ALL ONE'S MIGHT. THIS ONLY WILL PRESERVE IT.

1. Mencius said, "Benevolence subdues its opposite just as water subdues fire. Those, however, who nowadays practice benevolence do it as if with one cup of water they could save a whole wagon-load of fuel which was on fire, and when the flames were not extinguished, were to say that water cannot subdue fire. This conduct, moreover, greatly encourages those who are not benevolent.

2. "The final issue will simply be this—the loss of that small amount of benevolence."

XIX

BENEVOLENCE MUST BE MATURED.

Mencius said, "Of all seeds the best are the five kinds of grain, yet if they be not ripe, they are not equal to the *t'î* or the *pâi*. So, the value of benevolence depends entirely on its being brought to maturity."

XX

LEARNING MUST NOT BE BY HALVES.

1. Mencius said, "Î, in teaching men to shoot, made it a rule to draw the bow to the full, and his pupils also did the same.

2. "A master-workman, in teaching others, uses the compass and square, and his pupils do the same."

KÂO TSZE

PART II

I

THE IMPORTANCE OF OBSERVING THE RULES OF PROPRIETY, AND, WHEN THEY MAY BE DISREGARDED, THE EXCEPTION WILL BE FOUND TO PROVE THE RULE. EXTREME CASES MAY NOT BE PRESSED TO INVALIDATE THE PRINCIPLE.

1. A man of Zăn asked the disciple Wû-lû, saying, "Is an observance of the rules of propriety in regard to eating, or eating merely, the more important?" The answer was, "The observance of the rules of propriety is the more important."

2. "Is the gratifying the appetite of sex, or the doing so only according to the rules of propriety, the more important?" The answer again was, "The observance of the rules of propriety in the matter is the more important."

3. The man pursued, "If the result of eating only according to the rules of propriety will be death by starvation, while by disregarding those rules we may get food, must they still be observed in such a case? If according to the rule that he shall go in person to meet his wife a man cannot get married, while by disregarding that rule he may get married, must he still observe the rule in such a case?"

4. Wû-lû was unable to reply to these questions, and the next day he went to Tsâu, and told them to Mencius. Mencius said, "What difficulty is there in answering these inquiries?"

5. "If you do not adjust them at their lower extremities, but only put their tops on a level, a piece of wood an inch square may be made to be higher than the pointed peak of a high building.

6. "Gold is heavier than feathers—but does that saying have reference, on the one hand, to a single clasp of gold, and, on the other, to a wagon-load of feathers?

7. "If you take a case where the eating is of the utmost importance and the observing the rules of propriety is of little importance, and compare the things together, why stop with saying merely that the eating is more important? So, taking the case where the gratifying the appetite of sex is of the utmost importance and the observing the rules of propriety is of little importance, why stop with merely saying that the gratifying the appetite is the more important?

8. "Go and answer him thus, 'If, by twisting your elder brother's arm, and snatching from him what he is eating, you can get food for yourself, while, if you do not do so, you will not get anything to eat, will you so twist his arm? If by getting over your neighbor's wall, and dragging away his virgin daughter, you can get a wife, while if you do not do so, you will not be able to get a wife, will you so drag her away?'"

II

ALL MAY BECOME YÂOS AND SHUNS, AND TO BECOME SO,
THEY HAVE ONLY SINCERELY, AND IN THEMSELVES,
TO CULTIVATE YÂO AND SHUN'S PRINCIPLES AND WAYS.

1. Chiâo of Tsâo asked Mencius, saying, "It is said, 'All men may be Yâos and Shuns'—is it so?" Mencius replied, "It is."

2. Chiâo went on, "I have heard that King Wăn was ten cubits high, and T'ăng nine. Now I am nine cubits four inches in height. But I can do nothing but eat my millet. What am I to do to realize that saying?"

3. Mencius answered him, "What has this—the question of size—to do with the matter? It all lies simply in acting as such. Here is a man, whose strength was not equal to lift a duckling: he was then a man of no strength. But today he says, 'I can lift 3,000 catties' weight,' and he is a man of strength. And so, he who can lift the weight which Wû Hwo lifted is just another Wû Hwo. Why should a man make a want of ability the subject of his grief? It is only that he will not do the thing.

4. "To walk slowly, keeping behind his elders, is to perform the part of a younger. To walk quickly and precede his elders, is to violate the duty of a younger brother. Now, is it what a man cannot do—to walk slowly? It is what he does not do. The course of Yâo and Shun was simply that of filial piety and fraternal duty.

5. "Wear the clothes of Yâo, repeat the words of Yâo, and do the actions of Yâo, and you will just be a Yâo. And, if you wear the clothes of Chieh, repeat the words of Chieh, and do the actions of Chieh, you will just be a Chieh."

6. Chiâo said, "I shall be having an interview with the prince of Tsâu, and can ask him to let me have a house to lodge in. I wish to remain here, and receive instruction at your gate."

7. Mencius replied, "The way of truth is like a great road. It is not difficult to know it. The evil is only that men will not seek it. Do you go home and search for it, and you will have abundance of teachers."

III

EXPLANATION OF THE ODES HSIÂO P'ÂN AND K'ÂI FANG.
DISSATISFACTION WITH A PARENT IS NOT NECESSARILY UNFILIAL.

1. Kung-sun Ch'âu asked about an opinion of the scholar Kâo, saying, "Kâo observed, 'The Hsiâo P'ân is the ode of a little man.'" Mencius asked, "Why did he say so?" "Because of the murmuring which it expresses," was the reply.

2. Mencius answered, "How stupid was that old Kâo in dealing with the ode! There is a man here, and a native of Yüeh bends his bow to shoot him. I will advise him not to do so, but speaking calmly and smilingly—for no other reason but that he is not related to me. But if my own brother be bending his bow to shoot the man, then I will advise him not to do so, weeping and crying the while—for no other reason than that he is related to me. The dissatisfaction expressed in the Hsiâo P'ân is the working of relative affection, and that affection shows benevolence. Stupid indeed was old Kâo's criticism on the ode."

3. Ch'âu then said, "How is it that there is no dissatisfaction expressed in the K'âi Făng?"

4. Mencius replied, "The parent's fault referred to in the K'âi Fang is small; that referred to in the Hsiâo P'ân is great. Where the parent's fault was great, not to have murmured on account of it would have increased the want of natural affection. Where the parent's fault was small, to have murmured on account of it would have been to act like water which frets and foams about a stone that interrupts its course. To increase the want of natural affection would have been

unfilial, and to fret and foam in such a manner would also have been unfilial.

5. "Confucius said, 'Shun was indeed perfectly filial! And yet, when he was fifty, he was full of longing desire about his parents.'"

IV

MENCIUS'S WARNINGS TO SUNG K'ANG ON THE ERROR AND DANGER OF COUNSELING THE PRINCES FROM THE GROUND OF PROFIT, THE PROPER GROUND BEING THAT OF BENEVOLENCE AND RIGHTEOUSNESS.

1. Sung K'ang being about to go to Ch'û, Mencius met him in Shih-ch'iû.

2. "Master, where are you going?" asked Mencius.

3. K'ang replied, "I have heard that Ch'in and Ch'û are fighting together, and I am going to see the king of Ch'û and persuade him to cease hostilities. If he shall not be pleased with my advice, I shall go to see the king of Ch'in, and persuade him in the same way. Of the two kings I shall surely find that I can succeed with one of them."

4. Mencius said, "I will not venture to ask about the particulars, but I should like to hear the scope of your plan. What course will you take to try to persuade them?" K'ang answered, "I will tell them how unprofitable their course is to them." "Master," said Mencius, "your aim is great, but your argument is not good.

5. "If you, starting from the point of profit, offer your persuasive counsels to the kings of Ch'in and Ch'û, and if those kings are pleased with the consideration of profit so as to stop the movements of their armies, then all belonging to those armies will rejoice in the cessation of war, and find their pleasure in the pursuit of profit. Ministers will serve their sovereign for the profit of which they cherish the thought; sons will serve their fathers, and younger brothers will serve their elder brothers, from the same consideration: and the issue will be, that, abandoning benevolence and righteousness, sovereign and minister, father and son, younger brother and elder, will carry on all their intercourse with this thought of profit cherished in their breasts. But never has there been such a state of society, without ruin being the result of it.

6. "If you, starting from the ground of benevolence and righteousness, offer your counsels to the kings of Ch'in and Ch'û, and if those kings are pleased with the consideration of benevolence and righteousness so as to stop the operations of their armies, then all belonging to those armies will rejoice in the stopping from war, and find their pleasure in benevolence and righteousness. Ministers will serve their sovereign, cherishing the principles of benevolence and righteousness; sons will serve their fathers, and younger brothers will serve their elder brothers, in the same way: and so, sovereign and minister, father and son, elder brother and younger, abandoning the thought of profit, will cherish the principles of benevolence and righteousness, and carry on all their intercourse upon them. But never has there been such a state of society, without the State where it prevailed rising to the royal sway. Why must you use that word 'profit.'"

V

HOW MENCIUS REGULATED HIMSELF IN DIFFERENTLY ACKNOWLEDGING FAVORS WHICH HE RECEIVED.

1. When Mencius was residing in Tsâu, the younger brother of the chief of Zăn, who was guardian of Zăn at the time, paid his respects to him by a present of silks, which Mencius received, not going to acknowledge it. When he was sojourning in P'ing-lû, Ch'û, who was prime minister of the State, sent him a similar present, which he received in the same way.

2. Subsequently, going from Tsâu to Zăn, he visited the guardian; but when he went from Ping-lû to the capital of Ch'î, he did not visit the minister Ch'û. The disciple Wû-lû was glad, and said, "I have got an opportunity to obtain some instruction."

3. He asked accordingly, "Master, when you went to Zăn, you visited the chief's brother; and when you went to Ch'î, you did not visit Ch'û. Was it not because he is only the minister?"

4. Mencius replied, "No. It is said in the Book of History, 'In presenting an offering to a superior, most depends on the demonstrations of respect. If those demonstrations are not equal to the things offered, we say there is no offering, that is, there is no act of the will presenting the offering.'

5. "This is because the things so offered do not constitute an offering to a superior."

6. Wû-lû was pleased, and when someone asked him what Mencius meant, he said, "The younger of Zăn could not go to Tsâu, but the minister Ch'û might have gone to P'ing-lû."

VI

How Mencius replied to the insinuations of Shun-yü K'wan, condemning him for leaving office without accomplishing anything.

1. Shun-yü K'wan said, "He who makes fame and meritorious services his first objects, acts with a regard to others. He who makes them only secondary objects, acts with a regard to himself. You, master, were ranked among the three chief ministers of the State, but before your fame and services had reached either to the prince or the people, you have left your place. Is this indeed the way of the benevolent?"

2. Mencius replied, "There was Po'î—he abode in an inferior situation, and would not, with his virtue, serve a degenerate prince. There was Î Yin—he five times went to T'ăng, and five times went to Chieh. There was Hûi of Liû-hsiâ—he did not disdain to serve a vile prince, nor did he decline a small office. The courses pursued by those three worthies were different, but their aim was one. And what was their one aim? We must answer—'To be perfectly virtuous.' And so it is simply after this that superior men strive. Why must they all pursue the same course?"

3. K'wan pursued, "In the time of the duke Mû of Lû, the government was in the hands of Kung-î, while Tsze-liû and Tsze-sze were ministers. And yet, the dismemberment of Lû then increased exceedingly. Such was the case, a specimen how your men of virtue are of no advantage to a kingdom!"

4. Mencius said, "The prince of Yü did not use Pâi-lî Hsi, and thereby lost his State. The duke Mû of Chin used him, and became chief of all the princes. Ruin is the consequence of not employing men of virtue and talents—how can it rest with dismemberment merely?"

5. K'wan urged again, "Formerly, when Wang P'âo dwelt on the Ch'î, the people on the west of the Yellow River all became skillful at singing in his abrupt manner. When Mien Ch'ü lived in Kâo-T'ăng, the people in the parts of Ch'î on the west became skillful at singing

in his prolonged manner. The wives of Hwa Châu and Ch'î Liang bewailed their husbands so skillfully, that they changed the manners of the State. When there is the gift within, it manifests itself without. I have never seen the man who could do the deeds of a worthy, and did not realize the work of one. Therefore there are now no men of talents and virtue. If there were, I should know them."

6. Mencius answered, "When Confucius was chief minister of justice in Lû, the prince came not to follow his counsels. Soon after there was the solstitial sacrifice, and when a part of the flesh presented in sacrifice was not sent to him, he went away even without taking off his cap of ceremony. Those who did not know him supposed it was on account of the flesh. Those who knew him supposed that it was on account of the neglect of the usual ceremony. The fact was, that Confucius wanted to go away on occasion of some small offense, not wishing to do so without some apparent cause. All men cannot be expected to understand the conduct of a superior man."

VII

THE PROGRESS AND MANNER OF DEGENERACY FROM THE THREE KINGS TO THE FIVE CHIEFS OF THE PRINCES, AND FROM THE FIVE CHIEFS TO THE PRINCES AND OFFICERS OF MENCIUS'S TIME.

1. Mencius said, "The five chiefs of the princes were sinners against the three kings. The princes of the present day are sinners against the five chiefs. The great officers of the present day are sinners against the princes.

2. "The sovereign visited the princes, which was called 'A tour of Inspection.' The princes attended at the court of the sovereign, which was called 'Giving a report of office.' It was a custom in the spring to examine the plowing, and supply any deficiency of seed; and in autumn to examine the reaping, and assist where there was a deficiency of the crop. When the sovereign entered the boundaries of a State, if the new ground was being reclaimed, and the old fields well cultivated; if the old were nourished and the worthy honored; and if men of distinguished talents were placed in office: then the prince was rewarded—rewarded with an addition to his territory. On the other hand, if, on entering a State, the ground was found left wild or overrun with weeds; if the old were neglected and the worthy unhonored; and if the offices were filled with hard tax-gatherers: then the prince was reprimanded. If a prince once omitted his

attendance at court, he was punished by degradation of rank; if he did so a second time, be was deprived of a portion of his territory; if he did so a third time, the royal forces were set in motion, and he was removed from his government. Thus the sovereign commanded the punishment, but did not himself inflict it, while the princes inflicted the punishment, but did not command it. The five chiefs, however, dragged the princes to punish other princes, and hence I say that they were sinners against the three kings.

3. "Of the five chiefs the most powerful was the duke Hwan. At the assembly of the princes in K'wei-ch'iû, he bound the victim and placed the writing upon it, but did not slay it to smear their mouths with the blood. The first injunction in their agreement was — 'Slay the unfilial; change not the son who has been appointed heir; exalt not a concubine to be the wife.' The second was — 'Honor the worthy, and maintain the talented, to give distinction to the virtuous.' The third was — 'Respect the old, and be kind to the young. Be not forgetful of strangers and travelers.' The fourth was, 'Let not offices be hereditary, nor let officers be pluralists. In the selection of officers let the object be to get the proper men. Let not a ruler take it on himself to put to death a Great officer.' The fifth was — 'Follow no crooked policy in making embankments. Impose no restrictions on the sale of grain. Let there be no promotions without first announcing them to the sovereign.' It was then said, 'All we who have united in this agreement shall hereafter maintain amicable relations.' The princes of the present day all violate these five prohibitions, and therefore I say that the princes of the present day are sinners against the five chiefs.

4. "The crime of him who connives at, and aids, the wickedness of his prince is small, but the crime of him who anticipates and excites that wickedness is great. The officers of the present day all go to meet their sovereigns' wickedness, and therefore I say that the Great officers of the present day are sinners against the princes."

VIII

MENCIUS'S OPPOSITION TO THE WARLIKE AMBITION OF THE PRINCE OF LÛ AND HIS MINISTER SHĂN KÛ-LÎ.

1. The prince of Lû wanted to make the minister Shăn commander of his army.

2. Mencius said, "To employ an uninstructed people in war may be said to be destroying the people. A destroyer of the people would not have been tolerated in the times of Yâo and Shun.

3. "Though by a single battle you should subdue Ch'î, and get possession of Nan-yang, the thing ought not to be done."

4. Shǎn changed countenance, and said in displeasure, "This is what I, Kû-Lî, do not understand."

5. Mencius said, "I will lay the case plainly before you. The territory appropriated to the sovereign is 1,000 lî square. Without a thousand lî, he would not have sufficient for his entertainment of the princes. The territory appropriated to a Hâu is 100 lî square. Without 100 lî, he would not have sufficient wherewith to observe the statutes kept in his ancestral temple.

6. "When Châu-kung was invested with the principalily of Lû, it was a hundred lî square. The territory was indeed enough, but it was not more than 100 lî. When T'âi-kung was invested with the principality of Ch'î, it was 100 lî square. The territory was indeed enough, but it was not more than 100 lî.

7. "Now Lû is five times 100 lî square. If a true royal ruler were to arise, whether do you think that Lû would be diminished or increased by him?

8. "If it were merely taking the place from the one State to give it to the other, a benevolent man would not do it—how much less will he do so, when the end is to be sought by the slaughter of men!

9. "The way in which a superior man serves his prince contemplates simply the leading him in the right path, and directing his mind to benevolence."

IX

HOW THE MINISTERS OF MENCIUS'S TIME PANDERED TO THEIR SOVEREIGN'S THIRST FOR WEALTH.

1. Mencius said, "Those who nowadays serve their sovereigns say, 'We can for our sovereign enlarge the limits of the cultivated ground, and fill his treasuries and arsenals.' Such persons are nowadays called 'Good ministers,' but anciently they were called 'Robbers of the people.' If a sovereign follows not the right way, nor has his mind bent on benevolence, to seek to enrich him is to enrich a Chieh.

2. "Or they will say, 'We can for our sovereign form alliances with other States, so that our battles must be successful.' Such persons are nowadays called 'Good ministers,' but anciently they were called 'Robbers of the people.' If a sovereign follows not the right way, nor has his mind directed to benevolence, to seek to enrich him is to enrich a Chieh.

3. "Although a prince, pursuing the path of the present day, and not changing its practices, were to have the throne given to him, he could not retain it for a single morning."

X

AN ORDAINED STATE CAN ONLY SUBSIST WITH A PROPER SYSTEM OF TAXATION, AND THAT ORIGINATING WITH YÂO AND SHUN IS THE PROPER ONE FOR CHINA.

1. Pâi Kwei said, "I want to take a twentieth of the produce only as the tax. What do you think of it?"

2. Mencius said, "Your way would be that of the Mo.

3. "In a country of ten thousand families, would it do to have only one potter?" Kwei replied, "No. The vessels would not be enough to use."

4. Mencius went on, "In Mo all the five kinds of grain are not grown; it only produces the millet. There are no fortified cities, no edifices, no ancestral temples, no ceremonies of sacrifice; there are no princes requiring presents and entertainments; there is no system of officers with their various subordinates. On these accounts a tax of one-twentieth of the produce is sufficient there.

5. "But now it is the Middle Kingdom that we live in. To banish the relationships of men, and have no superior men—how can such a state of things be thought of?

6. "With but few potters a kingdom cannot subsist—how much less can it subsist without men of a higher rank than others?

7. "If we wish to make the taxation lighter than the system of Yâo and Shun, we shall just have a great Mo and a small Mo. If we wish to make it heavier, we shall just have the great Chieh and the small Chieh."

XI

PÂI KWEI'S PRESUMPTUOUS IDEA THAT HE COULD REGULATE THE
WATERS BETTER THAN YÜ DID.

1. Pâi Kwei said, "My management of the waters is superior to that of
    Yü."

2. Mencius replied, "You are wrong, Sir. Yü's regulation of the waters
    was according to the laws of water.

3. "He therefore made the four seas their receptacle, while you make
    the neighboring States their receptacle.

4. "Water flowing out of its channels is called an inundation. Inundating
    waters are a vast waste of water, and what a benevolent man detests.
    You are wrong, my good Sir."

XII

FAITH IN PRINCIPLES NECESSARY TO FIRMNESS IN ACTION.

Mencius said, "If a scholar have not faith, how shall he take a firm
hold of things?"

XIII

OF WHAT IMPORTANCE TO A MINISTER — TO GOVERNMENT —
IT IS TO LOVE WHAT IS GOOD.

1. The prince of Lû wanting to commit the administration of his
    government to the disciple Yo-ch'ăng, Mencius said, "When I heard
    of it, I was so glad that I could not sleep."

2. Kung-sun Ch'âu asked, "Is Yo-ch'ăng a man of vigor?" and was
    answered, "No." "Is he wise in council?" "No." "Is he possessed of
    much information?" "No."

3. "What then made you so glad that you could not sleep?"

4. "He is a man who loves what is good."

5. "Is the love of what is good sufficient?"

6. "The love of what is good is more than a sufficient qualification for
    the government of the kingdom — how much more is it so for the
    State of Lû!

7. "If a minister love what is good, all within the four seas will count 1,000 lì but a small distance, and will come and lay their good thoughts before him.

8. "If he do not love what is good, men will say, 'How self-conceited he looks? He is sayinq to himself, I know it.' The language and looks of that self-conceit will keep men off at a distance of 1,000 lì. When good men stop 1,000 lì off, calumniators, flatterers, and sycophants will make their appearance. When a minister lives among calumniators, flatterers, and sycophants, though he may wish the State to be well governed, is it possible for it to be so?"

XIV

GROUNDS OF TAKING AND LEAVING OFFICE.

1. The disciple Ch'ǎn said, "What were the principles on which superior men of old took office?" Mencius replied, "There were three cases in which they accepted office, and three in which they left it.

2. "If received with the utmost respect and all polite observances, and they could say to themselves that the prince would carry their words into practice, then they took office with him. Afterwards, although there might be no remission in the polite demeanor of the prince, if their words were not carried into practice, they would leave him.

3. "The second case was that in which, though the prince could not be expected at once to carry their words into practice, yet being received by him with the utmost respect, they took office with him. But afterwards, if there was a remission in his polite demeanor, they would leave him.

4. "The last case was that of the superior man who had nothing to eat, either morning or evening, and was so famished that he could not move out of his door. If the prince, on hearing of his state, said, 'I must fail in the great point—that of carrying his doctrines into practice, neither am I able to follow his words, but I am ashamed to allow him to die of want in my country'; the assistance offered in such a case might be received, but not beyond what was sufficient to avert death."

XV

TRIALS AND HARDSHIPS THE WAY IN WHICH HEAVEN PREPARES MEN FOR GREAT SERVICES.

1. Mencius said, "Shun rose from among the channeled fields. Fû Yüeh was called to office from the midst of his building frames; Chiâo-ko from his fish and salt; Kwan Î-wû from the hands of his jailer; Sun-shû Âo from his hiding by the sea-shore; and Pâi-lî Hsî from the market-place.

2. "Thus, when Heaven is about to confer a great office on any man, it first exercises his mind with suffering, and his sinews and bones with toil. It exposes his body to hunger, and subjects him to extreme poverty. It confounds his undertakings. By all these methods it stimulates his mind, hardens his nature, and supplies his incompetencies.

3. "Men for the most part err, and are afterwards able to reform. They are distressed in mind and perplexed in their thoughts, and then they arise to vigorous reformation. When things have been evidenced in men's looks, and set forth in their words, then they understand them.

4. "If a prince have not about his court families attached to the laws and worthy counselors, and if abroad there are not hostile States or other external calamities, his kingdom will generally come to ruin.

5. "From these things we see how life springs from sorrow and calamity, and death from ease and pleasure."

XVI

HOW A REFUSAL TO TEACH MAY BE TEACHING.

Mencius said, "There are many arts in teaching. I refuse, as inconsistent with my character, to teach a man, but I am only thereby still teaching him."

BOOK VII

TSIN SIN

PART I

I

BY THE STUDY OF OURSELVES WE COME TO THE KNOWLEDGE OF HEAVEN, AND HEAVEN IS SERVED BY OUR OBEYING OUR NATURE.

1. Mencius said, "He who has exhausted all his mental constitution knows his nature. Knowing his nature, he knows Heaven.

2. "To preserve one's mental constitution, and nourish one's nature, is the way to serve Heaven.

3. "When neither a premature death nor long life causes a man any double-mindedness, but he waits in the cultivation of his personal character for whatever issue — this is the way in which he establishes his Heaven-ordained being."

II

MAN'S DUTY AS AFFECTED BY THE DECREES OR APPOINTMENTS OF HEAVEN. WHAT MAY BE CORRECTLY DESCRIBED ASCRIBED THERETO AND WHAT NOT.

1. Mencius said, "There is an appointment for everything. A man should receive submissively what may be correctly ascribed thereto.

2. "Therefore, he who has the true idea of what is Heaven's appointment will not stand beneath a precipitous wall.

3. "Death sustained in the discharge of one's duties may correctly be ascribed to the appointment of Heaven.

4. "Death under handcuffs and fetters cannot correctly be so ascribed."

III

1. Mencius said, "When we get by our seeking and lose by our neglecting—in that case seeking is of use to getting, and the things sought for are those which are in ourselves.

2. "When the seeking is according to the proper course, and the getting is only as appointed—in that case the seeking is of no use to getting, and the things sought are without ourselves."

IV

1. Mencius said, "All things are already complete in us.

2. "There is no greater delight than to be conscious of sincerity on self-examination.

3. "If one acts with a vigorous effort at the law of reciprocity, when he seeks for the realization of perfect virtue, nothing can be closer than his approximation to it."

V

Mencius said, "To act without understanding, and to do so habitually without examination, pursuing the proper path all the life without knowing its nature—this is the way of multitudes."

VI

Mencius said, "A man may not be without shame. When one is ashamed of having been without shame, he will afterwards not have occasion to be ashamed."

VII

1. Mencius said, "The sense of shame is to a man of great importance.

2. "Those who form contrivances and versatile schemes distinguished for their artfulness, do not allow their sense of shame to come into action.

3. "When one differs from other men in not having this sense of shame, what will he have in common with them?"

VIII

HOW THE ANCIENT SCHOLARS MAINTAINED THE DIGNITY OF THEIR CHARACTER AND PRINCIPLES.

Mencius said, "The able and virtuous monarchs of antiquity loved virtue and forgot their power. And shall an exception be made of the able and virtuous scholars of antiquity, that they did not do the same? They delighted in their own principles, and were oblivious of the power of princes. Therefore, if kings and dukes did not show the utmost respect, and observe all forms of ceremony, they were not permitted to come frequently and visit them. If they thus found it not in their power to pay them frequent visits, how much less could they get to employ them as ministers?"

IX

HOW A PROFESSIONAL ADVISOR OF THE PRINCES MIGHT BE ALWAYS PERFECTLY SATISFIED. THE EXAMPLE OF ANTIQUITY.

1. Mencius said to Sung Kâu-ch'ien, "Are you fond, Sir, of traveling to the different courts? I will tell you about such traveling.

2. "If a prince acknowledge you and follow your counsels, be perfectly satisfied. If no one do so, be the same."

3. Kâu-ch'ien said, "What is to be done to secure this perfect satisfaction?" Mencius replied, "Honor virtue and delight in righteousness, and so you may always be perfectly satisfied.

4. "Therefore, a scholar, though poor, does not let go his righteousness; though prosperous, he does not leave his own path.

5. "Poor and not letting righteousness go—it is thus that the scholar holds possession of himself. Prosperous and not leaving the proper path—it is thus that the expectations of the people from him are not disappointed.

6. "When the men of antiquity realized their wishes, benefits were conferred by them on the people. If they did not realize their wishes,

they cultivated their personal character, and became illustrious in the world. If poor, they attended to their own virtue in solitude; if advanced to dignity, they made the whole kingdom virtuous as well."

X

HOW PEOPLE SHOULD GET THEIR INSPIRATION TO GOOD IN THEMSELVES.

Mencius said, "The mass of men wait for a King Wăn, and then they will receive a rousing impulse. Scholars distinguished from the mass, without a King Wăn, rouse themselves."

XI

NOT TO BE ELATED BY RICHES IS A PROOF OF SUPERIORITY.

Mencius said, "Add to a man the families of Han and Wei. If he then look upon himself without being elated, he is far beyond the mass of men."

XII

WHEN A RULER'S AIM IS EVIDENTLY THE PEOPLE'S GOOD, THEY WILL NOT MURMUR AT HIS HARSHEST MEASURES.

Mencius said, "Let the people be employed in the way which is intended to secure their ease, and though they be toiled, they will not murmur. Let them be put to death in the way which is intended to preserve their lives, and though they die, they will not murmur at him who puts them to death."

XIII

THE DIFFERENT INFLUENCE EXERCISED BY A CHIEF AMONG THE PRINCES, AND BY A TRUE SOVEREIGN.

1. Mencius said, "Under a chief, leading all the princes, the people look brisk and cheerful. Under a true sovereign, they have an air of deep contentment.

2. "Though he slay them, they do not murmur. When he benefits them, they do not think of his merit. From day to day they make progress towards what is good, without knowing who makes them do so.

3. "Wherever the superior man passes through, transformation follows; wherever he abides, his influence is of a spiritual nature. It flows abroad, above and beneath, like that of Heaven and Earth. How can it be said that he mends society but in a small way!"

XIV

1. Mencius said, "Kindly words do not enter so deeply into men as a reputation for kindness.

2. "Good government does not lay hold of the people so much as good instructions.

3. "Good government is feared by the people, while good instructions are loved by them. Good government gets the people's wealth, while good instructions get their hearts."

XV

BENEVOLENCE AND RIGHTEOUSNESS ARE NATURAL TO MAN,
PARTS OF HIS CONSTITUTION.

1. Mencius said, "The ability possessed by men without having been acquired by learning is intuitive ability, and the knowledge possessed by them without the exercise of thought is their intuitive knowledge.

2. "Children carried in the arms all know to love their parents, and when they are grown a little, they all know to love their elder brothers.

3. "Filial affection for parents is the working of benevolence. Respect for elders is the working of righteousness. There is no other reason for those feelings—they belong to all under heaven."

XVI

HOW WHAT SHUN WAS DISCOVERED ITSELF
IN HIS GREATEST OBSCURITY.

Mencius said, "When Shun was living amid the deep retired mountains, dwelling with the trees and rocks, and wandering among the deer and swine, the difference between him and the rude inhabitants of those remote hills appeared very small. But when he heard a single good word, or saw a single good action, he was like a stream or a river bursting its banks, and flowing out in an irresistible flood."

XVII

A MAN HAS BUT TO OBEY THE LAW IN HIMSELF.

Mencius said, "Let a man not do what his own sense of righteousness tells him not to do, and let him not desire what his sense of righteousness tells him not to desire—to act thus is all he has to do."

XVIII

THE BENEFITS OF TROUBLE AND AFFLICTION.

1. Mencius said, "Men who are possessed of intelligent virtue and prudence in affairs will generally be found to have been in sickness and troubles.

2. "They are the friendless minister and concubine's son, who keep their hearts under a sense of peril, and use deep precautions against calamity. On this account they become distinguished for their intelligence."

XIX

FOUR DIFFERENT CLASSES OF MINISTERS.

1. Mencius said, "There are persons who serve the prince—they serve the prince, that is, for the sake of his countenance and favor.

2. "There are ministers who seek the tranquility of the State, and find their pleasure in securing that tranquility.

3. "There are those who are the people of Heaven. They, judging that, if they were in office, they could carry out their principles, throughout the kingdom, proceed so to carry them out.

4. "There are those who are great men. They rectify themselves and others are rectified."

XX

THE THINGS WHICH THE SUPERIOR MAN DELIGHTS IN.

1. Mencius said, "The superior man has three things in which he delights, and to be ruler over the kingdom is not one of them.

2. "That his father and mother are both alive, and that the condition of his brothers affords no cause for anxiety—this is one delight.

3. "That, when looking up, he has no occasion for shame before Heaven, and, below, he has no occasion to blush before men—this is a second delight.

4. "That he can get from the whole kingdom the most talented individuals, and teach and nourish them—this is the third delight.

5. "The superior man has three things in which he delights, and to be ruler over the kingdom is not one of them."

XXI

MAN'S OWN NATURE THE MOST IMPORTANT THING TO HIM,
AND THE SOURCE OF HIS TRUE ENJOYMENT.

1. Mencius said, "Wide territory and a numerous people are desired by the superior man, but what he delights in is not here.

2. "To stand in the center of the kingdom, and tranquilize the people within the four seas—the superior man delights in this, but the highest enjoyment of his nature is not here.

3. "What belongs by his nature to the superior man cannot be increased by the largeness of his sphere of action, nor diminished by his dwelling in poverty and retirement—for this reason that it is determinately apportioned to him by Heaven.

4. "What belongs by his nature to the superior man are benevolence, righteousness, propriety, and knowledge. These are rooted in his heart; their growth and manifestation are a mild harmony appearing in the countenance, a rich fullness in the back, and the character imparted to the four limbs. Those limbs understand to arrange themselves, without being told."

XXII

THE GOVERNMENT OF KING WĂN
BY WHICH THE AGED WERE NOURISHED.

1. Mencius said, "Po-î, that he might avoid Châu, was dwelling on the coast of the northern sea when he heard of the rise of King Wăn. He roused himself and said, 'Why should I not go and follow him? I have heard that the chief of the West knows well how to nourish the old.' T'âi-kung, to avoid Châu, was dwelling on the coast of the eastern sea. When he heard of the rise of King Wăn, he said, 'Why should I not go and follow him? I have heard that the chief of the

West knows well how to nourish the old.' If there were a prince in the kingdom, who knew well how to nourish the old, all men of virtue would feel that he was the proper object for them to gather to.

2. "Around the homestead with its five *mâu*, the space beneath the walls was planted with mulberry trees, with which the women nourished silkworms, and thus the old were able to have silk to wear. Each family had five brood hens and two brood sows, which were kept to their breeding seasons, and thus the old were able to have flesh to eat. The husbandmen cultivated their farms of 100 *mâu*, and thus their families of eight mouths were secured against want.

3. "The expression, 'The chief of the West knows well how to nourish the old,' refers to his regulation of the fields and dwellings, his teaching them to plant the mulberry and nourish those animals, and his instructing the wives and children, so as to make them nourish their aged. At fifty, warmth cannot be maintained without silks, and at seventy flesh is necessary to satisfy the appetite. Persons not kept warm nor supplied with food are said to be starved and famished, but among the people of King Wăn, there were no aged who were starved or famished. This is the meaning of the expression in question."

XXIII

TO PROMOTE THE VIRTUE OF THE PEOPLE, THE FIRST CARE
OF A GOVERNMENT SHOULD BE TO CONSULT FOR THEIR
BEING WELL OFF.

1. Mencius said, "Let it be seen to that their fields of grain and hemp are well cultivated, and make the taxes on them light — so the people may be made rich.

2. "Let it be seen to that the people use their resources of food seasonably, and expend their wealth only on the prescribed ceremonies: so their wealth will be more than can be consumed.

3. "The people cannot live without water and fire, yet if you knock at a man's door in the dusk of the evening, and ask for water and fire, there is no man who will not give them, such is the abundance of these things. A sage governs the kingdom so as to cause pulse and grain to be as abundant as water and fire. When pulse and grain are as abundant as water and fire, how shall the people be other than virtuous?"

XXIV

HOW THE GREAT DOCTRINES OF THE SAGES DWARF ALL
SMALLER DOCTRINES, AND YET ARE TO BE ADVANCED TO
BY SUCCESSIVE STEPS.

1. Mencius said, "Confucius ascended the eastern hill, and Lû appeared to him small. He ascended the T'âi mountain, and all beneath the heavens appeared to him small. So he who has contemplated the sea, finds it difficult to think anything of other waters, and he who has wandered in the gate of the sage, finds it difficult to think anything of the words of others.

2. "There is an art in the contemplation of water. It is necessary to look at it as foaming in waves. The sun and moon being possessed of brilliancy, their light admitted even through an orifice illuminates.

3. "Flowing water is a thing which does not proceed till it has filled the hollows in its course. The student who has set his mind on the doctrines of the sage, does not advance to them but by completing one lesson after another."

XXV

THE DIFFERENT RESULTS TO WHICH THE LOVE OF GOOD
AND THE LOVE OF GAIN LEAD.

1. Mencius said, "He who rises at cock-crowing and addresses himself earnestly to the practice of virtue, is a disciple of Shun.

2. "He who rises at cock-crowing, and addresses himself earnestly to the pursuit of gain, is a disciple of Chih.

3. "If you want to know what separates Shun from Chih, it is simply this—the interval between the thought of gain and the thought of virtue."

XXVI

THE ERRORS OF YANG, MO, AND TSZE-MO.
OBSTINATE ADHERENCE TO A COURSE WHICH WE
MAY DEEM ABSTRACTLY RIGHT IS PERILOUS.

1. Mencius said, "The principle of the philosopher Yang was—'Each one for himself.' Though he might have benefited the whole kingdom by plucking out a single hair, he would not have done it.

2. "The philosopher Mo loves all equally. If by rubbing smooth his whole body from the crown to the heel, he could have benefited the kingdom, he would have done it.

3. "Tsze-mo holds a medium between these. By holding that medium, he is nearer the right. But by holding it without leaving room for the exigency of circumstances, it becomes like their holding their one point.

4. "The reason why I hate that holding to one point is the injury it does to the way of right principle. It takes up one point and disregards a hundred others."

XXVII

THE IMPORTANCE OF NOT ALLOWING THE MIND TO BE INJURED BY POVERTY AND MEAN CONDITION.

1. Mencius said, "The hungry think any food sweet, and the thirsty think the same of any drink, and thus they do not get the right taste of what they eat and drink. The hunger and thirst, in fact, injure their palate. And is it only the mouth and belly which are injured by hunger and thirst? Men's minds are also injured by them.

2. "If a man can prevent the evils of hunger and thirst from being any evils to his mind, he need not have any sorrow about not being equal to other men."

XXVIII

HÛI OF LIÛ-HSIÂ'S FIRMNESS.

Mencius said, "Hûi of Liû-Hsiâ would not for the three highest offices of State have changed his firm purpose of life."

XXIX

ONLY THAT LABOR IS TO BE PRIZED WHICH ACCOMPLISHES ITS OBJECT.

Mencius said, "A man with definite aims to be accomplished may be compared to one digging a well. To dig the well to a depth of seventy-two cubits, and stop without reaching the spring, is after all throwing away the well."

XXX

THE DIFFERENCE BETWEEN YÂO, SHUN, T'ĂNG, AND WÛ,
ON THE ONE HAND, AND THE FIVE CHIEFS, ON THE OTHER, IN
RELATION TO BENEVOLENCE AND RIGHTEOUSNESS.

1. Mencius said, "Benevolence and righteousness were natural to Yâo and Shun. T'ăng and Wû made them their own. The five chiefs of the princes feigned them.

2. "Having borrowed them long and not returned them, how could it be known they did not own them?"

XXXI

THE END MAY JUSTIFY THE MEANS,
BUT THE PRINCIPLE SHOULD NOT BE READILY APPLIED.

1. Kung-sun Ch'âu said, "Î Yin said, 'I cannot be near and see him so disobedient to reason,' and therewith he banished T'â-chiâ to T'ung. The people were much pleased. When T'â-chiâ became virtuous, he brought him back, and the people were again much pleased.

2. "When worthies are ministers, may they indeed banish their sovereigns in this way when they are not virtuous?"

3. Mencius replied, "If they have the same purpose as Î Yin, they may. If they have not the same purpose, it would be usurpation."

XXXII

THE SERVICES WHICH A SUPERIOR MAN RENDERS TO A COUNTRY
ENTITLE HIM, WITHOUT HIS DOING OFFICIAL DUTY, TO SUPPORT.

Kung-sun Ch'âu said, "It is said, in the Book of Poetry,

He will not eat the bread of idleness!

How is it that we see superior men eating without laboring?" Mencius replied, "When a superior man resides in a country, if its sovereign employ his counsels, he comes to tranquility, wealth and glory. If the young in it follow his instructions, they become filial, obedient to their elders, true-hearted, and faithful. What greater example can there be than this of not eating the bread of idleness?"

XXXIII

HOW A SCHOLAR PREPARES HIMSELF FOR THE DUTIES
TO WHICH HE ASPIRES.

1. The king's son, Tien, asked Mencius, saying, "What is the business of the unemployed scholar?"

2. Mencius replied, "To exalt his aim."

3. Tien asked again, "What do you mean by exalting the aim?" The answer was, "Setting it simply on benevolence and righteousness. He thinks how to put a single innocent person to death is contrary to benevolence; how to take what one has not a right to is contrary to righteousness; that one's dwelling should be benevolence; and one's path should be righteousness. Where else should he dwell? What other path should he pursue? When benevolence is the dwelling-place of the heart, and righteousness the path of the life, the business of a great man is complete."

XXXIV

HOW MEN JUDGE WRONGLY OF CHARACTER, OVERLOOKING,
IN THEIR ADMIRATION OF ONE STRIKING EXCELLENCE,
GREAT FAILURES AND DEFICIENCIES.

Mencius said, "Supposing that the kingdom of Ch'î were offered, contrary to righteousness, to Ch'ǎn Chung, he would not receive it, and all people believe in him, as a man of the highest worth. But this is only the righteousness which declines a dish of rice or a plate of soup. A man can have no greater crimes than to disown his parents and relatives, and the relations of sovereign and minister, superiors and inferiors. How can it be allowed to give a man credit for the great excellences because he possesses a small one?"

XXXV

WHAT SHUN AND HIS MINISTER OF CRIME WOULD HAVE DONE,
IF SHUN'S FATHER HAD COMMITTED A MURDER.

1. T'âo Ying asked, saying, "Shun being sovereign, and Kâo-yâo chief minister of justice, if Kû-sâu had murdered a man, what would have been done in the case?"

2. Mencius said, "Kâo-yâo would simply have apprehended him."

3. "But would not Shun have forbidden such a thing?"

4. "Indeed, how could Shun have forbidden it? Kâo-yâo had received the law from a proper source."

5. "In that case what would Shun have done?"

6. "Shun would have regarded abandoning the kingdom as throwing away a worn-out sandal. He would privately have taken his father on his back, and retired into concealment, living somewhere along the sea-coast. There he would have been all his life, cheerful and happy, forgetting the kingdom."

XXXVI

HOW ONE'S MATERIAL POSITION AFFECTS HIS AIR, AND MUCH MORE MAY MORAL CHARACTER BE EXPECTED TO DO SO.

1. Mencius, going from Fan to Ch'î, saw the king of Ch'î's son at a distance, and said with a deep sigh, "One's position alters the air, just as the nurture affects the body. Great is the influence of position! Are we not all men's sons in this respect?"

2. Mencius said, "The residence, the carriages and horses, and the dress of the king's son, are mostly the same as those of other men. That he looks so is occasioned by his position. How much more should a peculiar air distinguish him whose position is in the wide house of the world!

3. "When the prince of Lû went to Sung, he called out at the T'ieh-châi gate, and the keeper said, 'This is not our prince. How is it that his voice is so like that of our prince?' This was occasioned by nothing but the correspondence of their positions."

XXXVII

THAT HE BE RESPECTED IS ESSENTIAL TO A SCHOLAR'S ENGAGING IN THE SERVICE OF A PRINCE.

1. Mencius said, "To feed a scholar and not love him, is to treat him as a pig. To love him and not respect him, is to keep him as a domestic animal.

2. "Honoring and respecting are what exist before any offering of gifts.

3. "If there be honoring and respecting without the reality of them, a superior man may not be retained by such empty demonstrations."

XXXVIII

ONLY WITH A SAGE DOES THE BODY ACT ACCORDING
TO ITS DESIGN.

Mencius said, "The bodily organs with their functions belong to our Heaven-conferred nature. But a man must be a sage before he can satisfy the design of his bodily organization."

XXXIX

REPROOF OF KUNG-SUN CH'ÂU FOR ASSENTING TO THE PROPOSAL
TO SHORTEN THE PERIOD OF MOURNING.

1. The king Hsüan of Ch'î wanted to shorten the period of mourning. Kung-sun Ch'âu said, "To have one whole year's mourning is better than doing away with it altogether."

2. Mencius said, "That is just as if there were one twisting the arm of his elder brother, and you were merely to say to him 'Gently, gently, if you please.' Your only course should be to teach such a one filial piety and fraternal duty."

3. At that time, the mother of one of the king's sons had died, and his tutor asked for him that he might be allowed to observe a few months' mourning. Kung-sun Ch'âu asked, "What do you say of this?"

4. Mencius replied, "This is a case where the party wishes to complete the whole period, but finds it impossible to do so. The addition of even a single day is better than not mourning at all. I spoke of the case where there was no hindrance, and the party neglected the thing itself."

XL

HOW THE LESSONS OF THE SAGE REACH TO
ALL DIFFERENT CLASSES.

1. Mencius said, "There are five ways in which the superior man effects his teaching.

2. "There are some on whom his influence descends like seasonable rain.

3. "There are some whose virtue he perfects, and some of whose talents he assists the development.

4. "There are some whose inquiries he answers.

5. "There are some who privately cultivate and correct themselves.

6. "These five ways are the methods in which the superior man effects his teaching."

XLI

THE TEACHER OF TRUTH MAY NOT LOWER HIS LESSONS TO SUIT HIS LEARNERS.

1. Kung-sun Ch'âu said, "Lofty are your principles and admirable, but to learn them may well be likened to ascending the heavens — something which cannot be reached. Why not adapt your teaching so as to cause learners to consider them attainable, and so daily exert themselves!"

2. Mencius said, "A great artificer does not, for the sake of a stupid workman, alter or do away with the marking-line. Î did not, for the sake of a stupid archer, charge his rule for drawing the bow.

3. "The superior man draws the bow, but does not discharge the arrow, having seemed to leap with it to the mark; and he there stands exactly in the middle of the path. Those who are able, follow him."

XLII

ONE MUST LIVE OR DIE WITH HIS PRINCIPLES, ACTING FROM HIMSELF, NOT WITH REGARD TO OTHER MEN.

1. Mencius said, "When right principles prevail throughout the kingdom, one's principles must appear along with one's person. When right principles disappear from the kingdom, one's person must vanish along with one's principles.

2. "I have not heard of one's principles being dependent for their manifestation on other men."

XLIII

HOW MENCIUS REQUIRED THE SIMPLE PURSUIT OF TRUTH IN THOSE WHOM HE TAUGHT.

1. The disciple Kung-tû said, "When Kang of T'ăng made his appearance in your school, it seemed proper that a polite consideration should be paid to him, and yet you did not answer him. Why was that?"

2. Mencius replied, "I do not answer him who questions me presuming on his nobility, nor him who presumes on his talents, nor him who presumes on his age, nor him who presumes on services performed to me, nor him who presumes on old acquaintance. Two of those things were chargeable on Kăng of T'ăng."

XLIV

FAILURES IN EVIDENT DUTY WILL BE ACCOMPANIED BY
FAILURE IN ALL DUTY. PRECIPITATE ADVANCES ARE
FOLLOWED BY SPEEDY RETREATS.

1. Mencius said, "He who stops short where stopping is acknowledged to be not allowable, will stop short in everything. He who behaves shabbily to those whom he ought to treat well, will behave shabbily to all.

2. "He who advances with precipitation will retire with speed."

XLV

THE SUPERIOR MAN IS KIND TO CREATURES, LOVING TO OTHER
MEN, AND AFFECTIONATE TO HIS RELATIVES.

Mencius said, "In regard to inferior creatures, the superior man is kind to them, but not loving. In regard to people generally, he is loving to them, but not affectionate. He is affectionate to his parents, and lovingly disposed to people generally. He is lovingly disposed to people generally, and kind to creatures."

XLVI

AGAINST THE PRINCES OF HIS TIME WHO OCCUPIED THEMSELVES
WITH THE KNOWLEDGE OF, AND REGARD FOR, WHAT WAS OF
LITTLE IMPORTANCE.

1. Mencius said, "The wise embrace all knowledge, but they are most earnest about what is of the greatest importance. The benevolent embrace all in their love, but what they consider of the greatest importance is to cultivate an earnest affection for the virtuous. Even the wisdom of Yâo and Shun did not extend to everything, but they attended earnestly to what was important. Their benevolence did not show itself in acts of kindness to every man, but they earnestly cultivated an affection for the virtuous.

2. "Not to be able to keep the three years' mourning, and to be very particular about that of three months, or that of five months; to eat immoderately and swill down the soup, and at the same time to inquire about the precept not to tear the meat with the teeth—such things show what I call an ignorance of what is most important."

TSIN SIN

PART II

I

A STRONG CONDEMNATION OF KING HÛI OF LIANG, FOR
SACRIFICING TO HIS AMBITION HIS PEOPLE AND EVEN HIS SON.

1. Mencius said, "The opposite indeed of benevolent was the king Hûi of Liang! The benevolent, beginning with what they care for, proceed to what they do not care for. Those who are the opposite of benevolent, beginning with what they do not care for, proceed to what they care for."

2. Kung-sun Ch'âu said, "What do you mean?" Mencius answered, "The king Hûi of Liang, for the matter of territory, tore and destroyed his people, leading them to battle. Sustaining a great defeat, he would engage again, and afraid lest they should not be able to secure the victory, urged his son whom he loved till he sacrificed him with them. This is what I call—'beginning with what they do not care for, and proceeding to what they care for.'"

II

HOW ALL THE FIGHTINGS RECORDED IN THE CH'UN-CH'IÛ WERE
UNRIGHTEOUS: A WARNING TO THE CONTENDING STATES OF
MENCIUS'S TIME.

1. Mencius said, "In the 'Spring and Autumn' there are no righteous wars. Instances indeed there are of one war better than another.

2. "'Correction' is when the supreme authority punishes its subjects by force of arms. Hostile States do not correct one another."

III

WITH WHAT RESERVATION MENCIUS READ THE SHÛ-CHING.

1. Mencius said, "It would be better to be without the Book of History than to give entire credit to it.

2. "In the 'Completion of the War,' I select two or three passages only, which I believe.

3. "'The benevolent man has no enemy under heaven. When the prince the most benevolent was engaged against him who was the most the opposite, how could the blood of the people have flowed till it floated the pestles of the mortars?'"

IV

COUNSEL TO PRINCES NOT TO ALLOW THEMSELVES TO BE
DECEIVED BY MEN WHO WOULD ADVISE THEM TO WAR.

1. Mencius said, "There are men who say—'I am skillful at marshaling troops, I am skillful at conducting a battle!' They are great criminals.

2. "If the ruler of a State love benevolence, he will have no enemy in the kingdom.

3. "When T'ăng was executing his work of correction in the south, the rude tribes on the north murmured. When he was executing it in the east, the rude tribes on the west murmured. Their cry was—'Why does he make us last?'

4. "When King Wû punished Yin, he had only three hundred chariots of war, and three thousand life-guards.

5. "The king said, 'Do not fear. Let me give you repose. I am no enemy to the people!' On this, they bowed their heads to the earth, like the horns of animals falling off.

6. "'Royal correction' is but another word for rectifying. Each State wishing itself to be corrected, what need is there for fighting?"

V

REAL ATTAINMENT MUST BE MADE BY THE LEARNER FOR HIMSELF.

Mencius said, "A carpenter or a carriage-maker may give a man the circle and square, but cannot make him skillful in the use of them."

VI

THE EQUINAMITY OF SHUN IN POVERTY AND AS SOVEREIGN.

Mencius said, "Shun's manner of eating his parched grain and herbs was as if he were to be doing so all his life. When he became sovereign, and had the embroidered robes to wear, the lute to play, and the two daughters of Yâo to wait on him, he was as if those things belonged to him as a matter of course."

VII

HOW THE THOUGHT OF ITS CONSEQUENCES SHOULD MAKE MEN CAREFUL OF THEIR CONDUCT.

Mencius said, "From this time forth I know the heavy consequences of killing a man's near relations. When a man kills another's father, that other will kill his father; when a man kills another's elder brother, that other will kill his elder brother. So he does not himself indeed do the act, but there is only an interval between him and it."

VIII

THE BENEVOLENCE AND SELFISHNESS OF ANCIENT AND MODERN RULE CONTRASTED.

1. Mencius said, "Anciently, the establishment of the frontier-gates was to guard against violence.

2. "Nowadays, it is to exercise violence."

IX

A MAN'S INFLUENCE DEPENDS ON HIS PERSONAL EXAMPLE AND CONDUCT.

Mencius said, "If a man himself do not walk in the right path, it will not be walked in even by his wife and children. If he order men according to what is not the right way, he will not be able to get the obedience of even his wife and children."

X

CORRUPT TIMES ARE PROVIDED AGAINST BY ESTABLISHED VIRTUE.

Mencius said, "A bad year cannot prove the cause of death to him whose stores of grain are large; an age of corruption cannot confound him whose equipment of virtue is complete."

XI

A MAN'S TRUE DISPOSITION WILL OFTEN APPEAR IN SMALL MATTERS, WHEN A LOVE OF FAME MAY HAVE CARRIED HIM OVER GREAT DIFFICULTIES.

Mencius said, "A man who loves fame may be able to decline a State of a thousand chariots; but if he be not really the man to do such a thing, it will appear in his countenance, in the matter of a dish of rice or a platter of soup."

XII

THREE THINGS IMPORTANT IN THE ADMINISTRATION OF A STATE.

1. Mencius said, "If men of virtue and ability be not confided in, a State will become empty and void.

2. "Without the rules of propriety and distinctions of right, the high and the low will be thrown into confusion.

3. "Without the great principles of government and their various business, there will not be wealth sufficient for the expenditure."

XIII

ONLY BY BENEVOLENCE CAN THE THRONE BE GOT.

Mencius said, "There are instances of individuals without benevolence, who have got possession of a single State, but there has been no instance of the throne's being got by one without benevolence."

XIV

THE DIFFERENT ELEMENTS OF A NATION — THE PEOPLE, TUTELARY SPIRITS, AND SOVEREIGN, IN RESPECT OF THEIR IMPORTANCE.

1. Mencius said, "The people are the most important element in a nation; the spirits of the land and grain are the next; the sovereign is the lightest.

2. "Therefore to gain the peasantry is the way to become sovereign; to gain the sovereign is the way to become a prince of a State; to gain the prince of a State is the way to become a great officer.

3. "When a prince endangers the altars of the spirits of the land and grain, he is changed, and another appointed in his place.

4. "When the sacrificial victims have been perfect, the millet in its vessels all pure, and the sacrifices offered at their proper seasons, if yet there ensue drought, or the waters overflow, the spirits of the land and grain are changed, and others appointed in their place."

XV

THAT PO-î AND HÛI OF LIÛ-HSIÂ WERE SAGES PROVED BY THE PERMANENCE OF THEIR INFLUENCE.

Mencius said, "A sage is the teacher of a hundred generations: this is true of Po-î and Hûi of Liû-Hsiâ. Therefore when men now bear the character of Po-î, the corrupt become pure, and the weak acquire determination. When they hear the character of Hûi of Liû-Hsiâ, the mean become generous, and the niggardly become liberal. Those two made themselves distinguished a hundred generations ago, and after a hundred generations, those who hear of them, are all aroused in this manner. Could such effects be produced by them, if they had not been sages? And how much more did they affect those who were in contiguity with them, and felt their inspiring influence!"

XVI

THE RELATION OF BENEVOLENCE TO MAN.

Mencius said, "Benevolence is the distinguishing characteristic of man. As embodied in man's conduct, it is called the path of duty."

XVII

HOW CONFUCIUS'S LEAVING LÛ AND CH'Î WAS DIFFERENT.

Mencius said, "When Confucius was leaving Lû, he said, 'I will set out by-and-by'—this was the way in which to leave the State of his parents. When he was leaving Ch'î, he strained off with his hand the water in which his rice was being rinsed, took the rice, and went away—this was the way in which to leave a strange State."

XVIII

THE REASON OF CONFUCIUS'S BEING IN STRAITS BETWEEN CH'ĂN AND TS'ÂI.

Mencius said, "The reason why the superior man was reduced to straits between Ch'ăn and Ts'âi was because neither the princes of the time nor their ministers sympathized or communicated with him."

XIX

MENCIUS COMFORTS MO CH'Î UNDER CALUMNY
BY THE REFLECTION THAT IT WAS THE ORDINARY
LOT OF DISTINGUISHED MEN.

1. Mo Ch'î said, "Greatly am I from anything to depend upon from the mouths of men."

2. Mencius observed, "There is no harm in that. Scholars are more exposed than others to suffer from the mouths of men.

3. "It is said, in the Book of Poetry,

> My heart is disquieted and grieved,
> I am hated by the crowd of mean creatures.

This might have been said by Confucius. And again,

> Though he did not remove their wrath,
> He did not let fall his own fame.

This might be said of King Wăn."

XX

HOW THE ANCIENTS LED ON MEN BY THEIR EXAMPLE,
WHILE THE RULERS OF MENCIUS'S TIME TRIED TO URGE MEN
CONTRARY TO THEIR EXAMPLE.

Mencius said, "Anciently, men of virtue and talents by means of their own enlightenment made others enlightened. Nowadays, it is tried, while they are themselves in darkness, and by means of that darkness, to make others enlightened."

XXI

THAT THE CULTIVATION OF THE MIND MAY
NOT BE INTERMITTED.

Mencius said to the disciple Kâo, "There are the footpaths along the hills—if suddenly they be used, they become roads; and if, as suddenly they are not used, the wild grass fills them up. Now, the wild grass fills up your mind."

XXII

AN ABSURD REMARK OF THE DISCIPLE KÂO
ABOUT THE MUSIC OF YÜ AND KING WǍN.

1. The disciple Kâo said, "The music of Yü was better than that of King Wǎn."

2. Mencius observed, "On what ground do you say so?" and the other replied, "Because at the pivot the knob of Yü's bells is nearly worn through."

3. Mencius said, "How can that be a sufficient proof? Are the ruts at the gate of a city made by a single two-horsed chariot?"

XXIII

HOW MENCIUS KNEW WHERE TO STOP AND MAINTAIN HIS OWN
DIGNITY IN HIS INTERCOURSE WITH THE PRINCES.

1. When Ch'î was suffering from famine, Ch'ǎn Tsin said to Mencius, "The people are all thinking that you, Master, will again ask that the granary of T'ǎng be opened for them. I apprehend you will not do so a second time."

2. Mencius said, "To do it would be to act like Fǎng Fû. There was a man of that name in Tsin, famous for his skill in seizing tigers. Afterwards he became a scholar of reputation, and going once out to the wild country, he found the people all in pursuit of a tiger. The tiger took refuge in a corner of a hill, where no one dared to attack him, but when they saw Fǎng Fû, they ran and met him. Fǎng Fû immediately bared his arms, and descended from the carriage. The multitude were pleased with him, but those who were scholars laughed at him.

XXIV

HOW THE SUPERIOR MAN SUBJECTS THE GRATIFICATION OF HIS
NATURAL APPETITES TO THE WILL OF HEAVEN, AND PURSUES THE
DOING OF GOOD WITHOUT THINKING THAT THE AMOUNT WHICH
HE CAN DO MAY BE LIMITED BY THAT WILL.

1. Mencius said, "For the mouth to desire sweet tastes, the eye to desire beautiful colors, the ear to desire pleasant sounds, the nose to desire fragrant odors, and the four limbs to desire ease and rest —

these things are natural. But there is the appointment of Heaven in connection with them, and the superior man does not say of his pursuit of them, 'It is my nature.'

2. "The exercise of love between father and son, the observance of righteousness between sovereign and minister, the rules of ceremony between guest and host, the display of knowledge in recognizing the talented, and the fulfilling the heavenly course by the sage—these are the appointment of Heaven. But there is an adaptation of our nature for them. The superior man does not say, in reference to them, 'It is the appointment of Heaven.'"

XV

THE CHARACTER OF THE DISCIPLE YO-CHANG. DIFFERENT DEGREES OF ATTAINMENT IN CHARACTER, WHICH ARE TO BE AIMED AT.

1. Hâo-shang Pû-hâi asked, saying, "What sort of man is Yo-chăng?" Mencius replied, "He is a good man, a real man."

2. "What do you mean by 'a good man, a real man'?"

3. The reply was, "A man who commands our liking is what is called a good man.

4. "He whose goodness is part of himself is what is called a real man.

5. "He whose goodness has been filled up is what is called a beautiful man.

6. "He whose completed goodness is brightly displayed is what is called a great man.

7. "When this great man exercises a transforming influence, he is what is called a sage.

8. "When the sage is beyond our knowledge, he is what is called a spirit-man.

9. "Yo-chăng is between the two first characters, and below the four last."

XXVI

RECOVERED HERETICS SHOULD BE RECEIVED WITHOUT CASTING THEIR OLD ERRORS IN THEIR TEETH.

1. Mencius said, "Those who are fleeing from the errors of Mo naturally turn to Yang, and those who are fleeing from the errors of Yang naturally turn to orthodoxy. When they so turn, they should at once and simply be received.

2. "Those who nowadays dispute with the followers of Yang and Mo do so as if they were pursuing a stray pig, the leg of which, after they have got it to enter the pen, they proceed to tie."

XXVII

THE JUST EXACTIONS OF THE GOVERNMENT ARE TO BE MADE DISCRIMINATINGLY AND CONSIDERATELY.

Mencius said, "There are the exactions of hempen-cloth and silk, of grain, and of personal service. The prince requires but one of these at once, deferring the other two. If he require two of them at once, then the people die of hunger. If he require the three at once, then fathers and sons are separated."

XXVIII

THE PRECIOUS THINGS OF A PRINCE, AND THE DANGER OF OVERLOOKING THEM FOR OTHER THINGS.

Mencius said, "The precious things of a prince are three—the territory, the people, the government and its business. If one value as most precious pearls and jade, calamity is sure to befall him."

XXIX

HOW MENCIUS PREDICTED BEFOREHAND THE DEATH OF P'AN-CH'ĂNG KWO.

P'an-ch'ăng Kwo having obtained an official situation in Ch'î, Mencius said, "He is a dead man, that P'an-ch'ăng Kwo!" P'an-ch'ăng Kwo being put to death, the disciples asked, saying, "How did you know, Master, that he would meet with death?" Mencius replied, "He was a man, who had a little ability, but had not learned the great doctrines of the superior man. He was just qualified to bring death upon himself, but for nothing more."

XXX

THE GENEROUS SPIRIT OF MENCIUS IN DISPENSING HIS
INSTRUCTIONS.

1. When Mencius went to T'ăng, he was lodged in the Upper palace. A sandal in the process of making had been placed there in a window, and when the keeper of the palace came to look for it, he could not find it.

2. On this, someone asked Mencius, saying, "Is it thus that your followers pilfer?" Mencius replied, "Do you think that they came here to pilfer the sandal?" The man said, "I apprehend not. But you, Master, having arranged to give lessons, do not go back to inquire into the past, and you do not reject those who come to you. If they come with the mind to learn, you receive them without any more ado."

XXXI

A MAN HAS ONLY TO GIVE DEVELOPMENT TO THE PRINCIPLES
OF GOOD WHICH ARE IN HIM, AND SHOW THEMSELVES IN SOME
THINGS, TO BE ENTIRELY GOOD AND CORRECT.

1. Mencius said, "All men have some things which they cannot bear — extend that feeling to what they can bear, and benevolence will be the result. All men have some things which they will not do — extend that feeling to the things which they do, and righteousness will be the result.

2. "If a man can give full development to the feeling which makes him shrink from injuring others, his benevolence will be more than can be called into practice. If he can give full development to the feeling which refuses to break through, or jump over, a wall, his righteousness will be more than can be called into practice.

3. "If he can give full development to the real feeling of dislike with which he receives the salutation, 'Thou,' 'Thou,' he will act righteously in all places and circumstances.

4. "When a scholar speaks what he ought not to speak, by guile of speech seeking to gain some end; and when he does not speak what he ought to speak, by guile of silence seeking to gain some end — both these cases are of a piece with breaking through a neighbor's wall."

XXXII

AGAINST AIMING AT WHAT IS REMOTE, AND NEGLECTING WHAT IS
NEAR. WHAT ARE GOOD WORDS AND GOOD PRINCIPLES.

1. Mencius said, "Words which are simple, while their meaning is far-reaching, are good words. Principles which, as held, are compendious, while their application is extensive, are good principles. The words of the superior man do not go below the girdle, but great principles are contained in them.

2. "The principle which the superior man holds is that of personal cultivation, but the kingdom is thereby tranquilized.

3. "The disease of men is this: that they neglect their own fields, and go to weed the fields of others, and that what they require from others is great, while what they lay upon themselves is light."

XXXIII

THE PERFECT VIRTUE OF THE HIGHEST SAGES,
AND HOW OTHERS FOLLOW AFTER IT.

1. Mencius said, "Yâo and Shun were what they were by nature; T'ăng and Wû were so by returning to natural virtue.

2. "When all the movements, in the countenance and every turn of the body, are exactly what is proper, that shows the extreme degree of the complete virtue. Weeping for the dead should be from real sorrow, and not because of the living. The regular path of virtue is to be pursued without any bend, and from no view to emolument. The words should all be necessarily sincere, not with any desire to do what is right.

3. "The superior man performs the law of right, and thereby waits simply for what has been appointed."

XXXIV

HE WHO UNDERTAKES TO COUNSEL THE GREAT,
SHOULD BE MORALLY ABOVE THEM.

1. Mencius said, "Those who give counsel to the great should despise them, and not look at their pomp and display.

2. "Halls several times eight cubits high, with beams projecting several cubits—these, if my wishes were to be realized, I would not have.

Food spread before me over ten cubits square, and attendants and concubines to the amount of hundreds—these, though my wishes were realized, I would not have. Pleasure and wine, and the dash of hunting, with thousands of chariots following after me—these, though my wishes were realized, I would not have. What they esteem are what I would have nothing to do with; what I esteem are the rules of the ancients. Why should I stand in awe of them?"

XXXV

THE REGULATION OF THE DESIRES IS ESSENTIAL TO THE NOURISHMENT OF THE MIND.

Mencius said, "To nourish the mind there is nothing better than to make the desires few. Here is a man whose desires are few: in some things he may not be able to keep his heart, but they will be few. Here is a man whose desires are many: in some things he may be able to keep his heart, but they will be few."

XXXVI

THE FILIAL FEELING OF TSĂNG-TSZE SEEN IN HIS NOT EATING JUJUBES.

1. Mencius said, "Tsăng Hsî was fond of sheep-dates, and his son, the philosopher Tsăng, could not bear to eat sheep-dates."

2. Kung-sun Ch'âu asked, saying, "Which is best—minced meat and broiled meat, or sheep-dates?" Mencius said, "Mince and broiled meat, to be sure." Kung-sun Ch'âu went on, "Then why did the philosopher Tsăng eat mince and broiled meat, and would not eat sheep-dates?" Mencius answered, "For mince and broiled meat there is a common liking, while that for sheep-dates was peculiar. We avoid the name, but do not avoid the surname. The surname is common; the name is peculiar."

XXXVII

TO CALL TO THE PURSUIT OF THE RIGHT MEDIUM WAS THE OBJECT OF CONFUCIUS AND MENCIUS. VARIOUS CHARACTERS WHO FAIL TO PURSUE THIS, OR ARE OPPOSED TO IT.

1. Wăn Chăng asked, saying, "Confucius, when he was in Ch'ăn, said: 'Let me return. The scholars of my school are ambitious, but hasty. They are for advancing and seizing their object, but cannot forget

their early ways.' Why did Confucius, when he was in Ch'ăn, think of the ambitious scholars of Lû?"

2. Mencius replied, "Confucius not getting men pursuing the true medium, to whom he might communicate his instructions, determined to take the ardent and the cautiously-decided. The ardent would advance to seize their object; the cautiously-decided would keep themselves from certain things. It is not to be thought that Confucius did not wish to get men pursuing the true medium, but being unable to assure himself of finding such, he therefore thought of the next class."

3. "I venture to ask what sort of men they were who could be styled 'The ambitious'?"

4. "Such," replied Mencius, "as Ch'in Chăng, Tsăng Hsî, and Mû P'ei, were those whom Confucius styled 'ambitious.'"

5. "Why were they styled 'ambitious'?"

6. The reply was, "Their aim led them to talk magniloquently, saying, 'The ancients! The ancients!' But their actions, where we fairly compare them with their words, did not correspond with them.

7. "When he found also that he could not get such as were thus ambitious, he wanted to get scholars who would consider anything impure as beneath them. Those were the cautiously-decided, a class next to the former."

8. Chăng pursued his questioning, "Confucius said, 'They are only your good careful people of the villages at whom I feel no indignation, when they pass my door without entering my house. Your good careful people of the villages are the thieves of virtue.' What sort of people were they who could be styled 'Your good careful people of the villages'?"

9. Mencius replied, "They are those who say, 'Why are they so magniloquent? Their words have not respect to their actions and their actions have not respect to their words, but they say, "The ancients! The ancients!" Why do they act so peculiarly, and are so cold and distant? Born in this age, we should be of this age, to be good is all that is needed.' Eunuch-like, flattering their generation — such are your good careful men of the villages."

10. Wăn Chăng said, "Their whole village styles those men good and careful. In all their conduct they are so. How was it that Confucius considered them the thieves of virtue?"

11. Mencius replied, "If you would blame them, you find nothing to allege. If you would criticize them, you have nothing to criticize. They agree with the current customs. They consent with an impure age. Their principles have a semblance of right-heartedness and truth. Their conduct has a semblance of disinterestedness and purity. All men are pleased with them, and they think themselves right, so that it is impossible to proceed with them to the principles of Yâo and Shun. On this account they are called 'The thieves of virtue.'

12. "Confucius said, 'I hate a semblance which is not the reality. I hate the darnel, lest it be confounded with the corn. I hate glib-tonguedness, lest it be confounded with righteousness. I hate sharpness of tongue, lest it be confounded with sincerity. I hate the music of Chăng, lest it be confounded with the true music. I hate the reddish blue, lest it be confounded with vermilion. I hate your good careful men of the villages, lest they be confounded with the truly virtuous.'

13. "The superior man seeks simply to bring back the unchanging standard, and, that being correct, the masses are roused to virtue. When they are so aroused, forthwith perversities and glossed wickedness disappear."

XXXVIII

ON THE TRANSMISSION OF THE LINE OF DOCTRINE FROM YÂO TO MENCIUS'S OWN TIME.

1. Mencius said, "From Yâo and Shun down to T'ăng were 500 years and more. As to Yu and Kâo Yâo, they saw those earliest sages, and so knew their doctrines, while T'ăng heard their doctrines as transmitted, and so knew them.

2. "From T'ăng to King Wăn were 500 years and more. As to Î Yin, and Lâi Chû, they saw T'ăng and knew his doctrines, while King Wăn heard them as transmitted, and so knew them.

3. "From King Wăn to Confucius were 500 years and more. As to T'âi-kung Wang and San Î-shăng, they saw Wăn, and so knew his doctrines, while Confucius heard them as transmitted, and so knew them.

4. "From Confucius downwards until now, there are only 100 years and somewhat more. The distance in time from the sage is so far from being remote, and so very near at hand was the sage's residence. In these circumstances, is there no one to transmit his doctrines? Yea, is there no one to do so?"